Benchmark Papers on Energy

Series Editors:
R. Bruce Lindsay, Brown University
Mones E. Hawley, Professional Services International

PUBLISHED VOLUMES AND VOLUMES IN PREPARATION

ENERGY: Historical Development of the Concept / *R. Bruce Lindsay*
APPLICATIONS OF ENERGY: Nineteenth Century / *R. Bruce Lindsay*
COAL, PART I: Social, Economic, and Environmental Aspects / *Mones E. Hawley*
COAL, PART II: Scientific and Technical Aspects / *Mones E. Hawley*
THE SECOND LAW OF THERMODYNAMICS / *Joseph Kestin*
IRREVERSIBLE PROCESSES / *Joseph Kestin*
ATOMIC PHYSICS AND ENERGY / *Robert Lindsay*
ENERGY STORAGE / *W. V. Hassenzahl*
DYNAMICS AND CONTROL OF POWER SYSTEMS / *A. H. El-Abiad*
ENERGY CONTROL / *R. Bruce Lindsay*

Benchmark Papers
on Energy / 2

A BENCHMARK ® Books Series

APPLICATIONS OF
ENERGY
Nineteenth Century

Edited by

R. BRUCE LINDSAY
Brown University

Dowden, Hutchinson
& Ross, Inc.

STROUDSBURG, PENNSYLVANIA

Distributed by

HALSTED
PRESS

A Division of
John Wiley & Sons, Inc.

Copyright © 1976 by **Dowden, Hutchinson & Ross, Inc.**
Benchmark Papers on Energy, Volume 2
Library of Congress Catalog Card Number: 76-11739
ISBN: 0-87933-227-1

78 77 76   1 2 3 4 5
Manufactured in the United States of America.

LIBRARY OF CONGRESS CATALOGING IN PUBLICATION DATA
Main entry under title:
Applications of energy
  (Benchmark papers on energy / 2)
  Includes bibliographical references and indexes.
  1. Power (Mechanics)—Addresses, essays, lectures. 2. Force and energy—Addresses, essays, lectures. 3. Thermodynamics—Addresses, essays, lectures. I. Lindsay, Robert Bruce, 1900–
TJ163.9.A66   621   76-11739
ISBN 0-87933-227-1

Exclusive Distributor: **Halsted Press**
A Division of John Wiley & Sons, Inc.
ISBN: 0-470-15140-4

SERIES EDITOR'S PREFACE

The Benchmark Papers on Energy constitute two series of volumes that make available to the reader in carefully organized form important and seminal papers in the historical development of the concept of energy and its applications in all fields of science and technology, as well as its role in civilization in general. This concept is generally admitted to be the most far-reaching idea that the human mind has developed to date, and its fundamental significance for human life and society is everywhere evident.

The first seven volumes of the series contain papers that deal primarily with the evolution of the energy concept and its current applications in the various branches of science. These will be supplemented in the future by volumes that concentrate on the technological and industrial applications of the concept and its socioeconomic implications.

Each volume has been organized and edited by an authority in the area to which it pertains and offers the editor's careful selection of the appropriate seminal papers, that is, those articles which have significantly influenced further development of that phase of the whole subject. In this way, every aspect of the concept of energy is placed in appropriate perspective, and each volume represents an introduction and guide to further work.

Each volume includes an editorial introduction that summarizes the significance of the field being covered. Every article or group of articles is accompanied by editorial commentary, with explanatory notes where necessary. An adequate index is provided for ready reference. Articles in languages other than English are either translated or abstracted in English. It is the hope of the publisher and editors that these volumes will serve as a working library of the most important scientific, technological, and social literature connected with the idea of energy.

The present volume, *Applications of Energy: Nineteenth Century*, has been prepared by one of the series editors. Its aim is to continue the story begun in Volume 1 on the historical development of the energy concept by emphasizing the generalization of the concept that took place in the second half of the nineteenth century, beginning with the remarkable memoir of Helmholtz in 1847. The growing importance of the idea was exemplified by the many applications that rapidly followed in all branches of physics. The 27 articles reproduced here summarize these applications through the work of the leading authorities of that period, culminating in the contributions of Gibbs and Planck. Further volumes in the series will treat the more elaborate development of thermo-dynamics, particularly from the standpoint of the second law and its statistical interpretation. Application to chemistry and biology will also be the subject of subsequent volumes.

I am deeply indebted to Particia Galkowski and her colleagues in the Sciences Library of Brown University for valuable assistance in the location of source material. My sincere gratitude goes to Susan Desilets Proto, Christine Hall, and Barbara Fisher of the Physics Department of Brown University for typing the translated and editorial commentary material.

My greatest debt is to those great investigators of the past who have created and developed the concept of energy.

R. BRUCE LINDSAY

CONTENTS

Contents

Contents

CONTENTS BY AUTHOR

INTRODUCTION: GENERALIZATION OF THE CONCEPT OF ENERGY AND EARLY APPLICATIONS

By the year 1845, the idea of energy as an important concept in mechanics had been pretty well established in Western Europe through the labors of the great continental mathematicians and theoretical physicists of the eighteenth century. Its clarity and significance were indeed handicapped by a misleading terminology, which confused it with the idea of force, a concept itself suffering from some confusion, although by that time generally interpreted in the Newtonian sense. At the end of the period just indicated, the notion of the intimate relation between mechanical energy and heat had been stressed in the work of J. R. Mayer and J. P. Joule, casting grave doubt on the materialistic theory of heat (caloric) and strongly suggesting the utility of looking upon heat as a form of energy into which mechanical energy could be transformed, and vice versa. For an anthology of and commentary on the literature leading up to this situation, reference may be made to *Energy: Historical Development of the Concept*, edited by R. Bruce Lindsay (Vol. 1, Benchmark Papers on Energy, Dowden, Hutchinson & Ross, Inc., Stroudsburg, Pa., 1975; throughout this volume we shall refer to this work as Lindsay, *Energy: Concept*).

In the early 1840s the notions of a relation between heat and mechanical energy and a mechanical equivalent of heat were considered bizarre by many if not most physical scientists of prominence. This new idea was treated with indifference or in many cases with actual hostility. It was clear that to make serious headway as an important tool in the study of nature the concept of energy and its generalization would need the careful examination and technical

1

support of scientists of major reputation, a status not possessed by Mayer, Joule, and Colding, who had daréd to defy the current views. Things began to move rather quickly around 1850, when men like William Thomson (later Lord Kelvin) finally abandoned the caloric theory and came to the support of the mechanical theory of heat. There followed a flood of papers by Thomson, Rankine, Clausius, and others.

Interestingly enough, however, it was not, after all, a distinguished, mature scientist who provided the first analytically rigorous basis for generalization of the concept of energy, but a young surgeon in the Prussian Army, who like Mayer had been trained in medicine and was practically self-taught in mathematics and physics. This was Hermann von Helmholtz, who on July 23, 1847, gave a lecture before the Physical Society of Berlin with the title "Über die Erhaltung der Kraft." The elaboration of the lecture was privately printed later the same year as a brochure in Berlin, because it was not accepted for publication in the professional physics journal. In this memoir, one of the classics of science, Helmholtz provided a masterly introduction to the use of the concept of energy in the various branches of physical science. In this volume we reprint in two separate parts the whole of this article in English translation, with commentaries on its significance for subsequent developments.

It is the purpose of the present volume to trace the story of the applications of the idea of energy during the nineteenth century, following Helmholtz's pioneering memoir. We begin with excerpts from the work of Clausius, Thomson (Lord Kelvin), Rankine, Regnault, and Joule, in which what they called at that time the mechanical theory of heat was applied to the physical phenomena displayed by fluids subjected to the action of heat. This is followed by a treatment of the role of energy in cosmical physics (e.g., the heat of the sun), its place in electricity and magnetism, and its application to field physics, as in the behavior of elastic media and the electromagnetic field. We then think it worthwhile to pay some attention to what was called the science of energetics and the controversy connected with it. Finally, we pay our respects to the development of thermodynamics as a sophisticated theory. In a certain sense, all through this volume we shall be tracing the early history of this very important physical theory, with special emphasis, to be sure, on the first law, the conservation of energy, stated in its most general form by Clausius: "Die Energie der Welt ist constant." In this volume there is less emphasis on the equally important second law of thermodynamics, which is to be the subject of subsequent volumes in the series.

2

Part I

THE PIONEER WORK OF HELMHOLTZ

Editor's Comments
on Paper 1

1 HELMHOLTZ
On the Conservation of Energy

As was indicated in the introduction, Helmholtz's 1847 memoir was a landmark in the development of thermodynamics. At one stroke the author showed that by generalizing the concept of mechanical energy and adopting the principle of its conservation amid all the transformations it can undergo, one gains a tool of enormous power in understanding a very wide range of physical phenomena.

With the boldness of youth, Helmholtz announced at the very beginning of his essay that it was intended for the study of physicists. I presume his idea was that the concept of energy had developed primarily through the attempt to understand physical phenomena. Although his memoir came to be considered one of the classics of science, it received a very cool reception when first published. This is not surprising; the author was only an army surgeon and not a professional physicist. His formal educational background in this discipline was almost nil. However, Helmholtz, in spite of his youth, had made a thorough study of the mathematicians and theoretical physicists of the eighteenth century and had obtained a good grasp of their methods and results.

The author's ultimate aim is a very ambitious one, to set up very general principles from which all natural laws can be derived. He announces at the outset that he will actually base all his deductions on a single great principle, which can be expressed in two alternative forms. The first is that it is impossible to create what he calls *Arbeitskraft* and we now call "energy" by the merely mutual actions of natural bodies in unbounded space. This is one way of expressing the basis for the principle of the conservation of energy. But he insists that there is an alternative way of expressing this, that all interactions in nature can be explained by attractive and repulsive forces, whose intensity depends only on the distance separating the bodies acting on each other. It is interesting to note that Helmholtz here comes out strongly for an atomic theory of the constitution of matter. Of course, his statement is rather loose; he says nothing about the influence of the masses of the particles on

4

the interaction forces, or the existence of fundamental force constants, like the constant of universal graviation. Still the fundamental idea is there. He proceeds to show that his second basic assumption is indeed equivalent to the first. In the course of this he provides some philosophical considerations to serve as background. This is very significant, as it reminds us of the same tendency in Mayer. Nineteenth-century German scientists found it impossible to do physics without philosophizing, e.g., bringing in the principle of causality.

The first two chapters of Helmholtz's memoir are essentially a review of analytical dynamics, with emphasis on the conservation of *vis viva* and then its generalization to the principle of the conservation of mechanical energy. This was essentially a reproduction in nineteenth-century terminology of the earlier dynamics of the Bernoullis, Euler, and Lagrange. But the emphasis was on the demonstration that central forces (of attraction and repulsion) lead to mechanical energy conservation. In other words, Helmholtz essentially established the energy equation for such forces in a more specific fashion than had been done by Lagrange.

Helmholtz then goes on to apply the principle of the conservation of mechanical energy to various mechanical motions, e.g., the motion of the planets in the solar system under the action of the central force of gravitation. He also applies the principle to wave motion and associates the intensity of a wave with the energy it transfers from place to place.

The next step was to treat heat as a form of energy and to discard the caloric theory. This Helmholtz did by treating heat as a form of energy of motion of the particles (molecules and atoms) of which all matter is composed. He stopped short of developing a full-fledged atomic theory of matter. This had to await the labors of Joule, Maxwell, Clausus, and Boltzmann.

Finally, Helmholtz paid his respects to electrical and magnetic phenomena from the standpoint of the energy concept. Here he was dealing with comparatively new branches of physics and his task was very difficult. Nevertheless, he broke new and very significant ground and his suggestions bore fruit in subsequent development. Applications to this field and in particular to the work on electromagnetism, based on the earlier researches of Ampère and Faraday, form by far the larger part of his memoir. He followed up this material with his own later investigations in electrodynamics.

In the last page or two, Helmholtz has something to say about the possible application of the energy idea to living things. Here he goes by no means as far as Robert Mayer did in his famous 1845 memoir, "The Motions of Organisms and Their Relation to Metabolism" [reprinted in English translation in *Julius Robert Mayer—Prophet of Energy*, by R. B. Lindsay (Pergamon Press, Inc., Elmsford, N.Y., 1973, pp. 75–145)]. The first part of the memoir is reprinted in Lindsay, *Energy: Concept* (Paper 29B).

In Paper 1, Helmholtz makes no mention of Mayer. There is indeed no indication that at that time he had ever heard of Mayer. This is not surprising, considering the lack of dissemination of Mayer's writings.

Paper 1 is an English translation of the first four sections of Helmholtz's memoir, including his important discussion of the application of the energy idea to heat. We omit the sections on electricity and magnetism, but include his final paragraph. When Helmholtz's collected papers were published in 1882, he included several appendixes commenting on certain aspects of his 1847 memoir. We include the appendix referring to his ultimate recognition of the priority of Mayer.

Hermann von Helmholtz (1821–1894) was probably the most distinguished German physicist of the nineteenth century. Before he turned completely to physics at the age of 50, he had already developed an outstanding reputation as a physiologist, and his treatises on the eye and ear have remained classics in their field. He was a man of very wide interests and devoted much attention to mathematics, philosophy, and the arts.

1

On the Conservation of Energy

Hermann von Helmholtz

This article was translated expressly for this Benchmark volume by R. Bruce Lindsay, Brown University, from "Über die Erhaltung der Kraft," in H. von Helmholtz, Wissenschaftliche Abhandlungen, *Vol. 1, Johann Ambrosius Barth, Leipzig, 1892, pp. 12–41, 68–75.*

Introduction

The present work in its principal contents is directed to the attention of physicists. I have therefore preferred to present the basis of it independent of any philosophical foundation and purely in the form of a physical hypothesis. It is my desire to follow out the consequences of this assumption and to compare the consequences in the different branches of physics with the experimental laws of natural phenomena. The derivation of the laws in question can be attacked from two standpoints, i.e., either from the principle that it is impossible to create work [*Arbeitskraft*, or energy] by the mutual action of natural bodies in unbounded space, or from the assumption that all interactions in nature can be explained by attractive and repulsive forces, whose intensity depends only on the distance separating the bodies acting on each other. It is shown at the beginning of the paper that these two principles are really identical. However, they possess a still more essential meaning for the ultimate aim of physical science, as I shall endeavor to make clear in this introduction.

It is the task of this branch of science to seek for the laws by which individual natural phenomena can be referred to general rules and can, indeed, be derived from the latter. These rules, e.g., the law of the refraction and reflection of light, the law of Mariotte and Gay-Lussac for the volume of gases, are obviously not to be considered as general concepts by which all phenomena associated with them can be embraced. The search for such laws is the task of the experimental side of our sciences. The theoretical part of science, on the other hand, endeavors to find the unknown causes of phenomena from their visible effects. It tries to come to grips with the latter through the principle of causality.[1] In this business we must use (and with justification) the fundamental principle that every change taking place in nature must have a sufficient cause. The immediate causes to which we attribute natural phenomena can themselves be either inalterable or alterable. In the latter case, the same fundamental principle makes it necessary for us to seek for other causes for their alterability, and so on, until we have attained to the last causes, which act in accordance with an invariable law and which therefore at every instant produce the same effect under the same circumstances. The final aim of theoretical science is accordingly to discover the last invariable causes of natural events. Whether, indeed, all natural phenomena can be traced back in this way, and whether, accordingly, nature is completely understandable in a conceptual sense or

[1] See Appendix 1.

7

whether it involves changes that elude the law of causality, which fall into the realm of spontaneity, is a matter which cannot be decided here. In any case it is clear that science, whose purpose it is to understand nature, must proceed from the assumption of its understandability, and must carry out its investigations in accordance with this assumption until we are forced through incontrovertible facts to recognize its limitations.

Science regards the objects of the external world from the standpoint of two kinds of abstractions. First, we regard their mere existence, wholly apart from their actions on other objects or on our sense organs. As such the objects are characterized as *matter*. The existence of matter in itself is as something inert and without activity. In matter we distinguish spatial distribution and quantity (mass), which is considered to be externally invariable. We are not permitted to ascribe qualitative differences to matter. For if we speak of different kinds of matter, we locate the difference only in its actions on other matter, i.e., on the forces it exerts. Matter in itself can therefore undergo no other kind of change than spatial, i.e., what we call *motion*. The objects of nature, however, are not bereft of their effects, for we indeed recognize them only through the actions that they produce on our sense organs, it being understood that we ascribe the actions to something which produces them. Accordingly, if we wish to apply the concept of matter to real things, we must have recourse to a second abstraction, the possibility that matter can exert effects, i.e., has forces associated with it. It is to be noted that in their application to nature the concepts of matter and force are never to be separated. Pure matter in itself would be of no consequence for the rest of nature, since it could never produce any change in the latter or in our sense organs. A pure force might be thought to have existence, but then on the other hand should really not exist, because we have named the existing thing *matter*. It is just as incorrect to wish to explain matter as something real, and force as a mere abstract concept to which nothing real corresponds. Actually, both are abstractions from reality found in quite the same way. We cannot indeed perceive matter in and for itself but only through its forces.

We have seen above that natural phenomena are to be ascribed to invariable final causes. This demand is formulated in such a way that forces which do not depend explicitly on time must operate as the final causes. In chemical science, we have called *elements* those bits of matter with constant forces (indestructible qualities). If, however, we think of the universe as separated into elements with constant qualities, the only possible changes in such a system are spatial, i.e., motions, and the external relations through which the action of the forces is modified can still only be spatial. Accordingly, the forces can only be motion forces, dependent in their action only on spatial relations.

To put the matter succinctly, natural phenomena are to be ascribed to motions of matter under invariable motion forces, which depend only on spatial relations.

Motion is change of spatial relations. Spatial relations are possible only with respect to delimited space and not with respect to empty space, which has no differences among its parts. Hence, motion can be experienced only as the change in the spatial relations of at least two material bodies with respect to each other. Force considered as the cause of motion can accordingly only be inferred for the relation of at least two bodies with respect to each other. It is therefore to be defined as the effort of two masses to change their mutual relative position. However, the force that two whole masses exert on each other must be resolved into the mutual forces of all their component parts. Mechanics is therefore based on the forces of material points, i.e., the points of space filled with matter.[1] However, points have no spatial relation with respect to each other except their separation, for the direction of the line joining them can only be specified with respect to at least two other points. A force connected with motion can therefore only be the cause of a change in the distance of separation, i.e., either an attractive or a repulsive force. This also follows at once from the principle of sufficient reason. The forces that two masses exert on each other must necessarily be completely determined in magnitude and direction as soon as the positions of the masses are given. However, for two points, only one direction is uniquely determined and that is the line joining them. Consequently, the forces that they exert on each other must be directed along this line, and their magnitude can depend only on their distance of separation.

Thus, the task of physical science is to ascribe natural phenomena to time-invariant (i.e., not dependent explicitly on time) attractive and repulsive forces, whose magnitude depends solely on the distance of separation. The ability to carry out this task is at the same time the condition for the complete understanding of nature. Up to now analytical mechanics has not assumed this limitation on the concept of forces of motion; first, it has not been clear as to the origin of its fundamental principles. Second is the question of being able to calculate the resultant of compound forces in cases in which there has been no success in resolving them into simple forces. A large part of the general principles of motion of systems of masses holds only for the case in which these masses act on each other through attractive or repulsive forces. These principles are the principle of virtual velocities, the principle of the conservation of motion of the center of mass, that of the conservation of the plane of rotation and of the moment of rotation [*Ed. note:* moment of inertia] of a free system, and finally the principle of the conservation of *vis viva*. Of these principles only the first and the last have real application to terrestrial motions, because the others apply only to completely free systems. As we shall proceed to show, the first is a special case of the last, which therefore appears as the most general and important principle of mechanics.

Theoretical science, therefore, if it is not to be content with reaching only half-way toward an understanding of nature, must make its point of view agree with the requirement just presented about the nature of simple forces and their consequences. The task of understanding will be complete when once the ascription of the phenomena to simple forces is completed, and when at the same time it can be shown that the chosen process is the only one permitted by the phenomena. For then this process would be found to be the necessary way to understand nature. One would then be able to ascribe objective truth to it.

I. The Principle of Conservation of *Vis Viva*

We begin with the assumption that it is impossible with any combination of natural bodies continuously to create moving force out of nothing. From this principle,

---

[1] See Appendix 2.

Carnot and Clapeyron[1] derived theoretically a series of laws concerning the specific and latent heats of a great variety of substances, partly already well known and in part as yet not verified experimentally. It is the purpose of the present memoir to extend the principle in question to all branches of physics, in part to indicate the applicability of the principle in all those cases in which the phenomenological laws have already been established, and also in part to follow up further, with the help of this principle and in analogy with the better known cases, the laws of those phenomena that have so far not been completely investigated, and thereby lend assistance to experimentation.

The principle in question can be stated as follows. Let us contemplate a system of natural bodies that stand in a certain spatial relation with respect to each other and perform motions under the influence of their mutual interaction forces until they have reached a certain different configuration. We can then regard the velocities the bodies have gained as equivalent to a certain amount of mechanical work and transform them into such. If we now wish to make the same forces effective for a second time, to produce again the same amount of work we must in some way return the bodies to their original condition by the application of other forces available to us. For this we shall again have to expend a certain amount of work.

In this case, our principle demands that the quantity of work that is obtained when the system moves from its initial configuration into the second one, and that which is lost when the system returns to its initial configuration, must be precisely the same no matter what the method, the path, or the velocities involved in this transition may be. For if the work along any particular path were greater than that on another, we could employ the first to gain the work and then give back only a part of this in returning to the original configuration. Hence, in this way an indefinite amount of mechanical energy could be gained, leading to a perpetual motion machine, which would not only be able to keep itself in motion but provide external work.

If we ask for the mathematical expression for this principle, we find it in the well-known law of the conservation of *vis viva*. The quantities of work produced and expended can be expressed in terms of a mass m raised to a height h. The work then is mgh, where g is the intensity of the force of gravity. [*Ed. note:* We call g the acceleration of gravity in modern terminology.] To attain the height h when thrown vertically into the air, a body must have the initial velocity $\sqrt{2gh}$, and it will gain the same velocity when it falls down again. Accordingly, we have $\frac{1}{2}mv^2 = mgh$. Consequently, one half the quantity mv^2, which is called the *vis viva* [*Editor's Note:* Helmholtz uses the German equivalent expression *lebendige Kraft*] of the body of mass m, can also serve as a measure of the quantity of work. To provide better agreement with contemporary terminology, I propose to call $\frac{1}{2}mv^2$ the *vis viva* and thus make the latter equal to the quantity of work. For the earlier applications of *vis viva*, which were restricted to the principle just named, the change (i.e., inclusion of the factor $\frac{1}{2}$) is not significant. But it has certain advantages in what is to follow. With this interpretation, the principle of *vis viva* now says that, when an arbitrary number of movable mass points move only under the influence of forces

---

[1] Poggendorff's *Annalen*, 59, 446, 566.

10

due only to their mutual interaction or forces directed toward fixed centers, the sum of the *vis viva* quantities for all the mass points is the same at every time instant for which the points have the same relative positions with respect to each other or to the fixed force center, irrespective of the paths followed and the velocity changes in the motion. If we think of the *vis viva* as used to raise the various mass points of the system to certain heights, it follows from what we have just shown that the quantities of work done under the conditions cited must also be equal. However, this principle does not hold for all possible kinds of forces. In mechanics, the principle is commonly associated with the principle of virtual velocities, and this can be demonstrated only for material points subject to attractive and repulsive forces. To begin with, we shall show here that the principle of the conservation of *vis viva* holds only when the forces acting can be resolved into forces which act along the lines joining the material points, and in magnitude depend only on the distances separating the points. In mechanics such forces are usually called central forces. It follows, therefore, that in all actions of natural bodies on each other, in which the principle in question is to be applied to all the smallest parts of these bodies, it is such central forces that are to be treated as the simplest fundamental forces.

Let us first consider a single material point of mass m that moves under the influence of forces due to a collection of bodies attached to a rigid system A. Mechanics then shows us how to determine the position and velocity of the point at each instant of time. We shall therefore consider the time t as the independent variable and let x, y, and z be the coordinates of m with respect to a coordinate system fixed in A. Let the velocity of m in its path be q, and let the component velocities of m along the axes be, respectively, $u = dx/dt$, $v = dy/dt$, and $w = dz/dt$. Finally, take as the components of the forces acting

$$X = m\frac{du}{dt}, \qquad Y = m\frac{dv}{dt}, \qquad Z = m\frac{dw}{dt}.$$

Our principle now demands that $\frac{1}{2}mq^2$ and accordingly q^2 also will depend not merely on t but also on the x, y, z coordinates of m. Thus

$$d(q^2) = \frac{d(q^2)}{dx}\,dx + \frac{d(q^2)}{dy}\,dy + \frac{d(q^2)}{dz}\,dz. \qquad (1)$$

Since $q^2 = u^2 + v^2 + w^2$, we have

$$d(q^2) = 2u\,du + 2v\,dv + 2w\,dw.$$

If now we put dx/dt in place of u and $X\,dt/m$ in place of du, and similarly for the other components, we get

$$d(q^2) = \frac{2X}{m}\,dx + \frac{2Y}{m}\,dy + \frac{2Z}{m}\,dz. \qquad (2)$$

11

Since equations (1) and (2) hold for arbitrary dx, dy, and dz, it follows that

$$\frac{d(q^2)}{dx} = \frac{2X}{m}, \quad \frac{d(q^2)}{dy} = \frac{2Y}{m}, \quad \frac{d(q^2)}{dz} = \frac{2Z}{m}.$$

However, if q^2 is a function only of x, y, and z independent of time, it follows that the same is true of X, Y, and Z; i.e., the direction and magnitude of the force is a function only of the position of m in the system A.

If now in place of the system A we think of a single material point a, it follows from what has just been shown that the direction and magnitude of the force exerted on m by a will be determined only by the relative position of m with respect to a. Since the position of m with respect to a is determined only by their separation r, it follows that the force in both direction and magnitude must be a function of r. Let us now think of an arbitrary rectangular coordinate system with origin at a. We must therefore have

$$md(q^2) = 2X\, dx + 2Y\, dy + 2Z\, dz = 0 \qquad (3)$$

whenever

$$d(r^2) = 2x\, dx + 2y\, dy + 2z\, dz = 0,$$

i.e., whenever

$$dz = -\frac{x\, dx + y\, dy}{z}.$$

If we insert this in equation (3), we get

$$\left(X - \frac{x}{z} Z \right) dx + \left(Y - \frac{y}{z} Z \right) dy = 0.$$

For arbitrary dx and dy, therefore, we obtain

$$X = \frac{x}{z} Z \quad \text{and} \quad Y = \frac{y}{z} Z,$$

which means that the resultant force must be directed toward the origin of the coordinate system, i.e., toward the point a.

It therefore follows that for systems which obey the law of the conservation of *vis viva* the forces are central forces.

II. The Principle of the Conservation of Energy

[*Ed. note:* In the title of this section, Helmholtz still uses the word *Kraft*, where we should put energy. We shall therefore use the word energy whenever Helmholtz uses *Kraft* in the conservation sense.]

We now desire to give the law stated in Part I a more general expression when central forces are in question.

If ϕ is the intensity (magnitude) of the force in the r direction, it being assumed that ϕ is positive for attraction and negative for repulsion, we have

$$X = -\frac{x}{r}\phi, \quad Y = -\frac{y}{r}\phi, \quad Z = -\frac{z}{r}.\phi. \tag{1}$$

Hence, according to equation (2) of the previous section,

$$m\,d(q^2) = -\frac{2\phi}{r}(x\,dx + y\,dy + z\,dz)$$

and, accordingly,

$$\tfrac{1}{2}m\,d(q^2) = -\phi\,dr.$$

If Q and R, and q and r are corresponding path velocities and distances, respectively, we have

$$\tfrac{1}{2}mQ^2 - \tfrac{1}{2}mq^2 = -\int_r^R \phi\,dr. \tag{2}$$

If we examine this equation more closely, we see that the right side is the difference between the *vis viva* values for m in two different positions with respect to the origin. To find the meaning of $\int_r^R \phi\,dr$, we think of ϕ, which varies along r, as represented in terms of rectangular coordinates. Then the integral in question will denote the area of the plane surface included between the curve between the ordinates R and r and the axis of abscissas. Just as one can treat this area as the sum of all the infinitely many abscissas lying in the interval, so we may interpret the integral as the component of all the force intensities that are effective in the distances between R and r. We now call the forces that endeavor to move m, so long as they have not actually produced motion, *tension* forces [*Spannkräfte*] in contrast to the *vis viva* or living force of bodies in motion. In this notation, $\int_r^R \phi\,dr$ becomes the sum of all the tension forces between the distances R and r. The statement of the general principle of conservation involved then takes the following form: The increase in the *vis viva* of a mass point in its motion under the influence of a central force is equal to the sum of the tension forces associated with the change in the distance from the force center.

[*Ed. note:* The preceding statements are awkward and misleading from a mathematical point of view (if not indeed incorrect) and also unfortunate from the standpoint of terminology. The author's reference to the integral as an area is, of course, correct, but it is wrong to say that the area is the sum of an infinite number of abscissas, when it is really the limit of the sum of the infinitesimal areas erected along the axis of abscissas with ordinates ending on the ϕ curve. Moreover, to refer to this area as the *sum* of forces, which he calls tension forces, is unfortunate. Actually, it is the sum of quantities obtained by multiplying each ϕ by a small increment dr along r. We recognize this in modern terminology as the *work* done by ϕ in this interval of motion. It is curious that Helmholtz did not recognize and state the result in this way, for Coriolis in the late 1820s had already introduced the term *work* for such a product, and Carnot, whom Helmholtz cites, had denoted the product of an intensive quantity like pressure and an extensive quantity like change in volume as work done in the case of a gas. We recognize the theorem demonstrated by Helmholtz as the "work–kinetic energy" theorem of modern mechanics. Of course, this theorem was essentially derived by Euler for the special case of collisions around the middle of the eighteenth century, and it is clear that Daniel Bernoulli grasped its significance at about the same time. It was also mathematically implicit in Lagrange's *Mécanique Analytique*, although he did not choose to stress its physical significance.]

If we think of two points, subject to their mutual attractive force, originally at distance R from each other, they will move toward each other under the action of the force to the smaller distance r; hence their *vis viva* will increase. On the other hand, if the separation is increased, the *vis viva* must decrease, and finally be entirely exhausted. We can therefore in the case of attractive forces think of the sum of the tension forces for separations between $r = 0$ and $r = R$, i.e., $\int_0^R \phi \, dr$, as the *vis viva* that is used up. [*Ed. note:* Here again the use of tension force in place of work done makes the expression very awkward.] The reverse takes place in the case of repulsive forces. If the points are at separation distance R, by further separation they will gain *vis viva*. The still existing tension forces are those between $r = R$ and $r = \infty$, whereas the last are between $r = 0$ and $r = R$.

To generalize our law, let us think of an arbitrary number of material points with masses $m_1, m_2, m_3, \ldots$, with the general designation m_a, and with rectangular coordinates x_a, y_a, and z_a. Let the component forces acting on them be X_a, Y_a, and Z_a. Let the component velocities be u_a, v_a, and w_a, and the path velocity be q_a. The distance between the particles m_a and m_b will be r_{ab}, and the central force between them ϕ_{ab}. The equation of motion of m_n [in analogy with equation (1) of this section] will therefore be

$$X_n = \sum \left[(x_a - x_n) \frac{\phi_{an}}{r_{an}} \right] = m_n \frac{du_n}{dt},$$

$$Y_n = \sum \left[(y_a - y_n) \frac{\phi_{an}}{r_{an}} \right] = m_n \frac{dv_n}{dt},$$

$$Z_n = \sum \left[(z_a - z_n) \frac{\phi_{an}}{r_{an}} \right] = m_n \frac{dw_n}{dt},$$

where the summation sign $\sum$ relates to all terms originating by letting a take all values $1, 2, 3, \ldots$, except n.

Let us now multiply the first equation by $dx_a = u_a \, dt$, the second by $dy_a = v_a \, dt$, the third by $dz_a = w_a \, dt$, and think of the three equations set up for all individual points m_b. If we then add the equations, we get

14

$$\sum\left[(x_a - x_b)\,dx_b \cdot \frac{\phi_{ab}}{r_{ab}}\right] = \sum\left[\frac{1}{2}m_a\,d(u_a^2)\right],$$

$$\sum\left[(y_a - y_b)\,dy_b \cdot \frac{\phi_{ab}}{r_{ab}}\right] = \sum\left[\frac{1}{2}m_a\,d(v_a^2)\right],$$

$$\sum\left[(z_a - z_b)\,dz_b \cdot \frac{\phi_{ab}}{r_{ab}}\right] = \sum\left[\frac{1}{2}m_a\,d(w_a^2)\right].$$

The terms on the left are obtained if we put in place of a all the indexes $1, 2, 3, \ldots$, and for b all such indexes also which are greater or less than a. The sums therefore are divided into two parts; in one of these a is always greater than b, in the other it is always smaller. It is clear that for every term in the one part of the form

$$(x_p - x_q)\,dx_q \cdot \frac{\phi_{pq}}{r_{pq}}$$

there will be a term in the other part of the form

$$(x_q - x_p)\,dx_p\,\frac{\phi_{pq}}{r_{pq}},$$

which when added together yield

$$-(x_p - x_q)(dx_p - dx_q)\,\frac{\phi_{pq}}{r_{pq}}.$$

If we take account of this in adding all three sums on the left and set

$$\tfrac{1}{2}d[(x_a - x_b)^2 + (y_a - y_b)^2 + (z_a - z_b)^2] = r_{ab}\,dr_{ab},$$

we obtain

$$-\sum[\phi_{ab}\,dr_{ab}] = \sum[\tfrac{1}{2}m_a\,d(q_a^2)], \qquad (3)$$

or, integrating,

$$-\sum\left[\int_{r_{ab}}^{R_{ab}}\phi_{ab}\,dr_{ab}\right] = \sum[\tfrac{1}{2}m_aQ_a^2] - \sum[\tfrac{1}{2}m_aq_a^2], \qquad (4)$$

where R and Q go together and r and q, likewise. We have here on the left the sum of the expended tension forces for the entire system, and on the right the difference between the initial and final *vis viva* values for the whole system. We can now state the general law as follows: In all cases of the motion of free material points under

15

the influence of their mutual attractive or repulsive forces, whose magnitudes depend only on the separation of the points, the loss in the total tension force is always equal to the gain in *vis viva*, and vice versa. Accordingly, the *sum* of the tension forces and the *vis viva* values is always a constant. Expressed in this most general way, the law can be called the law of the conservation of energy. [*Ed. note:* If *Spannkraft* were translated as *work* done by the resultant forces, this would be the generalized work–kinetic energy theorem. Moreover, if the work could be put equal to a change in what we call the potential energy of the system, this theorem would be the generalized mechanical energy equation, in which the total energy is the sum of the kinetic and potential energy. It would then express the law of the conservation of mechanical energy. Lagrange had already set up such an equation in his *Mécanique Analytique*.]

In this derivation of the theorem, nothing is essentially changed if a portion of the points, which we may designate with the letter d, are assumed to be fixed, so that $q_d = 0$. The law then takes the form

$$\sum [\phi_{ab} \, dr_{ab}] + \sum [\phi_{ad} \, dr_{ad}] = - \sum [\tfrac{1}{2} m_b \, d(q_b^2)]. \tag{5}$$

It still remains to notice in what relation the principle of the conservation of mechanical energy (*Kraft*) stands with respect to the most general law of statics, i.e., the principle of virtual velocities. This indeed follows immediately from our equations (3) and (5). If equilibrium is to exist for a given configuration of the system, then all points remain at rest and have no tendency to move, so that $q_a = 0$ for all a and $dq_a = 0$ for all a. From equation (3) there then follows

$$\sum [(\phi_{ab} \, dr_{ab}] = 0. \tag{6}$$

If indeed forces act from outside the system, we have, from equation (5),

$$\sum [\phi_{ab} \, dr_{ab}] + \sum [\phi_{ad} \, dr_{ad}] = 0. \tag{7}$$

In these equations we are to understand that dr indicates changes in the separation distances produced by arbitrary small displacements of the system subject to the constraints on it. In the earlier deductions, we have seen that an increase in the *vis viva*, for example, in a transition from rest to motion, can only be brought about by the expenditure of tension force [*Ed. note:* work]. The last two equations, corresponding to this, say that under such conditions, when through no single possible direction of motion tension force can be expended [*Ed. note:* work done], the system when once at rest, will stay at rest.

It is well known that from the equations just set down all the equations of statics can be deduced. The most important consequence for the nature of acting forces is this: If we no longer allow the points of the system to have arbitrary displacements as if they were completely free, but assume that they are rigidly fastened together, so that in equation (7) all $dr_{ab} = 0$, we get the individual equations

16

$$\sum [\phi_{ab} \, dr_{ab}] = 0,$$

$$\sum [\phi_{ad} \, dr_{ad}] = 0;$$

then the external as well as the internal forces must be in equilibrium. Therefore, if an arbitrary collection of natural bodies is brought into a state of equilibrium by the action of external forces, the equilibrium will not be disturbed (1) if we think of the individual points of the system in this equilibrium configuration rigidly fastened to each other, and (2) if we then remove the forces with which they act on each other. From this there further follows: If the forces with which two points of the systems act on each other are replaced by two external forces in equilibrium, then the latter must maintain the equilibrium, if in place of the natural forces on the points a rigid connection between them is substituted. However, forces that act on two points along a fixed straight line are in equilibrium if only they act along this line and are equal and oppositely directed. It accordingly follows for the forces due to the points themselves, which are equal and opposite to the external forces, that the former must lie along the lines joining the points and must be attractive or repulsive.

We can summarize the principles just set up as follows:

1. As often as natural bodies act on each other by means of attractive or repulsive forces, which do not depend explicitly on time and velocity, the sum of the *vis viva* and tension forces (work done) must be a constant. The maximum work that can be won must then be a definite finite quantity.

2. If, on the other hand, natural bodies are acted on by forces that depend explicitly on time and velocity, or act in directions other than along the line separating two bodies acting on each other, arrangements of such bodies are possible in which force (energy) is either gained or lost at infinity.

3. In the equilibrium of a system of bodies under the action of central forces, the internal forces must be in equilibrium with each other and likewise the external forces, as soon as we think of the bodies as bound rigidly together, and it is only the whole system that is movable as a whole with respect to bodies outside it. A rigid system, therefore, can never be set in motion through the action of its internal forces, but only through the action of external forces. If indeed there were other than central forces acting, rigid aggregates of bodies could be arranged, which would move by themselves, without needing a relation to other bodies.[1]

III. Application of the Principle to Mechanical Theorems

We now take up the special applications of the law of the conservation of energy [*Ed. note:* mechanical energy is meant]. At first we have to mention briefly those cases in which the conservation of *vis viva* has already been used and is well known.

1. All motions that take place under the influence of the general law of gravitation, i.e., the heavenly bodies and heavy terrestrial bodies. In the former case the law corresponds to an increase in the velocity as the body approaches the central

---

[1] See Appendix 4.

body, and also to the constancy of its orbital major axis and its period of revolution. In the latter case it involves the well-known law that the terminal velocity of fall depends only on the height from which the fall takes place and not on the direction and shape of the path of fall, and that this velocity when it is not reduced by friction or inelastic collision is just sufficient to lift the body up again to the height from which it fell. That the height of fall of a given weight is used as a measure of the quantity of work done by our machines has already been mentioned.

2. The transfer of motions through incompressible solid and liquid bodies insofar as neither friction nor inelastic collisions take place. In this case our general principle is usually expressed as the rule that a motion propagated through a mechanical agent always decreases in force magnitude in the same proportion as it increases in velocity. For example, if we think of the situation in which a certain amount of work is done through the agency of a machine in raising a weight m with velocity c, and then imagine that with another device the weight nm is raised, this will be done with velocity c/n, so that in both cases the quantity of tension force [work] developed in the same time is represented by mgc, in which g is the intensity of gravity.

3. The motion of completely elastic solid and liquid bodies. The condition for complete elasticity may be taken to mean that a body changed in shape and volume can return to its original shape and volume, it being further assumed that there is no friction in its internal parts. It was in such cases that our principle was most early recognized and most often used. The most common application in the case of solids is that of elastic collisions, whose laws are easily deduced from our principle plus that of the conservation of the center of gravity. Another example is provided by the manifold elastic vibrations, which continue even with new collisions, until they are dissipated by internal friction or the transfer of energy to the surrounding medium. In the case of fluid bodies, even liquids (which are elastic with very large coefficients of elasticity and provided with an equilibrium configuration of the component particles) as well as gases (with lower coefficients of elasticity and without equilibrium configuration), in general all motions are transformed into propagation as waves. Examples are provided by the waves on the surface of liquids, sound waves, and probably light and radiant heat.

The *vis viva* of a single particle Δm in a medium being traversed by a wave train is apparently specified by the velocity that the particle has in the equilibrium configuration. The general wave equation determines the particle velocity u. If a^2 denotes the intensity of the wave, λ the wavelength, α the velocity of propagation, x the abscissa, and t the time, we have

$$u = a \cdot \cos\left[\frac{2}{\lambda}\pi(x - \alpha t)\right].$$

[*Ed. note:* The author is restricting his attention to a plane harmonic wave propagated in the x direction.] For the equilibrium position, $u = a$; consequently, the *vis viva* of the particle Δm during the wave motion is $\frac{1}{2}\Delta m \cdot a^2$, and is proportional to the intensity. If the waves spread out spherically from a central source, they set in motion more and more of the medium as they spread; consequently, the intensity must decrease if the total *vis viva* is to remain constant. Since the amount of

18

the medium embraced by the wave increases as the square of the distance from the source, the intensity must decrease in inverse proportion.

The laws of the reflection, refraction, and polarization of light at the interface of two media having different wave velocities were, as is well known, derived by Fresnel from the assumption that the motion of the particles at the interface is the same on both sides of the boundary and that there is conservation of *vis viva*. [*Ed. note:* See Lindsay, *Energy: Concept*, p. 171.] In the interference of two wave trains there is no loss of *vis viva*, but only a redistribution. Two wave trains with individual intensities a^2 and b^2 give all points they traverse the intensity $a^2 + b^2$, as long as they do not interfere. If there is interference, the points of maximum intensity have intensity $(a + b)^2$, or $2ab$ greater than the sum of the squares of a and b, whereas the points of minimum intensity have intensity $(a - b)^2$, or $2ab$ less than the same quantity.

The *vis viva* of elastic waves is destroyed only in those cases which we call their absorption. The absorption of sound waves takes place principally on impact with flexible inelastic bodies, like curtains and clothing. It is principally due to a transformation of the motion in the bodies that are struck and in loss through friction. It is not yet clear whether the motion is also dissipated by the friction of the air particles against each other in the medium being traversed. [*Ed. note:* The author has in mind the possible effect of viscosity on sound propagation in a fluid medium. This had already been demonstrated by G. G. Stokes in an article published in 1845, but Helmholtz obviously had not seen this when he prepared his memoir. See *Acoustics: Its Historical and Philosophical Development*, edited by R. Bruce Lindsay (Benchmark Series in Acoustics, Dowden, Hutchinson & Ross, Inc., Stroudsburg, Pa., 1973, pp. 262ff).] The absorption of heat radiation is accompanied by a proportional development of heat. We shall investigate in the next section the extent to which the latter corresponds to a certain energy (*Kraft*) equivalent. The conservation of energy would be maintained if as much heat as is lost by the radiating body reappears in the object that is irradiated, it being assumed that no leakage takes place and that no part of the radiation goes elsewhere than to the irradiated body in question. In investigations on heat radiation the theorem [*Ed. note:* of conservation of energy] has been assumed up to now, but no attempts at its verification are known to me. In the absorption of light radiation by partially transparent and wholly opaque bodies, we recognize three kinds of effects. First, phosphorescent bodies absorb light in such a way that they are able to emit it again as light. Second, nearly all, if not all, light radiation appears to produce heat. The objections to the assumption of the identity of the heat-producing, light-producing and chemical-reaction-producing spectral radiation appear to have been rather thoroughly dissipated in recent times.[1] However, the heat equivalent of the radiation-producing chemical and light effects appears to be remarkably small in comparison with its intensive effect on the eye. If indeed the fundamental identity of these rays that produce different effects should not be confirmed, then we must regard the nature of light motion as explained by some unknown mechanism. Third, the

[1] See Macedonio Melloni, Poggendorff's *Annalen*, **57**, p. 300. Also Brücks, **65**, p. 593.

absorbed light produces chemical effects. With respect to energy relations we must here distinguish two kinds of such effects; in one the light acts to trigger the activity of the chemical change, in analogy with the action of a catalyst, e.g., the action on a mixture of chlorine and hydrogen; in the second case, it works against the chemical reaction, e.g., in the decomposition of silver salts or in the effect of light on green plants. For most of these effects, however, the action of light is still so little understood that we can by no means judge the magnitude of the energy involved. It is only in the action on green plants that the energy seems to be significant both in magnitude and intensity.

IV. The Energy Equivalent of Heat

Those mechanical phenomena in which an absolute loss of energy has been assumed are the following:

1. The collision of inelastic bodies. For the most part, this is associated with a change in shape and an increase in density of the colliding bodies, and accordingly with an increase in tension forces (*Spannkräfte*). In repeated collisions of this kind we find a considerable development of heat, e.g., in the hammering of a piece of metal. Finally, a part of the motion is given off as sound to the surrounding solid and gaseous media.

2. Friction, both on the surfaces of two bodies rubbed against each other, as well as in the inside of bodies, whose shape is being changed, through the displacement of the smaller component parts with respect to each other. In the case of friction, there are also small changes in the molecular constitution of bodies, i.e., at the onset of their motions with respect to each other. Later the surfaces seem to accommodate themselves to such an extent to this situation that for further motion these changes must be considered as vanishingly small. In certain cases such changes do not show up at all, e.g., when fluids rub against each other or against solid bodies. In addition to such effects, however, thermal and electrical effects always take place.

In mechanics we are accustomed to represent friction as a force that opposes the motion then taking place and whose magnitude is a function of the velocity. Evidently, this conception is only a very incomplete expression made largely to facilitate calculations of a complicated effect in which a great variety of molecular forces interact with each other. From this viewpoint it followed that *vis viva* is completely destroyed, just as one assumed was the case with elastic collisions. [*Ed. note:* This appears to be a slip. Helmholtz evidently meant "inelastic" collisions.] This does not take into consideration, however, that, wholly aside from the increase in tension force in the bodies subject to collision and friction [*Ed. note:* we should say increase in potential energy], the heat developed represents a form of energy, through which we could produce mechanical effects. The production of electricity in such cases is also neglected, making itself evident through mechanical attractions or repulsions or through the development of heat. The question still remains whether the sum of these energies always corresponds to the lost mechanical energy. For the cases in which molecular changes and the development of electricity are for the most part avoided, this question would be whether for a certain loss in mechanical energy there always arises a definite quantity of heat, and to what extent a quantity of heat can be treated as corresponding to an equivalent mechanical energy. For the solution of the first question few investigations have so far been carried out. Joule[1] has investigated the quantities of heat developed by friction in water in narrow tubes as well as in a vessel in which the water was set in motion by a paddle wheel. In the first case he found that the heat which raises the temperature of 1 kilogram of water 1°C is equivalent to the work needed to raise 452 kilograms to a height of 1 meter. In the second case the 452 kilograms became 521 kilograms. However, his methods of measurement do not appear to be sufficiently adequate to deal with the experimental difficulty of his investigation, and hence these results can make no claim to accuracy. [*Ed. note:* Joule's early work was indeed subject to lack of precision, but by 1847, at the time Helmholtz wrote the present paper, Joule had achieved noteworthy accuracy. He had, of course, already determined the mechanical equivalent of heat electrically as early as 1843, and by 1845 had evaluated it in terms of the compression and expansion of gases. When in 1881, Helmholtz edited his 1847 memoir he paid his respects in a special note, not reproduced here, to the precision of Joule's later work. See Lindsay, *Energy: Concept*, p. 345]. Probably these [early results of Joule] are too high, for in Joule's arrangement part of the heat produced may well have been lost to observation; moreover, the possible loss of mechanical energy in other parts of the machinery was not taken into account.

Let us now turn to the further question, to what extent heat can correspond to an energy equivalent. The materialistic theory of heat [*Ed. note:* he means caloric] must necessarily consider the quantity of heat substance as constant. It can produce mechanical energy only through its striving to spread itself out. In this theory the energy equivalent of heat can consist only in the work done in the transfer of heat from a higher to a lower temperature. Carnot and Clapeyron have worked out the problem from this point of view, and all results from their assumptions have been experimentally confirmed, at least for gases and vapors.

To explain heat due to friction, the materialistic theory must either assume that the heat is conducted to the rubbed substance from the outside (W. Henry[2]) or, according to Berthollet, assume that the heat is due to the compression of the surface of the rubbed substance and the particles rubbed off. The first assumption is negated by the fact that no experiment has yet demonstrated that in the neighborhood of the particles rubbed off by the friction there is any development of cold corresponding to the heat generated. As far as the second is concerned, if we leave aside the fact that it must assume a large and improbable action of the scarcely perceptible increase in density produced by the hydraulic press, it is completely disproved by the friction of liquids, as well as by the investigations in which pieces of iron are made glowing and soft by hammering, and pieces of ice are melted by friction.[3] [*Ed. note:* Modern studies have indeed cast great doubt on this supposed experiment of Davy. See Lindsay, *Energy: Concept.*] The iron that has been made soft and the water that results from the melting of the ice cannot have remained in the

---

[1] J. P. Joule, On the Existence of an Equivalent Relation Between Heat and the Ordinary Forms of Mechanical Power, *Philosophical Magazine*, **27**, 205.
[2] *Memoirs of the Society of Manchester*, **5**, 2, (London, 1802).
[3] Humphry Davy, *Essay on Heat, Light and the Combination of Light.*

compressed state. In addition to this, the development of heat by means of electrical motions proves that the quantity of heat can actually be increased in an absolute sense. If we leave out of account frictional and voltaic electricity, since it might be assumed that through some connection between electricity and heat substance the latter was elicited from some source and transferred to the heated electrical conductor, there still remain to us two ways of producing electrical effects by a purely mechanical method in which heat does not at all appear, i.e., by induction and by the motion of magnets. If we have a positively charged electrified body completely isolated from the surroundings, which cannot lose its electricity, another insulated conductor brought near to the first will show the charge $+E$. [*Ed. note*: This is a slip. He means $-E$. See next note.] We can touch this to the inner side of the battery of Leyden jars. We then move the conductor away from the initially charged conductor, whereupon it acquires the free negative charge $-E$, which can be discharged by touching the outside of the first conductor, or it can be discharged into a battery of Leyden jars. [*Ed. note:* Helmholtz is here describing the process of electrostatic induction, but is unfortunately not doing it very well!] When the charge is *induced*, there is no net charge until the second conductor is grounded. By repetition of this process we can apparently charge an arbitrarily large battery as often as we wish, and through its discharge we develop heat, without having this disappear anywhere else. On the other hand, in this process we will have used up a certain amount of mechanical energy, because, in every removal of the negatively charged conductor from the originally positively charged one, the attraction between the two must be overcome by the performance of work. This is essentially the process used when a Leyden jar is charged by an electrophorus. The same situation holds for magnetoelectric machines. As long as the magnet and armature move with respect to each other, electric currents are produced and heat is developed in the accompanying circuit, and as long as the relative motion continues, a certain quantity of mechanical energy will be destroyed. It is clear that the bodies making up the machine can develop an indefinite amount of heat without having the lattter disappear anywhere else. That the magnetoelectric current develops heat and does not become cold in the part of the spiral directly under the influence of the magnet, Joule has endeavored to show by experiment.[1] From these facts it follows that the quantity of heat can be increased absolutely through the agency of mechanical force, and that therefore thermal phenomena cannot be attributed to a substance which produces these effects by its mere presence, but rather that they are brought about by changes, by motions, whether it be of some particular material or whether of some already well known ponderable and imponderable bodies, e.g., electricity or light ether. The entity that has primarily been called quantity of heat should therefore be the expression, first, of the quantity of *vis viva* of the heat motion and, second, of those tension forces on the atoms [*Ed. note:* potential energy] which by an alteration in their arrangements can bring about such motions. The first part corresponds to what has previously been called *free* heat, the second to that which has been named *latent* heat. We can now make an investigation to establish the concept of this motion more definitely; it would seem in general that a hypothesis

---

[1] *Philosophical Magazine* (1844).

in agreement with the viewpoint of Ampère would correspond best with the present state of science. If we think of bodies as made up of atoms, which themselves are composed of different component parts (chemical elements, electricity, etc.), for such an atom three kinds of motion can be distinguished: (1) displacement of the center of mass, (2) rotation about the center of mass, and (3) relative displacements of the component parts of an atom with respect to each other. The first two motions are produced by the forces of the neighboring atoms and are therefore propagated through these in the form of waves, a form of propagation that corresponds to the radiation of heat, although not to its conduction. The motions of the component parts of an atom with respect to each other are produced by the forces present inside the atom, and can only slowly be transferred to the neighboring atoms to set them in motion, just as one vibrating string can set another in vibration, although in the process it itself loses a certain amount of motion. This kind of propagation appears to be similar to what takes place in the conduction of heat. Moreover, it is in general clear that such motions in atoms can produce changes in molecular forces, e.g., expansion and change in the state of aggregation. There is indeed lacking to us any foothold whereby we may determine the nature of these motions. For our purposes, the possibility that heat phenomena can be considered as motion is sufficient. In this motion the conservation of energy will hold to the extent that the conservation of heat substance was previously held to do, i.e., in all phenomena of conduction and radiation from one body to another and in the binding and release of heat in changes of states of aggregation.

Of the different methods of heat production we have mentioned those involved in irradiation and in the action of mechanical forces. We shall discuss those due to electricity in detail later. There remains the production of heat by chemical processes. This has been explained previously as the release of heat substance, which had been *latent* in the bodies before undergoing chemical change. In accordance with this view, one has to assign to every simple body, as well as to every chemical compound (which can form compounds of still higher order), a definite quantity of latent heat, which necessarily belongs to its chemical constitution. From this there follows the law, which has indeed been partially verified by experience, that in the chemical combination of several substances to produce the same products the same quantity of heat is always produced, no matter in what order the combination takes place nor what in-between states occur.[1] According to our present point of view, the heat arising in chemical processes is the quantity of *vis viva* produced through the definite amount of chemical forces of attraction that act. The above law then becomes the expression for the principle of the conservation of energy for this case.

The condition and laws for the disappearance of heat have been investigated with no more thoroughness than those for its production, although such production undoubtedly takes place. Up to now we have known only the cases in which chemical compounds have been broken up or more dilute states of aggregation developed, with heat becoming latent. Whether heat disappears in the production of mechanical energy, which is a necessary postulate of the conservation of energy, has never yet been asked. For this I can only cite an investigation of Joule,[2] which appears

[1] Hess, in Poggendorff's *Annalen*, **50**, 392; **56**, 398.
[2] *Philosophical Magazine*, **26**, 369.

On the Conservation of Energy

to be trustworthy. He found that when air streamed out of a vessel of volume 136.5 cubic inches, in which it was compressed to 22 atmospheres, the surrounding water was cooled by 4.085°F. This was when the streaming took place into the atmosphere, i.e., when the air streaming out encountered resistance. On the other hand, when the streaming took place into a completely evacuated vessel of the same size placed in the same water bath as the first vessel, there was no temperature change. In this second case the air had no resistance to overcome and hence used up no mechanical energy.

We have now to investigate the relation between our point of view and the attempts of Clapeyron[1] and Holtzmann[2] to measure the energy equivalent of heat. Clapeyron bases his evaluation on the consideration that in the production of mechanical energy heat is used only through its transfer from a warmer to a colder body. He also assumed that the energy production is a maximum if the passage of the heat takes place between bodies of the same temperature, and that the temperature changes, however, are brought about by the compression and expansion of the heated bodies. This maximum, however, must be the same for all natural bodies that can produce mechanical work by heating and cooling. For, if it were different, we could take the body for which a certain amount of heat would produce a greater amount of mechanical energy and use this to get the energy, and could then use a part of this energy to make the other body act backward to take heat from the cooler to the warmer source. By repetition of this process, one could produce an indefinitely large amount of mechanical energy, it still being assumed that the quantity of heat did not change. Analytically, the law takes the following general form:

$$\frac{dq}{dv} \cdot \frac{dt}{dp} - \frac{dq}{dp} \cdot \frac{dt}{dv} = C.$$

Here q is the quantity of heat contained in one body, whose temperature is t. Both quantities are expressed as functions of v, the volume, and p, the pressure. The mechanical work which a unit of heat (that which heats 1 kilogram of water by 1°C) will do when it passes through a temperature difference of 1°C is $1/C$. This quantity should be the same for all natural bodies, but is variable with temperature. For gases the formula becomes

$$C = v\frac{dq}{dv} - p\frac{dq}{dp}.$$

Clapeyron's deductions from the general validity of this formula have, in the case of gases at any rate, led to analogies with plausible agreement with experiment. But his deduction of the law can be accepted only if the absolute quantity of heat is considered to be invariable. Besides, his special formula for gases, which is the only one supported by experience, also follows from the formula of Holtzmann, as we

[1] Poggendorff's *Annalen*, **59**, 446, 506.
[2] *Über die Wärme und Elasticität der Gase und Dämpfe*, Mannheim, 1845. An extract from this is in Poggendorff's *Annalen*, Supplement II.

24

shall show presently. From his more general formula he has sought to show only that the law following from it does not stand in contradiction to experience. This law is that, if the pressure on different bodies, taken at constant temperature, is raised by a small amount, quantities of heat are produced which are proportional to the expansion of the bodies by heat. I shall call attention here to only one (and that at least very improbable) consequence of this law, that the compression of water at its point of maximum density should produce no heat, whereas between this and the freezing point, it should produce cold.

Holtzmann proceeds from the consideration that when a certain quantity of heat enters a gas it can either produce a rise in temperature or expansion without a rise in temperature. The work done in this expansion he took as the mechanical equivalent of the heat, and calculated from the acoustical experiments of Dulong, giving the ratio of the two specific heats of a gas, that the heat to raise the temperature of 1 kilogram of water 1°C is equivalent to the work to raise 374 kilograms 1 meter. This kind of calculation is permissible from our standpoint only if the whole *vis viva* of the heat in question is really given up as mechanical energy, and, accordingly, that the sum of the *vis viva* and the tension forces [potential energy] i.e., the sum of the free and latent heats, is the same in the greatly expanded gas as in the gas before expansion at the same temperature. From this it follows that a gas which expands without doing any work must not suffer any change in temperature, as indeed appears to be the case from the experiment of Joule mentioned earlier. Moreover, the temperature rise and fall with compression and dilation under normal circumstances should result from a production of heat through mechanical energy, and conversely. The correctness of Holtzmann's law is attested by the large number of consequences drawn from it that agree with experiment, e.g., the derivation of the formula for the dependence of the elasticity of steam at different temperatures. [*Ed. note:* It is of particular interest that Helmholtz makes no mention here of the work of Julius Robert Mayer, who published the first theoretically calculated value for the mechanical equivalent of heat in 1842, using essentially the same method employed by Holtzmann three years later. It is not surprising that when he prepared his 1847 paper, Helmholtz had never heard of Mayer's work, which was not published in a regular physics journal. Nor was he familiar with Mayer's later and much more detailed memoir of 1845, which was privately printed and evidently not seen by the kind of people who would be likely to be impressed by its importance. Actually, in his 1845 memoir, Mayer covered much the same ground as Helmholtz in this 1847 paper, emphasizing the general significance of the concept of energy and applying it not only to physical phenomena of all kinds but to biological problems as well. Mayer's treatment was, to be sure, more qualitative than Helmholtz's. He did not possess the mathematical ability of Helmholtz. For a discussion of the relation of the work of Mayer to that of other workers in the early development of the concept of energy, see Lindsay, *Energy: Concept.* Also see *Julius Robert Mayer—Prophet of Energy*, by R. Bruce Lindsay (Pergamon Press, Inc., Elmsford, N.Y., 1973). In an appendix to the 1847 paper, which Helmholtz prepared in 1881, he discussed the work of Mayer and paid tribute to his priority. This appendix is printed at the end of this translation.]

Corresponding to Holtzmann's theoretical value of 374, Joule from his experimental researches obtained numbers like 481, 464, and 474, and later by his frictional experiments numbers like 452 and 521.

The formula of Holtzmann agrees with that of Clapeyron for gases. However, the undetermined function C in the latter formula now becomes definite; hence, the complete determination of the integral becomes possible. Holtzmann's formula thus becomes

$$\frac{pv}{a} = v\frac{dq}{dv} - p\frac{dq}{dp},$$

where a is the mechanical equivalent of heat. The formula of Clapeyron is

$$C = v\frac{dq}{dv} - p\frac{dq}{dp}.$$

They agree if $C = pv/a$ or since

$$pv = k(1 + \alpha t),$$

where α = the coefficient of thermal expansion and k is a constant, we have

$$\frac{1}{C} = \frac{a}{k(1 + \alpha t)}.$$

The values of $1/C$ calculated by Clapeyron agree rather well with those calculated from the above formula, as is shown in the following table.

Temperature (°C)	Calculated by Clapeyron			Holtzmann formula
	a	b	c	
0	1.410		1.586	1.544
35.5		1.365	1.292	1.366
78.8		1.208	1.142	1.198
100		1.115	1.102	1.129
156.8		1.076	1.072	0.904

The value under column a was calculated from the velocity of sound in air. The values under column b were computed from the latent heat of the vapors of ether, alcohol, water, and oil of turpentine at the indicated temperatures. Those under column c were computed from the expansive force of water vapor at the temperatures indicated. For gases, Holtzmann's formula appears to be doubtful. [*Ed. note:* The comparisons shown in the table are not very meaningful until one realizes that in Clapeyron's theory $1/C$ means the ratio of the specific heat at constant pressure to that at constant volume. For a better appreciation of the agreement, reference should be made to Clapeyron's article cited earlier. In particular, the letters a, b, and c in the table have nothing to do with physical quantities.]

APPENDIXES ADDED IN 1881

Appendix 1

The philosophical discussions in the introduction are strongly influenced by Kant's views on epistemology, which I am still inclined to consider as correct. It was only later that I made clear to myself that the principle of causality is indeed nothing else than the assumption that all nature phenomena are subject to laws. Law recognized as objective power we call energy (*Kraft*). According to the original significance of the word, *cause* is that entity which remains everlastingly unchanged behind the changes in phenomena, i.e., substance and the law by which it acts, i.e., energy. The impossibility mentioned of thinking of substances and energy as isolated from each other results simply from the fact that the law governing an effect presupposes conditions under which the law is effective. Energy separated from substance would make the objectivization of the law impossible.

Appendix 2

The necessity for the decomposition of forces into those which act on points can be deduced from the complete understandability of nature for masses on which the forces act, insofar as complete understanding of motion fails, unless the motion of each individual material point can be given. But the same necessity does not appear to me to exist for the masses from which the forces originate. I have already touched on this in the following sections of the paper. The discussions in parts I and II of the text are in part only justifiable if this decomposability of forces is taken for granted from the outset. That the motion-producing forces are as they were defined by Newton, which by the principle of parallelogram of forces are resultants of individual forces, which have their origin on individual mass elements, I can recognize as a natural law grounded in experience. It expresses a fact. The acceleration that a mass point experiences when several causes work together is the resultant (geometric sum) of those accelerations which the individual causes would have produced separately. Now we meet the empirical case in which two bodies, e.g., two magnets, act simultaneously on a third magnet and exert on it a force that is not simply the resultant of the forces with which each magnet would act by itself. In this case we make do with the assumption that each individual magnet brings about a change in the distribution of an imponderable, invisible substance. But here I can no longer consider the principle of understandability as sufficient for the conclusion that the effect of two or more individual causes of acceleration is necessarily to be found through the geometrical summation of the individual effects.

Electrodynamic theories that make the force between electrically charged bodies depend on their velocity and acceleration have abandoned the essential content of Newton's second law, as well as the further principle that the forces which two particles exert on each other are completely determined when the positions of the masses are given. Investigations in electrodynamics have up to now always been in contradiction to those mechanical principles of action and reaction and constancy of energy, which have hitherto been valid without exception in the realm of our experience. If for the electricity in conductors there may exist only unstable equilibrium, the uniqueness and definiteness of solutions of electrical problems will have vanished, and if force has to be made dependent on an absolute motion, i.e., on a changed relation of a mass to something which can never be the object of a possible perception, i.e., to empty space, it seems to me that this is an assumption which completely surrenders the possibility of a complete solution of the problems of science. In my opinion this ought to be allowed to happen only when all other theoretical possibilities have been exhausted.

Appendix 3

The often cited proof (as given in the text) for the necessity of central forces is not satisfactory for the case in which forces have to depend on velocities or accelerations, as Herr Lipschitz has called to my attention. Then we can write

$$X = \frac{dU}{dx} + Q\frac{dz}{dt} - R\frac{dy}{dt},$$

$$Y = \frac{dU}{dy} + R\frac{dx}{dt} - P\frac{dz}{dt},$$

$$Z = \frac{dU}{dz} + P\frac{dy}{dt} - Q\frac{dx}{dt},$$

where U is a function of the coordinates, and P, Q, R are arbitrary functions of the coordinates and their derivatives. Then we get

$$X \cdot \frac{dx}{dt} + Y\frac{dy}{dt} + Z\frac{dz}{dt} = \frac{dU}{dt} = \frac{d}{dt}\left(\tfrac{1}{2}mq^2\right).$$

Accordingly, the *vis viva* is a function of the coordinates. The additional terms added to the force components, as represented by the terms in P, Q, R, correspond to a resultant force that is perpendicular to the resultant velocity of the moving point. Such a force would change the curvature of the path but not the *vis viva*.

If we retain the validity of the law of action and reaction and the resolution into point forces, the general theorem in the text is correct. For the law in question permits only forces between a pair of points that in direction lie along the line joining the points and are equal and opposite in direction. The forces perpendicular to the velocities could only enter at the moments when both velocities were perpendicular to the line joining the particles.

Appendix 4

The theorem referred to here is also expressed too generally, since we must restrict the previous general theorem to the case in which action and reaction are equal and opposite. If we abandon the latter, the generalized electrodynamic law of Clausius includes a case in which forces depend on velocities and accelerations but do not develop energy at an infinite distance.

Appendix 5

There should be added here to the history of the discovery of the law of conservation of energy the fact that J. R. Mayer published in 1842 his paper "Über die Kräfte der unbelebten Natur," and in 1845 he brought out his memoir *Die organische Bewegung in ihrem Zusammenhang mit demm Stoffwechsel* (Heilbromn). In the first paper, Mayer expresses his conviction of the equivalence of heat and work, and the mechanical equivalent of heat is calculated in the same manner as used by Holtzmann and described in our text. [*Ed. note:* Holtzmann's work was much later than Mayer's.] Mayer got 365 kg for his value. The aim of Mayer's second essay is essentially the same as mine. It was only later that I learned of these works of Mayer. Since becoming acquainted with them, I have never let any occasion pass in discussing the law of conservation of energy without naming Mayer in the first rank of its discoverers.[1] I have also maintained to the best of my ability Mayer's claims against the friends of Joule, who were inclined to deny them wholly. A letter along these lines to Professor P. G. Tait was reprinted in the preface of his book *Sketch of Thermodynamics* (Edinburgh, 1868). I include it here.

I must say that the discoveries of Kirchhoff in this field [radiation and absorption] form one of the most instructive cases in the history of physics for the reason that many other previous investigations were right on the edge of his discoveries, so to speak. Kirchhoff's predecessors stood in the same relation to his discoveries more or less as Mayer, Colding, and Seguin stood to those of Joule and W. Thomson.

So far as Robert Mayer is concerned, I can at any rate understand the point of view you take with respect to him, but I cannot let the occasion pass without asserting that I am not entirely of the same opinion. The progress of the natural sciences depends on the development of ever new inductions from the observed facts and the comparison of the consequences of these inductions, insofar as they relate to new facts, with reality through the agency of experiment. There can be no doubt about the necessity of this second course. This second part often demands the expenditure of a lot of work and great ingenuity, and he who carries out such a task successfully deserves the highest credit. But the glory of discovery also belongs to him who found the new idea. After that, experimental test is a more mechanical kind of contribution. Moreover, one should not unconditionally demand that the discoverer of the idea is in duty bound to carry out the second stage of the work. If we took this attitude, we would have to denigrate the greatest part of the work of all mathematical physicists. Even W. Thomson carried out a series of theoretical researches on Carnot's law and its consequences before he set up a single experiment on them. And yet no one of us would think of valuing his work less on that account.

Robert Mayer was not in a position to carry out experimental researches. He was rebuffed by the physicists known to him. Several years later I suffered the same treatment. He could only with difficulty

[1] See my *Populäre wissenschaftliche Vorträge*, Part II, p. 112 (1854); the same, p. 141 (1862); the same, p. 194 (1869).

find a place for the publication of his first highly condensed presentation. You know that in consequence of this opposition to his views he incurred a nervous breakdown. It is difficult for us to go back and put ourselves into the trend of thought in the time he was working and to grasp how absolutely new the matter seemed then. I believe that even Joule had to fight for a long time for recognition of his discovery.

Although nobody can deny that Joule has done much more than Mayer and that in the first papers of the latter many details are unclear, I believe we must consider Mayer as a man who independently and by his own efforts has discovered those ideas which have conditioned the greatest advance in modern science; and his merit is not diminished by the fact that simultaneously with him another scientist in another country and in another realm of activity made the same discovery and later generalized it in more effective fashion.

In very recent times the adherents of metaphysical speculation have tried to consider the law of the conservation of energy as valid a priori and have therefore celebrated Mayer as a hero of pure thought. What they think of as the very highest point of Mayer's contributions, the metaphysically formulated apparent proof of the necessity of this law, will appear to every scientist accustomed to the usual scientific method as the weakest side of Mayer's explanation. It is doubtless the reason why Mayer's works remained for so long unknown in scientific circles. It was only after the conviction of the correctness of the law had broken a path for itself, largely through the masterly researches of Joule, that people became aware of Mayer's writings.

For the rest, this law [of conservation of energy], like all knowledge of phenomena in the real world, was really found inductively. It was a gradually established induction that no one can build a perpetual motion machine, i.e., produce energy independently without a corresponding consumption of something, in spite of many efforts to do this.

A long time ago the French Academy placed perpetual motion in the same category as the squaring of the circle and decided to receive no further alleged solutions. This must be considered under the circumstances as a widespread conviction. I myself have heard this conviction expressed even during my school days, and heard discussions of the incompleteness of the proof of this impossibility of perpetual motion. The question of the origin of animal heat demanded a most careful and complete discussion of all the facts connected with it. In investigating this field of work, I have always considered it as one deserving careful critique and not one to be thought of as an original single discovery concerning the priority for which there should be controversy. I was somewhat astonished at the resistance which I encountered [*Ed. note:* he evidently refers to his 1847 lecture and paper] in the articles of those familiar with the material I was dealing with. I was denied acceptance of my paper in Poggendorff's *Annalen*. Among the members of the Berlin Academy it was only the mathematician, C. G. J. Jacobi, who took my part. Fame and external acceptance in those days were not to be won with pushing new points of view, the contrary rather. My opponents of the metaphysical school strove to fasten on me a claim to priority which I did not deserve. That they were entirely wrong and that I made no claims to priority is made abundantly clear from the fact that I named in my essay the other investigators who had worked in the field, so far as I had learned of them. And wholly aside from the work which I mentioned in my paper, mainly that of Joule, there could in no case be any claim for priority on my part, even if such a claim made any sense in connection with a general principle like conservation of energy.

If my knowledge of the scientific literature in 1847 was incomplete, I can present the hope for forgiveness based on the fact that my paper was prepared in the city of Potsdam, in which my literary aids were restricted to the library of the gymnasium there, and that the *Fortschritte der Physik* of the Berlin Physical Society and other similar sources of help were not available to me. Today [1881] it has become very easy to remain oriented in the literature of physics.

Appendix 6

The concept of the potential of a body due to an electrical charge on itself has here a somewhat different meaning from that which it later received in the scientific literature. In the very meager literature available to me at the time, I could find no precedents for the use of this concept and therefore allowed myself to be guided in my development by the analogy of the potential of two different charges with respect to each other (V in the text). If one treats the carriers of the charges as congruent, and corresponding surface elements as charged equally, the potential V of the two can be formed. One can then think of the two bodies brought into congruence, whence V will become that which I have designated as W. In this procedure every pair of elementary charges e and ϵ is counted twice. The value of W calculated in this way is not the value of the work as it is set forth in the text of the paper. The latter is really $W/2$. In my later papers I have followed the appropriate usage of other authorities and have designated $W/2$ as the self-potential of the body.

Part II

CONTRIBUTIONS OF CLAUSIUS, THOMSON, RANKINE, REGNAULT, AND JOULE

Editor's Comments
on Papers 2 Through 8

During the two or three years following the appearance of Helmholtz's memoir of 1847, considerable activity led to results of importance for the applications of the concept of energy and the establishment of thermodynamics. These results are primarily associated with the names of Rudolf Clausius (1822–1888), William Thomson (later Lord Kelvin) (1824–1907), and William J. M. Rankine (1820–1872). In this connection we must also mention the name of

Henri Victor Regnault (1810–1878). Since Helmholtz's 1847 memoir did not appear in one of the standard and easily available scientific periodicals, it is doubtful that it stimulated any of the initial investigations of these four men. They were more directly influenced by the work of Carnot and Emile Clapeyron (who extended and interpreted Carnot's work), as well as by the earlier work of J. P. Joule and the writings of J. R. Mayer, the significance of whose calculation of the mechanical equivalent of heat had finally penetrated the minds of active (albeit conservative) physicists.

The essential problem faced by Clausius, Thomson, and Rankine was to reconcile the undeniably significant results of Carnot on the motive power of heat, based on the caloric theory, with the mechanical theory of heat advocated by Mayer and Joule. Thomson was so impressed with the importance of Carnot's famous memoir of 1824, "On the Motive Power of Fire" [reprinted in part in Lindsay, *Energy: Concept*, p. 228], with its introduction of the cycle idea in the action of a heat engine, and with its apparent dependence on the caloric theory of heat according to which work is done by an engine merely through the transfer of caloric from a higher to a lower temperature with no net disappearance of heat, that he (Thomson) found it hard to accept the work of Mayer and Joule. According to the views of the latter, heat must disappear in the performance of work by a heat engine. Thomson evidently thought at first that the invariance in the total amount of heat in the universe, which is a key idea in the caloric theory, was an integral and necessary part of Carnot's theory. In addition, Thomson was also sceptical of the theoretical validity of Mayer's calculations, as well as of the experimental precision of Joule's measurements.

The first person to grapple decisively with this problem was the German theoretical physicist Rudolf Clausius. In 1850 he published an article with the title (English translation) "On the Motive Power of Heat and on the Laws Which Can Be Deduced from It for the Theory of Heat" [Poggendorff's *Annalen der Physik und Chemie*, **79**, 368, 500 (1850)], in which he showed that it is perfectly possible to reconcile Carnot's theory in its essential aspects with the concept of the conservation of energy and the mechanical theory of heat. Clausius's article may be considered the first serious attempt to construct a theory of thermodynamics on a logical basis agreeing with experiment. The author uses freely the cycle idea of Carnot, which Helmholtz ignored. Clausius also wrote the first law of thermodynamics for gases in essentially the modern form, i.e., an elementary quantity of heat communicated to a gas goes in part to increase its internal energy (Clausius's function U), whereas the rest enables the gas to do a certain amount of external work. It is true that Clausius does not use the term "internal energy" or indeed make reference to the word "energy" at all, although he does speak of the heat of substances as due to the *vis viva* of their constituent particles. At the time of which we are writing, the word "energy" had not yet come into common use in the treatment of the relation between heat and work. In German, the word *Kraft* was still used for what we now term energy; similarly, in English, *force* was employed.

The modern thermodynamic significance of the two specific heats of a gas is clearly pointed out in Clausius's paper, which also presents the now standard derivation of the equation representing an adiabatic change in an ideal gas.

Paper 2 consists of the introduction and Part I of Clausius's memoir. The second part involves the second law of thermodynamics (which is treated in detail in another volume of the Benchmark Series on Energy), and discusses applications of thermodynamics to saturated vapor. Clausius ultimately included the substance of this memoir as well as the results of his later investigations in his impressive treatise *Die Mechanische Wärmetheorie* (two vols., Braunschweig, 1876). This became the first serious treatise on the theory of thermodynamics.

Rudolf Clausius is best known for his work in thermodynamics and the kinetic theory of gases. But he also made important contributions to static and current electricity, electrodynamics, and the properties of electrolytes. It is of interest to recall that in thermodynamics he was the inventor of the concept of entropy.

As has already been noted, William Thomson (later Lord Kelvin; in what follows we shall refer to him by the name by which he is now more familiarly known) became very much interested in the 1840s in the work of Carnot on heat engines, news of which percolated very slowly into scientific circles after its publication in 1824. In 1849, Kelvin published a lengthy paper devoted to an examination of Carnot's theory (with some critical remarks about Carnot's assumption of the indestructability of caloric) [*Transactions of the Royal Society of Edinburgh*, **16** (1849)]. In the meantime, his interest in the dynamical theory of heat had been aroused and the result was a long paper "On the Dynamical Theory of Heat, with Numerical Results Deduced from Mr Joule's Equivalent of a Thermal Unit, and M. Regnault's Observations on Steam" [*Transactions of the Royal Society of Edinburgh*, **20** (1851)]. In this paper [reprinted with certain additions in *Philosophical Magazine*, **4**(4), 105, 168, 424 (1852)] he accepted for the first time the mechanical theory of heat and the concept of a mechanical equivalent of heat. It is of interest to observe that he attributed the establishment of the mechanical theory to Sir Humphrey Davy and quotes from Davy's alleged experiment on the melting of ice by friction in a vacuum, about which historians of science have expressed great doubt. Kelvin makes no mention of Rumford and others who had a hand in supporting the mechanical theory. He does mention Mayer and Joule, although his reference to Mayer is not particularly gracious. In the original 1851 version of the paper, he makes no mention of Helmholtz's 1847 memoir, which at that time he had not seen. It had come to his attention when he reprinted his paper in the *Philosophical Magazine* in 1852, and he devotes a brief footnote to it.

Of particular interest is the first use in a serious scientific article of the term "thermodynamic," which was to provide a name for one of the most imposing of all scientific theories. From the standpoint of terminology, the paper is also noteworthy for the introduction of the term "mechanical energy," together with a definition of it.

Paper 3 consists of Kelvin's Introduction, the whole of Part I, and paragraphs 81 and 82 of Part II. The early part stresses the fundamental principles on which Kelvin feels thermodynamics must be based. We omit the detailed tabular material, which of course was very important for the experimental verification of the theory, but appears to be too specialized for our purpose here. Other applications of thermodynamics to specific physical phenomena, e.g., electricity, will appear in appropriate places in this volume.

Another contribution of Kelvin's that deserves attention at this place is his suggestion of an absolute temperature scale (Paper 4). Although this does not fit precisely into the development of the dynamical theory of heat and the concept of the conservation of energy, it did have an enormously important significance for heat measurement and hence indirectly affected the advance of the whole of thermodynamics. Obviously, without the concept of temperature nothing could be done, and without an absolute scale it would be impossible to compare measurements with different types of thermometers. It is interesting that Kelvin's proposal of an absolute thermometric scale was made on the basis of his study of Carnot's theory and while he was still an adherent of the caloric theory. This, however, did not get in the way of its adaptation to the mechanical theory. We reprint the whole of this paper, which appeared in *Philosophical Magazine* [33(3), 313 (1848)], as Paper 4. We also reproduce a later note (1854) concerning the relation of the paper to the dynamical theory of heat and providing a more correct viewpoint.

Lord Kelvin was an unusual combination of theoretical and experimental physicist and practical engineer. During his long academic career as professor of natural philosophy at the University of Glasgow, he touched upon in his researches practically every aspect of physics known in his time. On the practical side he is probably best known for his work on the Atlantic cable and his invention and production of precision electric measuring instruments.

We now turn to W. J. M. Rankine, the Scottish engineer who turned his attention to many fundamental problems in physics, but was for a number of years during the 1850s particularly concerned with the dynamical theory of heat and heat engines. Rankine early felt that the thermodynamic behavior of gases should be studied in terms of the mechanical energy of the constituent parts of the gas. In what may be considered his first important thermodynamic paper, "On the Mechanical Action of Heat, Especially in Gases and Vapours" [*Transactions of the Royal Society of Edinburgh*, **20** (1851), and in abbreviated form in *Philosophical Magazine*, 3(4), 61 (1851)], Rankine introduced the hypothesis of molecular vortices to account for the heat energy of a gas and developed some useful applications to gas theory. We do not reprint it here since it really forms a part of the development of the application of the concept of energy to atomic and molecular physics, which forms the subject of another volume in the Benchmark Series on Energy.

Paper 5 is Rankine's first elaborate paper on what may be considered thermodynamics proper (it was read before the Philosophical Society of Glasgow on January 5, 1853, and published in *Philosophical Magazine*). In Paper 5, Rankine explains what he means by actual energy (whose form for particles is kinetic energy, a term which had not yet come into general use at that time) and potential energy (with meaning very close to that now used in mechanics). He then states the law of the conservation of energy in terms of these two forms of energy. The purpose of this paper is to set up general equations governing the transformation of energy from one form to another in agreement with the conservation principle. His notation is, of course, somewhat unfamiliar, but it is easy to see that he was successfully setting forth a general point of view of great significance for subsequent developments. This becomes clearer when in the later part of Paper 5 he applies his general formulas to specific problems in heat as a form of energy. In this connection he defines the efficiency of a heat engine and ex-presses it in terms of the two temperatures between which the engine works. It will be noted that he uses the word "motive" or "expansive" power or "useful effect" for what is now called the work done by the engine.

In Paper 6, Rankine made another important contribution to the thermodynamics of heat engines (read before the Royal Society of London on January 19, 1854, and published in its journal the same year). Here, starting with James Watt's famous engine indi-cator diagrams, Rankine develops the theory of thermodynamic cycle curves in the pressure–volume plane in terms of heat com-municated to and work done by a heat engine. This formed the basis for his introduction of the well-known Rankine cycle as a more practical cycle for heat engines than the Carnot cycle. It also led him ultimately to produce a textbook, *A Manual on the Steam Engine and Other Prime Movers* (1859). We reprint the first seven subsections of the original. The rest of the article, which is a long one, involves mainly considerations on the efficiency of heat engines.

Rankine was professor of civil engineering and mechanics in the University of Glasgow from 1855 until his death in 1872.

We have already stated earlier in this commentary that Regnault's important work should not be overlooked, particularly in view of Kelvin's use of it. From about 1840 on, Regnault in Paris had been engaged in the experimental investigation of the thermal properties of gases. Although specific heat measurements for gases had been made long before, he was convinced that they were lacking in accuracy. Hence, he improved methods of measurement with a view to securing greater precision. At the same time he gave much thought to the relation between heat and mechanical work. He summarized his views in a paper of which our reprint (Paper 7) is an English translation of the first eight pages, dealing with Regnault's views on the role of energy in heat engines and prob-lems in the thermal behavior of gases. At the end of the extract we introduce an editorial note on the significance of Regnault's work on specific heat for Mayer's theoretical determination of the mechanical equivalent of heat.

Mention of Mayer's work leads to a consideration of another famous paper on the thermal properties of gases. When Mayer derived theoretically the value of the mechanical equivalent of heat, he felt that he had to use an assumption equivalent to the statement that in the free expansion of a gas into a vacuum there is no change in temperature. Actually, Mayer did not consider this as a pure hypothesis, since he believed that the French chemist Joseph Louis Gay-Lussac had demonstrated around 1801 the validity of the assumption through his experiments performed on the expansion of gases.

Evidently, the experiments of Gay-Lussac were not widely known in England. In 1845, J. P. Joule repeated the experiment and found [see *Philosophical Magazine*, **26**, 375, (1845)] results essentially in agreement with those of Gay-Lussac, although admittedly the experiment could lay no great claim to precision. This phenomenon has long been known as the Joule effect.

William Thomson (later Lord Kelvin), who was ever dubious of the validity of Mayer's calculation, took up the matter in earnest in 1852 and secured the collaboration of Joule in a long series of measurements. The results were reported in a group of joint papers by Joule and Thomson; publication extended over 10 years. These papers were collected and reprinted in Kelvin's *Mathematical and Physical Papers of William Thomson* (Vol. 1, Cambridge University Press, 1882, pp. 333–455), under the general title "On the Thermal Effects of Fluids in Motion."

Since the experiments on completely free expansion were not decisive, Joule and Thomson arranged to have the gas emerge through a porous cotton plug. The name "porous plug experiment" has stuck to their work ever since, although the effect they observed is called the Joule–Thomson effect. They found that in the expansion as thus controlled there is actually a temperature change, usually a small cooling, which is a function of the pressure difference on the two sides of the plug and of the temperature on the high-pressure side. The effect has been observed in countless experiments performed in the past 100 years under the most precise conditions. Both heating and cooling have been observed, depending on the gas used and the prevailing conditions. The cooling effect, when it occurs, is, of course, the basis for the liquefaction of gases. The porous plug experiment also serves as the basis for the determination of the absolute temperature of the freezing point of water.

Kelvin undoubtedly felt that the results which he and Joule obtained vitiated Mayer's assumption and hence made his theoretical calculation of the mechanical equivalent of heat invalid. In this he was mistaken. For an ideal gas the Joule–Thomson change in temperature is actually zero, and hence Mayer's calculation was theoretically unassailable insofar as he could assume that air at ordinary temperature and pressure acts like an ideal gas. At the time when he made his calculation there was no other reasonable assumption to make. His figures for specific heat were, of course, in error, but that did not render his method invalid.

The Joule–Thomson effect is without doubt one of the most important of all thermodynamic phenomena. Paper 8 is the Introduction and Part I (pages 333–356) of the Joule–Thomson article as it appeared in Kelvin's papers.

2

Reprinted by permission of the publisher from S. Carnot, *Reflections on the Motive Power of Fire and Other Papers*, E. Mendoza, ed., Dover Publications, Inc., New York, 1960, pp. 109–132

On the Motive Power of Heat, and on the Laws which can be Deduced from it for the Theory of Heat

Rudolf Clausius

SINCE heat was first used as a motive power in the steam-engine, thereby suggesting from practice that a certain quantity of work may be treated as equivalent to the heat needed to produce it, it was natural to assume also in theory a definite relation between a quantity of heat and the work which in any possible way can be produced by it, and to use this relation in drawing conclusions about the nature and the laws of heat itself. In fact, several fruitful investigations of this sort have already been made; yet I think that the subject is not yet exhausted, but on the other hand deserves the earnest attention of physicists, partly because serious objections can be raised to the conclusions that have already been reached, partly because other conclusions, which may readily be drawn and which will essentially contribute to the establishment and completion of the theory of heat, still remain entirely unnoticed or have not yet been stated with sufficient definiteness.

The most important of the researches here referred to was that of S. Carnot,* and the ideas of this author were afterwards given analytical form in a very skilful way by Clapeyron.† Carnot showed that whenever work is done by heat and no permanent change occurs in the condition of the working body, a certain quantity of heat passes from a hotter to a colder body. In the steam-engine, for example, by means of the steam which is developed in the boiler and precipitated in the condenser, heat is transferred from the grate to the condenser. This *transfer* he considered as

---

* *Réflexions sur la puissance motrice du feu, et sur les machines propres à développer cette puissance, par S. Carnot.* Paris, 1824. I have not been able to obtain a copy of this book, and am acquainted with it only through the work of Clapeyron and Thomson, from the latter of whom are quoted the extracts afterwards given.

† *Journ. de l'École Polytechnique*, vol. xix (1834), and *Pogg. Ann.*, vol. lix.

the heat change, corresponding to the work done. He says expressly that no heat is lost in the process, but that the *quantity of heat* remains unchanged, and adds: "This fact is not doubted; it was assumed at first without investigation, and then established in many cases by calorimetric measurements. To deny it would overthrow the whole theory of heat, of which it is the foundation." I am not aware, however, that it has been sufficiently proved by experiment that no loss of heat occurs when work is done; it may, perhaps, on the contrary, be asserted with more correctness that even if such a loss has not been proved directly, it has yet been shown by other facts to be not only admissible, but even highly probable. It it be assumed that heat, like a substance, cannot diminish in quantity, it must also be assumed that it cannot increase. It is, however, almost impossible to explain the heat produced by friction except as an increase in the quantity of heat. The careful investigations of Joule, in which heat is produced in several different ways by the application of mechanical work, have almost certainly proved not only the possibility of increasing the quantity of heat in any circumstances but also the law that the quantity of heat developed is proportional to the work expended in the operation. To this it must be added that other facts have lately become known which support the view, that heat is not a substance, but consists in a motion of the least parts of bodies. If this view is correct, it is admissible to apply to heat the general mechanical principle that a motion may be transformed into work, and in such a manner that the loss of *vis viva* is proportional to the work accomplished.

These facts, with which Carnot also was well acquainted, and the importance of which he has expressly recognized, almost compel us to accept the equivalence between heat and work, on the modified hypothesis that the accomplishment of work requires not merely a change in the distribution of heat, but also an actual consumption of heat, and that, conversely, heat can be developed again by the expenditure of work.

In a memoir recently published by Holtzmann,* it seems at first as if the author intended to consider the matter from this latter point of view. He says (p. 7): "The action of the heat supplied to the gas is either an elevation of temperature, in conjunction with an increase in its elasticity, or mechanical work, or

---

* *Ueber die Wärme und Elasticität der Gase und Dämpfe*, von C. Holtzmann, Mannheim, 1845; also Pogg. *Ann.*, vol. 72a.

a combination of both, and the mechanical work is the equivalent of the elevation of temperature. The heat can only be measured by its effects; of the two effects mentioned the mechanical work is the best adapted for this purpose, and it will accordingly be so used in what follows. I call the unit of heat the heat which by its entrance into a gas can do the mechanical work a—that is, to use definite units, which can lift a kilograms through 1 meter." Later (p. 12) he also calculates the numerical value of the constant a in the same way as Mayer had already done,[*] and obtains a number which corresponds with the heat equivalent obtained by Joule in other entirely different ways. In the further extension of his theory, however, in particular in the development of the equations from which his conclusions are drawn, he proceeds exactly as Clapeyron did, so that in this part of his work he tacitly assumes that the quantity of heat is constant.

The difference between the two methods of treatment has been much more clearly grasped by W. Thomson, who has extended Carnot's discussion by the use of the recent observations of Regnault on the tension and latent heat of water vapor.[†] He speaks of the obstacles which lie in the way of the unrestricted assumption of Carnot's theory, calling special attention to the researches of Joule, and also raises a fundamental objection which may be made against it. Though it may be true in any case of the production of work, when the working body has returned to the same condition as at first, that heat passes from a warmer to a colder body, yet on the other hand it is not generally true that whenever heat is transferred work is done. Heat can be transferred by simple conduction, and in all such cases, if the mere transfer of heat were the true equivalent of work, there would be a loss of working power in Nature, which is hardly conceivable. Nevertheless, he concludes that in the present state of the science the principle adopted by Carnot is still to be taken as the most probable basis for an investigation of the motive power of heat, saying: "If we abandon this principle, we meet with innumerable other difficulties—insuperable without further experimental investigation—and an entire reconstruction of the theory of heat from its foundation."[‡]

I believe that we should not be daunted by these difficulties,

---

[*] *Ann. der Chem. und Pharm.* of Wöhler and Liebig, vol. xlii., p. 239.

[†] *Transactions of the Royal Society of Edinburgh*, vol. xvi.

[‡] *Math. and Phys. Papers*, vol. i, p. 119, note.

but rather should familiarize ourselves as much as possible with the consequences of the idea that heat is a motion, since it is only in this way that we can obtain the means wherewith to confirm or to disprove it. Then, too, I do not think the difficulties are so serious as Thomson does, since even though we must make some changes in the usual form of presentation, yet I can find no contradiction with any proved facts. It is not at all necessary to discard Carnot's theory entirely, a step which we certainly would find it hard to take, since it has to some extent been conspicuously verified by experience. A careful examination shows that the new method does not stand in contradiction to the essential principle of Carnot, but only to the subsidiary statement *that no heat is lost*, since in the production of work it may very well be the case that at the same time a certain quantity of heat is consumed and another quantity transferred from a hotter to a colder body, and both quantities of heat stand in a definite relation to the work that is done. This will appear more plainly in the sequel, and it will there be shown that the consequences drawn from the two assumptions are not only consistent with one another, but are even mutually confirmatory.

I. CONSEQUENCES OF THE PRINCIPLE OF THE EQUIVALENCE OF HEAT AND WORK

We shall not consider here the kind of motion which can be conceived of as taking place within bodies, further than to assume in general that the particles of bodies are in motion, and that their heat is the measure of their *vis viva*, or rather still more generally, we shall only lay down a principle conditioned by that assumption as a fundamental principle, in the words: In all cases in which work is produced by the agency of heat, a quantity of heat is consumed which is proportional to the work done; and, conversely, by the expenditure of an equal quantity of work an equal quantity of heat is produced.

Before we proceed to the mathematical treatment of this principle, some immediate consequences may be premised which affect our whole method of treatment, and which may be understood without the more definite demonstration which will be given them later by our calculations.

It is common to speak of the *total heat* of bodies, especially of gases and vapors, by which term is understood the sum of the free and latent heat, and to assume that this is a quantity dependent only on the actual condition of the body considered, so that, if all its other physical properties, its temperature, its density, etc., are known, the total heat contained in it is completely determined. This assumption, however, is no longer admissible if our principle is adopted. Suppose that we are given a body in a definite state— for example, a quantity of gas with the temperature t_0 and the volume v_0—and that we subject it to various changes of temperature and volume, which are such, however, as to bring it at last to its original state again. According to the common assumption, its total heat will again be the same as at first, from which it follows that if during one part of its changes heat is communicated to it from without, the same quantity of heat must be given up by it in the other part of its changes. Now with every change of volume a certain amount of work must be done by the gas or upon it, since by its expansion it overcomes an external pressure, and since its compression can be brought about only by an exertion of external pressure. If, therefore, among the changes to which it has been subjected there are changes of volume, work must be done upon it and by it. It is not necessary, however, that at the end of the operation, when it is again brought to its original state, the work done by it shall on the whole equal that done upon it, so that the two quantities of work shall counterbalance each other. There may be an excess of one or the other of these quantities of work, since the compression may take place at a higher or lower temperature than the expansion, as will be more definitely shown later on. To this excess of work done by the gas or upon it there must correspond, by our principle, a proportional excess of heat consumed or produced, and the gas cannot give up to the surrounding medium the same amount of heat as it receives.

The same contradiction to the ordinary assumption about the *total heat* may be presented in another way. If the gas at t_0 and v_0 is brought to the higher temperature t_1 and the larger volume v_1, the quantity of heat which must be imparted to it is, on that assumption, independent of the way in which the change is brought about; from our principle, however, it is different, according as the gas is first heated while its volume, v_0, is constant, and then allowed to expand at the constant temperature t_1, or is first expanded at the constant temperature t_0, and then heated, or as the expansion and heating are interchanged in any other way or even occur together, since in all these cases the work done by the gas is different.

In the same way, if a quantity of water at the temperature t_0 is changed into vapor at the temperature t_1 and of the volume v_1, it will make a difference in the amount of heat needed if the water as such is first heated to t_1 and then evaporated, or if it is evaporated at t_0 and the vapor then brought to the required volume and temperature, v_1 and t_1, or finally if the evaporation occurs at any intermediate temperature.

From these considerations and from the immediate application of the principle, it may easily be seen what conception must be formed of *latent* heat. Using again the example already employed, we distinguish in the quantity of heat which must be imparted to the water during its changes the *free* and *latent* heat. Of these, however, we may consider only the former as really present in the vapor that has been formed. The latter is not merely, as its name implies, *concealed* from our perception, but it is *nowhere present*; it is *consumed* during the changes in doing work.

In the heat consumed we must still introduce a distinction— that is to say, the work done is of two kinds. First, there is a certain amount of work done in overcoming the mutual attractions of the particles of the water, and in separating them to such a distance from one another that they are in the state of vapor. Secondly, the vapor during its evolution must push back an external pressure in order to make room for itself. The former work we shall call the *internal*, the latter, the *external* work, and shall partition the latent heat accordingly.

It can make no difference with respect to the *internal* work whether the evaporation goes on at t_0 or at t_1, or at any intermediate temperature, since we must consider the attractive force of the particles, which is to be overcome, as invariable.*

The *external* work, on the other hand, is regulated by the pressure as dependent on the temperature. Of course the same is true in general as in this special example, and therefore if it was said above that the quantity of heat which must be imparted to a body, to

---

* It cannot be raised, as an objection to this statement, that water at t_1 has less cohesion than at t_0, and that therefore less work would be needed to overcome it. For a certain amount of work is used in diminishing the cohesion, which is done while the water as such is heated, and this must be reckoned in with that done during the evaporation. It follows at once that only a part of the heat, which the water takes up from without while it is being heated, is to be considered as free heat, while the remainder is used in diminishing the cohesion. This view is also consistent with the circumstance that water has so much greater a specific heat than ice, and probably also than its vapor.

bring it from one condition to another, depended not merely on its initial and final conditions, but also on the way in which the change takes place, this statement refers only to that part of the *latent* heat which corresponds to the *external* work. The other part of the *latent* heat, as also the *free* heat, are independent of the way in which the changes take place.

If now the vapor at t_1 and v_1 is again transformed into water, work will thereby be *expended*, since the particles again yield to their attractions and approach each other, and the external pressure again advances. Corresponding to this, heat must be *produced*, and the so-called liberated heat which appears during the operation does not merely come out of concealment but is actually made new. The heat produced in this reversed operation need not be equal to that used in the direct one, but that part which corresponds to the *external* work may be greater or less according to circumstances.

We shall now turn to the mathematical discussion of the subject, in which we shall restrict ourselves to the consideration of the *permanent gases* and of *vapors at their maximum density*, since these cases, in consequence of the extensive knowledge we have of them, are most easily submitted to calculation, and besides that are the most interesting.

Let there be given a certain quantity, say a unit of weight, of a *permanent gas*. To determine its present condition, three magnitudes must be known: the pressure upon it, its volume, and its temperature. These magnitudes are in a mutual relationship, which is expressed by the combined laws of Mariotte and Gay-Lussac,* and may be represented by the equation:

$$(\text{I.}) \qquad\qquad pv = R\,(a+t),$$

where p, v, and t represent the pressure, volume, and temperature of the gas in its present condition, a is a constant, the same for all gases, and R is also a constant, which in its complete form is $\dfrac{p_0\,v_0}{a+t_0}$, if p_0, v_0, and t_0 are the corresponding values of the three magnitudes already mentioned for any other condition of the gas. This last constant is in so far different for the different gases that it is inversely proportional to their specific gravities.

It is true that Regnault has lately shown by a very careful

---

* This law will hereafter, for brevity, be called the M. and G. law, and Mariotte's law will be called the M. law.

investigation that this law is not strictly accurate, yet the departures from it are in the case of the permanent gases very small, and only become of consequence in the case of those gases which can be condensed into liquids. From this it seems to follow that the law holds with greater accuracy the more removed the gas is from its condensation point with respect to pressure and temperature. We may therefore, while the accuracy of the law for the permanent gases in their ordinary condition is so great that it can be treated as complete in most investigations, think of a limiting condition for each gas, in which the accuracy of the law is actually complete. We shall, in what follows, when we treat the permanent gases as such, assume this ideal condition.

According to the concordant investigations of Regnault and Magnus, the value of $\frac{1}{a}$ for atmospheric air is equal to 0.003665, if the temperature is reckoned in centigrade degrees from the freezing-point. Since, however, as has been mentioned, the gases do not follow the M. and G. law exactly, the same value of $\frac{1}{a}$ will not always be obtained, if the measurements are made in different circumstances. The number here given holds for the case when air is taken at 0° under the pressure of *one* atmosphere, and heated to 100° at constant volume, and the increase of its expansive force observed. If, on the other hand, the pressure is kept constant, and the increase of its volume observed, the somewhat greater number 0.003670 is obtained. Further, the numbers increase if the experiment is tried under a pressure higher than the atmospheric pressure, while they diminish somewhat for lower pressures. It is not therefore possible to decide with certainty on the number which should be adopted for the gas in the ideal condition in which naturally all differences must disappear; yet the number 0.003665 will surely not be far from the truth, especially since this number very nearly obtains in the case of hydrogen, which probably approaches the most nearly of all the gases the ideal condition, and for which the changes are in the opposite sense to those of the other gases. If we therefore adopt this value of $\frac{1}{a}$ we obtain

$$a = 273.$$

In consequence of equation (I.) we can treat any one of the three magnitudes p, v, and t—for example, p—as a function of the two others, v and t. These latter then are the independent variables by which the condition of the gas is fixed. We shall now seek to determine how the magnitudes which relate to the quantities of heat depend on these two variables.

If any body changes its volume, mechanical work will in general be either produced or expended. It is, however, in most cases impossible to determine this exactly, since besides the *external* work there is generally an unknown amount of *internal* work done. To avoid this difficulty, Carnot employed the ingenious method already referred to of allowing the body to undergo its various changes in succession, which are so arranged that it returns at last exactly to its original condition. In this case, if *internal* work is done in some of the changes, it is exactly compensated for in the others, and we may be sure that the *external* work, which remains over after the changes are completed, is all the work that has been done. Clapeyron has represented this process graphically in a very clear way, and we shall follow his presentation now for the permanent gases, with a slight alteration rendered necessary by our principle.

In the figure, let the abscissa *oe* represent the volume and the ordinate *ea* the pressure on a unit weight of gas, in a condition in which its temperature $= t$. We assume that the gas is contained in an extensible envelope, which, however, cannot exchange heat with it. If, now, it is allowed to expand in this envelope, its temperature would fall if no heat were imparted to it. To avoid this, let it be put in contact, during its expansion, with a body, A, which is kept at the constant temperature t, and which imparts just so much heat to the gas that its temperature also remains equal to t. During this expansion at constant temperature, its pressure diminishes according to the M. law, and may be represented by the ordinate of a curve, *ab*, which is a portion of an equilateral hyperbola. When the volume of the gas has increased in this way from *oe* to *of*, the body A is removed, and the expansion is allowed to continue without the introduction of more heat. The temperature will then fall, and the pressure diminish more rapidly than before. The law which is followed in this part of the process may be represented by the curve *bc*. When the volume of the gas has increased in this way from *of* to *og*, and its temperature has fallen from t to τ, we begin to compress it, in order to restore it again to its original volume *oe*. If it were left to itself its temperature would again rise. This, however, we do not permit, but bring it in contact with a body B, at the constant temperature τ, to which it at once gives up

50

the heat that is produced, so that it keeps the temperature τ; and while it is in contact with this body we compress it so far (by the amount *gh*) that the remaining compression *he* is exactly sufficient to raise its temperature from τ to *t*, if during this last compression

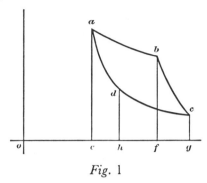

Fig. 1

it gives up no heat.   During the former compression the pressure increases according to the M. law, and is represented by the portion *cd* of an equilateral hyperbola.   During the latter, on the other hand, the increase is more rapid and is represented by the curve *da*.   This curve must end exactly at *a*, for since at the end of the operation the volume and temperature have again their original values, the same must be true of the pressure also, which is a function of them both.   The gas is therefore in the same condition again as it was at the beginning.

Now, to determine the work produced by these changes, for the reasons already given, we need to direct our attention only to the *external* work.   During the expansion the gas *does* work, which is determined by the integral of the product of the differential of the volume into the corresponding pressure, and is therefore represented geometrically by the quadrilaterals *eabf* and *fbcg*.   During the compression, on the other hand, work is *expended*, which is represented similarly by the quadrilaterals *gcdh* and *hdae*.   The excess of the former quantity of work over the latter is to be looked on as the whole work produced during the changes, and this is represented by the quadrilateral *abcd*.

If the process above described is carried out in the reverse order, the same magnitude, *abcd*, is obtained as the excess of the work *expended* over the work *done*.

In order to make an analytical application of the method just described, we will assume that all the changes which the gas undergoes are *infinitely small*. We may then treat the curves obtained as straight lines, as they are represented in the accompanying figure. We may also, in determining the area of the quadrilateral *abcd*, consider it a parallelogram, since the error arising therefrom can only be a quantity of the *third* order, while the area itself is a quantity of the *second* order. On this assumption, as may easily be seen, the area may be represented by the product *ef · bk*, if *k* is the point in which the ordinate *bf* cuts the lower side of the quadrilateral. The magnitude *bk* is the increase of the pressure, while

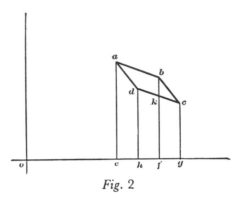

Fig. 2

the gas at the constant volume *of* has its temperature raised from τ to t—that is, by the differential $t - \tau = dt$. This magnitude may be at once expressed by the aid of equation (I.) in terms of v and t, and is

$$dp = \frac{Rdt}{v}.$$

If, further, we denote the increase of volume *ef* by dv, we obtain the area of the quadrilateral, and so, also,

(1)   *The work done* $= \dfrac{Rdvdt}{v}.$

We must now determine the heat consumed in these changes. The quantity of heat which must be communicated to a gas, while it is brought from any former condition in a definite way to that condition in which its volume $= v$ and its temperature $= t$, may be called Q, and the changes of volume in the above process, which must here be considered separately, may be represented as follows:

ef by dv, *hg* by $d'v$, *eh* by δv, and *fg* by $\delta'v$. During an expansion from the volume $oe = v$ to the volume $of = v + dv$ at the constant temperature t, the gas must receive the quantity of heat

$$\left(\frac{dQ}{dv}\right) dv,$$

and correspondingly, during an expansion from $oh = v + \delta v$ to $og = v + \delta v + d'v$ at the temperature $t - dt$, the quantity of heat,

$$\left[\left(\frac{dQ}{dv}\right) + \frac{d}{dv}\left(\frac{dQ}{dv}\right) \delta v - \frac{d}{dt}\left(\frac{dQ}{dv}\right) dt\right] d'v.$$

In the case before us this latter quantity must be taken as negative in the calculation, because the real process was a compression instead of the expansion assumed. During the expansion from *of* to *og* and the compression from *oh* to *oe*, the gas has neither gained nor lost heat, and hence the quantity of heat which the gas has received in excess of that which it has given up—that is, the *heat consumed*

$$(2) \qquad = \left(\frac{dQ}{dv}\right) dv - \left[\left(\frac{dQ}{dv}\right) + \frac{d}{dv}\left(\frac{dQ}{dv}\right) \delta v - \frac{d}{dt}\left(\frac{dQ}{dv}\right) dt\right] d'v.$$

The magnitudes δv and $d'v$ must be eliminated from this expression. For this purpose we have first, immediately from the inspection of the figure, the following equation:

$$dv + \delta'v = \delta v + d'v.$$

From the condition that during the compression from *oh* to *oe*, and therefore also conversely during an expansion from *oe* to *oh* occurring under the same conditions, and similarly during the expansion from *of* to *og*, both of which occasion a fall of temperature by the amount dt, the gas neither receives nor gives up heat, we obtain the equations

$$\left(\frac{dQ}{dv}\right) \delta v - \left(\frac{dQ}{dt}\right) dt = 0,$$

$$\left[\left(\frac{dQ}{dv}\right) + \frac{d}{dv}\left(\frac{dQ}{dv}\right) dv\right] \delta'v - \left[\left(\frac{dQ}{dt}\right) + \frac{d}{dv}\left(\frac{dQ}{dt}\right) dv\right] dt = 0.$$

Eliminating from these three equations and equation (2) the three magnitudes $d'v$, δv, and $\delta'v$, and also neglecting in the development those terms which, in respect of the differentials, are of a higher order than the second, we obtain

$$(3) \qquad \textit{The heat consumed} = \left[\frac{d}{dt}\left(\frac{dQ}{dv}\right) - \frac{d}{dv}\left(\frac{dQ}{dt}\right)\right] dv dt.$$

If we now return to our principle, that to produce a certain amount of work the expenditure of a proportional quantity of heat is necessary, we can establish the formula

(4)
$$\frac{\text{The heat consumed}}{\text{The work done}} = A,$$

where *A is a constant, which denotes the heat equivalent for the unit of work.* The expressions (1) and (3) substituted in this equation give

$$\frac{\left[\frac{d}{dt}\left(\frac{dQ}{dv}\right) - \frac{d}{dv}\left(\frac{dQ}{dt}\right)\right]dvdt}{\dfrac{R \cdot dvdt}{v}} = A,$$

or

(II.)
$$\frac{d}{dt}\left(\frac{dQ}{dv}\right) - \frac{d}{dv}\left(\frac{dQ}{dt}\right) = \frac{AR}{v}.$$

We may consider this equation as the analytical expression of our fundamental principle applied to the case of permanent gases. It shows that Q cannot be a function of v and t, if these variables are independent of each other. For if it were, then by the well-known law of the differential calculus, that if a function of two variables is differentiated with respect to both of them, the order of differentiation is indifferent, the right-hand side of the equation should be equal to zero.

The equation may also be brought into the form of a *complete* differential equation,

(II.*a*)
$$dQ = dU + A \cdot R \frac{a+t}{v} \, dv,$$

in which U is an arbitrary function of v and t. This differential equation is naturally not integrable, but becomes so only if a second relation is given between the variables, by which t may be treated as a function of v. The reason for this is found in the last term, and this corresponds exactly to the *external* work done during the change, since the differential of this work is pdv, from which we obtain

$$\frac{R(a+t)}{v} \, dv,$$

if we eliminate p by means of (I.).

We have thus obtained from equation (II.*a*) what was introduced before as an immediate consequence of our principle, that the total amount of heat received by the gas during a change of volume and temperature can be separated into two parts, one of which, *U*, which comprises the *free* heat that has entered and the heat *consumed* in doing *internal* work, if any such work has been done, has the properties which are commonly assigned to the total heat, of being a function of *v* and *t*, and of being therefore fully determined by the initial and final conditions of the gas, between which the transformation has taken place; while the other part, which comprises the heat *consumed* in doing *external* work, is dependent not only on the terminal conditions, but on the whole course of the changes between these conditions.

Before we undertake to prepare this equation for further conclusions, we shall develop the analytical expression of our fundamental principle for the case of vapors at their maximum density.

In this case we have no right to apply the M. and G. law, and so must restrict ourselves to the principle alone. In order to obtain an equation from it, we again use the method given by Carnot and graphically presented by Clapeyron, with a slight modification. Consider a liquid contained in a vessel impenetrable by heat, of which, however, only a part is filled by the liquid, while the rest is left free for the vapor, which is at the maximum density corresponding to its temperature, *t*. The total volume of both liquid and vapor is represented in the accompanying figure by the abscissa *oe*, and the pressure of the vapor by the ordinate *ea*. Let the vessel now yield to the pressure and enlarge in volume while the liquid and vapor are in contact with a body *A*, at the constant temperature *t*. As the volume increases, more liquid evaporates, but the heat which thus becomes latent is supplied from the body *A*, so that the temperature, and so also the pressure, of the vapor remain unchanged. If in this way the total volume is increased from *oe* to *of*, an amount of external work is done which is represented by the rectangle *eabf*. Now remove the body *A* and let the vessel increase in volume still further, while heat can neither enter nor leave it. In this processs the vapor already present will expand, and also new vapor will be produced, and in consequence the temperature will fall and the pressure diminish. Let this process go on until the temperature has changed from *t* or *τ*, and the volume has become *og*. If the fall of pressure during this expansion is represented by the curve *bc*, the external work done in the process = *fbcg*.

Now diminish the volume of the vessel, in order to bring the liquid with its vapor back to its original total volume, *oe*; and let this compression take place, in part, in contact with the body *B* at the temperature *τ*, into which body all the heat set free by the

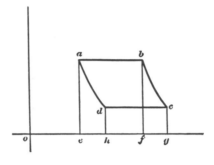

Fig. 3

condensation of the vapor will pass, so that the temperature remains constant and = *τ*, in part without this body, so that the temperature rises. Let the operation be so managed that the first part of the compression is carried out only so far (to *oh*) that the volume *he* still remaining is exactly such that compression through it will raise the temperature from *τ* to *t* again. During the former diminution of volume the pressure remains invariable, = *gc*, and the external work employed is equal to the rectangle *gcdh*. During the latter diminution of volume the pressure increases and is represented by the curve *da*, which must end exactly at the point *a*, since the original pressure, *ea*, must correspond to the original temperature, *t*. The work employed in this last operation is = *hdae*. At the end of the operation the liquid and vapor are again in the same condition as at the beginning, so that the excess of the *external* work done over that employed is also the *total* work done. It is represented by the quadrilateral *abcd*, and its area must also be set equal to the *heat consumed* during the same time.

For our purposes we again assume that the changes just described are infinitely small, and on this assumption represent the whole process by the accompanying figure, in which the curves *ad* and *bc* which occur in Fig. 3 have become straight lines. So far as the area of the quadrilateral *abcd* is concerned, it may again be considered a parallelogram, and may be represented by the product *ef · bk*.

If, now, the pressure of the vapor at the temperature t and at its maximum tension is represented by p, and if the temperature difference $t - \tau$ is represented by dt, we have

$$bk = \frac{dp}{dt}\, dt.$$

The line *ef* represents the increase of volume, which occurs in consequence of the passage of a certain quantity of liquid, which may be

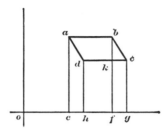

Fig. 4

called dm, over into vapor. Representing now the volume of a unit weight of the vapor at its maximum density at the temperature t by s, and the volume of the same quantity of liquid at the temperature t by σ, we have evidently

$$ef = (s - \sigma)\, dm,$$

and consequently the area of the quadrilateral, or

(5)   *The work done* $= (s - \sigma) \dfrac{dp}{dt}\, dmdt.$

In order to represent the quantities of heat concerned, we will introduce the following symbols. The quantity of heat which becomes latent when a unit weight of the liquid evaporates at the temperature t and under the corresponding pressure, is called τ, and the specific heat of the liquid is called c. Both of these quantities, as well as also s, σ, and $\dfrac{dp}{dt}$, are to be considered functions of t. Finally, let us denote by hdt the quantity of heat which must be imparted to a unit weight of the vapor if its temperature is raised from t to $t + dt$, while it is so compressed that it is again at the maximum density for this temperature without the precipitation of any part of it. The quantity h is likewise a function of t. It will, for the present, be left undetermined whether it has a positive or negative value.

If we now denote by μ the mass of liquid originally present in the vessel, and by m the mass of vapor, and further by dm the mass which evaporates during the expansion from oe to of, and by $d'm$ the mass which condenses during the compression from og to oh, the heat which becomes latent in the first operation and is taken from the body A is

$$rdm,$$

and that which is set free in the second operation and is given to the body B is

$$\left(r - \frac{dr}{dt}\,dt\right) d'm.$$

In the other expansion and in the other compression heat is neither gained nor lost, so that, at the end of the process,

(6)   *The heat consumed* $= rdm - \left(r - \dfrac{dr}{dt}\,dt\right) d'm.$

In this expression the differential $d'm$ must be replaced by dm and dt. For this purpose we make use of the conditions under which the second expansion and the second compression occurred. The mass of vapor, which condenses during the compression from oh to oe, and which would be evolved by the corresponding expansion from oe to oh, may be represented by δm, and that which is evolved by the expansion from of to og by $\delta'm$. We then have at once, since at the end of the process the same mass of liquid μ and the mass of vapor m must be present as at the beginning, the equation

$$dm + \delta'm = d'm + \delta m.$$

Further, we obtain for the expansion from oe to oh, since in it the temperature of the mass of liquid μ and the mass of vapor m must be lowered by dt without the emission of heat, the equation

$$r\delta m - \mu \cdot cdt - m \cdot hdt = 0;$$

and similarly for the expansion from of to og, by substituting $\mu - dm$ and $m + dm$ for μ and m, and $\delta'm$ for δm,

$$r\delta'm - (\mu - dm)cdt - (m + dm)hdt = 0.$$

58

If from these three equations and (6) we eliminate the magnitudes $d'm$, δm, and $\delta'm$, and reject terms of higher order than the second, we have

(7)   *The heat consumed* $= \left(\dfrac{dr}{dt} + c - h\right) dmdt.$

The formulas (7) and (5) must now be connected in the same way as that used in the case of the permanent gases, that is,

$$\frac{\left(\dfrac{dr}{dt} + c - h\right) dmdt}{(s - \sigma)\dfrac{dp}{dt} dmdt} = A,$$

and we obtain as the analytical expression of the fundamental principle in the case of vapors at their maximum density the equation

(III.) $\dfrac{dr}{dt} + c - h = A(s - \sigma)\dfrac{dp}{dt}.$

If, instead of using our principle, we adopt the assumption that the quantity of heat is *constant*, we must replace (III.), as appears from (7), by

(8) $\dfrac{dr}{dt} + c - h = 0.$

This equation has been used, if not exactly in the same form, at least in its general sense, to obtain a value for the magnitude h. So long as Watt's law is considered true for water, that the sum of the free and latent heats of a quantity of vapor at its maximum density is equal for all temperatures, and that therefore

$$\frac{dr}{dt} + c = 0,$$

it must be concluded that for this liquid $h = 0$. This conclusion has, in fact, often been stated as correct, in that it has been said that if a quantity of vapor is at its maximum density, and then compressed or expanded in a vessel impermeable by heat, it remains at its maximum density. But since Regnault* has corrected Watt's law by substituting for it the approximate relation

$$\frac{dr}{dt} + c = 0.305,$$

* *Mém. de l'Acad.*, xxi, the 9th and 10th memoirs.

the equation (8) gives for h the value 0.305. It would therefore follow that the quantity of vapor formerly considered in the vessel impermeable by heat would be partly condensed by compression, and on expansion would not remain at the maximum density, since its temperature would not fall in a way to correspond to the diminution of pressure.

It is entirely different if we replace equation (8) by (III.). The expression on the right-hand side is, from its nature, always positive, and it therefore follows that h must be less than 0.305. It will subsequently appear that the value of this expression is so great that h is negative. We must therefore conclude that the quantity of vapor before mentioned is partly condensed, not by *compression*, but by *expansion*, and that by compression its temperature rises at a greater rate than the density increases, so that it does not remain at its maximum density.

It must be admitted that this result is exactly opposed to the common view already referred to; yet I do not believe that it is contradicted by any experimental fact. Indeed, it is more consistent than the former view with the behavior of steam as observed by Pambour. Pambour* found that the steam which issues from a locomotive after it has done its work always has the temperature at which the tension, observed at the same time, is a maximum. From this it follows either that $h = 0$, as it was once thought to be, because this assumption agreed with Watt's law, accepted as probably true, or that h is *negative*. For if h were *positive*, the temperature of the vapor, when released, would be too high in comparison with its tension, and that could not have escaped Pambour's notice. If, on the other hand, h is *negative*, according to our former statement, there can never arise from this cause too low a temperature, but a part of the steam must become liquid, so as to maintain the rest at the proper temperature. This part need not be great, since a small quantity of vapor sets free on condensation a relatively large quantity of heat, and the water formed will probably be carried on mechanically by the rest of the steam, and will in such researches pass unnoticed, the more likely as it might be thought, if it were to be observed, that it was water from the boiler carried out mechanically.

The results thus far obtained have been deduced from the fundamental principle without any further hypothesis. The equation

---

* *Traité des Locomotives*, second edition, and *Théorie des Machines à Vapeur*, second edition.

(II.*a*) obtained for permanent gases may, however, be made much more fruitful by the help of an obvious subsidiary hypothesis. The gases show in their various relations, especially in the relation expressed by the M. and G. law between volume, pressure, and temperature, so great a regularity of behavior that we are naturally led to take the view that the mutual attraction of the particles, which acts within solid and liquid bodies, no longer acts in gases, so that while in the case of other bodies the heat which produces expansion must overcome not only the external pressure but the internal attraction as well, in the case of gases it has to do only with the external pressure.   If this is the case, then during the expansion of a gas only so much heat becomes *latent* as is used in doing *external work*.   There is, further, no reason to think that a gas, if it expands at constant temperature, contains more *free* heat than before.   If this be admitted, we have the law: *a permanent gas, when expanded at constant temperature, takes up only so much heat as is consumed in doing external work during the expansion.*   This law is probably true for any gas with the same degree of exactness as that attained by the M. and G. law applied to it.

From this it follows at once that

(9)
$$\left(\frac{dQ}{dv}\right) = A \cdot R \frac{a+t}{v},$$

since, as already noticed, $R \dfrac{a+t}{v} dv$ represents the external work done during the expansion dv.   It follows that the function U which occurs in (11.*a*) does not contain v, and the equation therefore takes the form

(II.*b*)
$$dQ = cdt + AR \frac{a+t}{v} dv,$$

where c can be a function of t only.   It is even probable that this magnitude c, which represents the specific heat of the gas at constant volume, is a constant.

Now in order to apply this equation to special cases, we must introduce the relation between the variables Q, t, and v, which is obtained from the conditions of each separate case, into the equation, and so make it integrable.   We shall here consider only a few simple examples of this sort, which are either interesting in themselves or become so by comparison with other theorems already announced.

We may first obtain the specific heats of the gas at constant volume and at constant pressure if in (II.*b*) we set $v = $ const., and $p = $ const. In the former case, $dv = 0$, and (II.*b*) becomes

(10)
$$\frac{dQ}{dt} = c.$$

In the latter case, we obtain from the condition $p = $ const., by the help of equation (I.),

$$dv = \frac{Rdt}{p},$$

or

$$\frac{dv}{v} = \frac{dt}{a+t};$$

and this, substituted in (II.*b*), gives

(10*a*)
$$\frac{dQ}{dt} = c' = c + AR,$$

if we denote by c' the specific heat at constant pressure.

It appears, therefore, that the *difference of the two specific heats of any gas is a constant magnitude, AR*. This magnitude also involves a simple relation among the different gases. The complete expression for R is $\frac{p_0 v_0}{a+t_0}$, where p_0, v_0, and t_0 are any three corresponding values of p, v, and t for a unit of weight of the gas considered, and it therefore follows, as has already been mentioned in connection with the adoption of equation (I.), that R is inversely proportional to the specific gravity of the gas, and hence also that the same statement must hold for the difference $c' - c = AR$, since A is the same for all gases.

If we reckon the specific heat of the gas, not with respect to the unit of *weight*, but, as is more convenient, with respect to the unit of *volume*, we need only divide c and c' by v_0, if the volumes are taken at the temperature t_0 and pressure p_0. Designating these quotients by γ and γ', we obtain

(11)
$$\gamma' - \gamma = \frac{A \cdot R}{v_0} = A\frac{p_0}{a+t_0}.$$

In this last quantity nothing appears which is dependent on the particular nature of the gas, and *the difference of the specific heats referred to the unit of volume is therefore the same for all gases.*

This law was deduced by Clapeyron from Carnot's theory, though the constancy of the difference $c' - c$, which we have deduced before, is not found in this work, where the expression given for it still has the form of a function of the temperature.

If we divide equation (11) on both sides by γ, we have

$$(12) \qquad\qquad k - 1 = \frac{A}{\gamma} \cdot \frac{p_0}{a + t_0},$$

in which k, for the sake of brevity, is used for the quotient $\frac{\gamma'}{\gamma}$, or, what amounts to the same thing, for the quotient $\frac{c'}{c}$. This quantity has acquired special importance in science from the theoretical discussion by Laplace of the propagation of sound in air. *The excess of this quotient over unity is therefore, for the different gases, inversely proportional to the specific heats of the same at constant volume, if these are referred to the unit of volume.* This law has, in fact, been found by Dulong from experiment* to be so nearly accurate that he has assumed it, in view of its theoretical probability, to be strictly accurate, and has therefore employed it, conversely, to calculate the specific heats of the different gases from the values of k determined by observation. It must, however, be remarked that the law is only theoretically justified when the M. and G. law holds, which is not the case with sufficient exactness for all the gases employed by Dulong.

If it is now assumed that the specific heat of gases at constant volume c is constant, which has been stated above to be very probable, the same follows for the specific heat at constant pressure, and consequently *the quotient of the two specific heats* $\frac{c'}{c} = k$ *is a constant.*

This law, which Poisson has already assumed as correct on the strength of the experiments of Gay-Lussac and Welter, and has made the basis of his investigations on the tension and heat of gases,† is therefore in good agreement with our present theory, while it would not be possible on Carnot's theory as hitherto developed.

If in equation (II.*b*) we set $Q = $ const., we obtain the following equation between v and t:

$$(13) \qquad\qquad c\,dt + A \cdot R \, \frac{a + t}{v} \, dv = 0,$$

---

* *Ann. de Chim. et de Phys.*, xli, and Pogg. *Ann.*, xvi.
† *Traité de Mécanique*, second edition, vol. ii, p. 646.

which gives, if c is considered constant,

$$v \frac{A \cdot R}{c} \cdot (a+t) = \text{const.},$$

or, since from equation (10a), $\frac{AR}{c} = \frac{c'}{c} - 1 = k - 1,$

$$v^{k-1}(a+t) = \text{const.}$$

Hence we have, if v_0, t_0, and p_0 are three corresponding values of v, t and p,

(14)
$$\frac{a+t}{a+t_0} = \left(\frac{v_0}{v}\right)^{k-1.}$$

If we substitute in this relation the pressure p first for v and then for t by means of equation (I.), we obtain

(15)
$$\left(\frac{a+t}{a+t_0}\right)^k = \left(\frac{p}{p_0}\right)^{k-1}$$

(16)
$$\frac{p}{p_0} = \left(\frac{v_0}{v}\right)^{k.}$$

These are the relations which hold between volume, temperature, and pressure, if a quantity of gas is compressed or expanded within an envelope impermeable by heat. These equations agree precisely with those which have been developed by Poisson for the same case,* which depends upon the fact that he also treated k as a constant.

Finally, if we set $t = \text{const.}$ in equation (II.b), the first term on the right drops out, and there remains

(17)
$$dQ = AR \frac{a+t}{v} dv,$$

from which we have

$$Q = AR(a+t) \log v + \text{const.},$$

or, if we denote by v_0, p_0, t_0, and Q_0 the values of v, p, t, and Q, which hold at the beginning of the change of volume,

(18)
$$Q - Q_0 = AR(a+t_0) \log \frac{v}{v_0}.$$

From this follows the law also developed by Carnot: *If a gas changes its volume without changing its temperature, the quantities of heat evolved or*

---

* *Traité de Mécanique*, vol. ii, p. 647.

absorbed are in arithmetical progression, while the volumes are in geometrical progression.

Further, if we substitute for R in (18) the complete expression $\dfrac{p_0 v_0}{a + t_0}$, we have

$$(19) \qquad\qquad Q - Q_0 = A p_0 v_0 \log \frac{v}{v_0}.$$

If now we apply this equation to the different gases, not by using equal *weights* of them, but such quantities as have at the outset equal volumes, v_0, it becomes in all its parts independent of the special nature of the gas, and agrees with the well-known law which Dulong proposed, guided by the above-mentioned simple relation of the magnitude $k - 1$, *that all gases, if equal volumes of them are taken at the same temperature and under the same pressure, and if they are then compressed or expanded by an equal fraction of their volumes, either evolve or absorb an equal quantity of heat.* Equation (19) is, however, much more general. It states in addition, *that the quantity of heat is independent oj the temperature at which the volume of the gas is altered,* if only the quantity of the gas employed is always determined so that the original volume v_0 is always the same at the different temperatures; and it states further, that *if the original pressure is different in the different cases, the quantities of heat are proportional to it.*

[*Ed. note:* material omitted]

3

Reprinted from *Mathematical and Physical Papers of William Thomson*, Vol. 1, Cambridge University Press, London, 1882, pp. 174–192, 222–223

ART. XLVIII. ON THE DYNAMICAL THEORY OF HEAT, WITH NUMERICAL RESULTS DEDUCED FROM MR JOULE'S EQUIVALENT OF A THERMAL UNIT, AND M. REGNAULT'S OBSERVATIONS ON STEAM.

William Thomson (Lord Kelvin)

[*Transactions of the Royal Society of Edinburgh*, March, 1851, *and Phil. Mag.* IV. 1852.]

Introductory Notice.

1. SIR HUMPHRY DAVY, by his experiment of melting two pieces of ice by rubbing them together, established the following proposition:—"The phenomena of repulsion are not dependent on a peculiar elastic fluid for their existence, or caloric does not exist." And he concludes that heat consists of a motion excited among the particles of bodies. "To distinguish this motion from others, and to signify the cause of our sensation of heat," and of the expansion or expansive pressure produced in matter by heat, "the name *repulsive* motion has been adopted *."

2. The dynamical theory of heat, thus established by Sir Humphry Davy, is extended to radiant heat by the discovery of phenomena, especially those of the polarization of radiant heat, which render it excessively probable that heat propagated through "vacant space," or through diathermanic substances, consists of waves of transverse vibrations in an all-pervading medium.

---

* From Davy's first work, entitled *An Essay on Heat, Light, and the Combinations of Light*, published in 1799, in "Contributions to Physical and Medical Knowledge, principally from the West of England, collected by Thomas Beddoes, M.D.," and republished in Dr Davy's edition of his brother's collected works, Vol. II. Lond. 1836.

3. The recent discoveries made by Mayer and Joule*, of the generation of heat through the friction of fluids in motion, and by the magneto-electric excitation of galvanic currents, would either of them be sufficient to demonstrate the immateriality of heat; and would so afford, if required, a perfect confirmation of Sir Humphry Davy's views.

4. Considering it as thus established, that heat is not a substance, but a dynamical form of mechanical effect, we perceive that there must be an equivalence between mechanical work and heat, as between cause and effect. The first published statement of this principle appears to be in Mayer's *Bemerkungen über die Kräfte der unbelebten Natur†*, which contains some correct views regarding the mutual convertibility of heat and mechanical effect, along with a false analogy between the approach of a weight to the earth and a diminution of the volume of a continuous substance, on which an attempt is founded to find numerically the mechanical equivalent of a given quantity of heat. In a paper published about fourteen months later, "On the Calorific Effects of Magneto-Electricity and the Mechanical Value of Heat‡," Mr Joule of Manchester expresses very distinctly the consequences regarding the mutual convertibility of heat and mechanical effect which follow from the fact, that heat is not a substance but a state of motion; and investigates on unquestionable principles the "absolute numerical relations," according to which heat is connected with mechanical power; verifying experimentally, that whenever heat is generated from purely mechanical action, and no other effect produced, whether it be by means of the friction of fluids or by the magneto-electric excitation of galvanic currents, the same quantity is generated by the same amount of work spent; and determining the actual amount of work, in foot-pounds,

---

* In May, 1842, Mayer announced in the *Annalen* of Wöhler and Liebig, that he had raised the temperature of water from 12° to 13° Cent. by agitating it. In August, 1843, Joule announced to the British Association "That heat is evolved by the passage of water through narrow tubes;" and that he had "obtained one degree of heat per lb. of water from a mechanical force capable of raising 770 lbs. to the height of one foot;" and that heat is generated when work is spent in turning a magneto-electric machine, or an electro-magnetic engine. (See his paper "On the Calorific Effects of Magneto-Electricity, and on the Mechanical Value of Heat."— *Phil. Mag.*, Vol. XXIII., 1843.)

† *Annalen* of Wöhler and Liebig, May, 1842.

‡ British Association, August, 1843; and *Phil. Mag.*, Sept., 1843.

required to generate a unit of heat, which he calls "the mechanical equivalent of heat." Since the publication of that paper, Mr Joule has made numerous series of experiments for determining with as much accuracy as possible the mechanical equivalent of heat so defined, and has given accounts of them in various communications to the British Association, to the *Philosophical Magazine*, to the Royal Society, and to the French Institute.

5. Important contributions to the dynamical theory of heat have recently been made by Rankine and Clausius; who, by mathematical reasoning analogous to Carnot's on the motive power of heat, but founded on an axiom contrary to his fundamental axiom, have arrived at some remarkable conclusions. The researches of these authors have been published in the *Transactions* of this Society, and in Poggendorff's *Annalen*, during the past year; and they are more particularly referred to below in connexion with corresponding parts of the investigations at present laid before the Royal Society.

[Various statements regarding animal heat, and the heat of combustion and chemical combination, are made in the writings of Liebig (as, for instance, the statement quoted in the foot-note added to § 18 below), which virtually imply the convertibility of heat into mechanical effect, and which are inconsistent with any other than the dynamical theory of heat.]

6. The object of the present paper is threefold:—

(1) To show what modifications of the conclusions arrived at by Carnot, and by others who have followed his peculiar mode of reasoning regarding the motive power of heat, must be made when the hypothesis of the dynamical theory, contrary as it is to Carnot's fundamental hypothesis, is adopted.

(2) To point out the significance in the dynamical theory, of the numerical results deduced from Regnault's observations on steam, and communicated about two years ago to the Society, with an account of Carnot's theory, by the author of the present paper; and to show that by taking these numbers (subject to correction when accurate experimental data regarding the density of saturated steam shall have been afforded), in connexion with Joule's mechanical equivalent of a thermal unit, a complete theory

of the motive power of heat, within the temperature limits of the experimental data, is obtained.

(3) To point out some remarkable relations connecting the physical properties of all substances, established by reasoning analogous to that of Carnot, but founded in part on the contrary principle of the dynamical theory.

PART I.

Fundamental Principles in the Theory of the Motive Power of Heat.

7. According to an obvious principle, first introduced, however, into the theory of the motive power of heat by Carnot, mechanical effect produced in any process cannot be said to have been derived from a purely thermal source, unless at the end of the process all the materials used are in precisely the same physical and mechanical circumstances as they were at the beginning. In some conceivable "thermo-dynamic engines," as for instance Faraday's floating magnet, or Barlow's "wheel and axle," made to rotate and perform work uniformly by means of a current continuously excited by heat communicated to two metals in contact, or the thermo-electric rotatory apparatus devised by Marsh, which has been actually constructed; this condition is fulfilled at every instant. On the other hand, in all thermo-dynamic engines, founded on electrical agency, in which discontinuous galvanic currents, or pieces of soft iron in a variable state of magnetization, are used, and in all engines founded on the alternate expansions and contractions of media, there are really alterations in the condition of materials; but, in accordance with the principle sta'ed above, these alterations must be strictly periodical. In any such engine, the series of motions performed during a period, at the end of which the materials are restored to precisely the same condition as that in which they existed at the beginning, constitutes what will be called a complete cycle of its operations. Whenever in what follows, *the work done* or *the mechanical effect produced* by a thermo-dynamic engine is mentioned without qualification, it must be understood that the mechanical effect produced, either in a non-varying engine, or in a complete cycle, or any number of complete cycles of a periodical engine, is meant.

8. The *source of heat* will always be supposed to be a hot body at a given constant temperature, put in contact with some part of the engine; and when any part of the engine is to be kept from rising in temperature (which can only be done by drawing off whatever heat is deposited in it), this will be supposed to be done by putting a cold body, which will be called the refrigerator, at a given constant temperature in contact with it.

9.   The whole theory of the motive power of heat is founded on the two following propositions, due respectively to Joule, and to Carnot and Clausius.

PROP. I. (Joule).—When equal quantities of mechanical effect are produced by any means whatever from purely thermal sources, or lost in purely thermal effects, equal quantities of heat are put out of existence or are generated.

PROP. II. (Carnot and Clausius).—If an engine be such that, when it is worked backwards, the physical and mechanical agencies in every part of its motions are all reversed, it produces as much mechanical effect as can be produced by any thermo-dynamic engine, with the same temperatures of source and refrigerator, from a given quantity of heat.

10.   The former proposition is shown to be included in the general "principle of mechanical effect," and is so established beyond all doubt by the following demonstration.

11.   By whatever direct effect the heat gained or lost by a body in any conceivable circumstances is tested, the measurement of its quantity may always be founded on a determination of the quantity of some standard substance, which it or any equal quantity of heat could raise from one standard temperature to another; the test of equality between two quantities of heat being their capability of raising equal quantities of any substance from any temperature to the same higher temperature.   Now, according to the dynamical theory of heat, the temperature of a substance can only be raised by working upon it in some way so as to produce increased thermal motions within it, besides effecting any modifications in the mutual distances or arrangements of its particles which may accompany a change of temperature.   The work necessary to produce this total mechanical effect is of course proportional to the quantity of the substance raised from one

70

standard temperature to another; and therefore when a body, or a group of bodies, or a machine, parts with or receives heat, there is in reality mechanical effect produced from it, or taken into it, to an extent precisely proportional to the quantity of heat which it emits or absorbs. But the work which any external forces do upon it, the work done by its own molecular forces, and the amount by which the half *vis viva* of the thermal motions of all its parts is diminished, must together be equal to the mechanical effect produced from it; and consequently, to the mechanical equivalent of the heat which it emits (which will be positive or negative, according as the sum of those terms is positive or negative). Now let there be either no molecular change or alteration of temperature in any part of the body, or, by a cycle of operations, let the temperature and physical condition be restored exactly to what they were at the beginning; the second and third of the three parts of the work which it has to produce vanish; and we conclude that the heat which it emits or absorbs will be the thermal equivalent of the work done upon it by external forces, or done by it against external forces; which is the proposition to be proved.

12.   The demonstration of the second proposition is founded on the following axiom:—

It is impossible, by means of inanimate material agency, to derive mechanical effect from any portion of matter by cooling it below the temperature of the coldest of the surrounding objects*.

13.   To demonstrate the second proposition, let A and B be two thermo-dynamic engines, of which B satisfies the conditions expressed in the enunciation; and let, if possible, A derive more work from a given quantity of heat than B, when their sources and refrigerators are at the same temperatures, respectively. Then on account of the condition of complete *reversibility* in all its operations which it fulfils, B may be worked backwards, and made to restore any quantity of heat to its source, by the expenditure of the amount of work which, by its forward action, it would derive from the same quantity of heat. If, therefore, B be

---

* If this axiom be denied for all temperatures, it would have to be admitted that a self-acting machine might be set to work and produce mechanical effect by cooling the sea or earth, with no limit but the total loss of heat from the earth and sea, or, in reality, from the whole material world.

worked backwards, and made to restore to the source of A (which we may suppose to be adjustable to the engine B) as much heat as has been drawn from it during a certain period of the working of A, a smaller amount of work will be spent thus than was gained by the working of A. Hence, if such a series of operations of A forwards and of B backwards be continued either alternately or simultaneously, there will result a continued production of work without any continued abstraction of heat from the source; and, by Prop. I., it follows that there must be more heat abstracted from the refrigerator by the working of B backwards than is deposited in it by A. Now it is obvious that A might be made to spend part of its work in working B backwards, and the whole might be made self-acting. Also, there being no heat either taken from or given to the source on the whole, all the surrounding bodies and space except the refrigerator might, without interfering with any of the conditions which have been assumed, be made of the same temperature as the source, whatever that may be. We should thus have a self-acting machine, capable of drawing heat constantly from a body surrounded by others at a higher temperature, and converting it into mechanical effect. But this is contrary to the axiom, and therefore we conclude that the hypothesis that A derives more mechanical effect from the same quantity of heat drawn from the source than B, is false. Hence no engine whatever, with source and refrigerator at the same temperatures, can get more work from a given quantity of heat introduced than any engine which satisfies the condition of reversibility, which was to be proved.

14. This proposition was first enunciated by Carnot, being the expression of his criterion of a perfect thermo-dynamic engine[*]. He proved it by demonstrating that a negation of it would require the admission that there might be a self-acting machine constructed which would produce mechanical effect indefinitely, without any source either in heat or the consumption of materials, or any other physical agency; but this demonstration involves, fundamentally, the assumption that, in "a complete cycle of operations," the medium parts with exactly the same quantity of heat as it receives. A very strong expression of doubt regarding the truth of this assumption, as a universal principle, is given by

---

[*] Account of Carnot's *Theory*, § 13.

Carnot himself[*]; and that it is false, where mechanical work is, on the whole, either gained or spent in the operations, may (as I have tried to show above) be considered to be perfectly certain. It must then be admitted that Carnot's original demonstration utterly fails, but we cannot infer that the proposition concluded is false. The truth of the conclusion appeared to me, indeed, so probable, that I took it in connexion with Joule's principle, on account of which Carnot's demonstration of it fails, as the foundation of an investigation of the motive power of heat in air-engines or steam-engines through finite ranges of temperature, and obtained about a year ago results, of which the substance is given in the second part of the paper at present communicated to the Royal Society. It was not until the commencement of the present year that I found the demonstration given above, by which the truth of the proposition is established upon an axiom (§ 12) which I think will be generally admitted. It is with no wish to claim priority that I make these statements, as the merit of first establishing the proposition upon correct principles is entirely due to Clausius, who published his demonstration of it in the month of May last year, in the second part of his paper on the motive power of heat[†]. I may be allowed to add, that I have given the demonstration exactly as it occurred to me before I know that Clausius had either enunciated or demonstrated the proposition. The following is the axiom on which Clausius' demonstration is founded :—

It is impossible for a self-acting machine, unaided by any external agency, to convey heat from one body to another at a higher temperature.

It is easily shown, that, although this and the axiom I have used are different in form, either is a consequence of the other. The reasoning in each demonstration is strictly analogous to that which Carnot orginally gave.

15. A complete theory of the motive power of heat would consist of the application of the two propositions demonstrated above, to every possible method of producing mechanical effect from thermal agency[‡]. As yet this has not been done for the

---

[*] Account of Carnot's *Theory*, § 6.

[†] Poggendorff's *Annalen*, referred to above.

[‡] "There are at present known two, and only two, distinct ways in which

electrical method, as far as regards the criterion of a perfect engine implied in the second proposition, and probably cannot be done without certain limitations; but the application of the first proposition has been very thoroughly investigated, and verified experimentally by Mr Joule in his researches "On the Calorific Effects of Magneto-Electricity;" and on it is founded one of his ways of determining experimentally the mechanical equivalent of heat. Thus, from his discovery of the laws of generation of heat in the galvanic circuit*, it follows that when mechanical work by means of a magneto-electric machine is the source of the galvanism, the heat generated in any given portion of the fixed part of the circuit is proportional to the whole work spent; and from his experimental demonstration that heat is developed in any moving part of the circuit at exactly the same rate as if it were at rest, and traversed by a current of the same strength, he is enabled to conclude—

(1)   That heat may be created by working a magneto-electric machine.

(2)   That if the current excited be not allowed to produce any other than thermal effects, the total quantity of heat produced is in all circumstances exactly proportional to the quantity of work spent.

16.   Again, the admirable discovery of Peltier, that cold is produced by an electrical current passing from bismuth to antimony, is referred to by Joule†, as showing how it may be proved

mechanical effect can be obtained from heat.   One of these is by the alterations of volume which bodies experience through the action of heat ; the other is through the medium of electric agency."—"Account of Carnot's Theory," § 4.   (*Transactions*, Vol. xvi. part 5.)

* That, in a given fixed part of the circuit, the heat evolved in a given time is proportional to the square of the strength of the current, and for different fixed parts, with the same strength of current, the quantities of heat evolved in equal times are as the resistances.   A paper by Mr Joule, containing demonstrations of these laws, and of others on the relations of the chemical and thermal agencies concerned, was communicated to the Royal Society on the 17th of December, 1840, but was not published in the *Transactions*.   (See abstract containing a statement of the laws quoted above, in the *Philosophical Magazine*, Vol. xviii. p. 308.)   It was published in the *Philosophical Magazine* in October, 1841 (Vol. xix. p. 260).

† [Note of March 20, 1852, added in *Phil. Mag.* reprint.   In the introduction to his paper on the "Calorific Effects of Magneto-Electricity," &c., *Phil. Mag.*, 1843.

I take this opportunity of mentioning that I have only recently become ac-

that, when an electrical current is continuously produced from a purely thermal source, the quantities of heat evolved electrically in the different homogeneous parts of the circuit are only compensations for a loss from the junctions of the different metals, or that, when the effect of the current is entirely thermal, there must be just as much heat emitted from the parts not affected by the source as is taken from the source.

17.   Lastly*, when a current produced by thermal agency is made to work an engine and produce mechanical effect, there will be less heat emitted from the parts of the circuit not affected by the source than is taken in from the source, by an amount precisely equivalent to the mechanical effect produced; since Joule demonstrates experimentally, that a current from any kind of

quainted with Helmholtz's admirable treatise on the principle of mechanical effect (*Ueber die Erhaltung der Kraft*, von Dr H. Helmholtz. Berlin. G. Reimer, 1847), having seen it for the first time on the 20th of January of this year; and that I should have had occasion to refer to it on this, and on numerous other points of the dynamical theory of heat, the mechanical theory of electrolysis, the theory of electro-magnetic induction, and the mechanical theory of thermo-electric currents, in various papers communicated to the Royal Society of Edinburgh, and to this Magazine, had I been acquainted with it in time.—W. T., March 20, 1852.]

* This reasoning was suggested to me by the following passage contained in a letter which I received from Mr Joule on the 8th of July, 1847. "In Peltier's experiment on cold produced at the bismuth and antimony solder, we have an instance of the conversion of heat into the mechanical force of the current," which must have been meant as an answer to a remark I had made, that no evidence could be adduced to show that heat is ever put out of existence. I now fully admit the force of that answer; but it would require a proof that there is more heat put out of existence at the heated soldering [or in this and other parts of the circuit] than is created at the cold soldering [and the remainder of the circuit, when a machine is driven by the current] to make the "evidence" be *experimental*. That this is the case I think is certain, because the statements of § 16 in the text are demonstrated consequences of the first fundamental proposition; but it is still to be remarked, that neither in this nor in any other case of the production of mechanical effect from purely thermal agency, has the ceasing to exist of an equivalent quantity of heat been demonstrated otherwise than theoretically. It would be a very great step in the experimental illustration (or *verification*, for those who consider such to be necessary) of the dynamical theory of heat, to actually show in any one case a loss of heat; and it might be done by operating through a very considerable range of temperatures with a good air-engine or steam-engine, not allowed to waste its work in friction. As will be seen in Part. II. of this paper, no experiment of any kind could show a considerable loss of heat without employing bodies differing considerably in temperature; for instance, a loss of as much as ·098, or about one-tenth of the whole heat used, if the temperature of all the bodies used be between 0° and 30° Cent.

source driving an engine, produces in the engine just as much less heat than it would produce in a fixed wire exercising the same resistance as is equivalent to the mechanical effect produced by the engine.

18. The quality of thermal effects, resulting from equal causes through very different means, is beautifully illustrated by the following statement, drawn from Mr Joule's paper on magneto-electricity*.

Let there be three equal and similar galvanic batteries furnished with equal and similar electrodes; let A_1 and B_1 be the terminations of the electrodes (or wires connected with the two poles) of the first battery, A_2 and B_2 the terminations of the corresponding electrodes of the second, and A_3 and B_3 of the third battery. Let A_1 and B_1 be connected with the extremities of a long fixed wire; let A_2 and B_2 be connected with the "poles" of an electrolytic apparatus for the decomposition of water; and let A_3 and B_3 be connected with the *poles* (or *ports* as they might be called) of an electro-magnetic engine. Then if the length of the wire between A_1 and B_1, and the speed of the engine between A_3 and B_3, be so adjusted that the strength of the current (which for simplicity we may suppose to be continuous and perfectly uniform in each case) may be the same in the three circuits, there will be more heat given out in any time in the wire between A_1 and B_1 than in the electrolytic apparatus between A_2 and B_2, or the working engine between A_3 and B_3. But if the hydrogen were allowed to burn in the oxygen, within the electrolytic vessel, and the engine to waste all its work without producing any other than thermal effects (as it would do, for instance, if all its work were spent in continuously agitating a limited fluid mass), the total heat emitted would be precisely the same in each of these two pieces of apparatus as in the wire between A_1 and B_1. It is worthy of remark that these propositions are *rigorously* true, being demonstrable consequences of the fundamental principle of the dynamical theory of heat, which have been discovered by Joule,

---

* In this paper reference is made to his previous paper "On the Heat of Electrolysis" (published in Vol. vii. part 2, of the second series of the Literary and Philosophical Society of Manchester) for experimental demonstration of those parts of the theory in which chemical action is concerned.

and illustrated and verified most copiously in his experimental researches*.

19.   Both the fundamental propositions may be applied in a perfectly rigorous manner to the second of the known methods of producing mechanical effect from thermal agency. This application of the first of the two fundamental propositions has already been published by Rankine and Clausius; and that of the second, as Clausius showed in his published paper, is simply Carnot's unmodified investigation of the relation between the mechanical effect produced and the thermal circumstance from which it originates, in the case of an expansive engine working within an infinitely small range of temperatures. The simplest investigation of the consequences of the first proposition on this application, which has occurred to me, is the following, being merely the modification of an analytical expression of Carnot's axiom regarding the permanence of heat, which was given in my former paper†, required to make it express, not Carnot's axiom, but Joule's.

20.   Let us suppose a mass‡ of any substance, occupying a volume v, under a pressure p uniform in all directions, and at a temperature t, to expand in volume to $v + dv$, and to rise in tem-

---

[* Note of March 20, 1852, added in *Phil. Mag.* reprint. I have recently met with the following passage in Liebig's *Animal Chemistry* (3rd edit. London, 1846, p. 43), in which the dynamical theory of the heat both of combustion and of the galvanic battery is indicated, if not fully expressed:—"When we kindle a fire under a steam-engine, and employ the power obtained to produce heat by friction, it is impossible that the heat thus obtained can ever be greater than that which was required to heat the boiler; and if we use the galvanic current to produce heat, the amount of heat obtained is never in any circumstances greater than we might have by the combustion of the zinc which has been dissolved in the acid."

A paper "On the Heat of Chemical Combination," by Dr Thomas Woods, published last October in the *Philosophical Magazine*, contains an independent and direct experimental demonstration of the proposition stated in the text regarding the comparative thermal effects in a fixed metallic wire, and an electrolytic vessel for the decomposition of water, produced by a galvanic current.—W. T., March 20, 1852.]

† "Account of Carnot's Theory," foot-note on § 26.

‡ This may have parts consisting of different substances, or of the same substance in different states, provided the temperature of all be the same. See below Part III., § 53—56.

perature to $t + dt$. The quantity of work which it will produce will be

$$pdv;$$

and the quantity of heat which must be added to it to make its temperature rise during the expansion to $t + dt$ may be denoted by

$$Mdv + Ndt.$$

The mechanical equivalent of this is

$$J(Mdv + Ndt),$$

if J denote the mechanical equivalent of a unit of heat. hence the mechanical measure of the total external effect produced in the circumstances is

$$(p - JM)\, dv - JNdt.$$

The total external effect, after any finite amount of expansion, accompanied by any continuous change of temperature, has taken place, will consequently be, in mechanical terms,

$$\int \{(p - JM)\, dv - JNdt\};$$

where we must suppose t to vary with v, so as to be the actual temperature of the medium at each instant, and the integration with reference to v must be performed between limits corresponding to the initial and final volumes. Now if, at any subsequent time, the volume and temperature of the medium become what they were at the beginning, however arbitrarily they may have been made to vary in the period, the total external effect must, according to Prop. I., amount to nothing; and hence

$$(p - JM)\, dv - JNdt*$$

must be the differential of a function of two independent variables, or we must have

$$\frac{d(p - JM)}{dt} = \frac{d(-JN)}{dv} \quad \cdots\cdots\cdots\cdots (1),$$

this being merely the analytical expression of the condition, that the preceding integral may vanish in every case in which the

[* The integral function $\int \{(JM - p)\, dv + JNdt\}$ may obviously be called the *mechanical energy* of the fluid mass; as (when the constant of integration is properly assigned) it expresses the whole work the fluid has in it to produce. The consideration of this function is the subject of a short paper communicated to the Royal Society of Edinburgh, Dec. 15, 1851, as an appendix to the paper at present republished; (see below Part v. §§ 81—96).]

initial and final values of v and t are the same, respectively. Observing that J is an absolute constant, we may put the result into the form

$$\frac{dp}{dt} = J\left(\frac{dM}{dt} - \frac{dN}{dv}\right) \dots \dots \dots (2).$$

This equation expresses, in a perfectly comprehensive manner, the application of the first fundamental proposition to the thermal and mechanical circumstances of any substance whatever, under uniform pressure in all directions, when subjected to any possible variations of temperature, volume and pressure.

21. The corresponding application of the second fundamental proposition is completely expressed by the equation

$$\frac{dp}{dt} = \mu M \dots \dots \dots \dots (3),$$

where μ denotes what is called "Carnot's function," a quantity which has an absolute value, the same for all substances for any given temperature, but which may vary with the temperature in a manner that can only be determined by experiment. To prove this proposition, it may be remarked in the first place that Prop. II. could not be true for every case in which the temperature of the refrigerator differs infinitely little from that of the source, without being true universally. Now, if a substance be allowed first to expand from v to $v + dv$, its temperature being kept constantly t; if, secondly, it be allowed to expand further, without either emitting or absorbing heat till its temperature goes down through an infinitely small range, to $t - \tau$; if, thirdly, it be compressed at the constant temperature $t - \tau$, so much (actually by an amount differing from dv by only an infinitely small quantity of the second order), that when, fourthly, the volume is further diminished to v without the medium's being allowed to either emit or absorb heat, its temperature may be exactly t; it may be considered as constituting a thermo-dynamic engine which fulfils Carnot's condition of complete reversibility. Hence, by Prop. II., it must produce the same amount of work for the same quantity of heat absorbed in the first operation, as any other substance similarly operated upon through the same range of temperatures. But $\frac{dp}{dt}\, \tau \,.\, dv$ is obviously the whole work done in the complete cycle, and (by the definition of M in § 20) Mdv is the quantity of heat absorbed in the first operation. Hence the value of

$$\frac{\frac{dp}{dt}\tau . dv}{Mdv}, \quad \text{or} \quad \frac{\frac{dp}{dt}}{M}\tau,$$

must be the same for all substances, with the same values of t and τ; or, since τ is not involved except as a factor, we must have

$$\frac{\frac{dp}{dt}}{M} = \mu \dots\dots\dots\dots\dots\dots(4),$$

where μ depends only on t; from which we conclude the proposition which was to be proved.

[Note of Nov. 9, 1881. Elimination of $\dfrac{dp}{dt}$ by (2) from (4) gives

$$\frac{J\left(\frac{dM}{dt} - \frac{dN}{dv}\right)}{M} = \mu \dots\dots\dots\dots\dots(4'),$$

a very convenient and important formula.]

22.   The very remarkable theorem that $\dfrac{\frac{dp}{dt}}{M}$ must be the same for all substances at the same temperature, was first given (although not in precisely the same terms) by Carnot, and demonstrated by him, according to the principles he adopted. We have now seen that its truth may be satisfactorily established without adopting the false part of his principles. Hence all Carnot's conclusions, and all conclusions derived by others from his theory, which depend merely on equation (3), require no modification when the dynamical theory is adopted. Thus, all the conclusions contained in Sections I., II., and III., of the Appendix to my "Account of Carnot's Theory" [Art. XLI. §§ 43—53 above], and in the paper immediately following it in the *Transactions* [and in the present reprint], entitled "Theoretical Considerations on the Effect of Pressure in Lowering the Freezing Point of Water," by my elder brother, still hold. Also, we see that Carnot's expression for the mechanical effect derivable from a given quantity of heat by means of a perfect engine in which the range of temperatures is infinitely small, expresses truly the greatest effect

which can possibly be obtained in the circumstances; although
it is in reality only an infinitely small fraction of the whole
mechanical equivalent of the heat supplied; the remainder being
irrecoverably lost to man, and therefore "wasted," although not
annihilated.

23.   On the other hand, the expression for the mechanical
effect obtainable from a given quantity of heat entering an engine
from a "source" at a given temperature, when the range down
to the temperature of the cold part of the engine or the "refrigerator" is finite, will differ most materially from that of Carnot ;
since, a finite quantity of mechanical effect being now obtained
from a finite quantity of heat entering the engine, a finite fraction
of this quantity must be converted from heat into mechanical
effect.   The investigation of this expression, with numerical determinations founded on the numbers deduced from Regnault's
observations on steam, which are shown in Tables I. and II of my
former paper, constitutes the second part of the paper at present
communicated.

PART II.

*On the Motive Power of Heat through Finite Ranges of
Temperature.*

24.   It is required to determine the quantity of work which a
perfect engine, supplied from a source at any temperature, *S*, and
parting with its waste heat to a refrigerator at any lower temperature, *T*, will produce from a given quantity, *H*, of heat drawn
from the source.

25.   We may suppose the engine to consist of an infinite
number of perfect engines, each working within an infinitely small
range of temperature, and arranged in a series of which the source
of the first is the given source, the refrigerator of the last the
given refrigerator, and the refrigerator of each intermediate engine
is the source of that which follows it in the series.   Each of these
engines will, in any time, emit just as much less heat to its
refrigerator than is supplied to it from its source, as is the equivalent of the mechanical work which it produces.   Hence if t and
$t + dt$ denote respectively the temperatures of the refrigerator and

source of one of the intermediate engines, and if q denote the quantity of heat which this engine discha: ges into its refrigerator in any time, and $q + dq$ the quantity which it draws from its source in the same time, the quantity of work which it produces in that time will be Jdq according to Prop. I., and it will also be $q\mu dt$ according to the expression of Prop. II., investigated in § 21; and therefore we must have

$$Jdq := q\mu dt.$$

Hence, supposing that the quantity of heat supplied from the first source, in the time considered is H, we find by integration

$$\log \frac{H}{q} = \frac{1}{J} \int_t^S \mu dt.$$

But the value of q, when $t = T$, is the final remainder discharged into the refrigerator at the temperature T; and therefore, if this be denoted by R, we have

$$\log \frac{H}{R} = \frac{1}{J} \int_T^S \mu dt \dots\dots\dots\dots\dots(5);$$

from which we deduce

$$R = H \epsilon^{-\frac{1}{J} \int_T^S \mu dt} \dots\dots\dots\dots\dots(6).$$

Now the whole amount of work produced will be the mechanical equivalent of the quantity of heat lost; and, therefore, if this be denoted by W, we have

$$W = J(H - R) \dots\dots\dots\dots\dots(7),$$

and consequently, by (6),

$$W = JH \{1 - \epsilon^{-\frac{1}{J} \int_T^S \mu dt}\} \dots\dots\dots\dots\dots(8).$$

26. To compare this with the expression $H \int_T^S \mu dt$, for the duty indicated by Carnot's theory*, we may expand the exponential in the preceding equation, by the usual series. We thus

find

$$\left. \begin{array}{c} W = \left(1 - \dfrac{\theta}{1 \cdot 2} + \dfrac{\theta^2}{1 \cdot 2 \cdot 3} - \&c.\right) . H \int_T^S \mu dt \\[2mm] \theta = \dfrac{1}{J} \int_T^S \mu dt \end{array} \right\} \dots\dots(9),$$

where

---

* "Account," &c., Equation 7, § 31. [Art. XLI. above.]

This shows that the work really produced, which always falls short of the duty indicated by Carnot's theory, approaches more and more nearly to it as the range is diminished; and ultimately, when the range is infinitely small, is the same as if Carnot's theory required no modification, which agrees with the conclusion stated above in § 22.

27. Again, equation (8) shows that the real duty of a given quantity of heat supplied from the source increases with every increase of the range; but that instead of increasing indefinitely in proportion to $\int_{T}^{S} \mu dt$, as Carnot's theory makes it do, it never reaches the value JH, but approximates to this limit, as $\int_{T}^{S} \mu dt$ is increased without limit. Hence Carnot's remark* regarding the practical advantage that may be anticipated from the use of the air-engine, or from any method by which the range of temperatures may be increased, loses only a part of its importance, while a much more satisfactory view than his of the practical problem is afforded. Thus we see that, although the full equivalent of mechanical effect cannot be obtained even by means of a perfect engine, yet when the actual source of heat is at a high enough temperature above the surrounding objects, we may get more and more nearly the whole of the admitted heat converted into mechanical effect, by simply increasing the effective range of temperature in the engine.

28. The preceding investigation (§ 25) shows that the value of Carnot's function, μ, for all temperatures within the range of the engine, and the absolute value of Joule's equivalent, J, are enough of data to calculate the amount of mechanical effect of a perfect engine of any kind, whether a steam-engine, an air-engine, or even a thermo-electric engine; since, according to the axiom stated in § 12, and the demonstration of Prop. II., no inanimate material agency could produce more mechanical effect from a given quantity of heat, with a given available range of temperatures, than an engine satisfying the criterion stated in the enunciation of the proposition.

* "Account," &c. Appendix, Section IV. [Art. XLI. above.]

29. The mechanical equivalent of a thermal unit Fahrenheit, or the quantity of heat necessary to raise the temperature of a pound of water from 32° to 33° Fahr., has been determined by Joule in foot-pounds at Manchester, and the value which he gives as his best determination is 772·69. Mr Rankine takes, as the result of Joule's determination 772, which he estimates must be within $\frac{1}{300}$ of its own amount, of the truth. If we take $772\frac{2}{5}$ as the number, we find, by multiplying it by $\frac{9}{5}$, 1390 as the equivalent of the thermal unit Centigrade, which is taken as the value of J in the numerical applications contained in the present paper. [Note of Jan. 12, 1882. Joule's recent redetermination gives 771·8 Manchester foot-pounds as the work required to warm 1 lb. of water from 32° to 33° Fahr.]

[*Ed. note:* material omitted]

PART V.

On the Quantities of Mechanical Energy contained in a Fluid in Different States, as to Temperature and Density †.

81. A body which is either emitting heat, or altering its dimensions against resisting forces, is doing work upon matter external to it The mechanical effect of this work in one case is the excitation of thermal motions, and in the other the overcoming of resistances. The body must itself be altering in its circumstances, so as to contain a less store of work within it by an amount precisely equal to the aggregate value of the mechanical effects produced ; and conversely, the aggregate value of the mechanical effects produced must depend solely on the initial and final states of the body, and is therefore the same whatever be the intermediate states through which the body passes, provided the *initial* and *final* states be the same.

82. The total mechanical energy of a body might be defined as the mechanical value of all the effect it would produce in heat emitted and in resistances overcome, if it were cooled to the

† From the *Transactions of the Royal Society of Edinburgh*, Vol. xx. Part 3; read December 15, 1851.

utmost, and allowed to contract indefinitely or to expand inde-finitely according as the forces between its particles are attractive or repulsive, when the thermal motions within it are all stopped ; but in our present state of ignorance regarding perfect cold, and the nature of molecular forces, we cannot determine this "total mechanical energy" for any portion of matter, nor even can we be sure that it is not infinitely great for a finite portion of matter.   Hence it is convenient to choose a certain state as standard for the body under consideration, and to use the un-qualified term, *mechanical energy*, with reference to this standard state ; so that the "mechanical energy of a body in a given state" will denote the mechanical value of the effects the body would produce in passing from the state in which it is given, to the standard state, or the mechanical value of the whole agency that would be required to bring the body from the standard state to the state in which it is given.

[*Ed. note:* material omitted]

4

Reprinted from *Mathematical and Physical Papers of William Thomson*, Vol. 1, Cambridge University Press, London, 1882, pp. 100–106, 234–236

Art. XXXIX. On an Absolute Thermometric Scale founded on Carnot's Theory of the Motive Power of Heat*, and calculated from Regnault's observations†.

William Thomson (Lord Kelvin)

[*Cambridge Philosophical Society Proceedings for June 5, 1848; and Phil. Mag., Oct. 1848.*]

THE determination of temperature has long been recognized as a problem of the greatest importance in physical science. It has accordingly been made a subject of most careful attention, and, especially in late years, of very elaborate and refined experimental researches‡; and we are thus at present in possession of as complete a practical solution of the problem as can be desired, even for the most accurate investigations. The theory of thermometry is however as yet far from being in so satisfactory a state. The principle to be followed in constructing a thermometric scale might at first sight seem to be obvious, as it might appear that a perfect thermometer would indicate equal additions of heat, as corresponding to equal elevations of temperature, estimated by the numbered divisions of its scale. It is however now recognized (from the variations in the specific heats of bodies) as an experimentally demonstrated fact that thermometry under this condition is impossible,

---

* Published in 1824 in a work entitled *Réflexions sur la Puissance Motrice du Feu*, by M. S. Carnot. Having never met with the original work, it is only through a paper by M. Clapeyron, on the same subject, published in the *Journal de l'École Polytechnique*, Vol. XIV. 1834, and translated in the first volume of Taylor's *Scientific Memoirs*, that the Author has become acquainted with Carnot's Theory.—W. T. [Note of Nov. 5th, 1881. A few months later through the kindness of my late colleague Prof. Lewis Gordon, I received a copy of Carnot's original work and was thus enabled to give to the Royal Society of Edinburgh my "Account of Carnot's theory" which is reprinted as Art. XLI. below. The original work has since been republished, with a biographical notice, Paris, 1878.]

† An account of the first part of a series of researches undertaken by M. Regnault by order of the French Government, for ascertaining the various physical data of importance in the Theory of the Steam Engine, is just published in the *Mémoires de l'Institut*, of which it constitutes the twenty-first volume (1847). The second part of the researches has not yet been published. [Note of Nov. 5, 1881. The continuation of these researches has now been published: thus we have for the whole series, Vol. I. in 1847; Vol. II. in 1862; and Vol. III. in 1870.]

‡ A very important section of Regnault's work is devoted to this object.

and we are left without any principle on which to found **an** absolute thermometric scale.

Next in importance to the primary establishment of an absolute scale, independently of the properties of any particular kind of matter, is the fixing upon an arbitrary system of thermometry, according to which results of observations made by different experimenters, in various positions and circumstances, may be exactly compared. This object is very fully attained by means of thermometers constructed and graduated according to the clearly defined methods adopted by the best instrument-makers of the present day, when the rigorous experimental processes which have been indicated, especially by Regnault, for interpreting their indications in a comparable way, are followed. The particular kind of thermometer which is least liable to uncertain variations of any kind is that founded on the expansion of air, and this is therefore generally adopted as the standard for the comparison of thermometers of all constructions. Hence the scale which is at present employed for estimating temperature is that of the air-thermometer; and in accurate researches care is always taken to reduce to this scale the indications of the instrument actually used, whatever may be its specific construction and graduation.

The principle according to which the scale of the air-thermometer is graduated, is simply that equal absolute expansions of the mass of air or gas in the instrument, under a constant pressure, shall indicate equal differences of the numbers on the scale ; the length of a "degree" being determined by allowing a given number for the interval between the freezing- and the boiling-points. Now it is found by Regnault that various thermometers, constructed with air under different pressures, or with different gases, give indications which coincide so closely, that, unless when certain gases, such as sulphurous acid, which approach the physical condition of vapours at saturation, are made use of, the variations are inappreciable*. This remarkable circumstance enhances very much the practical value of the air-thermometer; but still a

---

* Regnault, *Relation des Expériences*, &c., Fourth Memoir, First Part. The differences, it is remarked by Regnault, would be much more sensible if the graduation were effected on the supposition that the coefficients of expansion of the different gases are equal, instead of being founded on the principle laid down in the text, according to which the freezing- and boiling-points are experimentally determined for each thermometer.

rigorous standard can only be defined by fixing upon a certain gas at a determinate pressure, as the thermometric substance. Although we have thus a strict principle for constructing a *definite* system for the estimation of temperature, yet as reference is essentially made to a specific body as the standard thermometric substance, we cannot consider that we have arrived at an *absolute* scale, and we can only regard, in strictness, the scale actually adopted as *an arbitrary series of numbered points of reference sufficiently close for the requirements of practical thermometry.*

In the present state of physical science, therefore, a question of extreme interest arises: *Is there any principle on which an absolute thermometric scale can be founded?* It appears to me that Carnot's theory of the motive power of heat enables us to give an affirmative answer.

The relation between motive power and heat, as established by Carnot, is such that *quantities of heat,* and *intervals of temperature,* are involved as the sole elements in the expression for the amount of mechanical effect to be obtained through the agency of heat; and since we have, independently, a definite system for the measurement of quantities of heat, we are thus furnished with a measure for intervals according to which absolute differences of temperature may be estimated. To make this intelligible, a few words in explanation of Carnot's theory must be given; but for a full account of this most valuable contribution to physical science, the reader is referred to either of the works mentioned above (the original treatise by Carnot, and Clapeyron's paper on the same subject.

In the present state of science no operation is known by which heat can be absorbed, without either elevating the temperature of matter, or becoming latent and producing some alteration in the physical condition of the body into which it is absorbed; and the conversion of heat (or *caloric*) into mechanical effect is probably impossible*, certainly undiscovered. In actual engines for ob-

---

* This opinion seems to be nearly universally held by those who have written on the subject. A contrary opinion however has been advocated by Mr Joule of Manchester; some very remarkable discoveries which he has made with reference to the *generation* of heat by the friction of fluids in motion, and some known experiments with magneto-electric machines, seeming to indicate an actual conversion of mechanical effect into caloric. No experiment however is adduced in which the converse operation is exhibited; but it must be confessed that as yet much is involved in mystery with reference to these fundamental questions of natural philosophy.

taining mechanical effect through the agency of heat, we must consequently look for the source of power, not in any absorption and conversion, but merely in a transmission of heat. Now Carnot, starting from universally acknowledged physical principles, demonstrates that it is by the *letting down* of heat from a hot body to a cold body, through the medium of an engine (a steam-engine, or an air-engine for instance), that mechanical effect is to be obtained; and conversely, he proves that the same amount of heat may, by the expenditure of an equal amount of labouring force, be *raised* from the cold to the hot body (the engine being in this case *worked backwards*); just as mechanical effect may be obtained by the descent of water let down by a water-wheel, and by spending labouring force in turning the wheel backwards, or in working a pump, water may be elevated to a higher level. The amount of mechanical effect to be obtained by the transmission of a given quantity of heat, through the medium of any kind of engine in which the economy is perfect, will depend, as Carnot demonstrates, not on the specific nature of the substance employed as the medium of transmission of heat in the engine, but solely on the interval between the temperature of the two bodies between which the heat is transferred.

Carnot examines in detail the ideal construction of an air-engine and of a steam-engine, in which, besides the condition of perfect economy being satisfied, the machine is so arranged, that at the close of a complete operation the substance (air in one case and water in the other) employed is restored to precisely the same physical condition as at the commencement. He thus shews on what elements, capable of experimental determination, either with reference to air, or with reference to a liquid and its vapour, the absolute amount of mechanical effect due to the transmission of a unit of heat from a hot body to a cold body, through any given interval of the thermometric scale, may be ascertained. In M. Clapeyron's paper various experimental data, confessedly very imperfect, are brought forward, and the amounts of mechanical effect due to a unit of heat descending a degree of the air-thermometer, in various parts of the scale, are calculated from them, according to Carnot's expressions. The results so obtained indicate very decidedly, that what we may with much propriety call *the value of a degree* (estimated by the mechanical effect to be obtained from the descent of a unit of heat through it) of the air-thermometer depends on the part of the scale in which it is taken, being less for high than for low temperatures[*].

The characteristic property of the scale which I now propose is, that all degrees have the same value; that is, that a unit of heat descending from a body A at the temperature T° of this scale, to a body B at the temperature $(T-1)^\circ$, would give out the same mechanical effect, whatever be the number T. This may justly be termed an absolute scale, since its characteristic is quite independent of the physical properties of any specific substance.

To compare this scale with that of the air-thermometer, the *values* (according to the principle of estimation stated above) of degrees of the air-thermometer must be known. Now an expression, obtained by Carnot from the consideration of his ideal steam-engine, enables us to calculate these values, when the latent heat of a given volume and the pressure of saturated vapour at any temperature are experimentally determined. The determination of these elements is the principal object of Regnault's great work, already referred to, but at present his researches are not complete. In the first part, which alone has been as yet published, the latent heats of a given *weight*, and the pressures of saturated vapour, at all temperatures between 0° and 230° (Cent. of the air-thermometer), have been ascertained; but it would be necessary in addition to know the densities of saturated vapour at different temperatures, to enable us to determine the latent heat of a given volume at any temperature. M. Regnault announces his intention of instituting researches for this object; but till the results are made known, we have no way of completing the data necessary for the present problem, except by estimating the density of saturated vapour at any temperature (the corresponding pressure being known by Regnault's researches already published) according to the approximate laws of compressibility and expansion (the laws

---

[*] This is what we might anticipate, when we reflect that infinite cold must correspond to a finite number of degrees of the air-thermometer below zero; since, if we push the strict principle of graduation, stated above, sufficiently far, we should arrive at a point corresponding to the volume of air being reduced to nothing, which would be marked as -273° of the scale ($-100/\cdot366$, if $\cdot366$ be the coefficient of expansion); and therefore -273° of the air-thermometer is a point which cannot be reached at any finite temperature, however low.

of Mariotte and Gay-Lussac, or Boyle and Dalton). Within the limits of natural temperature in ordinary climates, the density of saturated vapour is actually found by Regnault (*Études Hygrométriques* in the *Annales de Chimie*) to verify very closely these laws; and we have reason to believe from experiments which have been made by Gay-Lussac and others, that as high as the temperature 100° there can be no considerable deviation; but our estimate of the density of saturated vapour, founded on these laws, may be very erroneous at such high temperatures as 230°. Hence a completely satisfactory calculation of the proposed scale cannot be made till after the additional experimental data shall have been obtained; but with the data which we actually possess, we may make an approximate comparison of the new scale with that of the air-thermometer, which at least between 0° and 100° will be tolerably satisfactory.

The labour of performing the necessary calculations for effecting a comparison of the proposed scale with that of the air-thermometer, between the limits 0° and 230° of the latter, has been kindly undertaken by Mr William Steele, lately of Glasgow College, now of St Peter's College, Cambridge. His results in tabulated forms were laid before the Society, with a diagram, in which the comparison between the two scales is represented graphically. In the first table*, the amounts of mechanical effect due to the descent of a unit of heat through the successive degrees of the air-thermometer are exhibited. The unit of heat adopted is the quantity necessary to elevate the temperature of a kilogramme of water from 0° to 1° of the air-thermometer; and the unit of mechanical effect is a metre-kilogramme; that is, a kilogramme raised a metre high.

In the second table, the temperatures according to the proposed scale, which correspond to the different degrees of the air-thermometer from 0° to 230°, are exhibited. [The arbitrary points which coincide on the two scales are 0° and 100°].

Note.—If we add together the first hundred numbers given in the first table, we find 135·7 for the amount of work due to a unit of heat descending from a body A at 100° to B at 0°. Now 79 such units of heat would, according to Dr Black (his result being

---

* [Note of Nov. 4, 1881. This table (reduced from metres to feet) was repeated in my "Account of Carnot's Theory of the Motive power of Heat," republished as Article XLI. below, in § 38 of which it will be found.]

very slightly corrected by Regnault), melt a kilogramme of ice. Hence if the heat necessary to melt a pound of ice be now taken as unity, and if a *metre-pound* be taken as the unit of mechanical effect, the amount of work to be obtained by the descent of a unit of heat from 100° to 0° is $79 \times 135\cdot7$, or 10,700 nearly. This is the same as 35,100 foot pounds, which is a little more than the work of a one-horse-power engine (33,000 foot pounds) in a minute; and consequently, if we had a steam-engine working with perfect economy at one-horse-power, the boiler being at the temperature 100°, and the condenser kept at 0° by a constant supply of ice, rather less than a pound of ice would be melted in a minute.

[Note of Nov. 4, 1881. This paper was wholly founded on Carnot's uncorrected theory, according to which the quantity of heat taken in in the hot part of the engine, (the boiler of the steam engine for instance), was supposed to be equal to that abstracted from the cold part (the condenser of the steam engine), in a complete period of the regular action of the engine, when every varying temperature, in every part of the apparatus, has become strictly periodic. The reconciliation of Carnot's theory with what is now known to be the true nature of heat is fully discussed in Article XLVIII. below; and in §§ 24—41 of that article, are shewn in detail the consequently required corrections of the thermodynamic estimates of the present article. These corrections however do not in any way affect the absolute scale for thermometry which forms the subject of the present article. Its relation to the practically more convenient scale (agreeing with air thermometers nearly enough for most purposes, throughout the range from the lowest temperatures hitherto measured, to the highest that can exist so far as we know) which I gave subsequently, Dynamical Theory of Heat (Art. XLVIII. below), Part VI., §§ 99, 100; *Trans. R. S. E.*, May, 1854: and Article 'Heat,' §§ 35—38, 47—67, *Encyclopædia Britannica*, is shewn in the following formula:

$$\theta = 100\,\frac{\log t - \log 273}{\log 373 - \log 273},$$

where θ and t are the reckonings of one and the same temperature, according to my first and according to my second thermodynamic absolute scale.]

[*Ed. note:* Lord Kelvin realized that his original 1848 article on the absolute thermometric scale had certain shortcomings, so in his later paper "On the dynamical theory of heat...," which was published in parts over a number of years, he included (1851) another brief note on his scale, paying due regard to the two fundamental principles of thermodynamics as he felt them to be established at that time. This note describes the scale essentially as it is used today. The brief note is reproduced as follows.]

98. Before entering on the treatment of the special subject, it is convenient to recall the fundamental laws of the dynamical theory of heat, and it is necessary to explain the thermometric assumption by which temperature is now to be measured.

The conditions under which heat and mechanical work are mutually convertible by means of any material system, subjected either to a continuous uniform action, or to a cycle of operations at the end of which the physical conditions of all its parts are the same as at the beginning, are subject to the following laws:—

Law I.—The material system must give out exactly as much energy as it takes in, either in heat or mechanical work.

Law II.—If every part of the action, and all its effects, be perfectly reversible, and if all the localities of the system by which heat is either emitted or taken in, be at one or other of two temperatures, the aggregate amount of heat taken in or emitted at the higher temperature, must exceed the amount emitted or taken in at the lower temperature, always in the same ratio when these temperatures are the same, whatever be the particular substance or arrangement of the material system, and whatever be the particular nature of the operations to which it is subject.

99. *Definition of temperature* and *general thermometric assumption.*—If two bodies be put in contact, and neither gives heat to the other, their temperatures are said to be the same; but if one gives heat to the other, its temperature is said to be higher.

The temperatures of two bodies are proportional to the quantities of heat respectively taken in and given out in localities at one temperature and at the other, respectively, by a material system subjected to a complete cycle of perfectly reversible thermo-dynamic operations, and not allowed to part with or take in heat at any other temperature: or, the absolute values of two temperatures are to one another in the proportion of the heat taken in to the heat rejected in a perfect thermo-dynamic engine working with a source and refrigerator at the higher and lower of the temperatures respectively.

100. *Convention for thermometric unit, and determination of absolute temperatures of fixed points in terms of it.*

Two fixed points of temperature being chosen according to Sir Isaac Newton's suggestion, by particular effects on a particular substance or substances, the difference of these temperatures is to be called unity, or any number of units or degrees as may be found convenient. The particular convention is, that the difference of temperatures between the freezing- and boiling-points of water under standard atmospheric pressure shall be called 100 degrees. The determination of the absolute temperatures of the fixed points is then to be effected by means of observations indicating the economy of a perfect thermo-dynamic engine, with the higher and the lower respectively as the temperatures of its source and refrigerator. The kind of observation best adapted for this object was originated by Mr Joule, whose work in 1844* laid the founda-

* "On the Changes of Temperature occasioned by the Rarefaction and Condensation of Air," see *Proceedings* of the Royal Society, June 1844; or, for the paper in full. *Phil. Mag.,* May 1845.

tion of the theory, and opened the experimental investigation; and it has been carried out by him, in conjunction with myself, within the last two years, in accordance with the plan proposed in Part IV.* of the present series. The best result, as regards this determination, which we have yet been able to obtain is, that the temperature of freezing water is 273·7 on the absolute scale; that of the boiling-point being consequently 373·7†. Further details regarding the new thermometric system will be found in a joint communication to be made by Mr Joule and myself to the Royal Society of London before the close of the present session.

[*Ed. note:* material omitted]

---

* "On a Method of discovering experimentally the Relation between the Heat Produced and the Work Spent in the Compression of a Gas." *Trans. R.S.E.*, April 1851; or *Phil. Mag.* 1852, second half-year.

† [Note of Dec. 1881. Later results show that these numbers are more accurately 273·1 and 373·1. Article on Heat by the author, *Encyc. Brit.*; also published separately under the title "Heat," Edinburgh, Black, 1880.]

5

Reprinted from *Phil. Mag.*, 5(4), 106–117 (1853)

On the General Law of the Transformation of Energy

William John Macquorn Rankine

(1.) IN this investigation the term *energy* is used to comprehend every affection of substances which constitutes or is commensurable with a power of producing change in opposition to resistance, and includes ordinary motion and mechanical power, chemical action, heat, light, electricity, magnetism, and all other powers, known or unknown, which are convertible or commensurable with these. All conceivable forms of energy may be distinguished into two kinds; actual or sensible, and potential or latent.

Actual energy is a measurable, transferable, and transformable affection of a substance, the presence of which causes the substance to tend to change its state in one or more respects; by the occurrence of which changes, actual energy disappears, and is replaced by

Potential energy, which is measured by the amount of a change in the condition of a substance, and that of the tendency or force whereby that change is produced (or, what is the same thing, of the resistance overcome in producing it), taken jointly.

If the change whereby potential energy has been developed be exactly reversed, then as the potential energy disappears, the actual energy which had previously disappeared is reproduced.

The law of the conservation of energy is already known, viz. that the sum of the actual and potential energies in the universe is unchangeable.

The object of the present investigation is to find the law of the *transformation of energy*, according to which all transformations of energy between the actual and potential states take place.

(2.) To reduce the problem to its simplest form, let us in the first place consider the mutual transformation of one form only of actual energy, and one form only of potential energy.

Let V denote one measurable state, condition, or mode of existence of the substance under consideration, whose magnitude increases when the kind of potential energy in question is developed.

Let U denote this potential energy.

Let P be the tendency or force whereby the state V tends to increase, which is opposed by an equal resistance.

Then when the state V undergoes a small increase dV, the potential energy developed or given out is

$$\left. \begin{aligned} d\mathrm{U} &= \mathrm{P}d\mathrm{V} = \frac{d\mathrm{U}}{d\mathrm{V}} \cdot d\mathrm{V}, \\ \mathrm{P} &= \frac{d\mathrm{U}}{d\mathrm{V}}. \end{aligned} \right\} \quad \ldots \ldots (\mathrm{A})$$

so that

* Communicated by the Author, having been read to the Philosophical Society of Glasgow, January 5, 1853.

Let Q denote the quantity, present in the substance, of the kind of actual energy under consideration. It is required to find how much of the potential energy of the kind U, developed by a small increase of the state V, is produced by transformation of actual energy of the kind Q, whose total quantity (to avoid complication of the problem) is supposed to be maintained constant by the communication of actual energy from external substances.

The quantity of potential energy of the form U which is produced by transformation from the actual form Q, is the effect of the presence of the total energy Q in the substance during the change dV.

To find this effect, let the total energy Q be conceived to be divided into an indefinite number of indefinitely small parts dQ, and let the effect of one be computed separately. To do this, let any one of the parts dQ be abstracted from the total energy Q; and let the effect of this be to diminish the development of power dU by the quantity d^2U. Then

$$\frac{d^2U}{dQdV} \cdot dVdQ$$

is the effect, in development of potential energy, of the presence in the substance of the small portion dQ of actual energy; and as all the small portions of actual energy are similarly circumstanced, the potential energy which is developed by the change dV, in consequence of the presence of the whole actual energy Q, bears the same ratio to the whole energy Q which the above quantity bears to the portion dQ; that is to say, the conversion of energy from the actual form Q, to the potential form U during the change dV, is represented by

$$Q \cdot \frac{d^2U}{dQdV} \cdot dV \quad . \quad . \quad . \quad . \quad . \quad . \quad (1)$$

(3.) Next let us suppose, that not only the state V varies, but the total quantity of energy Q also; and let us investigate what quantity of actual energy of the form Q must be communicated to the substance to produce simultaneously the variations dQ and dV.

First, there is the energy which remains in the actual form, directly producing the increase dQ in the total quantity Q.

Secondly, there is the energy (not yet determined) which may be transformed from the actual to some invisible potential form in consequence of the change dQ only. Let this be denoted by LdQ. The nature of this quantity may be best conceived by considering that the energy Q is itself a *state* of the substance, to effect a change in which a resistance L may have to be overcome.

Thirdly, there is the energy already determined and expressed in the formula (1), which is transformed from the actual to the potential form in consequence of the change of state dV.

The sum of those three quantities is as follows :

$$d \cdot Q = (1 + L)dQ + Q \cdot \frac{d^2 U}{dQ dV} \cdot dV. \quad \cdot \quad \cdot \quad (2)$$

If from this expression be subtracted the potential energy developed, that is to say, given out in overcoming resistance,

$$\frac{dU}{dV} \cdot dV,$$

the result will be the algebraical sum of the energies, actual and potential, acquired on the whole by the substance in passing from the total actual energy Q and state V to the total actual energy $Q + dQ$ and state $V + dV$; viz.

$$d\Psi = d \cdot Q - \frac{dU}{dV} \cdot dV = (1 + L)dQ + \left(Q\frac{d}{dQ} - 1 \right) \frac{dU}{dV} \cdot dV. \quad \cdot \quad (B)$$

Now this quantity must be the same, whether the change dQ or the change dV be made first, or both simultaneously; otherwise by varying the order of making those changes, the sum of energy in the universe, actual and potential, might be changed, which is impossible.   Therefore the above expression must be the complete differential of a function of the energy Q and state V ; that is to say,

$$\frac{dL}{dV} = \frac{d}{dQ}\left(Q\frac{d}{dQ} - 1 \right)\frac{dU}{dV} = Q\frac{d^2}{dQ^2} \cdot \frac{dU}{dV};$$

consequently

$$L = f' \cdot (Q) + Q \cdot \frac{d^2 U}{dQ^2},$$

$f'(Q)$ being a function of Q only, to be determined by experiment, of which $f(Q)$ is the primitive.

Thus we obtain, for the total energy, actual and potential, acquired by the substance, in consequence of the changes of total actual energy from Q to $Q + dQ$, and of state, from V to $V + dV$, the formula

$$\begin{aligned} d\Psi = d \cdot Q - d \cdot U &= \left(1 + f' \cdot (Q) + Q\frac{d^2 U}{dQ^2} \right)dQ + \left(Q\frac{d}{dQ} - 1 \right)\frac{dU}{dV} \cdot dV \\ &= d \cdot \left\{ Q + f(Q) + \left(Q\frac{d}{dQ} - 1 \right) \int \frac{dU}{dV} \cdot dV \right\}, \end{aligned} \quad (3)$$

in which the symbol $d.U$ is used to denote the total potential energy really developed; while $\int \frac{dU}{dV} \cdot dV$ is a *partial integral* computed for each value of Q, as if that value were constant.

This equation is the complete expression of the *law of the transformation of energy*, from any one actual form Q to any one potential form U, developed by increase of the state V.

By analysing it, we find that, besides the simple increase of actual energy dQ, which retains its form, the substance receives

$$\left(f'(Q) + Q\frac{d^2U}{dQ^2}\right)dQ \text{ of actual energy which disappears;}$$

$$Q\frac{d^2U}{dQdV}\cdot dV \text{ which is directly transformed into potential}$$
energy of the kind U;

and that it gives out the potential energy dU $=$ PdV.

(4.) The extension of these principles to any number of kinds of actual energy,

$$Q_\alpha, \quad Q_\beta, \quad Q_\gamma, \text{ \&c.} \ldots Q_\mu, \text{ \&c.,}$$

and any number of kinds of potential energy,

$$U_a = \int P_a dV_a; \; U_b = \int P_b dV_b; \; U_c = \int P_c dV_c, \text{\&c} \ldots U_m = \int P_m dV_m \text{\&c.,}$$

developed by changes in the states or conditions

$$V_a, \quad V_b, \quad V_c, \quad \text{\&c.} \ldots V_m, \text{ \&c.,}$$

leads to the following results:—

The quantity of any given kind of actual energy, Q_μ, which disappears, is

$$\left(f'(Q_\mu) + Q_\mu \Sigma \cdot \frac{d^2U}{dQ_\mu{}^2}\right)dQ_\mu,$$

the sum extending to all the forms of potential energy.

The quantity converted from any given actual form, Q_μ, to any given potential form U_m, is

$$Q_\mu \frac{d^2U_m}{dQ_\mu dV_m}\cdot dV_m.$$

Hence the algebraical sum of the energies acquired and given out by the substance is

$$d\Psi = \Sigma d.Q - \Sigma d.U = \Sigma.\left(1 + f'(Q) + Q.\Sigma \cdot \frac{d^2U}{dQ^2}\right)dQ + \Sigma$$
$$\left(\Sigma.Q\frac{d}{dQ} - 1\right)\frac{dU}{dV}dV = d.\left\{\Sigma Q + \Sigma f(Q) + \Sigma\Sigma.Q\frac{d}{dQ}\right.$$
$$\left.\int\frac{dU}{dV}\cdot dV - \Sigma.\int\frac{dU}{dV}dV\right\}. \quad \ldots \ldots \quad (4)$$

This equation is the complete expression of the *law of the mutual transformation of actual and potential energy of all possible kinds.*

The data requisite for its application to any physical problem are, the nature and value of the function $f(Q)$ for each kind of actual energy of $\dfrac{dU}{dV}$ for each kind of potential energy, and of $\dfrac{d^2U}{dQdV}$ and $\dfrac{d^2U}{dQ^2}$ for each combination by pairs of an actual with a potential energy.

(5.) Abstract and metaphysical as the principles and reasoning of this paper may appear, they are of immediate practical utility.

When applied to the mutual transformation of visible motion with the power arising from attractive and repulsive forces, the equation 3 becomes identical.

It is in the theory of those forms of energy which manifest themselves to us only by their effects, such as heat and electricity, that this law becomes useful.   It enables us, when power is produced by the consumption of one or more of those energies, to analyse the effect produced, to refer each portion to the kind of energy by which it is caused, and thus to determine how much of any given kind of energy must disappear in order to produce a given change in the condition of a substance.

An important consequence of the formula (1) is as follows :—

If the tendency, $\dfrac{dU}{dV}$, of the state V to increase is proportional simply to the actual energy present, Q, then

$$\frac{d^2U}{dQdV} = \frac{1}{Q} \cdot \frac{dU}{dV};$$

and consequently

$$Q \frac{d^2U}{dQdV} \cdot dV = dU ; \quad . \quad . \quad . \quad . \quad (5)$$

that is to say, *when the tendency to the production of potential energy is simply proportional to the actual energy present, then is the actual energy converted into potential energy the exact equivalent of the whole potential energy produced.*

(6.) Another important consequence of the formulæ (1) and (3) is as follows :—If a substance be made to undergo a change of condition, and be brought back to its primitive condition by a process not the exact reverse of the former process, then will there be a certain amount of permanent conversion of energy between the actual and potential forms.   That the permanent conversion from the actual to the potential form may be the greatest possible in proportion to the actual energy supplied from without, the changes of condition must be so regulated that none of the actual energy received or given out by the substance shall be employed in changing the total actual energy present in it, the whole being consumed or produced by transformation to or from the potential form.

To effect this, the following operations must be performed. The actual energy being maintained in the substance at the constant value Q_1, let it undergo a change of state from V_A to V_B. Then the actual energy supplied from without, which is all converted into potential energy, is

$$H_1 = Q_1 \cdot \frac{d}{dQ} \int_{V_A}^{V_B} \frac{dU}{dV} \, dV$$
$$= Q_1 (F_B - F_A),$$

where F denotes the function $\dfrac{d}{dQ} \int \dfrac{dU}{dV} \, dV$.

Let the actual energy now be reduced to a lower amount, Q_2, entirely by transformation to the potential form, without transfer of actual energy to other substances. That this may be the case, we must have, according to equation (2),

$$O = d \cdot Q = d\{Q + f(Q)\} + Q \, d \cdot F;$$

or if F_C be the value of F at the end of the operation,

$$F_B - F_C = \int_{Q_2}^{Q_2} \frac{d(Q + f(Q))}{Q}. \qquad \qquad \text{(C)}$$

Let F_D be a fourth value of F, such that
$$F_A - F_D = F_B - F_C; \text{ and consequently } F_C - F_D = F_B - F_A. \text{ (D)}$$
Then the substance having the actual energy Q_2 maintained constant, and its condition changed until F becomes F_D, the following quantity of energy must be retransformed from the potential to the actual state, and transferred to other substances:

$$H_2 = Q_2(F_C - F_D) = Q_2(F_B - F_A).$$

The substance being then brought back to its original condition, viz.

$$Q = Q_1 \text{ and } F = F_A,$$

without receiving or emitting actual energy, the following quantity of energy will at the end of the operation have been permanently transformed from the actual to the potential condition,

$$H_1 - H_2 = (Q_1 - Q_2)(F_B - F_A), \qquad \cdot \quad \cdot \quad \cdot \quad \text{(6)}$$

which bears the following proportion to the whole quantity of actual energy received by the substance from without,

$$\frac{H_1 - H_2}{H_1} = \frac{Q_1 - Q_2}{Q_1}; \qquad \cdot \quad \cdot \quad \cdot \quad \cdot \quad \text{(7)}$$

that is to say,—

The greatest quantity of energy which can be permanently converted from the actual to the potential state by causing a substance to undergo a cycle of changes, bears the same proportion to the whole actual energy communicated to the substance from without, which the excess of the actual energy present in the substance during the reception of actual energy, above the actual energy present during the emission of actual energy, bears to the former of these two quantities.

This is the general law of the action of all possible machines, which work by the transformation of energy of all kinds, known or unknown.

Application to Heat.

(7.) Having described in detail the application of these principles to the theory of expansive heat, in the sixth section of a paper on the Mechanical Action of Heat, communicated to the Royal Society of Edinburgh, I shall here give merely an outline of the principal points of that application.

Expansive heat may be defined to be *a species of actual energy, the presence of which in a body gives it a tendency to expand.*

To adapt the preceding formulæ to this kind of energy, we must affix the following interpretation to the symbols.

Let Q denote the quantity of heat in a body, as measured by an equivalent quantity of mechanical power ;

V the volume of the body, whose tendency to increase is represented by

P, the expansive pressure, in units of force per unit of surface.

Then $dU = PdV$ is the expansive power or potential energy developed by a small expansion dV ; and during this expansion the following quantity of heat becomes latent, that is to say, is converted into expansive power, according to equation (1),

$$Q \cdot \frac{d^2U}{dQ dV} \cdot dV = Q \cdot \frac{dP}{dQ} dV.$$

According to the principle laid down in the fifth article, if any substance exists in which the expansive pressure is simply proportional to the quantity of heat present, then the heat which disappears in expanding that substance is the exact equivalent of the power developed. In all known substances, however, even those in the gaseous state, the expansive pressure deviates from this law ; and accordingly the difference

$$\left(Q \frac{dP}{dQ} - P \right) dV$$

represents the power expended in overcoming cohesive force, diminished by that which is produced by such elasticity as the body may possess independently of heat.

The recent experiments of Mr. Joule and Professor William Thomson on the thermic phænomena of currents of air, give values of this quantity under various circumstances as to temperature and density ; and after calculating from formulæ deduced from M. Regnault's experiments the effect of cohesive force, I have found that they indicate that perfect gases possess an elasticity, independent of heat, corresponding to that due to about $2^{\circ} \cdot 1$ of the Centigrade thermometer; that is to say, that the temperature of total privation of heat is about $2^{\circ} \cdot 1$ Centigrade above the absolute zero of a perfect gas-thermometer, or $272\frac{1}{2}^{\circ}$ Centigrade below the freezing-point.

In applying the law of the efficiency of machines to the case of expansive heat, we must put the following interpretation on the symbols :—

Let Q_1 denote the total heat present in the expanding body during the period of receiving heat from without;

Q_2 the total heat during the period of emitting heat;

H_1 the whole heat received;

H_2 the whole heat emitted; so that

$H_1 - H_2$ is the useful effect of the engine, or the heat permanently converted into expansive power; then the proportion of the useful effect to the whole heat received is, as in equation (7),

$$\frac{H_1 - H_2}{H_1} = \frac{Q_1 - Q_2}{Q_1}.$$

If we admit the principle, which appears to me to be demonstrable, that the heat present in a body varies with temperature according to the same law for all substances, the above formula leads immediately to Carnot's law, as modified by Messrs. Clausius and Thomson. If we, further, adopt the hypothesis that expansive heat consists in vortices or eddies in atmospheres surrounding centres of molecular attraction, we are led to the conclusion, which is borne out by our present experimental knowledge so far as it extends, that the quantity of heat in a body is proportional simply to the temperature, as measured from the point of total privation of heat already mentioned. Let κ denote the position of this point on the thermometric scale; then the greatest proportion of heat which can be rendered effective by any expansive engine, receiving heat at the temperature τ_1 and emitting it at τ_2, is

$$\frac{\tau_1 - \tau_2}{\tau_1 - \kappa}, \qquad \cdots \cdots \quad (8)$$

being the formula which, in the fifth section of a paper on the Mechanical Action of Heat, I have deduced directly from the hypothesis above mentioned.

Application to Current Electricity.

(8.) In order to apply the general law of the transformation of energy and its consequences to current electricity, we must consider in the first place how the actual energy present in a closed electric circuit is to be measured.

We know that when a closed electric circuit is not employed to produce any extraneous effect, such as induction, magnetism, or chemical analysis, its whole actual energy is expended in producing heat. We also know, through the experiments of Messrs. Riess and Joule, that the heat generated by an electric current in unity of time under such circumstances is proportional to the function called the *quantity* of the current multiplied by the function called the electromotive force. Hence we must adopt for the symbol Q the following signification,

$$Q = Mu, \quad \dots \quad \dots \quad (9)$$

where u is the quantity of the current, and M the electromotive force, measured in such a manner that their product shall represent the heat generated in unity of time in the circuit when no other effect is produced.

It is further known, that when no effect is produced but heat, the quantity of the current is equal to the electromotive force divided by a function called the resistance of the circuit; that is to say, under these circumstances

$$u = \frac{M}{R}, \quad \dots \quad \dots \quad (E)$$

where R is that resistance; and that in all cases, whether other effects are produced or not, the heat generated is represented by the square of the quantity of the current multiplied by the resistance, or

$$H = Ru^2. \quad \dots \quad \dots \quad (F)$$

Chemical affinity constitutes a kind of potential energy, which is converted into the actual energy of electricity when substances combine. To determine the law of this transformation, we have the following facts:—The electromotive force depends on the nature of the substances which combine, and is moreover proportional to the number of surfaces in the circuit at which the combination takes place in the proper direction. Let n be this number, K a specific coefficient, then

$$M = Kn. \quad \dots \quad \dots \quad (G)$$

The quantity of the current depends also on the nature of the substances, and is proportional to the quantities of them which enter into combination at any one surface. Let z be the amount of compound formed in unity of time, k a specific coefficient; then

$$u = kz. \quad \dots \quad \dots \quad (H)$$

Consequently

$$Q = Mu = Kknz; \quad \dots \quad (10)$$

from which it appears, that if the principles which we have laid down as experimental data be rigorously correct, electrical actual energy and chemical energy are simply proportional to each other, and the amount of electrical actual energy produced in a circuit is the exact equivalent of the chemical potential energy which disappears.

Let us next examine the transformation of electrical actual energy into the potential energy of magnetism by means of soft iron; and for this purpose let a horse-shoe bar be magnetized by means of a coil encircling it, in which is a current of the energy

$$Q = Mu = Ru^2.$$

Let the keeper be at a fixed distance x from the bar, and let the amount of their mutual attraction be

$$P \cdot \phi x.$$

Then it is known by the experiments of Messrs. Joule, Lenz, and Jacobi, that within certain limits the coefficient P is proportional, for a given length and arrangement of coil, to the square of the quantity of the current, all other things being supposed constant; that is to say, it is simply proportional to the electrical actual energy; therefore, within those limits, the electrical actual energy which disappears in producing magnetic potential energy is the exact equivalent of the magnetic energy developed.

When the electric current exceeds a certain quantity as compared with the transverse section of the bar, Mr. Joule has proved that the magnetic attraction no longer increases in the exact ratio of the electrical energy, but more slowly. The conclusion to be drawn from this is somewhat remarkable. The total attraction between the bar and its keeper being proportional to P, the portion which causes electrical energy to disappear when it acts is proportional to $Q \dfrac{dP}{dQ}$, which being smaller than P, the difference, represented by $P - Q \dfrac{dP}{dQ}$, is the coefficient of a portion of magnetic attraction which acts in raising weights like that of a permanent magnet, without causing electrical actual energy to disappear. It is probable that the action of this portion of magnetism is accompanied by some peculiar variations in the molecular condition of the iron.

(9.) In order to apply the general law of the efficiency of machines to the mechanical action of electro-chemical energy, we have only to conceive for the purpose of this calculation that the reception and discharge of actual energy, which really take place at the same instant, are performed during alternate instants. Then Q_1 will represent the energy corresponding to the chemical action in the battery in unity of time, and Q_2 that corresponding to the heat discharged in unity of time, and

$$\frac{Q_1 - Q_2}{Q_1} = \frac{M - Ru}{M}, \quad \cdots \quad (11)$$

the proportion of the total energy received which is converted into mechanical power.

This formula, deduced from an abstract principle by interpreting its symbols according to experimental data, agrees with results arrived at by Professor William Thomson and Mr. Joule from the special consideration of electro-chemical and magnetic forces.

If we take for granted (what is not absolutely certain) that the resistance of the circuit in an electro-magnetic engine is the same whether it is performing work or not, then let u_0 be the quantity of the current which would take place if the engine were not working, and we obtain the following value of the electromotive force,

$$M = Ru_0,$$

which reduces the above formula (11) to the following :

$$\frac{Q_1 - Q_2}{Q_1} = \frac{u_0 - u}{u_0}. \quad \cdots \quad (11A)$$

This is the formula given in a paper " On the Œconomical Production of Mechanical Effect from Chemical Forces " (Manchester Transactions, vol. x.), by Mr. Joule, who points out its analogy to the corresponding formula for heat. We have seen that they are particular cases of a universal principle.

To determine the mean quantity of current u in equation (11), we have the following data. Let v be the mean value of the function $\phi x \frac{dx}{dt}$, and

$$Pv$$

the mean amount of power developed by magnetic force in unity of time ; then, m being a coefficient depending on the length and arrangement of coils round the bar, we have

$$P = mu^2,$$

and consequently

$$Pv = mu^2 v$$

is the electric energy converted into mechanical power in unity of time. Adding to this Ru^2, the quantity converted into heat, and equating the sum to the total production of electrical energy, we have

$$Mu = (R + mv)u^2,$$

and the quantity of the current is found to be

$$u = \frac{M}{R + mv}. \quad \cdots \quad (K)$$

This reduces equation (11) to the following,

$$\frac{Q_1 - Q_2}{Q_1} = 1 - \frac{R}{R + mv}; \quad . \quad . \quad . \quad (12)$$

which shows that the ratio of the effect of an electro-magnetic engine, working by the induction of magnetism in a soft iron bar, to the power expended, approaches unity as the velocity increases without limit; but at the same time the actual performance diminishes indefinitely.

(10.) The foregoing examples illustrate the method of applying the general law of the transformation of energy to some of those forms with which we are most familiar, by interpreting the symbols according to the properties of the kinds of energy under consideration with which we are made acquainted by experiment. The examples are necessarily of a simple kind; but I purpose to apply the same principles to determine the laws of more complicated phænomena.

Glasgow, December 31, 1852.

6

Reprinted from *Phil. Trans. Roy. Soc. London*, **144**, 115–123 (1854)

On the Geometrical Representation of the Expansive Action of Heat, and the Theory of Thermo-dynamic Engines. By WILLIAM JOHN MACQUORN RANKINE, C.E., F.R.SS. Lond. and Edin. &c.

Received December 5, 1853,—Read January 19, 1854.

SECTION I.—INTRODUCTION AND GENERAL THEOREMS.

(Article 1.) THE first application of a geometrical diagram to represent the expansive action of Heat was made by JAMES WATT, when he contrived the well-known Steam-Engine Indicator, subsequently altered and improved by others in various ways. As the diagram described by WATT's Indicator is the type of all diagrams representing the expansive action of heat, its general nature is exhibited in fig. 1.

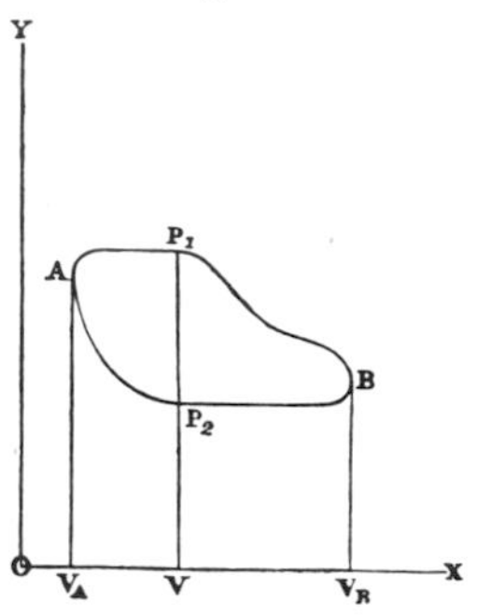

Let abscissæ, measured along, or parallel to, the axis OX represent the volumes successively assumed by a given mass of an elastic substance, by whose alternate expansion and contraction heat is made to produce motive power; OV_A and OV_B being the least and greatest volumes which the substance is made to assume, and OV any intermediate volume. For brevity's sake, these quantities will be denoted by V_A, V_B, and V, respectively. Then $V_B - V_A$ may represent the space traversed by the piston of an engine during a single stroke.

Fig. 1.

Let ordinates, measured parallel to the axis OY and at right angles to OX, denote the expansive pressures successively exerted by the substance at the volumes denoted by the abscissæ. During the increase of volume from V_A to V_B, the pressure, in order that motive power may be produced, must be, on the whole, greater than during the diminution of volume from V_B to V_A; so that, for instance, the ordinates VP_1 and VP_2, or the symbols P_1 and P_2, may represent the pressures corresponding to a given volume V during the expansion and contraction of the substance respectively.

Then the area of the curvilinear figure, or *Indicator-diagram*, AP_1BP_2A, will represent the motive power, or " Potential Energy," *developed* or *given out* during a complete stroke, or cycle of changes of volume of the elastic substance. The algebraical expression for this area is

$$\int_{V_A}^{V_B} (P_1 - P_2) dV. \quad \cdot \quad \cdot \quad \cdot \quad \cdot \quad \cdot \quad \cdot \quad \cdot \quad \cdot \quad \cdot \quad \cdot \quad \cdot \quad (1.)$$

108

The practical use of such diagrams, in ascertaining the power and the mode of action of the steam in steam-engines, where the curve AP_1BP_2A is described by a pencil attached to a pressure-gauge, on a card whose motion corresponds with that of the piston, is sufficiently well known.

(2.) It appears that the earliest application of *diagrams of energy* (as they may be called) to prove and illustrate the theoretical principles of the mechanical action of heat, was made either by CARNÔT, or by M. CLAPEYRON in his account of CARNÔT's theory ; but the conclusions of those authors were in a great measure vitiated by the assumption of the substantiality of heat.

In the fifth section of a paper on the Mechanical Action of Heat, published in the Transactions of the Royal Society of Edinburgh, vol. xx., a diagram of energy is employed to demonstrate the general law of the economy of heat in thermo-dynamic engines according to the correct principle of the action of such machines, viz. that the area of the diagram represents at once the potential energy or motive power which is developed at each stroke, and the mechanical equivalent of the actual energy, or heat, which permanently disappears.

As the principles of the expansive action of heat are capable of being presented to the mind more clearly by the aid of diagrams of energy than by means of words and algebraical symbols alone, I purpose, in the present paper, to apply those diagrams, partly to the illustration and demonstration of propositions already proved by other means, but chiefly to the solution of new questions, especially those relating to the action of heat in all classes of engines, whether worked by air, or by steam, or by any other material ; so as to present, in a systematic form, those theoretical principles which are applicable to all methods of transforming heat to motive power by means of the changes of volume of an elastic substance.

Throughout the whole of this investigation, quantities of heat, and coefficients of specific heat, are expressed, not by units of temperature in a unit of weight of water, but by equivalent quantities of mechanical power, stated in foot-pounds, according to the ratio established by Mr. JOULE's experiments on friction (Phil. Trans. 1850) ; that is to say,

772 foot-pounds per degree of FAHR., or
1389·6 foot-pounds per Centigrade degree,

applied to one pound of liquid water at atmospheric temperatures.

(3.) *Of Isothermal Curves, and Curves of No Transmission of Heat.*

A curve described on a diagram of energy, such that its ordinates represent the pressures of a homogeneous substance corresponding to various volumes, while the total *sensible* or *actual heat* present in the body is maintained at a constant value, denoted, for example, by Q, may be called the *Isothermal Curve of Q* for the given substance. (See fig. 2.) Suppose, for instance, that the co-ordinates of the point A, V_A and P_A, represent respectively a volume and a pressure of a given substance, at which the actual heat is Q ; and the co-ordinates of the point B, viz. V_B and P_B, another volume and pressure at which the actual heat is the same; then are the points A and B situated on the same isothermal curve QQ.

On the other hand, let the substance be allowed to expand from the volume and pressure V_A, P_A, without receiving or emitting heat; and when it reaches a certain volume, V_C, let the pressure be represented by P_C, which is less than the pressure would have been had the actual heat been maintained constant, because, by expansion, heat is made to disappear. Then C will be a point on a certain curve NN passing through A, which may be called a *Curve of No Transmission.*

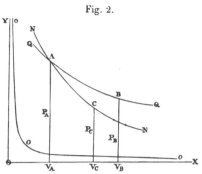

Fig. 2.

It is to be understood that, during the process last described, the potential energy developed during the expansion, and which is represented by the area ACV_cV_A, is entirely communicated to external substances; for if any part of it were expended in agitating the particles of the expanding substance, a portion of heat would be reproduced by friction.

If *o o o* be a curve whose ordinates represent the pressures corresponding to various volumes when the substance is absolutely destitute of heat, then this curve, which may be called the *Curve of Absolute Cold*, is at once an isothermal curve and a curve of no transmission.

So far as we yet know, the curve of absolute cold is, for all substances, an asymptote to all the other isothermal curves and curves of no transmission, which approach it and each other indefinitely as the volume of the substance increases without limit.

NOTE.—The following remarks are intended to render more clear the precise meaning of the term *Total Actual Heat.*

The Total Actual Heat of a given mass of a given substance at a given temperature, is the quantity of Physical Energy present in the mass *in the form of Heat* under the given circumstances.

If, for the purpose of illustrating this definition, we assume the hypothesis that heat consists in molecular revolutions of a particular kind, then the Total Actual Heat of a mass is measured by the mechanical power corresponding to the *vis viva* of those revolutions, and is represented by

$$\frac{1}{2}\Sigma.mv^2,$$

m being the mass of any circulating molecule, and v^2 the mean-square of its velocity.

But the meaning of the term Total Actual Heat may also be illustrated without the aid of any hypothesis.

For this purpose, let us take the ascertained fact of the production of heat by the expenditure of mechanical power in friction, according to the numerical proportion determined by Mr. JOULE ; and let E denote the quantity of mechanical power which must be expended in friction, in order to raise the temperature of unity of weight of a given substance from that of absolute privation of heat to a given temperature τ.

During this operation, let the several elements of the external surface of the mass undergo changes of relative position expressed by the variations of quantities denoted generally by p, and let the increase of each such quantity as p be resisted by an externally-applied force such as P.

Then during the elevation of temperature from absolute cold to τ, the energy converted to the potential form in overcoming the external pressures P will be

$$\Sigma . \int P dp.$$

Also let the internal particles of the mass undergo changes of relative position expressed by the variations of quantities denoted generally by r, and let the increase of each such quantity as r be resisted by an internal molecular force such as R.

Then the energy converted to the potential form in overcoming internal molecular forces will be

$$\Sigma . \int R dr.$$

Subtracting these quantities of energy converted to the potential form by means of external pressures and internal forces, from the whole power converted into heat by friction in order to raise the temperature of the mass from that of absolute privation of heat to the given temperature τ, we find the following result :—

$$Q = E - \Sigma . \int P dp - \Sigma . \int R dr ;$$

and this remainder is the quantity of energy which *retains the form of heat*, in unity of weight of the given substance at the given temperature ; that is to say, the Total Actual Heat.

It is obvious that Total Actual Heat cannot be ascertained directly ; first, because the temperature of total privation of heat is unattainable ; and secondly, because the molecular forces R are unknown.

It can, however, be determined indirectly from the latent heat of expansion of the substance. For the heat which disappears during the expansion of unity of weight of an elastic substance at constant actual heat from the volume V_A to the volume V_B, under the constant or variable pressure P, is expressed (as will be shown in the sequel) by

$$Q . \frac{d}{dQ} \int_{V_A}^{V_B} P dV ;$$

so that from a sufficient number of experiments on the amount of heat transformed to potential energy by the expansion of a given substance, the relations, for that substance, between pressure, volume, and Total Actual Heat, may be determined.

(4.) PROPOSITION I.—THEOREM. *The Mechanical Equivalent of the Heat absorbed or given out by a substance in passing from one given state as to pressure and volume to another given state, through a series of states represented by the co-ordinates of a given curve on a diagram of energy, is represented by the area included between the given curve and two curves of no transmission of heat drawn from its extremities, and indefinitely prolonged in the direction representing increase of volume.*

(Demonstration) (see fig. 3). Let the co-ordinates of any two points, A and B, represent respectively the volumes and pressures of the substance in any two condi-

Fig. 3.

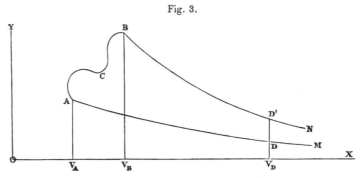

tions ; and let a curve of any figure, ACB, represent, by the co-ordinates of its points, an arbitrary succession of volumes and pressures through which the substance is made to pass, in changing from the condition A to the condition B. From the points A and B respectively, let two curves of no transmission AM, BN, extend indefinitely towards X ; then the area referred to in the enunciation is that contained between the given arbitrary curve ACB and the two indefinitely prolonged curves of no transmission ; areas above the curve AM being considered as representing heat absorbed by the substance, and those below, heat given out.

To fix the ideas, let us in the first place suppose the area MACBN to be situated above AM. After the substance has reached the state B, let it be expanded according to the curve of no transmission BN, until its volume and pressure are represented by the co-ordinates of the point D'. Next, let the volume V_D be maintained constant, while heat is abstracted until the pressure falls so as to be represented by the ordinate of the point D, situated on the curve of no transmission AM. Finally, let the substance be compressed, according to this curve of no transmission, until it recovers its primitive condition A. Then the area ACBD'DA, which represents the whole potential energy developed by the substance during one cycle of operations, represents also the heat which disappears, that is, the difference between the heat absorbed by the substance during the change from A to B, and emitted during the change from D' to D ; for if this were not so, the cycle of operations would alter the amount of energy in the universe, which is impossible.

The further the ordinate V_DDD' is removed in the direction of X, the smaller does the heat emitted during the change from D' to D become ; and consequently, the more nearly does the area ACBD'DA approximate to the equivalent of the heat absorbed during the change from A to B ; to which, therefore, the area of the indefinitely-prolonged diagram MACBN is exactly equal. Q.E.D.

It is easy to see how a similar demonstration could have been applied, *mutatis mutandis*, had the area lain below the curve AM. It is evident also, that when this area lies, part above and part below the line AM, the difference between these two parts represents the difference between the heat absorbed and the heat emitted during different parts of the operation.

(5.) *First Corollary.*—THEOREM. *The difference between the whole heat absorbed, and the whole expansive power developed, during the operation represented by any curve, such as* ACB, *on a diagram of energy, depends on the initial and final conditions of the substance alone, and not on the intermediate process.*

(Demonstration.)   In fig. 3, draw the ordinates AV_A, BV_B parallel to OY.   Then the area V_AACBV_B represents the expansive power developed during the operation ACB ; and it is evident that the difference between this area and the indefinitely-prolonged area MACBN, which represents the heat received by the substance, depends simply on the positions of the points A and B, which denote the initial and final conditions of the substance as to volume and pressure, and not on the form of the curve ACB, which represents the intermediate process. Q.E.D.

To express this result symbolically, it is to be considered, that the excess of the heat or actual energy *received* by the substance above the expansive power or potential energy *given out* and exerted on external bodies, in passing from the condition A to the condition B, is equal to the whole energy *stored up* in the substance during this operation, which consists of two parts, viz.—

Actual energy ; being the increase of the actual or sensible heat of the substance in passing from the condition A to the condition B, which is to be represented by this expression,

$$\Delta . Q = Q_B - Q_A ;$$

Potential energy ; being the power which is stored up in producing changes of molecular arrangement during this process ; and which, it appears from the Theorem just proved, must be represented, like the actual energy, by the difference between a function of the volume and pressure corresponding to A, and the analogous function of the volume and pressure corresponding to B ; that is to say, by an expression of the form,

$$\Delta S = S_B - S_A.$$

Let $H_{A,B} = $ area MACBN represent the heat received by the substance during the operation ACB, and

$$\int_{V_A}^{V_B} PdV = \text{area } V_A ACBV_B$$

the power or potential energy, given out.

Then the theorem of this article is expressed as follows :—

$$H_{A,B} - \int_{V_A}^{V_B} PdV = Q_B - Q_A + S_B - S_A = \Delta Q + \Delta.S \quad . \quad . \quad . \quad (2.)$$

being a form of the General Equation of the Expansive Action of Heat, in which the *Potential of Molecular Action*, S, remains to be determined.

(6.) *Second Corollary* (see fig. 4).—The *Latent Heat of Expansion* of a substance, from one given volume V_A to another V_B, for a given amount of actual heat **Q** ; that

Fig. 4.

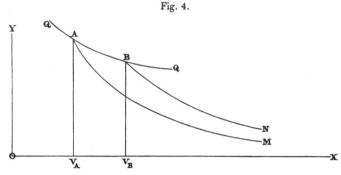

is to say, the heat which must be absorbed by the substance in expanding from the volume V_A to the volume V_B, in order that the actual heat **Q** may be maintained constant, is represented geometrically as follows. Let **QQ** be the isothermal curve of the given actual heat **Q** on the diagram of energy; A, B two points on this curve, whose co-ordinates represent the two given volumes and the corresponding pressures. Through A and B draw the two curves of no transmission AM, BN, produced indefinitely in the direction of X. Then the area contained between the portion of isothermal curve AB, and the indefinitely-produced curves AM, BN, represents the mechanical equivalent of the latent heat sought, whose symbolical expression is formed from Equation 2 by making $Q_B - Q_A = 0$, and is as follows :—

$$H_{A,B} \text{ (for } Q = \text{const.)} = \int_{V_A}^{V_B} PdV + S_B - S_A. \quad . \quad . \quad . \quad . \quad . \quad (3.)$$

114

SECTION II.—PROPOSITIONS RELATIVE TO HOMOGENEOUS SUBSTANCES.

(7.) PROPOSITION II.—THEOREM. *In fig. 5, let* A_1A_2M, B_1B_2N *be any two curves of no transmission, indefinitely extended in the direction of* X, *intersected in the points,*

Fig. 5.

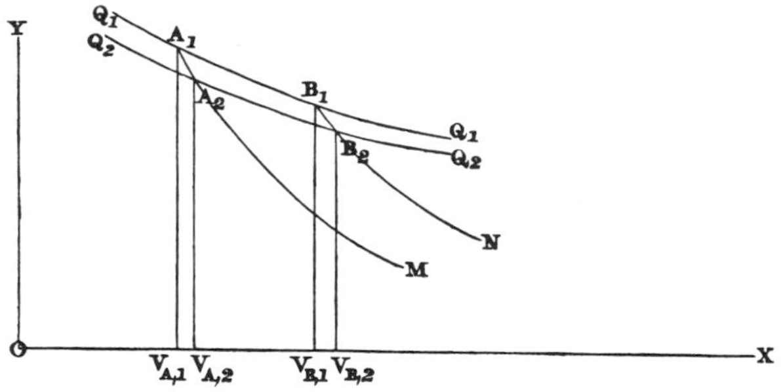

A_1, B_1, A_2, B_2, *by two isothermal curves,* $Q_1A_1B_1Q_1$, $Q_2A_2B_2Q_2$, *which are indefinitely near to each other; that is to say, which correspond to two quantities of actual heat,* Q_1 *and* Q_2, *differing by an indefinitely small quantity* $Q_1 - Q_2 = \delta Q$.

Then the elementary quadrilateral area, $A_1B_1B_2A_2$, *bears to the whole indefinitely-prolonged area* MA_1B_1N, *the same proportion which the indefinitely small difference of actual heat* δQ *bears to the whole actual heat* Q_1; *or*

$$\frac{\text{area } A_1B_1B_2A_2}{\text{area } MA_1B_1N} = \frac{\delta Q}{Q_1}.$$

(Demonstration.)   Draw the ordinates $A_1V_{A_1}$, $A_2V_{A_2}$, $B_1V_{B_1}$, $B_1V_{B_2}$ Suppose, in the first place, that δQ is an aliquot part of Q_1, obtained by dividing the latter quantity by a very large integer n, which we are at liberty to increase without limit.

The entire indefinitely-prolonged area MA_1B_1N represents a quantity of heat which is converted into potential energy during the expansion of the substance from V_{A_1} to V_{B_1}, in consequence of the continued presence of the total actual heat Q_1; for if no heat were present no such conversion would take place. *Mutatis mutandis,* a similar statement may be made respecting the area MA_2B_2N. By increasing without limit the number n and diminishing δQ, we may make the expansion from V_{A_2} to V_{B_2} as nearly as we please an identical phenomenon with the expansion from V_{A_1} to V_{B_1}. The quadrilateral $A_1B_1B_2A_2$ represents the diminution of conversion of heat to potential energy, which results from the abstraction of any one whatsoever of the n small equal parts δQ into which the actual heat Q_1 is supposed to be divided, and it therefore represents the effect, in conversion of heat to potential energy, of the presence of any one of those small portions of actual heat. And as all those portions δQ are similar and similarly circumstanced, the effect of the presence of the whole actual heat Q_1 in causing conversion of heat to potential energy, will be simply the sum of the effects of all its small portions, and will bear the same ratio to the effect of one of those small portions, which the whole actual heat bears to the small portion.   Thus, by virtue of the general law enunciated below and assumed as an axiom, the theorem is proved when δQ is an aliquot part of Q_1; but δQ is either an aliquot part, or a sum of aliquot parts, or may be indefinitely approximated to by a series of aliquot parts; so that the theorem is universally true. Q.E.D.

The symbolical expression of this theorem is as follows. When the actual heat Q_1, at any given volume, is varied by the indefinitely small quantity δQ, let the pressure vary by the indefinitely small quantity $\frac{dP}{dQ}\,\delta Q$; then the area of the quadrilateral $A_1B_1B_2A_2$ will be represented by

$$\delta Q . \int_{V_{A,1}}^{V_{B,1}} \frac{dP}{dQ} dV,$$

and consequently, that of the whole figure MA_1B_1N, or the latent heat of expansion from $V_{A,1}$ to $V_{B,1}$, at Q_1, by

$$H_1 = Q_1 \int_{V_{A1}}^{V_{B1}} \frac{dP}{dQ} dV ; \quad \cdot \quad \cdot \quad \cdot \quad \cdot \quad \cdot \quad \cdot \quad \cdot \quad \cdot \quad (4.)$$

a result identical with that expressed in the sixth section of a paper published in the Transactions of the Royal Society of Edinburgh, vol. xx.

The demonstration of this theorem is an example of a special application of the following

GENERAL LAW OF THE TRANSFORMATION OF ENERGY.

The effect of the presence, in a substance, of a quantity of Actual Energy, in causing transformation of Energy, is the sum of the effects of all its parts :—
a law first enunciated in a paper read by me to the Philosophical Society of Glasgow on the 5th of January, 1853.

(8.) GENERAL EQUATION OF THE EXPANSIVE ACTION OF HEAT.

The two expressions for the Latent Heat of Expansion at constant Actual Heat, given in equations 3 and 4 respectively, being equated, furnish the means of determining the potential energy of molecular action S, so far as it depends on volume, and thus of giving a definite form to the general equation 2.

The two expressions referred to may be thus stated in words :—

I. The heat which disappears in producing a given expansion, while the actual heat present in the substance is maintained constant, is equivalent to the sum of the potential energy given out in the form of expansive power, and the potential energy stored up by means of molecular attractions.

II. It is also equivalent to the potential energy due to the action during the expansion, of a pressure $Q\frac{dP}{dQ}$, at each instant equal to what the pressure would be, if its actual rate of variation with heat at the instant in question were a constant coefficient, expressing the ratio of the whole pressure to the whole actual heat present.

7

The Specific Heats of Elastic Fluids
Henri Victor Regnault

*This excerpt was translated expressly for this Benchmark
volume by R. Bruce Lindsay, Brown University, from
"Recherches sur les chaleurs spécifiques des fluides
élastiques," Compt. Rend., 36, 676–683 (1853)*

For the last 12 years I have occupied myself in collecting the elements
necessary for the solution of the general problem which can be stated
as follows:

Given a certain quantity of heat, what is the work one can obtain theoretically in applying it to the production and dilatation of different elastic
fluids under practically realizable circumstances?

The complete solution of this problem would give the true theory
not only of steam engines as they exist today, but also that of engines in
which water vapor is replaced by another vapor or even by a permanent
elastic fluid whose elasticity is increased by heat.

At the time when I began these researches the question seemed to
me more simple than it does today. Starting with scientific ideas then
admitted, it was easy to define precisely the various elements that entered
into it, and I visualized procedures with whose aid I could hope to find
one after another the laws and to determine numerical values. But, as
usually happens in the observational sciences, the further I proceeded
with my studies, the wider their circle grew. The questions that at first
appeared to me to be very simple have now become very complicated,
and perhaps I would not have had the courage to begin the subject if in
the beginning I had understood all the difficulties.

It has been believed until very recently that the quantities of heat
emitted or absorbed by a given elastic fluid would be equal when the
fluid passes from a given initial state back to this same state, no matter
how the transition is carried out. In a word, it was taken for granted
that quantities of heat depend only on initial and final conditions of
temperature and pressure, and that they were independent of the
intermediate states through which the fluid passed. In 1824, S. Carnot
published a work entitled "Reflections on the Motive Power of Fire,"
which at first attracted little attention. In this he set forth the principle
that the work done by a heat engine is due to the passage of heat
from a hotter source, which gives off heat, to a cooler condenser,
which receives the heat. M. Clapeyron has made calculations based
on Carnot's principle and has shown that the quantities of heat gained
or lost by a given gas depend not only on the initial and final states,
but also on the intermediate states through which the gas has passed.

The mechanical theory of heat has found favor during the last few years, and at the moment it is engaging the attention of many mathematicians. But Carnot's principle has had to undergo an important modification: i.e., heat can be transformed into mechanical work and conversely mechanical work can be transformed into heat. In Carnot's theory, the heat possessed by the elastic fluid that enters the engine is all present in the elastic fluid which leaves it or proceeds to the condenser. Mechanical work is done by the simple passage of the heat from the heat reservoir to the condenser in traversing the engine. In the new theory, this quantity of heat does not remain entirely in the form of heat: a part disappears during its passage through the engine, and the work produced is in every case proportional to the quantity of heat that is lost. Thus, in a steam engine, with or without a condenser or with or without expansion of the steam, the mechanical work produced by the engine is proportional to the difference between the quantity of heat possessed by the steam at its entrance into the engine and that which it keeps as it leaves the engine or at the moment of condensation. In this theory, to obtain from a given quantity of heat the maximum mechanical effect, it is necessary to arrange things so that this loss of heat shall be as large as possible, i.e., the elastic force retained by the expanded steam at the moment when it enters the condenser shall be as small as possible. But in every case, in the operation of a steam engine the quantity of heat utilized for mechanical work will be only a very small fraction of that which it is necessary to communicate to the boiler. In an expansion steam engine, without a condenser, in which the steam enters at a pressure of 5 atmospheres and leaves at a pressure of 1 atmosphere, the quantity of heat possessed by the steam at its entrance, in my experiments, was about 653 units, and that retained at its egress was 637. According to the theory I have been discussing, the quantity of heat utilized for mechanical work would be 653 – 637 = 16 units, i.e., only one fortieth of the quantity of heat given to the boiler. In a condensing engine receiving saturated vapor at 5 atmospheres and in which the condenser presents a constant elastic force of 55 millimeters of mercury, the quantity of heat in the entering steam was still 653 units, and that which the steam possessed at the moment of condensation, i.e., where it was lost for any possible mechanical effect, was now 619 units. The heat utilized for work was then 34 units, or a little more than one twentieth of the heat given to the boiler.

One will then obtain a greater fraction of heat utilized for mechanical work either by superheating the steam before its entry into the engine or by lowering as much as possible the temperature of condensation. But the latter scheme is difficult to realize in practice. It would force one to increase considerably the quantity of cold water used for the condensation, and hence effectively cut down the net work done and render possible restoration to the boiler of less heated water. One can more easily achieve the same end by arranging for a smaller expansion of the steam in the engine and in condensing this steam by the injection of a very volatile liquid, like ether or chloroform. The heat possessed by the steam at the moment of this condensation, and of which only a very small part would be transformed into mechanical work, passes into the more volatile liquid, which it changes into vapor at high pressure. By passing this vapor into a second engine, where it expands to such an elastic force that the injection water can practically lead it into the condenser, a portion of the heat is transformed into work. Calculation based on numerical values resulting from my experiments shows that this quantity of heat is much greater than that which could have been obtained by a larger expansion of steam in the first engine. In this way, one can easily explain the economic gain to be obtained from two coupled engines, the one using steam and the other ether or chloroform vapor, on which experiments were made several years ago.

In air engines, in which the work is produced by dilatation due to the heat given to the gas in the engine or by the increase produced in its elastic force, the work done at each stroke of the piston will always be proportional to the difference between the quantity of heat in the entering and leaving air, i.e., in the loss of heat experienced by the air in passing through the engine. But as in Ericson's system, the heat in the air leaving the engine can be fed back into the engine through the new air entering it. Hence, one sees that, theoretically at least, in these last engines all the heat provided is used in the production of work, whereas in the better steam engines the heat utilized for work is only one twentieth of the heat provided. It is understood, of course, that I here neglect all external heat losses and mechanical losses which are met with in practice.

Joule, Thomson, and Rankine in England and Mayer and Clausius in Germany, often starting out from different points of view, have developed analytically the mechanical theory of heat and have sought to deduce from it the laws of all the phenomena relating to elastic fluids. As for myself, I have for a long time taught in my university lectures analogous ideas to which I have been led by my experimental researches on elastic fluids. In these researches I continually ran into anomalies that appeared to me inexplicable in the light of previously accepted theories. To give an idea of this, I shall cite some simple examples.

First example: (1) A mass of gas under a pressure of 10 atmospheres is enclosed in a space whose volume is suddenly doubled. The pressure drops to 5 atmospheres.

(2) Two reservoirs of equal volume are placed in a given calorimeter. The one is full of gas at a pressure of 10 atmospheres. The second is completely empty (vacuum). One suddenly estblishes a connection between the two reservoirs. The gas expands to double its volume, and the pressure is reduced again to 5 atmospheres.

Thus in the two experiments just mentioned the initial and final conditions of the gas are the same. But this identity of conditions is

119

accompanied by very different calorific results: in the first case one observes a considerable cooling; in the second case the calorimeter does not show the least change in temperature.

Second example: (1) A mass M of gas under atmospheric pressure traverses a coiled pipe in which it is heated to 100 degrees temperature and then goes through a calorimeter whose initial temperature was 0 degrees. The temperature of the calorimeter is raised by t degrees.

(2) The same mass of gas under a pressure of 10 atmospheres traverses the coiled pipe, where it is heated to 100 degrees, and then goes to the calorimeter with original temperature 0 degrees and at the same pressure. The temperature of the calorimeter is raised by t' degrees. Experiments show that t' is not very different from t.

(3) The same mass of gas under a pressure of 10 atmospheres traverses the same coiled pipe, where it is heated to 100 degrees, but in reaching the calorimeter (still kept initially at 0 degrees) the gas is expanded and moves under atmospheric pressure so that it leaves the calorimeter in temperature equilibrium with the latter and in pressure equilibrium with the ambient atmosphere. The temperature of the calorimeter is then observed to be increased by t''.

According to previously held theories, the quantity of heat given up by the gas in experiment (3) ought to be equal to that in experiment (2), diminished by the quantity of heat that has been absorbed by the gas during the very large dilatation to which it has been subjected. The experiment shows, on the contrary, that the temperature t'' is greater than t' and t.

I could multiply these cases, but then I should be anticipating what I shall have to say later. I shall delay this exposition to the time when I expect to publish the results of all the experiments I have made on the compression and expansion of gases.

However this may be, the examples which I have just cited are sufficient to demonstrate that one ought to be very careful about conclusions drawn from experiments in which elastic fluids are in motion, are subject to changes in elasticity, and produce mechanical work, which is often difficult to estimate; for the heating effects produced depend in great measure on the order and manner in which the changes are made.

Unfortunately, it is easy to set up a physical theory in general terms, but it is very difficult to specify it with precision so as not only to connect it with all the facts already known in the science, but also to deduce those facts which have hitherto escaped observation. The wave theory of light, established by Fresnel, provides a good example in present-day physics. If one puts in equation form the problems of heat looked at from the mechanical point of view, one is led as in all analogous problems to an equation involving partial derivatives of the second order in several variables that are unknown functions of each other. These functions represent the true physical laws, which it is necessary to know in order to find the complete solution of the problem. The integration of the equation introduces arbitrary functions whose nature must be discovered in order to compare the results given by the equation to those given by direct experience, and to laws that are deduced from experience. Unfortunately, in researches on heat, direct experiments are rarely applicable to simple phenomena. Ordinarily, they involve complex questions that depend on several laws at once, and usually it is difficult to pick out the part which relates to each of these. The experimenter should then seek to modify the circumstances under which he works in such a way as to vary as far as possible in his isolated experiments the part relating to each of the elementary phenomena and the law connected with it. He will thus obtain condition equations that can be of great help in the discovery of the general theory, for the latter, whatever it may be, must always agree with these equations.

It is from this point of view that I have carried out my researches, and I always endeavor to define the conditions under which I work in the most precise way, so that one can always draw conclusions from my experiments no matter what the theory was to which they seemed to lead.

In 1847, I published the first part of my investigations; they formed Volume 21 of the *Memoirs* of the Academy. Since that time I have never stopped pursuing them. But the experimental observations they demanded were so numerous and the numerical calculations so long and laborious that it would have been impossible to carry them out if they had been left to my individual efforts. I have been greatly helped by M. Izarn, who had already been associated with the first part of my work, as well as by a young mining engineer, M. Descos, whom the Minister of Public Works has kindly allowed to join me during the past two years in order to facilitate the conclusion of my labors. I here take occasion to express to them publicly my appreciation of the indefatigable zeal with which they have assisted me. The subjects of my new experiments are the following:

1. The relations existing between temperature and elastic forces of a large number of saturated vapors, over a range from the weakest elastic force up to 12 atmospheres.

2. The elastic forces of the same saturated vapors and also when they are in purely gaseous form.

3. The elastic forces at saturation of vapors produced from liquid mixtures.

4. The latent heat of these vapors under various pressures from the lowest up to from 8 to 10 atmospheres.

5. The latent heat of vaporization of these same substances in the gaseous state.

6. The specific heats of permanent gases and of vapors under different pressures.

7. The quantities of heat absorbed or emitted by the compression and dilatation of gases, whether the dilatation takes place in a space whose volume increases, or whether it takes place by passing through a capillary opening in a thin wall or through a long capillary tube.

8. The quantities of heat absorbed by a gas when during its expansion it does mechanical work that is entirely dissipated in the interior of the calorimeter or of which the greater part is utilized outside.

9. Finally, the densities of saturated vapors under various pressures.

The experiments which relate to these different questions, with the exception of the last, are nearly completed. But since it will still take me a good deal of time to put these in order and to discuss them with the care they deserve, I propose to present the general results from time to time to the Academy, hoping ultimately to publish them in their entirety.

I shall communicate today the results of my researches on the heat capacity of elastic fluids.

[*Ed. Note:* The remainder of this paper contains a critical account of earlier work on the specific heats of gases by such people as Gay-Lussac, Lavoisier and Laplace, Dalton, Clement and Desormes, De-Laroche and Berard, and Dulong, most of which Regnault considers was erroneous. He then gives in tabular form the numerical values he himself obtained for the specific heats at constant pressure of the "permanent" gases like oxygen, hydrogen, nitrogen, etc., as well as values for many compound gases like ammonia, ether, etc.

From the historic point of view as regards the mechanical theory of heat and the concept of energy, Regnault's most significant result was his re-measurements of the specific heat at constant pressure of air between −30 and 225°C, for which he found the value 0.238 calories per gram °C in place of the previously accepted value of DeLaroche and Berard, 0.267 calories per gram °C. This was the value Mayer used in his theoretical calculation of the mechanical equivalent of heat J in 1842, thus obtaining a value of J somewhat lower than Joule later measured. If Regnault's more correct value of the specific heat had been available to Mayer, he would have calculated a value of J in practically complete agreement with Joule's best experimental value.]

8

Reprinted from *Mathematical and Physical Papers of William Thomson*, Vol. 1, Cambridge University Press, London, 1882, pp. 333–356

ART. XLIX.   On the Thermal Effects of Fluids in Motion.

By J. P. Joule and W. Thomson.

PRELIMINARY.

On the Thermal Effects experienced by Air in rushing through small Apertures*.

[*Phil. Mag.* 2nd half year, 1852.]

THE hypothesis that the heat evolved from air compressed and kept at a constant temperature is mechanically equivalent to the work spent in effecting the compression, assumed by Mayer as the foundation for an estimate of the numerical relation between quantities of heat and mechanical work, and adopted by Holtzmann, Clausius, and other writers, was made the subject of an experimental research by Mr Joule†, and verified as at least approximately true for air at ordinary atmospheric temperatures. A theoretical investigation, founded on a conclusion of Carnot's‡, which requires no modification§ in the dynamical theory of heat, also leads to a verification of Mayer's hypothesis within limits of accuracy as close as those which can be attributed to Mr Joule's experimental tests.   But the same investigation establishes the conclusion, that that hypothesis cannot be rigorously true except for one definite temperature within the range of Regnault's experiments on the pressure and latent heat of saturated aqueous vapour, unless the density of the vapour both differs considerably at the temperature 100° Cent. from what it is usually supposed to be, and for other temperatures and pressures presents great discrepancies from the gaseous laws.   No experiments, however,

---

* Communicated by the Authors; having been read to the British Association at Belfast, Sept. 3, 1852.

† *Phil. Mag.* May 1845, p. 375, "On the Changes of Temperature produced by the Rarefaction and Condensation of Air."

‡ *Transactions of the Royal Society of Edinburgh* (April, 1849), Vol. xvi. part 5, "Appendix to Account of Carnot's Theory," §§ 46—51.

§ *Trans. Royal Soc. Edinb.* (March, 1851), Vol. xx. part 2, or *Phil. Mag.* Aug. 1852, "On the Dynamical Theory of Heat," § 30.

which have yet been published on the density of saturated aqueous vapour are of sufficient accuracy to admit of an unconditional statement of the indications of theory regarding the truth of Mayer's hypothesis, which cannot therefore be considered to have been hitherto sufficiently tested either experimentally or theoretically. The experiments described in the present communication were commenced by the authors jointly in Manchester last May. The results which have been already obtained, although they appear to establish beyond doubt a very considerable discrepancy from Mayer's hypothesis for temperatures from 40° to 170° Fahr., are far from satisfactory; but as the authors are convinced that, without apparatus on a much larger scale, and a much more ample source of mechanical work than has hitherto been available to them, they could not get as complete and accurate results as are to be desired, they think it right at present to publish an account of the progress they have made in the inquiry.

The following brief statement of the proposed method, and the principles on which it is founded, is drawn from §§ 77, 78 of Part IV. of the series of articles on the Dynamical Theory of Heat [Art. XLVIII. above] republished in this Magazine from the *Transactions of the Royal Society of Edinburgh* in 1851* (Vol. XX. part 2, pp. 296, 297).

Let air be forced continuously and as uniformly as possible, by means of a forcing-pump, through a long tube, open to the atmosphere at the far end, and nearly stopped in one place so as to leave, for a short space, only an extremely narrow passage, on each side of which, and in every other part of the tube, the passage is comparatively very wide; and let us suppose, first, that the air in rushing through the narrow passage is not allowed to gain any heat from, nor (if it had any tendency to do so) to part with any to, the surrounding matter. Then, if Mayer's hypothesis were true, the air after leaving the narrow passage would have exactly the same temperature as it had before reaching it. If, on the contrary, the air experiences either a cooling or a heating effect in the circumstances, we may infer that the heat produced by the fluid friction in the rapids, or, which is the same, the thermal equivalent of the work done by the air in expanding from its state of high pressure on one side of the narrow passage to the state of atmospheric pressure which it has after passing the rapids,

* See also "Dynamical Theory of Heat," part 5, *Trans. Roy. Soc. Edinb.* 1852.

is in one case less, and in the other more, than sufficient to compensate the cold due to the expansion; and the hypothesis in question would be disproved.

The apparatus consisted principally of a forcing-pump of $10\frac{1}{2}$ inches stroke and $1\frac{3}{8}$ internal diameter, worked by a hand-lever, and adapted to pump air, through a strong copper vessel* of 136 cubic inches capacity (used for the purpose of equalizing the pressure of the air), into one end of a spiral leaden pipe 24 feet long and $\frac{5}{16}$ths of an inch in diameter, provided with a stop-cock at its other end. The spiral was in all the experiments kept immersed in a large water-bath.

In the first series of experiments, the temperature of the bath was kept as nearly as possible the same as that of the surrounding atmosphere; and the stop-cock, which was kept just above the surface of the water, had a vulcanized india-rubber tube tied to its mouth. The forcing-pump was worked uniformly, and the stop-cock was kept so nearly closed as to sustain a pressure of from two to five atmospheres within the spiral. A thermometer placed in the vulcanized india-rubber tube, with its bulb near the stop-cock, always showed a somewhat lower temperature than another placed in the water-bath†; and it was concluded that the air had experienced a cooling effect in passing through the stop-cock.

To diminish the effects which might be anticipated from the conduction of heat through the solid matter round the narrow passage, a strong vulcanized india-rubber tube, a few inches long, and of considerably less diameter than the former, was tied on the mouth of the stop-cock in place of that one which was removed, and tied over the mouth of the narrower. The stop-cock was now kept wide open, and the narrow passage was obtained by

---

* This and the forcing-pump are parts of the apparatus used by Mr Joule in his original experiments on air. See *Phil. Mag.* May, 1845.

† When the forcing-pump is worked so as to keep up a uniform pressure in the spiral, and the water of the bath is stirred so as to be at a uniform temperature throughout, this temperature will be, with almost perfect accuracy, the temperature of the air as it approaches the stop-cock. It is to be remarked, however, that when, by altering the aperture of the stop-cock, or the rate of working the pump, the pressure within the spiral is altered, even although not very suddenly, the air throughout the spiral, up to the narrow passage, alters in temperature on account of the expansion or condensation which it is experiencing, and there is an immediate corresponding alteration in the temperature of the stream of air flowing from *the rapids*, which produces often a most sensible effect on the thermometer in the issuing stream.

squeezing the double india-rubber tube by means of a pair of wooden pincers applied to compress the inner tube very near its end, through the other surrounding it. The two thermometers were placed, one, as before, in the bath, and the other in the wide india-rubber tube, with its bulb let down so as to be close to the end of the narrower one within. It was still found that, the forcing-pump being worked as before, when the pincers were applied so as to keep up a steady pressure of two atmospheres or more in the spiral, the thermometer placed in the current of air flowing from the narrow passage showed a lower temperature than that of the air in the spiral, as shown by the other. Sometimes the whole of the narrow india-rubber tube, the wooden pincers, and several inches of the wider tube containing the thermometer, were kept below the surface of the bath, and still the cooling effect was observed; and this even when hot water, at a temperature of about 150° F., was used, although in this case the observed cooling effect was less than when the temperature of the bath was lower.

As it was considered possible that the cooling effects observed in these experiments might be due wholly or partly to the air reaching the thermometer-bulb before it had lost all the *vis viva* produced by the expansion in the narrow passage, and consequently before the full equivalent of heat had been produced by the friction, and as some influence (although this might be expected to diminish the cooling effect) must have been produced by the conduction of heat through the solid matter round the air, especially about the narrow passage, an attempt was made to determine the whole thermal effect by means of a calorimetrical apparatus applied externally. For this purpose the india-rubber tubes were removed, and the stop-cock was again had recourse to for producing the narrow passage. A piece of small block-tin tube, about 10 inches long, was attached to the mouth of the stop-cock, and was bent into a spiral, as close round the stop-cock as it could be conveniently arranged. A portion of the block-tin pipe was unbent from the principal spiral, and was bent down so as to allow the stop-cock to be removed from the water-bath, and to be immersed with the exit spiral in a small glass jar filled with water. The forcing-pump was now worked at a uniform rate, with the stop-cock nearly closed, for a quarter of an hour, and then nearly open for a quarter of an hour, and so on for several alternations. The temperatures of the water in the large bath and in the glass jar were observed at frequent stated intervals during these experiments; but, instead of there being any cooling effect discovered when the stop-cock was nearly closed, there was found to be a slight elevation of temperature during every period of the experiments, averaging nominally ·06525° F. for four periods of a quarter of an hour when the stop-cock was nearly closed, and ·06533° when it was wide open, or, within the limits of the accuracy of the observations, ·065° in each case; a rise due, no doubt, to the rising temperature of the surrounding atmosphere during the series of experiments. Hence the results appear at first sight only negative; but it is to be remarked that, the temperature of the bath having been on an average $3\frac{1}{2}$° F. lower than that of the water in the glass jar, the natural rise of temperature in the glass jar must have been somewhat checked by the air coming from the principal spiral; and had there been no cooling effect due to rushing through the stop-cock when it was nearly closed, would have been more checked when the stop-cock was wide open than when it was nearly closed, as the same number of strokes of the pump must have sent considerably more air through the apparatus in one case than in the other. A cooling effect on the whole, due to the rushing through the nearly closed stop-cock, is thus indicated, if not satisfactorily proved.

Other calorimetric experiments were made with the stop-cock immersed in water in one glass jar, and the air from it, conducted by a vulcanized india-rubber tube, to flow through a small spiral of block-tin pipe immersed in a second glass jar of equal capacity; and it was found that the water in the jar round the stop-cock was cooled, while that in the other, containing the exit spiral, was heated, during the working of the pump, with the stop-cock nearly closed, and a pressure of about three atmospheres in the principal spiral. The explanation of this curious result is clearly, that the water round the stop-cock supplied a little heat to the air in the first part of the rapids, where it has been cooled by expansion and has not yet received all the heat of the friction, and that the heat so obtained, along with the heat produced by friction throughout the rapids, raises the temperature of the air a little above what it would have had if no heat had been gained from without; so that about the end of the rapids the air has a temperature a little above that of the surrounding water, and is led, under the protection of the india-rubber tube, to the exit spiral with a slightly elevated temperature. This is what would *necessarily* happen in any case of an arrangement such as that described, if Mayer's hypothesis were strictly true; but then the quantity of heat emitted to the water in the second glass jar, from the air in passing through the exit spiral, would be exactly equal to that taken by conduction through the stop-cock from the water in the first. In reality, according to the discrepancy from Mayer's hypothesis, which the other experiments described in this communication appear to establish, there must have been somewhat more heat taken in by conduction through the stop-cock than was emitted by it in flowing through the exit spiral; but the experiments were not of sufficient accuracy, and were affected by too many disturbing circumstances, to allow this difference to be tested.

To obtain a decisive test of the discrepancy from Mayer's hypothesis, indicated by the experiments which have been described, and to obtain either comparative or absolute determinations of its amount for different temperatures, some alterations in the apparatus, especially with regard to the narrow passage and the thermometer for the temperature of the air flowing from it, were found to be necessary by Mr Joule, who continued the research alone, and made the experiments described in what follows.

A piece of brass piping, a (see the accompanying sketch drawn half the actual size), was soldered to the termination of the leaden spiral, and a bit of calf-skin leather, b, having been tightly bound over its end, it was found that the natural pores of the leather were sufficient to allow of a uniform and conveniently rapid flow of air from the receiver. By protecting the end over which the leather diaphragm was bound with a piece of vulcanized india-rubber tube, c, the former could be immersed to the depth of about two inches in the bath of water. A small thermometer*, having a spherical bulb $\frac{1}{6}$th of an inch in diameter, was placed within the india-rubber tube, the bulb being allowed to rest on the central part of the leather diaphragm†.

* We had two of these thermometers, one of which had Fahrenheit's, the other an arbitrary scale.

† The bulb was kept in this position for convenience sake, but it was ascertained that the effects were not perceptibly diminished when it was raised $\frac{1}{4}$ of an inch above the diaphragm.

In making the experiments, the pump was worked at a uniform rate until the pressure of the air in the spiral and the

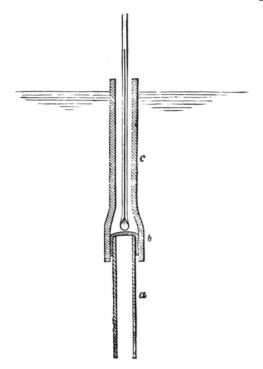

temperature of the thermometer had become sensibly constant. The water of the bath was at the same time constantly stirred, and by various devices kept as uniform as possible during each series of experiments. The temperature of the stream of air having been observed, the same thermometer was immediately plunged into the bath to ascertain its temperature, the difference between the two readings giving of course the cooling effect of the rushing air.

According to theory*, the cooling effect for a given tempera-

* See "Account of Carnot's Theory," Appendix II. [Art. XLI. above], *Trans. Roy. Soc. Edinb.* Jan. 1849, Vol. XVI. p. 566; and "Dynamical Theory," § 75 [Art. XLVIII. above], *Trans. Roy. Soc. Edinb.* April, 1851, Vol. XX. p. 296; or *Phil. Mag.* Dec. 1852. The numbers shown in the table of § 51 of the former paper being used in the formula of § 75 of the latter, and 1390 being used for J, we find (according to the numerical data used formerly for deriving numerical results from the theory) how much heat would have to be added to each pound of the issuing stream of air to bring it back to the temperature it had when approaching the narrow passage; and this number, divided by ·24, the specific heat of air under constant pressure, would be the depression of temperature (in Centigrade degrees) actually experienced by the air when no heat is communicated to it in or after the rapids.

ture would be independent of the kind of aperture and of the copiousness of the stream, and would be simply proportional to the logarithm of the pressure, if the insulation of the current against gain or loss of heat from the surrounding matter were perfect, and if the thermometer be so placed in the issuing stream as to be quite out of the *rapids*. On this account the values of the cooling effect divided by the logarithm of the pressure were calculated, and are shown in the last columns of the tables of results given below. When this was done for the first two series of experiments, the discrepancies (see columns 5 of the first two of the tables given below) were found to be so great, and especially among the results of the different experiments for the higher temperature of 160° F., all made with the pressure and other circumstances as nearly as possible the same, so irregular, that great uncertainty was felt as to the numerical results, which must obviously have been much affected by purely accidental circumstances. At the same time it was noticed, that in the case of Series 1, in which the temperature of the bath was always as nearly as possible that of the atmosphere, and different pressures were used, the discrepancies showed a somewhat regular tendency of the value of the cooling effect divided by the logarithm of the pressure to increase with the pressure; which was probably owing to the circumstance that the stream was more copious, and that less of the cooling effect was lost (as some probably was in every case) by the conduction of heat from without, the higher the pressure under which the air approached the narrow passage. Hence in all the subsequent experiments the quantity of air pumped through per second was noted.

The following Tables show the results obtained from ten series of experiments conducted in the manner described:

Series 1.

Col. 1.	Col. 2.	Col. 3.	Col. 4.	Col. 5*.
Quantity of air pumped in cubic inches per second.	Temperature of bath.	Pressure of air in atmospheres.	Cooling effect.	Cooling effect divided by logarithm of pressure.
A.	T.	P.	D.	$\dfrac{D}{\log P}$.
Not noted.	61°	1·79	0·5°	1·98°
Not noted.	61	2·64	0·9	2·13
Not noted.	61	2·9	0·7	1·51
Not noted.	61	3·22	1·5	2·95
Not noted.	61	3·4	1·4	2·64
Not noted.	61	3·61	1·4	2·51
Not noted.	61	3·61	1·3	2·33
Not noted.	61	3·61	1·4	2·51
Not noted.	61	3·84	1·5	2·57
Not noted.	61	4·11	1·7	2·77
Mean	61	......	......	2·39

Series 2.

Not noted.	160	2·64	0·264	0·62
Not noted.	160	2·64	0·396	0·94
Not noted.	160	2·64	0·66	1·56
Not noted.	160	2·64	0·528	1·25
Not noted.	160	2·64	0·66	1·56
Mean	160	2·64	0·502	1·18

Series 3.

5·6	170·8	3·61	0·396	0·71
5·6	170·8	4·11	0·528	0·86
5·6	170·8	4·11	0·66	1·08
5·6	170·8	4·11	0·726	1·18
5·6	170·8	4·26	0·66	1·05
8·4	170·8	4·78	0·858	1·26
8·4	170·8	4·98	0·858	1·23
Mean 6·4	170·8	4·28	0·67	1·05

Series 4.

5·6	37·8	3·4	0·8	1·51
5·6	38·8	3·4	1·1	2·07
5·6	37·9	3·61	0·6	1·08
5·6	44·4	3·04	1·1	2·28
5·6	45·3	3·04	0·9	1·86
5·6	46·3	3·04	1·0	2·07
Mean 5·6	41·75	......	......	1·81

* The true value of $\dfrac{D}{\log P}$ for any particular temperature would be the depression of temperature that would be experienced by air approaching the narrow passage at that temperature and under ten atmospheres of pressure, since P is measured in atmospheres, and the *common* logarithm is taken.

Table (*continued*).

Series 5.

Col. 1.	Col. 2.	Col. 3.	Col. 4.	Col. 5.
Quantity of air pumped in cubic inches per second.	Temperature of bath.	Pressure of air in atmospheres.	Cooling effect.	Cooling effect divided by logarithm of pressure.
A.	T.	P.	D.	$\dfrac{D}{\log P}$.
8·4	46·8	3·84	1·2	2·06
8·4	38·7	4·11	1·8	2·93
8·4	39·3	4·11	1·8	2·93
Mean 8·4	41·6	......	......	2·64

Series 6.

11·2	39·7	4·4	1·7	2·64
11·2	40·9	4·4	1·9	2·95
11·2	41·9	4·4	1·5	2·33
11·2	43	4·4	1·5	2·33
Mean 11·2	41·38	4·4	1·65	2·56

Series 7.

1·4	64·1	1·9	0·3	1·08
1·4	64·2	1·87	0·45	1·65
1·4	64·0	1·9	0·4	1·43
1·4	64·2	1·9	0·5	1·79
1·4	64·3	1·9	0·45	1·61
Mean 1·4	64·16	1·894	0·42	1·51

Series 8.

2·8	64·2	2·41	0·5	1·31
2·8	64·3	2·41	0·5	1·31
2·8	64·5	2·41	0·5	1·31
2·8	64·7	2·41	0·7	1·83
2·8	64·7	2·41	0·6	1·57
Mean 2·8	64·48	2·41	0·56	1·46

Series 9.

5·6	64·6	2·9	0·8	1·73
5·6	64·7	2·9	0·8	1·73
5·6	64·8	3·04	0·8	1·66
5·6	65·0	2·97	0·7	1·48
Mean 5·6	64·775	......	......	1·65

Series 10.

11·2	65·	4·11	1·2	1·95
11·2	65·1	4·11	1·3	2·12
11·2	65·1	4·11	1·4	2·28
Mean 11·2	65·06	4·11	1·3	2·12

The numbers in the last column of any one of these tables show, by their discrepancies, how much uncertainty there must be in the results on account of purely accidental circumstances.

The following table is arranged, with double argument of temperature and of quantity of air passing per second, to show a comparison of the means of the different series (Series 3 being divided into two, one consisting of the first five experiments, and the other of the remaining two).

Table of Mean Values of $\dfrac{D}{\log P}$ in different Series of Experiments.

		Quantity of air passing per second.				
		1·4	2·8	5·6	8·4	11·2
Temperature of bath.	41½	......	......	1·81	2·64	2·56
	64½	1·51	1·46	1·65	......	2·12
	171	......	......	·98	1·25	......

The general increase of the numbers from left to right in this table shows that very much of the cooling effect must be lost on account of the insufficiency of the current of air. This loss might possibly be diminished by improving the thermal insulation of the current in and after the rapids; but it appears probable that it could be reduced sufficiently to admit of satisfactory observations being made, only by using a much more copious current of air than could be obtained with the apparatus hitherto employed.

The decrease of the numbers from the upper to the lower spaces, especially in the one complete vertical column (that under the argument 5·6), shows that the cooling effect is less to a remarkable degree for the higher than for the lower temperatures. Even from 41° to 65° F. the diminution is most sensible; and at 171° the cooling effect appears to be only about half as much as at 41°.

The best results for the different temperatures are probably those shown under the arguments 8·4 and 11·2, being those obtained from the most copious currents; but it is probable that they all fall considerably short of the true values of $\dfrac{D}{\log P}$ for the actual temperatures; and we may consider it as perfectly established by the experiments described above, that *there is a final cooling effect produced by air rushing through a small aperture at any temperature up to* 170° F., and that *the amount of this cooling effect decreases as the temperature is augmented.* Now according to the theoretical views on this subject brought forward in the papers on "Carnot's Theory" [Art. XLI. above], and "On the Dynamical Theory of Heat" [Art. XLVIII. above], already referred to, a cooling effect was expected for low temperatures; and the amount of this effect was expected to be the *less* the *higher* the temperature; expectations which have therefore been perfectly confirmed by experiment. But since the excess of the heat of compression above the thermal equivalent of the work was, in the theoretical investigation, found to diminish to zero* as the temperature is raised to about 33° Cent., or 92° Fahr., and to be negative for all higher temperatures, a *heating* instead of a *cooling* effect would be found for such a temperature as 171° F., if the data regarding saturated steam used in obtaining numerical results from the theory were correct. All of these data except the *density* had been obtained from Regnault's very exact experimental determinations; and we may consequently consider it as nearly certain, that the true values of the density of saturated aqueous vapour differ considerably from those which were assumed. Thus, if the error is to be accounted for by the *density* alone, the fact of there being any cooling effect in the air experiments at 171° Fahr. (77° Cent.) shows that the density of saturated aqueous vapour at that temperature must be greater than it was assumed to be in the ratio of something more than 1416 to 1390, or must be more than 1·019 of what it was assumed to be : and, since the experiments render it almost if not absolutely certain, that even at 100° Cent. air rushing through a small aperture would produce a final cooling effect, it is probable that the density of steam at the ordinary boiling-point, instead of being about $\frac{1}{1693\cdot5}$, as it is generally supposed to be, must be something more than $\frac{1430\cdot6}{1390}$ of this; that is, must exceed $\frac{1}{1645}$.

With a view to ascertain what effect would be produced in the case of the air rushing violently against the thermometer-bulb, the leather diaphragm was now perforated with a fine needle, and

---

* See the table in § 51 of the "Account of Carnot's Theory" [Art. XLI. above], from which it appears that the element tabulated would have the value 1390, or that of the mechanical equivalent of the thermal unit, at about 33° Cent.

the bulb placed on the orifice so as to cause the air to rush between the leather and the sides of the bulb. With this arrangement the following results were obtained:—

Series 11.

A.	T.	P.	D.	$\frac{\log P}{D}$.
11·2	64°	3·22	3·5°	6·90°
11·2	64	3·31	3·5	6·73
11·2	64	3·61	3·8	6·82
11·2	64	2·30	4·0	11·05
11·2	64	3·31	6·1	11·73
11·2	64	2·58	4·7	11·41
11·2	64	4·78	5·3	7·80
11·2	64	1·9	4·0	14·34
Mean 11·2	64	......	......	9·60

The great irregularities in the last column of the above table are owing to the difficulty of keeping the bulb of the thermometer in exactly the same place over the orifice. The least variation would occasion an immediate and considerable change of temperature; and when the bulb was removed to only $\frac{1}{4}$ of an inch above the orifice, the cooling effects were reduced to the amount observed when the natural pores alone of the leather were employed. There can be no doubt but that the reason why the cooling effects experienced by the thermometer-bulb were greater in these experiments than in the former is, that in these it was exposed to the current of air in localities in which a sensible portion of the mechanical effect of the work done by the expansion had not been converted into heat by friction, but still existed in the form of *vis viva* of fluid motion. Hence this series of experiments confirms the theoretical anticipations formerly published* regarding the condition of the air in *the rapids* caused by flowing through a small aperture.

---

* See "Dynamical Theory," § 77 [Art. XLVIII. above], *Trans. Royal Soc. Edinb.* April, 1851; or *Phil. Mag.* Dec. 1852.

[From *Transactions of the Royal Society*, June, 1853.]

PART I.

IN a paper communicated to the Royal Society, June 20, 1844, "On the Changes of Temperature produced by the Rarefaction and Condensation of Air*," Mr Joule pointed out the dynamical cause of the principal phenomena, and described the experiments upon which his conclusions were founded. Subsequently Professor Thomson pointed out that the accordance discovered in that investigation between the work spent and the mechanical equivalent of the heat evolved in the compression of air may be only approximate, and in a paper communicated to the Royal Society of Edinburgh in April, 1851, "On a Method of discovering experimentally the relation between the Mechanical Work spent, and the Heat produced by the compression of a Gaseous Fluid†" [Art. XLVIII. above, §§ 61—80], proposed the method of experimenting adopted in the present investigation, by means of which we have already arrived at partial results‡. This method consists in forcing the compressed elastic fluid through a mass of porous non-conducting material, and observing the consequent change of temperature in the elastic fluid. The porous plug was adopted instead of a single orifice, in order that the work done by the expanding fluid may be immediately spent in friction, without any appreciable portion of it being even temporarily employed to generate ordinary *vis viva*, or being devoted to produce sound. The non-conducting material was chosen to diminish as much as possible all loss of thermal effect by conduction, either from the air on one side to the air on the other side of the plug, or between the plug and the surrounding matter.

A principal object of the researches is to determine the value of μ, Carnot's function. If the gas fulfilled perfectly the laws of compression and expansion ordinarly assumed, we should have§

$$\frac{1}{\mu} = \frac{1/E + t}{J} + \frac{K\delta}{Ep_0u_0 \log P},$$

---

* *Philosophical Magazine*, May, 1845, p. 369.

† *Transactions of the Royal Society, Edinburgh*, April 21, 1851.

‡ *Philosophical Magazine*, Dec. 1852, p. 481.

§ Dynamical Theory of Heat, (equation 7), § 80 [Art. XLVIII. above], *Transactions of the Royal Society of Edinburgh*, April 21, 1851.

where J is the mechanical equivalent of the thermal unit; p_0u_0 the product of the pressure in pounds on the square foot into the volume in cubic feet of a pound of the gas at $0°$ Cent.; P is the ratio of the pressure on the high pressure side to that on the other side of the plug; δ is the observed cooling effect; t the temperature Cent. of the bath, and K the thermal capacity of a pound of the gas under constant pressure equal to that on the low pressure side of the gas. To establish this equation it is only necessary to remark that $K\delta$ is the heat that would have to be added to each pound of the exit stream of air, to bring it to the temperature of the bath, and is the same (according to the general principle of mechanical energy) as would have to be added to it in passing through the plug, to make it leave the plug with its temperature unaltered. We have therefore $K\delta = -H$, in terms of the notation used in the passage referred to.

On the above hypothesis (that the gas fulfils the laws of compression and expansion ordinarily assumed) $\delta/\log P$ would be the same for all values of P; but Regnault has shown that the hypothesis is not rigorously true for atmospheric air, and our experiments show that $\delta/\log P$ increases with P. Hence, in reducing the experiments, a correction must be first applied to take into account the deviations, as far as they are known, of the fluid used, from the gaseous laws, and then the value of μ may be determined. The formula by which this is to be done is the following (Dynamical Theory of Heat [Art. XLVIII. above], equation (f), § 74, or equation (17), § 95, and (8), § 88)—

$$\frac{1}{\mu} = \frac{\frac{1}{J}\{w - (p'u' - pu)\} + K\delta}{\frac{dw}{dt}},$$

where $$w = \int_u^{u'} pdv,$$

u and u' denoting the volumes of a pound of the gas at the high pressure and low pressure respectively, and at the same temperature (that of the bath), and v the volume of a pound of it at that temperature, when at any intermediate pressure p. An expression for w for any temperature may be derived from an empirical formula for the compressibility of air at that temperature, and between the limits of pressure in the experiment.

The apparatus, which we have been enabled to provide by the assistance of a grant from the Royal Society, consists mainly of a pump, by which air may be forced into a series of tubes acting at at once as a receiver of the elastic fluid, and as a means of communicating to it any required temperature ; nozzles, and plugs of porous material being employed to discharge the air against the bulb of a thermometer.

The pump *a*, fig. 1, consists of a cast-iron cylinder of 6 inches internal diameter, in which a piston, fig. 2, fitted with spiral

Fig. 1.

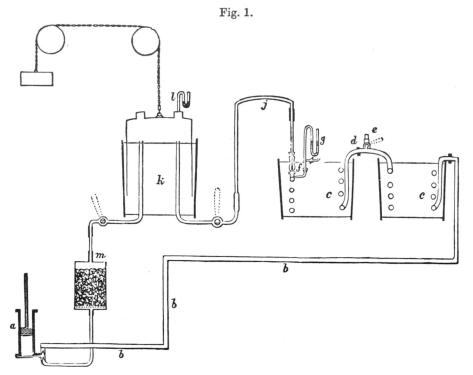

metallic packing (of antifriction metal), works by the direct action of the beam of a steam-engine through a stroke of 22 inches. The pump is single-acting, the air entering at the base of the cylinder during the up-stroke, and being expelled thence into the receiving tubes by the down-stroke. The governor of the steam-engine limits the number of complete strokes of the pump to 27 per minute. The valves, fig. 3, consist of loose spheres of brass 0·6 of an inch in diameter, which fall by their own gravity over orifices 0·45 of an inch diameter. The cylinder and valves in connection with it are immersed in water to prevent the wear and tear which might arise from a variable or too elevated temperature.

Wrought-iron tubing, *bb*, fig. 1, of 2 inches internal diameter, conducts the compressed air horizontally a distance of 6 feet, thence vertically to an elevation of 18 feet, where another length of 23 feet conveys it to the copper tubing, cc; the junction being

Fig. 3.

Fig. 2.

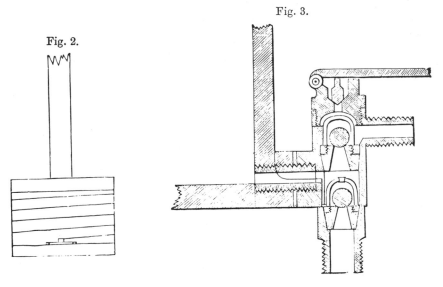

effected by means of a coupling-joint. The copper tubing, which is of 2 inches internal diameter and 74 feet in length, is arranged in two coils, each being immersed in a wooden vessel of 4 feet

Fig. 4.

diameter, from the bottom and sides of which it is kept at a distance of 6 inches. The coils are connected by means of a coupling-joint d, near which a stop-cock, e, is placed, in order to let a portion of air escape when it is wanted to reduce the pressure. The terminal coil has a flange, f, to which any required nozzle may be attached by means of screw-bolts. Near the flange, a small pipe, g, is screwed, at the termination of which a calibrated glass tube bent (as shown in fig. 4), and partly filled with mercury, is tightly secured. A

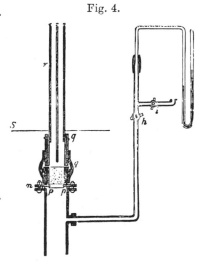

stop-cock at h, and another in a small branch pipe at i, permit the air at any time to be let off, so as to examine the state of the gauge when uninfluenced by any except atmospheric pressure. The branch pipe is also employed in collecting a small portion of air for chemical analysis during each experiment. A pipe, j, is so suspended, that by means of india-rubber junctions, a communication can readily be made to convey the air issuing from the nozzle into the gas-meter, k, which has a capacity of 40 cubic feet, and is carefully graduated by calibration. A bent glass tube, l, inserted in the top of the meter, and containing a little water, indicates the slight difference which sometimes exists between the pressure of air in the meter and that of the external atmosphere. When required, a wrought-iron pipe, m, 1 inch in diameter, is used to convey the elastic fluid from the meter to the desiccating apparatus, and thence to the pump so as to circulate through the entire apparatus.

We have already pointed out the different thermal effects to be anticipated from the rushing of air from a single narrow orifice. They are *cold*, on the one hand, from the expenditure of heat in labouring force to communicate rapid motion to the air by means of expansion; and *heat*, on the other, in consequence of the *vis viva* of the rushing air being reconverted into heat. The two opposite effects nearly neutralize each other at 2 or 3 inches distance from the orifice, leaving however a slight preponderance of cooling effect; but close to the orifice the variations of temperature are excessive, as will be made manifest by the following experiments.

A thin plate of copper, having a hole of $\frac{1}{20}$th of an inch diameter, drilled in the centre, was bolted to the flange, an india-rubber washer making the joint air-tight. At the ordinary velocity of the pump the orifice was sufficient to discharge the whole quantity of air when its pressure arrived at 124 lbs. on the square inch. When however lower pressures were tried, the stop-cock e was kept partially open. The thermometer used was one with a spherical bulb 0·15 of an inch in diameter. Holding it as close to the orifice as possible without touching the metal, the following observations were made at various pressures, the temperature of the water in which the coils were immersed being 22° Cent. The air was dried and deprived of carbonic acid by passing it, previous to entering the pump, through a vessel $4\frac{1}{2}$ feet long and 20 inches diameter, filled with quick-lime.

Total pressure of the air in lbs. on the square inch.	Temperature Centigrade.	Depression below temperature of bath.
124	8·58	13·42
72	11·65	10·35
31	16·25	5·75

The heating effect was exhibited as follows :—The bulb of the thermometer was inserted into a piece of conical gutta percha pipe in such a manner that an extremely narrow passage was allowed between the interior surface of the pipe and the bulb. Thus armed, the thermometer was held, as represented by fig. 5, at half an inch distance from the orifice, when the following results were obtained :—

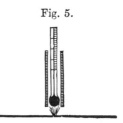

Fig. 5.

Total pressure of the air in lbs. on the square inch.	Temperature Centigrade.	Elevation above temperature of bath.
124	45°·75	23°·75
71	39·23	17·23
31	26·2	4·20

It must be remarked, that the above recorded thermal effects are not to be taken as representing the maximum results to be derived from the rushing air at the pressures named. The determination of these, in the form of experiment above given, is prevented by several circumstances. In particular it must be observed, that the cooling effects must have been reduced in consequence of the heat evolved by the friction of the rushing air against the bulb of the thermometer. The heating effects, resulting as they do from the absorption and conversion into heat of the *vis viva* of the rushing air, depend very much upon the narrowness of the space between the thermometer and gutta percha pipe. We intend further on to return to this subject, but in the mean time will mention three forms of experiment whereby the heating effect is very strikingly and instructively exhibited.

Experiment 1.—The finger and thumb are brought over the orifice, as represented in fig. 6, so that by gradually closing them the stream of air is pinched. It is found that the effort to close the finger and thumb is opposed by considerable force, which increases with the pressure applied. At the same time a strong tremulous motion is felt and a shrill noise is heard, whilst the heat produced in five or six seconds necessitates the termination of the experiment.

Fig. 6.

Experiment 2.—Fig. 7. The finger is placed over the orifice and pressed until a thin stratum of air escapes between the copper-plate and the finger. In this case the burning heat of the rushing air is equally remarkable in spite of the proximity of the finger to the cold metal.

Fig. 7.

Experiment 3.—Fig. 8. A piece of thick india-rubber is pressed by the finger over the narrow orifice so as to allow a thin stream of air to rush between the india-rubber and the plate of copper. In this case the india-rubber is speedily raised to a temperature which prevents its being handled comfortably.

Fig. 8.

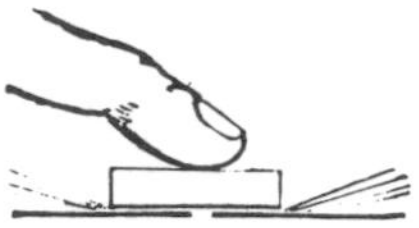

We have now adduced enough to illustrate the immense and sudden changes of temperature which exist in the "rapids" of a current of air, changes which point out the necessity of employing a porous plug, in order that when the air arrives at the thermometer its state may be reduced to a uniform condition.

Fig. 9.

Figs. 4 and 9 represent our first arrangement for the porous plug, where n is a brass casting with flange to bolt to the copper tube. It has eight studs, o, and eight holes, pp, drilled into the inner part of the flange. The studs and holes furnish the means of securing the porous material (in the present instance of cotton wool) in its place, by binding it down tightly with twine. Immediate contact between the cotton and metal is prevented by the insertion of a piece of india-rubber tubing; qqq are three pieces of india-rubber tube inserted within each other, the inner one communicating with a glass tube r, through which the divisions of the thermometer may be seen, and which serves to convey the air to the meter. In the experiments about to be given, the thermometer was in immediate contact with the cotton plug as represented in the figure, and the nozzle was immersed in the bath up to the line s. The weight of the cotton wool in the dry state was 251 grs., its specific gravity 1·404, and being compressed into a space 1½ inch in diameter and 1·9 inch long, the opening left for the passage of air must have been equal in volume to a pipe of 1·33 of an inch diameter.

142

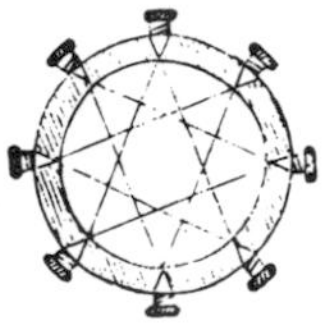

First series of experiments.   Atmospheric air dried and deprived of carbonic acid by quick-lime.   Gauge 73·6 ; barom.
30·04 = 14·695 lbs. pressure per square inch.

Gauge.	Total pressure in lbs. per square inch.	Cubic inches of air passed per minute reduced to atmospheric pressure.	Temperature of bath * ascertained by Thermometer No. 1, in Centigrade degrees.	Temperature of the issuing air, ascertained by Thermometer No. 2.	Cooling effect.
37·5 37·5 38 37·8 $\Big\}$ 37·7	35·854	12703	445 445·5 445·9 446 $\Big\}$ 445·6 $= 18°2676$	414 414 414·6 414·8 $\Big\}$ 414·35 $= 17°8298$	0·4378
38 38 37·8 38 $\Big\}$ 37·9	35·647	12703	446·1 446·6 446·8 447·1 $\Big\}$ 446·65 $= 18·3128$	415·4 416 416·8 417·6 $\Big\}$ 416·45 $= 17·9295$	0·3833
38 37·75 37·5 37·5 $\Big\}$ 37·69	35·866	12703	447·2 447·5 447·8 448 $\Big\}$ 447·62 $= 18·3545$	418 418·2 418·4 418 $\Big\}$ 418·15 $= 18·0110$	0·3435

A Liebig tube containing sulphuric acid, specific gravity 1·8,
gained 0·03 of a grain by passing through it, during the experiment, 100 cubic inches of air.

The observations above tabulated were made at intervals of
two or three minutes.   It will be observed that the cooling effect
appeared to be greater at the commencement than at the termination of the series.   This may be attributed in a great measure
to the drying of the cotton, which was found to contain at least
5 per cent. of moisture after exposure to the atmosphere.   There was
also another source of interference with the accuracy of the results
owing to a considerable oscillation of pressure arising from the action
of the pump.   We had remarked that when the number of strokes
of the engine was suddenly reduced from twenty-seven to twenty-
five per minute, a depression of the thermometer equal to some
hundredths of a degree Cent. took place, a circumstance evidently
owing to the entire mass of air in the coils and cotton plugs
suffering dilatation without allowing time for the escape of the
consequent thermal effect.   Hence it was found absolutely essential

---

* By varying the temperature of the water in which the coils were immersed, it
was found that the temperature of the water surrounding the first coil exercised no
perceptible influence, the temperature of the rushing air being entirely regulated by
that of the terminal coil.   However, the precaution was taken of keeping both coils
at nearly the same temperature.

to keep the pump working at a perfectly uniform rate. For a similar reason it was also most important to prevent the oscillations of pressure due to the action of the pump, particularly as it appeared obvious that the heat evolved by the sudden increase of pressure, on the admission of a fresh supply of air from the pump, would arrive at the thermometer in a larger proportion than the cold produced by the subsequent gradual dilatation. In fact, on making an experiment in which the air was kept at a low pressure, by opening a stop-cock provided for the purpose, the oscillations of pressure amounting to $\frac{1}{20}$th of the whole, it was found that an apparent heating effect, equal to $0°\cdot2$ Cent., was produced instead of a small cooling effect.

It became therefore necessary to obviate the above source of error, and the method first employed with that view, was to place a diaphragm of copper with a hole in its centre $\frac{1}{4}$th of an inch in diameter at the junction between the iron and copper pipes. The oscillation being thus reduced, so as to be hardly perceptible, we made the following observations.

Second series of experiments. Atmospheric air dried and deprived of carbonic acid by quick-lime. Gauge $73\cdot75$; barometer $30\cdot162 = 14\cdot755$ lbs. pressure per square inch; thermometer $19°\cdot3$ Cent.

Gauge.	Total pressure in lbs. per square inch.	Cubic inches of air issuing per minute at atmospheric pressure.	Temperature of bath by Thermometer No. 1, degrees Centigrade.	Temperature of issuing air by Thermometer No. 2, degrees Centigrade.	Cooling effect.
39 38·6 38·5 }38·65 38·5	36·069	11796	467 467 467 }167·02 = 19·186 467·1	434·6 435 435 }434·9 = 18·810 435	0·377
38·5 38·8 38·8 }38·79 38·75	35·912	11796	467·1 467·2 467·2 }467·2 = 19·194 467·3	435·1 435·4 435·6 }435·37 = 18·832 435·4	0·362
38·8 38·8 38·8 }38·8 38·8	35·900	11796	467·3 467·4 467·4 }467·37 = 19·202 467·4	435·6 435·8 435·9 }435·82 = 18·854 436	0·348

Suspecting that particles of the sperm oil employed for lubricating the pump were carried mechanically to the cotton plug and interfered with the results, we now substituted a box with

144

perforated caps, filled with cotton wool, for the diaphragm used in the last series. With this arrangement the pressure was kept as uniform as with the other, and all solid and liquid particles were kept back by filtration.

Third series of experiments. Atmospheric air dried and deprived of carbonic acid by quick-lime*, and filtered through cotton. Gauge 73·7; thermometer 21°·7 Cent.; barometer 30·10 = 14·71 lbs. on the square inch.

Time of observation.	Gauge.	Total pressure in lbs. per square inch.	Cubic inches of air issuing per minute at atmospheric pressure.	Temperature of bath by Thermometer No. 1, in degrees Centigrade.	Temperature of the issuing air by Thermometer No. 2, in degrees Centigrade.	Cooling effect.
m 3	39			357·7	337·3?	
6	39·1			357·8	337·8	
9	39·5	39·2	34·410	11784	358	357·92 = 14·506	338	337·89 = 14·183	0·323
12	39·2			358·2	338·4	
15	39·1			358·7	333·8	
16	39·35			358·9	338·7	
18	39·1	39·19	34·418	11784	359·1	358·97 = 14·552	339	338·85 = 14·230	0·322
21	39·2			359·2	338·9	
23	39·2			359·4	339·25	
25	39·1			359·7	339·8	
28	39·2	39·18	34·426	11784	359·8	359·72 = 14·584	339·7	339·69 = 14·270	0·314
30	39·2			360	340	
32	39·5			360·1	340	
34	39·3			360·2	340·2	
36	39·25	39·34	34·279	11784	360·4	360·27 = 14·607	340·4	340·25 = 14·296	0·311
38	39·3			360·4	340·4	

The stop-cock for reducing pressure being now partially opened, the observations were continued as follows :—

* The use of quick-lime as a desiccating agent was suggested to us by Mr Thomas Ransome. It answered its purpose admirably after it had fallen a little by use, so as to be finely subdivided. The perfection of its action was shown by the desiccating cylinder remaining, after having been used two hours, cold at the lower part, while the upper part for about 9 inches was made very hot. The analysis of the air passed during the third series of experiments showed that one of the Liebig tubes had gained no weight whatever; and in one instance we have observed that the sulphuric acid of 1·8 specific gravity, actually lost weight, apparently indicating that the air dried by quick-lime was able to remove water from acid of that density.

Time of observation.	Gauge.	Total pressure in lbs. per square inch.	Temperature of bath by Thermometer No. 1, in degrees Centigrade.	Temperature of the issuing air by Thermometer No. 2, in degrees Centigrade.	Cooling effect.
h m					
50	55·1		361·7	344·	
52	55·1		361·9	344·8	
54	55·1		361·9	345·3	
55	55·1		361·9	345·8	
57	55·1		362·1	346·0	
59	55·1	55·12 / 22·876	362·3 / 362·26 = 14·693	346·4 / 346·19 = 14·579	0·114
1 1	55·1		362·4	346·9	
3	55·1		362·7	347·2	
5	55·1		362·7	347·6	
7	55·3		363	347·9	
11	54·3		363·3	348·9	
13	54·4		363·3	348·9	
15	54·4		363·5	349·2	
17	54·7		363·7	349·4	
19	54·5	54·51 / 23·217	363·9 / 363·82 = 14·760	350· / 349·74 = 14·749	0·011
20	54·5		364·1	350·	
22	54·6		364·2	350·3	
24	54·6		364·2	350·4	
26	54·6		364·2	350·6	
30	54·6		375·	356·4	
32	54·6		375·4	358·2	
33	54·2		375·4	359·4	
35	54·3		375·5	359·8	
37	54·4		375·8	360·	
39	54·6	54·38 / 23·277	375·7 / 375·7 = 15·270	360·1 / 360 = 15·238	0·032
40	54·3		375·8	360·3	
42	54·5		376·	360·4	

During the above experiment 100 cubic inches of the air was slowly passed through two Liebig tubes containing sulphuric acid, specific gravity 1·8. The first tube gained 0·006 of a grain, the second remained at exactly the same weight.

P.S.   Oct. 14, 1853.—The apparently anomalous results contained in the last Table have been fully explained, and shown to depend on the alteration of pressure which took place towards the beginning of the interval of time from 42m to 50m, by subsequent researches which we hope soon to lay before the Royal Society.

Part III

ENERGY IN COSMICAL PHYSICS

Editor's Comments
on Papers 9 Through 11

One outstanding physical problem of the nineteenth century was the origin and maintenance of the sun's heat. The importance of this heat for life and all other activities on earth was early recognized, although the time during which the solar system had been in existence with the sun at its center was the subject of much controversy during this period. It was clear, at any rate, that the source of the sun's heat could hardly be normal chemical combination as it prevails on earth, for even with the smallest reasonable estimated time for the sun's existence it would on this basis long since have burned itself out. This stimulated the search for alternative theories of the origin and maintenance of this heat to provide a longer life span. The problem took a more promising turn with the development of the mechanical theory of heat and the generalization of the concept of energy.

Julius Robert Mayer, whose early papers on the mechanical theory of heat are reprinted in Lindsay, *Energy: Concept* (Papers 29A and 29B), felt that he had the answer to the problem. In 1848 he published in Heilbronn the paper "Beiträge zur Dynamik des Himmels in populärer Darstellung." This was most recently reprinted in English translation with the title "Celestial Dynamics" in *Julius Robert Mayer—Prophet of Energy*, by R. Bruce Lindsay (Pergamon Press, Inc., Elmsford, N.Y., 1973, pp. 148–196). We reprint here as Paper 9 the first part of this essay. In this paper Mayer reviews the whole problem of the sun's heat, giving the numerical values of the emission as they were available in his day. The units strike us as a bit bizarre, but it is clear that he had an adequate grasp of the facts. Mayer easily showed that chemical combustion is wholly inadequate to account for the maintenance of the solar heat. He then turned to the hypothesis that meteors falling from outer space into the sun are a possible source. Astronomical evidence convinced him that such bodies exist as cosmic debris in enormous numbers within the confines of the solar system. Each meteor (called in the translation inaccurately, in terms of modern terminology, an asteroid) in falling into the sun, either directly or through a curved path that draws ever nearer the sun's surface, ultimately changes its mechanical energy into heat. Mayer was able to calculate the amount of meteoric material that by falling into the sun could maintain the sun's heat, and found that this was not difficult to account for in terms of the astronomical evidence. The resulting increase in the mass of the sun would seem to have provided a critical problem, since astronomers were reluctant to consider any appreciable increase of this kind because of its ultimate effect on the motion of the earth and other planets. Mayer was aware of this but felt he could still guarantee constancy of the solar mass by assuming that what the sun gained from the meteors it would lose through radiation. This may well have been the first time before Einstein that mass was associated with radiant energy.

Although Mayer had earlier sent a paper containing an abbreviated version of his solar heat theory to the Paris Academy, its receipt was never acknowledged. It is not surprising that his idea received scant attention in European scientific circles. It had evidently not come to the attention of William Thomson (Lord Kelvin) when in 1854 he presented to the Royal Society of Edinburgh his own version of the meteoric theory, which at first he put forward with enthusiasm. This communication was printed in the *Transactions* of the society in April, 1854, (Paper 10). Kelvin's presentation followed Mayer's ideas very closely. He did include some interesting tabular material on the mechanical energy of objects revolving around the sun. We reprint here that portion of the original containing the main features of the author's support of the meteoric hypothesis. The remainder of the paper consists of appendixes added at later times. They reflect Kelvin's second thoughts on the whole problem. By 1871 he had completely abandoned what he then refers to as "Mayer's Theory" (he finally acknowledged Mayer's priority), coming to the conclusion that it was in conflict with astronomical evidence concerning the constancy of the earth's motion. It seems fairly clear that he had never read the whole of Mayer's account. At any rate, he gave up the battle to try to account for the maintenance of the solar heat. Part of his reason indeed was spectroscopic and possessed considerable validity. He finally concluded that the sun "is simply an incandescent body gradually cooling down." This must be considered a strange conclusion in the light of the existence of another theory, the contraction hypothesis put forward by Helmholtz only six years after the appearance of Mayer's 1848 memoir.

It was at a popular (in the German meaning of the term) lecture delivered in 1854 in Königsberg, where he was at that time a professor of physiology in the university, that Helmholtz set forth his theory. This was undoubtedly stimulated by the nebular hypothesis of Kant and Laplace for the origin of the solar system. Helmholtz realized that in the contraction of matter toward a massive center by gravitational action, mechanical energy disappears and, according to the principle of the conservation of energy, an equivalent amount of heat must be produced. Using simple mechanical energy calculations for motion of matter in a gravitational field, Helmholtz was able to show that an almost insignificant contraction in the sun's radius and surface area per year could readily maintain the sun's radiation at its current level.

The reference to the contraction theory is contained in the English translation of Helmholtz's Königsberg lecture made by John Tyndall under the title "The Interaction of the Natural Forces" and reprinted in Helmholtz's *Popular Lectures on Scientific Subjects* (D. Appleton and Co., New York, 1897, pp. 153–196). We reprint here as Paper 11 the relevant passage about the contraction theory, including Helmholtz's illustrative calculations (pp. 173–196).

Even after Kelvin's renunciation of the views of Mayer and Helmholtz attributing the maintenance of solar heat to the direct transformations of mechanical energy into heat, Helmholtz's contraction theory continued to command considerable respect. It was the time demands of geology and evolution that proved its undoing. In the twentieth century the nuclear fusion process is the favorite theory, and it certainly can provide an ample energy supply. It still involves an energy-transformation process, leaning as it does on the famous mass–energy relation of the Einstein theory of relativity. Of course, the contraction postulated by Helmholtz must still go on, and, if the sun's mass and size are to remain constant, must be compensated by processes taking place inside the sun. The whole problem of solar heat and stellar heat in general is an admirable example of the role of energy in physical processes, first developed in the nineteenth century and still demanding attention in the twentieth.

9

Reprinted from *The Correlation and Conservation of Forces*, E. L. Youmans, ed.,
D. Appleton and Co., New York, 1886, pp. 259–286

Celestial Dynamics

Julius Robert Mayer

I.—INTRODUCTION.

EVERY incandescent and luminous body diminishes in temperature and luminosity in the same degree as it radiates light and heat, and at last, provided its loss be not repaired from some other source of these agencies, becomes cold and non-luminous.

For light, like sound, consists of vibrations which are communicated by the luminous or sounding body to a surrounding medium. It is perfectly clear that a body can only excite such vibrations in another substance when its own particles undergo a similar movement; for there is no cause for undulatory motion when a body is in a state of rest, or in a state of equilibrium with the medium by which it is surrounded. If a bell or a string is to be sounded, an external force must be applied; and this is the cause of the sound.

It the vibratory motion of a string could take place without any resistance, it would vibrate for all time; but in this case no sound could be produced, because sound is essentially the propagation of motion; and in the same degree as the

151

string communicates its vibrations to the surrounding and re-sisting medium its own motion becomes weaker and weaker, until at last it sinks into a state of rest.

The sun has often and appropriately been compared to an incessantly sounding bell. But by what means is the power of this body kept up in undiminished force so as to enable him to send forth his rays into the universe in such a grand and magnificent manner? What are the causes which counteract or prevent his exhaustion, and thus save the planetary system from darkness and deadly cold?

Some endeavoured to approach " the grand secret," as Sir Wm. Herschel calls this question, by the assumption that the rays of the sun, being themselves perfectly cold, merely cause the " substance" of heat, supposed to be contained in bodies, to pass from a state of rest into a state of motion, and that in order to send forth such cold rays the sun need not be a hot body, so that, in spite of the infinite development of light, the cooling of the sun was a matter not to be thought of.

It is plain that nothing is gained by such an explanation; for, not to speak of the hypothetical " substance" of heat, assumed to be at one time at rest and at another time in motion, now cold and then hot, it is a well-founded fact that the sun does not radiate a cold phosphorescent light, but a light capable of warming bodies intensely; and to ascribe such rays to a cold body is at once at variance with reason and experience.

Of course such and similar hypotheses could not satisfy the demands of exact science, and I will therefore try to explain in a more satisfactory manner than has been done up to this time the connexion between the sun's radiation and its effects. In doing so, I have to claim the indulgence of scientific men, who are acquainted with the difficulties of my task.

II.—SOURCES OF HEAT.

BEFORE we turn our attention to the special subject of this paper, it will be necessary to consider the means by which light and heat are produced. Heat may be obtained from very different sources. Combustion, fermentation, putrefaction, slaking of lime, the decomposition of chloride of nitrogen and of gun-cotton, &c. &c., are all of them sources of heat. The electric spark, the voltaic current, friction, percussion, and the vital processes are also accompanied by the evolution of this agent.

A general law of nature, which knows of no exception, is the following :—In order to obtain heat, something must be expended; this something, however different it may be in other respects, can always be referred to one of two categories : either it consists of some material expended in a chemical process, or of some sort of mechanical work.

When substances endowed with considerable chemical affinity for each other combine chemically, much heat is developed during the process. We shall estimate the quantity of heat thus set free by the number of kilogrammes of water which it would heat 1° C. The quantity of heat necessary to raise one kilogramme of water one degree is called a unit of heat.

It has been established by numerous experiments that the combustion of one kilogramme of dry charcoal in oxygen, so as to form carbonic acid, yields 7200 units of heat, which fact may be briefly expressed by saying that charcoal furnishes 7200° degrees of heat.

Superior coal yields 6000°, perfectly dry wood from 3300° to 3900°, sulphur 2700, and hydrogen $34,600^\circ$ of heat.

According to experience, the number of units of heat only depends on the quantity of matter which is consumed, and not on the conditions under which the burning takes place. The same amount of heat is given out whether the combustion proceeds slowly or quickly, in atmospheric air or in pure oxygen gas. If in one case a metal be burnt in air and the amount of heat directly measured, and in another instance the same quantity of metal be oxidized in a galvanic battery, the heat being developed in some other place—say, the wire which conducts the current,—in both of these experiments the same quantity of heat will be observed.

The same law also holds good for the production of heat by mechanical means. The amount of heat obtained is only dependent on the quantity of power consumed, and is quite independent of the manner in which this power has been expended. If, therefore, the amount of heat which is produced by certain mechanical work is known, the quantity which will be obtained by any other amount of mechanical work can easily be found by calculation. It is of no consequence whether this work consists in the compression, percussion, or friction of bodies.

The amount of mechanical work done by a force may be expressed by a weight, and the height to which this weight would be raised by the same force. The mathematical expression for "work done," that is to say, a measure for this work, is obtained by multiplying the height expressed in feet or other units by the number of pounds or kilogrammes lifted to this height.

We shall take one kilogramme as the unit of weight, and one metre as the unit of height, and we thus obtain the weight of one kilogramme raised to the height of one metre as a unit measure of mechanical work performed. This measure we shall call a kilogrammetre, and adopt for it the symbol Km.

Mechanical work may likewise be measured by the velocity obtained by a given weight in passing from a state of rest into that of motion. The work done is then expressed by the product obtained by the multiplication of the weight by the square of its velocity. The first method, however, because it is the more convenient, is the one usually adopted; and the numbers obtained therefrom may easily be expressed in other units.

The product resulting from the multiplication of the number of units of weight and measures of height, or, as it is called, the product of mass and height, as well as the product of the mass and the square of its velocity, are called "*vis viva* of motion," "mechanical effect," dynamical effect," "work done," "*quantité de travail*," &c. &c.

The amount of mechanical work necessary for the heating of 1 kilogramme of water 1° C has been determined by experiment to be = 367 Km; therefore Km = 0·00273 units of heat.*

A mass which has fallen through a height of 367 metres possesses a velocity of 84·8 metres in one second; a mass, therefore, moving with this velocity originates 1° C. of heat when its motion is lost by percussion, friction, &c. If the velocity be two or three times as great, 4° or 9° of heat will be developed. Generally speaking, when the velocity is *c* metres, the corresponding development of heat will be expressed by the formula

$$0·000139° \times c^2.$$

* This essay was published in 1845. At that time de la Roche and Berard's determination of the specific heat of air was generally accepted. If the physical constants used by Mayer be corrected according to the results of more recent investigation, the mechanical equivalent of heat is found to be 771·4 foot-pounds. Mr. Joule finds it = 772 foot-pounds.— TR.

III.—MEASURE OF THE SUN'S HEAT.

THE actinometer is an instrument invented by Sir John Herschel for the purpose of measuring the heating effect produced by the sun's rays. It is essentially a thermometer with a large cylindrical bulb filled with a blue liquid, which is acted upon by the sun's rays, and the expansion of which is measured by a graduated scale.

From observations made with this instrument, Sir John Herschel calculates the amount of heat received from the sun to be sufficient to melt annually at the surface of the.globe a crust of ice 29·2 metres in thickness.

Pouillet has recently shown by some careful experiments with the lens pyrheliometer, an instrument invented by himself, that every square centimetre of the surface of our globe receives, on an average, in one minute an amount of solar heat which would raise the temperature of one gramme of water 0·4408°. Not much more than one-half of this quantity of heat, however, reaches the solid surface of our globe, since a considerable portion of it is absorbed by our atmosphere. The layer of ice which, according to Pouillet, could be melted by the solar heat which yearly reaches our globe would have a thickness of 30·89 metres.

A square metre of our earth's surface receives, therefore, according to Pouillet's results, which we shall adopt in the following pages, on an average in one minute 4·408 units of heat. The whole surface of the earth is = 9,260,500 geographical square miles*; consequently the earth receives in one minute 2247 billions of units of heat from the sun.

In order to obtain smaller numbers, we shall call the quantity of heat necessary to raise a cubic mile of water 1°

* The geographical mile = 7420 metres, and one English mile = 1608 metres.

C. in temperature, a cubic mile of heat. Since one cubic mile of water weighs 408·54 billions of kilogrammes, a cubic mile of heat contains 408·54 billions of units of heat. The effect produced by the rays of the sun on the surface of the earth in one minute is therefore 5·5 cubic miles of heat.

Let us imagine the sun to be surrounded by a hollow sphere whose radius is equal to the mean distance of the earth from the sun, or 20,589,000 geographical miles ; the surface of this sphere would be equal to 5326 billions of square miles. The surface obtained by the intersection of this hollow sphere and our globe, or the base of the cone of solar light which reaches our earth, stands to the whole surface of this hollow sphere as $\frac{9,200,500}{4}$: 5326 billions, or as 1 to 2300 millions. This is the ratio of the heat received by our globe to the whole amount of heat sent forth from the sun, which latter in one minute amounts to 12,650 millions of cubic miles of heat.

This amazing radiation ought, unless the loss is by some means made good, to cool considerably even a body of the magnitude of the sun.

If we assume the sun to be endowed with the same capacity for heat as a mass of water of the same volume, and its loss of heat by radiation to affect uniformly its whole mass, the temperature of the sun ought to decrease 1°·8 C. yearly, and for the historic time of 5000 years this loss would consequently amount to 9000° C.

A uniform cooling of the whole of the sun's huge mass cannot, however, take place ; on the contrary, if the radiation were to occur at the expense of a given store of heat or radiant power, the sun would become covered in a short space of time with a cold crust, whereby radiation would be brought to an end. Considering the continued activity of the sun through countless centuries, we may assume with mathematical certainty the existence of some compensating influence to make good its enormous loss.

Is this restoring agency a chemical process?

If such were the case, the most favourable assumption would be to suppose the whole mass of the sun to be one lump of coal, the combustion of every kilogramme of which produces 6000 units of heat. Then the sun would only be able to sustain for forty-six centuries its present expenditure of light and heat, not to mention the oxygen necessary to keep up such an immense combustion, and other unfavourable circumstances.

The revolution of the sun on his axis has been suggested as the cause of his radiating energy. A closer examination proves this hypothesis also to be untenable.

Rapid rotation, without friction or resistance, cannot in itself alone be regarded as a cause of light and heat, especially as the sun is in no way to be distinguished from the other bodies of our system by velocity of axial rotation. The sun turns on his axis in about twenty-five days, and his diameter is nearly 112 times as great as that of the earth, from which it follows that a point on the solar equator travels but a little more than four times as quickly as a point on the earth's equator. The largest planet of the solar system, whose diameter is about $\frac{1}{10}$th that of the sun, turns on its axis in less than ten hours; a point on its equator revolves about six times quicker than one on the solar equator. The outer ring of Saturn exceeds the sun's equator more than ten times in velocity of rotation. Nevertheless no generation of light or heat is observed on our globe, on Jupiter, or on the ring of Saturn.

It might be thought that friction, though undeveloped in the case of the other celestial bodies, might be engende ed by the sun's rotation, and that such friction might generate enormous quantities of heat. But for the production of frictior two bodies, at least, are always necessary which are in immediate contact with one another, and which move with different velocities or in different directions. Friction, moreover has a tendency to produce equal motion of the two rubbing bodies; and when this is attained, the generation of heat ceases. If now the sun be the one moving body, where is the other? and if the second body exist, what power prevents it from assuming the same rotary motion as the sun?

But could even these difficulties be disregarded, a weightier and more formidable obstacle opposes this hypothesis. The known volume and mass of the sun allow us to calculate the *vis viva* which he possesses in consequence of his rotation. Assuming his density to be uniform throughout his mass, and his period of rotation twenty-five days, it is equal to 182,300 quintillions of kilogrammetres (Km). But for one unit of heat generated, 367 Km are consumed; consequently the whole rotation-effect of the sun could only cover the expenditure of heat for the space of 183 years.

The space of our solar system is filled with a great number of ponderable objects, which have a tendency to move towards the centre of gravity of the sun; and in so doing, their rate of motion is more and more accelerated.

A mass, without motion, placed within the sphere of the sun's attraction, will obey this attraction, and, if there be no disturbing influences, will fall in a straight line into the sun. In reality, however, such a rectilinear path can scarcely occur, as may be shown by experiment.

Let a weight be suspended by a string so that it can only touch the floor in one point. Lift the weight up to a certain height, and at the same time stretch the string out to its full length; if the weight be now allowed to fall, it will be observed, almost in every case, not to reach at once the point on the floor towards which it tends to move, but to move round this point for some time in a curved line.

The reason of this phenomenon is that the slightest deviation of the weight from its shortest route towards the point on the floor, caused by some disturbing influence such as the resistance of the air against a not perfectly uniform surface, will maintain itself as long as motion lasts. It is nevertheless possible for the weight to move at once to the point ; the probability of its doing so, however, becomes the less as the height from which it is allowed to drop increases, or the string, by means of which it is suspended, is lengthened.

Similar laws influence the movements of bodies in the space of the solar system. The height of the fall is here represented by the original distance from the sun at which the body begins to move ; the length of the string by the sun's attraction, which increases when the distance decreases ; and the small surface of contact on the floor by the area of the section of the sun's sphere. If now a cosmical mass within the physical limits of the sun's sphere of attraction begins its fall towards that heavenly body, it will be disturbed in its long path for many centuries, at first by the nearest fixed stars, and afterwards by the bodies of the solar system. Motion of such a mass in a straight line, or its perpendicular fall into the sun, would, therefore, under such conditions, be impossible. The observed movement of all planetary bodies in closed curves agrees with this.

We shall now return to the example of the weight suspended by a string and oscillating round a point towards which it is attracted. The diameters of the orbits described by this weight are observed to be nearly equal ; continued observation, however, shows that these diameters gradually diminish in length, so that the weight will by degrees approach the point in which it can touch the floor. The weight, however, touches the floor not in a mathematical point, but in a small surface ; as soon, therefore, as the diameter of the curve in which the weight moves is equal to the diameter of this surface, the weight will touch the floor. This final contact is no accidental or improbable event, but a necessary phenomenon caused by the resistance which the oscillating mass constantly suffers from the air and friction. If all resistance could be annihilated, the motion of the weight would of course continue in equal oscillations.

The same law holds good for celestial bodies.

The movements of celestial bodies in an absolute vacuum would be as uniform as those of a mathematical pendulum, whereas a resisting medium pervading all space would cause the planets to move in shorter and shorter orbits, and at last to fall into the sun.

Assuming such a resisting medium, these wandering celestial bodies must have on the periphery of the solar system their cradle, and in its centre their grave ; and however long the duration, and however great the number of their revolutions may be, as many masses will on the average in a certain time arrive at the sun as formerly in a like period of time came within his sphere of attraction.

All these bodies plunge with a violent impetus into their common grave. Since no cause exists without an effect, each of these cosmical masses will, like a weight falling to the earth, produce by its percussion an amount of heat proportional to its *vis viva*.

From the idea of a sun whose attraction acts throughout space, of ponderable bodies scattered throughout the universe, and of a resisting æther, another idea necessarily follows— that, namely, of a continual and inexhaustible generation of heat on the central body of this cosmical system.

Whether such a conception be realized in our solar system —whether, in other words, the wonderful and permanent evolution of light and heat be caused by the uninterrupted fall of cosmical matter into the sun—will now be more closely examined.

The existence of matter in a primordial condition (*Urmaterie*), moving about in the universe, and assumed to follow the attraction of the nearest stellar system, will scarcely be denied by astronomers and physicists ; for the richness of surrounding nature, as well as the aspect of the starry heavens, prevents the belief that the wide space which separates our solar system from the regions governed by the other fixed

stars is a vacant solitude destitute of matter. We sha.
leave, however, all suppositions concerning subjects so distant
from us both in time and space, and confine our attention ex
clusively to what may be learnt from the observation of the
existing state of things.

Besides the fourteen known planets with their eighteen
satellites, a great many other cosmical masses move within
the space of the planetary system, of which the comets deserve to be mentioned first.

Kepler's celebrated statement that " there are more comets in the heavens than fish in the ocean," is founded on the
fact that, of all the comets belonging to our solar system,
comparatively few can be seen by the inhabitants of the earth,
and therefore the not inconsiderable number of actually observed comets obliges us, according to the rules of the calculus of probabilities, to assume the existence of a great many
more beyond the sphere of our vision.

Besides planets, satellites, and comets, another class of
celestial bodies exists within our solar system. These are
masses which, on account of their smallness, may be considered as cosmical atoms, and which Arago has appropriately
called asteroids. They, like the planets and the comets, are
governed by gravity, and move in elliptical orbits round the
sun. When accident brings them into the immediate neighbourhood of the earth, they produce the phenomena of shoot-
ing-stars and fireballs.

It has been shown by repeated observation, that on a
bright night twenty minutes seldom elapse without a shooting-
star being visible to an observer in any situation. At certain
times these meteors are observed in astonishingly great numbers; during the meteoric shower at Boston, which lasted
nine hours, when they were said to fall " crowded together
like snow-flakes," they were estimated as at least 240,000.
On the whole, the number of asteroids which come near the
earth in the space of a year must be computed to be many

thousands of millions. This, without doubt, is only a small fraction of the number of asteroids that move round the sun, which number, according to the rules of the calculus of probabilities, approaches the infinite.

As has been already stated, on the existence of a resisting æther it depends whether the celestial bodies, the planets, the comets, and the asteroids move at constant mean distances round the sun, or whether they are constantly approaching that central body.

Scientific men do not doubt the existence of such an æther. Littrow, amongst others, expresses himself on this point as follows :—" The assumption that the planets and the comets move in an absolute vacuum can in no way be admitted. Even if the space between celestial bodies contained no other matter than that necessary for the existence of light (whether light be considered as emission of matter or the undulations of a universal æther), this alone is sufficient to alter the motion of the planets in the course of time and the arrangement of the whole system itself; the fall of all the planets and the comets into the sun and the destruction of the present state of the solar system must be the final results of this action."

A direct proof of the existence of such a resisting medium has been furnished by the academician Encke. He found that the comet named after him, which revolves round the sun in the short space of 1207 days, shows a regular acceleration of its motion, in consequence of which the time of each revolution is shortened by about six hours.

From the great density and magnitude of the planets, the shortening of the diameters of their orbits proceeds, as might be expected, very slowly, and is up to the present time inappreciable. The smaller the cosmical masses are, on the contrary, other circumstances remaining the same, the faster they move towards the sun; it may therefore happen that in a space of time wherein the mean distance of the earth from the sun would diminish one metre, a small asteroid would travel more than one thousand miles towards the central body.

As cosmical masses stream from all sides in immense numbers towards the sun, it follows that they must become more and more crowded together as they approach thereto. The conjecture at once suggests itself that the zodiacal light, the nebulous light of vast dimensions which surrounds the sun, owes its origin to such closely-packed asteroids. However it may be, this much is certain, that this phenomenon is caused by matter which moves according to the same laws as the planets round the sun, and it consequently follows that the whole mass which originates the zodiacal light is continually approaching the sun and falling into it.

This light does not surround the sun uniformly on all sides; that is to say, it has not the form of a sphere, but that of a thin convex lens, the greater diameter of which is in the plane of the solar equator, and accordingly it has to an observer on our globe a pyramidal form. Such lenticular distribution of the masses in the universe is repeated in a remarkable manner in the disposition of the planets and the fixed stars.

From the great number of cometary masses and asteroids and the zodiacal light on the one hand, and the existence of a resisting æther on the other, it necessarily follows that ponderable matter must continually be arriving on the solar surface. The effect produced by these masses evidently depends on their final velocity; and, in order to determine the latter, we shall discuss some of the elements of the theory of gravitation.

The final velocity of a weight attracted by and moving towards a celestial body will become greater as the height through which the weight falls increases. This velocity, however, if it be only produced by the fall, cannot exceed a certain magnitude; it has a maximum, the value of which depends on the volume and mass of the attracting celestial body

Let r be the radius of a spherical and solid celestial body and g the velocity at the end of the first second of a weight falling on the surface of this body; then the greatest velocity which this weight can obtain by its fall towards the celestial body, or the velocity with which it will arrive at its surface after a fall from an infinite height, is $\sqrt{2gr}$ in one second. This number, wherein g and r are expressed in metres, we shall call G.

For our globe the value of g is 9·8164 . . and that of r 6,369,800; and consequently on our earth

$$G = \sqrt{(2 \times 9{\cdot}8164 \times 6{,}369{,}800)} = 11{,}183.$$

The solar radius is 112·05 times that of the earth, and the velocity produced by gravity on the sun's surface is 28·36 times greater than the same velocity on the surface of our globe; the greatest velocity therefore which a body could obtain in consequence of the solar attraction, or

$$G = \sqrt{(28{\cdot}36 \times 112{\cdot}05)} \times 11{,}183 = 630{,}400;$$

that is, this maximum velocity is equal to 630,400 metres, or 85 geographical miles in one second.

By the help of this constant number, which may be called the *characteristic* of the solar system, the velocity of a body in central motion may easily be determined at any point of its orbit. Let a be the mean distance of the planetary body from the centre of gravity of the sun, or the greater semidiameter of its orbit (the radius of the sun being taken as unity); and let h be the distance of the same body at any point of its orbit from the centre of gravity of the sun; then the velocity, expressed in metres, of the planet at the distance h is

$$G \times \sqrt{\frac{2a-h}{2a \times h}}.$$

At the moment the planet comes in contact with the solar surface, h is equal to 1, and its velocity is therefore

$$G \times \sqrt{\frac{2a-1}{2a}}.$$

165

It follows from this formula that the smaller $2a$ (or the major axis of the orbit of a planetary body) becomes, the less will be its velocity when it reaches the sun. This velocity, like the major axis, has a minimum; for so long as the planet moves outside the sun, its major axis cannot be shorter than the diameter of the sun, or, taking the solar radius as a unit, the quantity $2a$ can never be less than 2. The smallest velocity with which we can imagine a cosmical body to arrive on the surface of the sun is consequently

$$G \times \sqrt{\frac{1}{2}} = 445,750,$$

or a velocity of 60 geographical miles in one second.

For this smallest value the orbit of the asteroid is circular; for a larger value it becomes elliptical, until finally, with increasing excentricity, when the value of $2a$ approaches infinity, the orbit becomes a parabola. In the last case the velocity is

$$G \times \sqrt{\frac{\infty - 1}{\infty}} = G,$$

or, 85 geographical miles in one second.

If the value of the major axis become negative, or the orbit assume the form of a hyperbola, the velocity may increase without end. But this could only happen when cosmical masses enter the space of the solar system with a projected velocity, or when masses, having missed the sun's surface, move into the universe and never return; hence a velocity greater than G can only be regarded as a rare exception, and we shall therefore only consider velocities comprised within the limits of 60 and 80 miles.*

The final velocity with which a weight moving in a

---

* The relative velocity also with which an asteroid reaches the solar surface depends in some degree on the velocity of the sun's rotation. This, however, as well as the rotatory effect of the asteroid, is without moment, and may be neglected.

straight line towards the centre of the sun arrives at the solar surface is expressed by the formula

$$c = G \times \sqrt{\frac{h-1}{h}},$$

wherein c expresses the final velocity in metres, and h the original distance from the centre of the sun in terms of solar radius. If this formula be compared with the foregoing, it will be seen that a mass which, after moving in central motion, arrives at the sun's surface has the same velocity as it would possess had it fallen perpendicularly into the sun from a distance* equal to the major axis of its orbit; whence it is apparent that a planet, on arriving at the sun, moves at least as quickly as a weight which falls freely towards the sun from a distance as great as the solar radius, or 96,000 geographical miles.

What thermal effect corresponds to such velocities? Is the effect sufficiently great to play an important part in the immense development of heat on the sun?

This crucial question may be easily answered by help of the preceding considerations. According to the formula given at the end of Chapter II., the degree of heat generated by percussion is

$$= 0 \cdot 000139^{\circ} \times c^{2},$$

where c denotes the velocity of the striking body expressed in metres. The velocity of an asteroid when it strikes the sun measures from 445,750 to 630,400 metres; the caloric effect of the percussion is consequently equal to from $27\frac{1}{2}$ to 55 millions of degrees of heat†.

An asteroid, therefore, by its fall into the sun developes

---

* This distance is to be counted from the centre of the sun.

† Throughout this memoir the degrees of heat are expressed in the Centigrade scale. Unless stated to the contrary, the measures of length are given in geographical miles. A geographical mile = 7420 metres, and an English mile = 1608 metres.—Tr.

from 4600 to 9200 times as much heat as would be generated by the combustion of an equal mass of coal.

IV.—ORIGIN OF THE SUN'S HEAT.

THE question why the planets move in curved orbits, one of the grandest of problems, was solved by Newton in consequence, it is believed, of his reflecting on the fall of an apple. This story is not improbable, for we are on the right track for the discovery of truth when once we clearly recognize that between great and small no qualitative but only a quantitative difference exists—when we resist the suggestions of an ever active imagination, and look for the same laws in the greatest as well as in the smallest processes of nature.

This universal range is the essence of a law of nature, and the touchstone of the correctness of human theories. We observe the fall of an apple, and investigate the law which governs this phenomenon; for the earth we substitute the sun, and for the apple a planet, and thus possess ourselves of the key to the mechanics of the heavens.

As the same laws prevail in the greater as well as in the smaller processes of nature, Newton's method may be used in solving the problem of the origin of the sun's heat. We know the connexion between the space through which a body falls, the velocity, the *vis viva*, and the generation of heat on the surface of this globe; if we again substitute for the earth the sun, with a mass 350,000 greater, and for a height of a few metres celestial distances, we obtain a generation of heat exceeding all terrestrial measures. And since we have sufficient reason to assume the actual existence of such mechanical processes in the heavens, we find therein the only tenable explanation of the origin of the heat of the sun.

The fact that the development of heat by mechanical means on the surface of our globe is, as a rule, not so great, and cannot be so great as the generation of the same agent by chemical means, as by combustion, follows from the laws already discussed; and this fact cannot be used as an argument against the assumption of a greater development of heat by a greater expenditure of mechanical work. It has been shown that the heat generated by a weight falling from a height of 367 metres is only $\frac{1}{6000}$th part of the heat produced by the combustion of the same weight of coal; just as small is the amount of heat developed by a weight moving with the not inconsiderable velocity of 85 metres in one second. But, according to the laws of mechanics, the effect is proportional to the square of the velocity; if therefore the weight move 100 times faster, or with a velocity of 8500 metres in one second, it will produce a greater effect than the combustion of an equal quantity of coal.

It is true that so great a velocity cannot be obtained by human means; everyday experience, however, shows the development of high degrees of temperature by mechanical processes.

In the common flint and steel, the particles of steel which are struck off are sufficiently heated to burn in air. A few blows directed by a skilful blacksmith with a sledge-hammer against a piece of cold metal may raise the temperature of the metal at the points of collision to redness.

The new crank of a steamer, whilst being polished by friction, becomes red-hot, several buckets of water being required to cool it down to its ordinary temperature.

When a railway train passes with even less than its ordinary velocity along a very sharp curve of the line, sparks are observed in consequence of the friction against the rails.

One of the grandest constructions for the production of motion by human art is the channel in which the wood was allowed to glide down from the steep and lofty sides of Mount

Pilatus into the plain below. This wooden channel which was built about thirty years ago by the engineer Rupp, was 9 English miles in length; the largest trees were shot down it from the top to the bottom of the mountain in about two minutes and a half. The momentum possessed by the trees on their escaping at their journey's end from the channel was sufficiently great to bury their thicker ends in the ground to the depth of from 6 to 8 metres. To prevent the wood getting too hot and taking fire, water was conducted in many places into the channel.

This stupendous mechanical process, when compared with cosmical processes on the sun, appears infinitely small. In the latter case it is the mass of the sun which attracts, and in lieu of the height of Mount Pilatus we have distances of a hundred thousand and more miles; the amount of heat generated by cosmical falls is therefore at least 9 million times greater than in our terrestrial example.

Rays of heat on passing through glass and other transparent bodies undergo partial absorption, which differs in degree, however, according to the temperature of the source from which the heat is derived. Heat radiated from sources less warm than boiling water is almost completely stopped by thin plates of glass. As the temperature of a source of heat increases, its rays pass more copiously through diathermic bodies. A plate of glass, for example, weakens the rays of a red-hot substance, even when the latter is placed very close to it, much more than it does those emanating at a much greater distance from a white-hot body. If the quality of the sun's rays be examined in this respect, their diathermic energy is found to be far superior to that of all artificial sources of heat. The temperature of the focus of a concave metallic reflector in which the sun's light has been collected is only diminished from one-seventh to one-eighth by the interposition of a screen of glass. If the same experiment be made with an artificial and luminous source of heat, it is found that, though the focus be very hot when the screen is away, the interposition of the latter cuts off nearly all the heat; moreover, the focus will not recover its former temperature when reflector and screen are placed sufficiently near to the source of heat to make the focus appear brighter than it did in the former position without the glass screen.

The empirical law, that the diathermic energy of heat increases with the temperature of the source from which the heat is radiated, teaches us that the sun's surface must be much hotter than the most powerful process of combustion could render it.

Other methods furnish the same conclusion. If we imagine the sun to be surrounded by a hollow sphere, it is clear that the inner surface of this sphere must receive all the heat radiated from the sun. At the distance of our globe from the sun, such a sphere would have a radius 215 times as great, and an area 46,000 times as large as the sun himself; those luminous and calorific rays, therefore, which meet this spherical surface at right angles retain only $\frac{1}{46.000}$th part of their original intensity. If it be further considered that our atmosphere absorbs a part of the solar rays, it is clear that the rays which reach the tropics of our earth at noonday can only possess from $\frac{1}{50,000}$th to $\frac{1}{60,000}$th of the power with which they started. These rays, when gathered from a surface of from 5 to 6 square metres, and concentrated in an area of one square centimetre, would produce about the temperature which exists on the sun, a temperature more than sufficient to vaporize platinum, rhodium, and similar metals.

The radiation calculated in Chapter III. likewise proves the enormous temperature of the solar surface. From the determination mentioned therein, it follows that each square centimetre of the sun's surface loses by radiation about 80 units of heat per minute—an immense quantity in comparison with terrestrial radiations.

A correct theory of the origin of the sun's heat must explain the cause of such enormous temperatures. This explanation can be deduced from the foregoing statements. According to Pouillet, the temperature at which bodies appear intensely white-hot is about 1500° C. The heat generated by the combustion of one kilogramme of hydrogen is, as determined by Dulong, 34,500, and according to the more recent experiments of Grassi, 34,666 units of heat. One part of hydrogen combines with eight parts of oxygen to form water; hence one kilogramme of these two gases mixed in this ratio would produce 3850°.

Let us now compare this heat with the amount of the same agent generated by the fall of an asteroid into the sun. Without taking into account the low specific heat of such masses when compared with that of water, we find the heat developed by the asteroid to be from 7000 to 15,000 times greater than that of the oxyhydrogen mixture. From data like these, the extraordinary diathermic energy of the sun's rays, the immense radiation from his surface, and the high temperature in the focus of the reflector are easily accounted for.

The facts above mentioned show that, unless we assume on the sun the existence of matter with unheard of chemical properties as a *deus ex machina*, no chemical process could maintain the present high radiation of the sun; it also follows from the above results, that the chemical nature of bodies which fall into the sun does not in the least affect our conclusions; the effect produced by the most inflammable substance would not differ by one-thousandth part from that resulting from the fall of matter possessing but feeble chemical affinities. As the brightest artificial light appears dark in comparison with the sun's light, so the mechanical processes of the heavens throw into the shade the most powerful chemical actions.

The quality of the sun's rays, as dependent on his temper

ature, is of the greatest importance to mankind. If the solar heat were originated by a chemical process, and amounted near its source to a temperature of a few thousand degrees, it would be possible for the light to reach us, whilst the greater part of the more important calorific rays would be absorbed by the higher strata of our atmosphere and then returned to the universe.

In consequence of the high temperature of the sun, however, our atmosphere is highly diathermic to his rays, so that the latter reach the surface of our earth and warm it. The comparatively low temperature of the terrestrial surface is the cause why the heat cannot easily radiate back through the atmosphere into the universe. The atmosphere acts, therefore, like an envelope, which is easily pierced by the solar rays, but which offers considerable resistance to the radiant heat escaping from our earth; its action resembles that of a valve which allows liquid to pass freely in one, but stops the flow in the opposite direction.

The action of the atmosphere is of the greatest importance as regards climate and meteorological processes. It must raise the mean temperature of the earth's surface. After the setting of the sun—in fact, in all places where his rays do not reach the surface, the temperature of the earth would soon be as low as that of the universe, if the atmosphere were removed, or if it did not exist. Even the powerful solar rays in the tropics would be unable to preserve water in its liquid state.

Between the great cold which would reign at all times and in all places, and the moderate warmth which in reality exists on our globe, intermediate temperatures may be imagined; and it is easily seen that the mean temperature would decrease if the atmosphere were to become more and more rare. Such a rarefaction of a valve-like acting atmosphere actually takes place as we ascend higher and higher above

the level of the sea, and it is accordingly and necessarily ac
companied by a corresponding diminution of temperature.

This well-known fact of the lower mean temperature of
places of greater altitude has led to the strangest hypotheses.
The sun's rays were not supposed to contain all the conditions
for warming a body, but to set in motion the "substance"
of heat contained in the earth. This "substance" of heat,
cold when at rest, was attracted by the earth, and was therefore found in greater abundance near the centre of the globe.
This view, it was thought, explained why the warming power
of the sun was so much weaker at the top of a mountain than
at the bottom, and why, in spite of his immense radiation, he
retained his full powers.

This belief, which especially prevails amongst imperfectly
informed people, and which will scarcely succumb to correct
views, is directly contradicted by the excellent experiments
made by Pouillet at different altitudes with the pyrheliometer.
These experiments show that, everything else being equal,
the generation of heat by the solar rays is more powerful in
higher altitudes than near the surface of our globe, and that
consequently a portion of these rays is absorbed on their passage through the atmosphere. Why, in spite of this partial
absorption, the mean temperature of low altitudes is nevertheless higher than it is in more elevated positions, is explained by the fact that the atmosphere stops to a far greater
degree the calorific rays emanating from the earth than it
does those from the sun.

V.—CONSTANCY OF THE SUN'S MASS.

NEWTON, as is well known, considered light to be the
emission of luminous particles from the sun. In the continued emission of light this great philosopher saw a cause tend-

ing to diminish the solar mass; and he assumed, in order to make good this loss, comets and other cosmical masses to be continually falling into the central body.

If we express this view of Newton's in the language of the undulatory theory, which is now universally accepted, we obtain the results developed in the preceding pages. It is true that our theory does not accept a peculiar "substance" of light or of heat; nevertheless, according to it, the radiation of light and heat consists also in purely material processes, in a sort of motion, in the vibrations of ponderable resisting substances. Quiescence is darkness and death; motion is light and life.

An undulating motion proceeding from a point or a plane and excited in an unlimited medium, cannot be imagined apart from another simultaneous motion, a translation of the particles themselves;* it therefore follows, not only from the emission, but also from the undulatory theory, that radiation continually diminishes the mass of the sun. Why, nevertheless, the mass of the sun does not really diminish has already been stated.

The radiation of the sun is a centrifugal action equivalent to a centripetal motion.

The caloric effect of the centrifugal action of the sun can be found by direct observation; it amounts, according to Chapter III., in one minute to 12,650 millions of cubic miles of heat, or 5·17 quadrillions of units of heat. In Chapter IV. it has been shown that one kilogramme of the mass of an asteroid originates from 27·5 to 55 millions of units of heat; the quantity of cosmical masses, therefore, which falls every minute into the sun amounts to from 94,000 to 188,000 billions of kilogrammes.

To obtain this remarkable result, we made use of a method

* This centrifugal motion is perhaps the cause of the repulsion of the tails on comets when in the neighbourhood of the sun, as observed by Bessel

which is common in physical inquiries. Observation of the moon's motion reveals to us the external form of the earth. The physicist determines with the torsion-balance the weight of a planet, just as the merchant finds the weight of a parcel of goods, whilst the pendulum has become a magic power in the hands of the geologist, enabling him to discover cavities in the bowels of the earth. Our case is similar to these. By observation and calculation of the velocity of sound in our atmosphere, we obtain the ratio of the specific heat of air under constant pressure and under constant volume, and by the help of this number we determine the quantity of heat generated by mechanical work. The heat which arrives from the sun in a given time on a small surface of our globe serves as a basis for the calculation of the whole radiating effect of the sun; and the result of a series of observations and well-founded conclusions is the quantitative determination of those cosmical masses which the sun receives from the space through which he sends forth his rays.

Measured by terrestrial standards, the ascertained number of so many billions of kilogrammes per minute appears incredible. This quantity, however, may be brought nearer to our comprehension by comparison with other cosmical magnitudes. The nearest celestial body to us (the moon) has a mass of about 90,000 trillions of kilogrammes, and it would therefore cover the expenditure of the sun for from one to two years. The mass of the earth would afford nourishment to the sun for a period of from 60 to 120 years.

To facilitate the appreciation of the masses and the distances occurring in the planetary system, Herschel draws the following picture. Let the sun be represented by a globe 1 metre in diameter. The nearest planet (Mercury) will be about as large as a pepper-corn, $3\frac{1}{2}$ millimetres in thickness, at a distance of 40 metres. 78 and 107 metres distant from the sun will move Venus and the Earth, each 9 millimetres in diameter, or a little larger than a pea. Not much more than a quarter of a metre from the Earth will be the Moon, the size of a mustard seed, $2\frac{1}{2}$ millimetres in diameter. Mars, at a distance of 160 metres, will have about half the diameter of the Earth ; and the smaller planets (Vesta, Hebe, Astrea, Juno, Pallas, Ceres, &c.), at a distance of from 250 to 300 metres from the sun, will resemble particles of sand. Jupiter and Saturn, 560 and 1000 metres distant from the centre, will be represented by oranges, 10 and 9 centimetres in diameter. Uranus, of the size of a nut 4 centimetres across, will be 2000 metres ; and Neptune, as large as an apple 6 centimetres in diameter, will be nearly twice as distant, or about half a geographical mile away from the sun. From Neptune to the nearest fixed star will be more than 2000 geographical miles.

To complete this picture, it is necessary to imagine finely divided matter grouped in a diversified manner, moving slowly and gradually towards the large central globe, and on its arrival attaching itself thereto ; this matter, when favourably illuminated by the sun, represents itself to us as the zodiacal light. This nebulous substance forms also an important part of a creation in which nothing is by chance, but wherein all is arranged with Divine foresight and wisdom.

The surface of the sun measures 115,000 millions of square miles, or $6\frac{1}{3}$ trillions of square metres ; the mass of matter which in the shape of asteroids falls into the sun every minute is from 94,000 to 188,000 billions of kilogrammes ; one square metre of solar surface, therefore, receives on an average from 15 to 30 grammes of matter per minute.

To compare this process with a terrestrial phenomenon, a gentle rain may be considered which sends down in one hour a layer of water 1 millimetre in thickness (during a thunderstorm the rainfall is often from ten to fifteen times this quantity), this amounts on a square metre to 17 grammes per minute.

The continual bombardment of the sun by these cosmical masses ought to increase its volume as well as its mass, if centripetal action only existed. The increase of volume, could scarcely be appreciated by man ; for if the specific gravity of these cosmical masses be assumed to be the same as that of the sun, the enlargement of his apparent diameter to the extent of one second, the smallest appreciable magnitude, would require from 33,000 to 66,000 years.

Not quite so inappreciable would be the increase of the mass of the sun. If this mass, or the weight of the sun, were augmented, an acceleration of the motion of the planets in their orbits would be the consequence, whereby their times of revolution round the central body would be shortened. The mass of the sun is 2·1 quintillions of kilogrammes ; and the mass of the cosmical matter annually arriving at the sun stands to the above as 1 to from 21 — 42 millions. Such an augmentation of the weight of the sun ought to shorten the sidereal year from $\frac{1}{42,000,000}$th to $\frac{1}{85,000,000}$th of its length, or from $\frac{3}{4}$ths to $\frac{3}{8}$ths of a second.

The observations of astronomers do not agree with this conclusion ; we must therefore fall back on the theory men tioned at the beginning of this chapter, which assumes that the sun, like the ocean, is constantly losing and receiving equal quantities of matter. This harmonizes with the suppo sition that the *vis viva* of the universe is a constant quantity

[*Ed. note:* material omitted]

Reprinted from *Mathematical and Physical Papers of William Thomson*, Vol. 2, Cambridge University Press, London, 1884, pp. 1–16

ART. LXVI.   ON THE MECHANICAL ENERGIES OF THE SOLAR SYSTEM.

William Thomson (Lord Kelvin)

[From *Edinb. Roy. Soc. Trans.* April, 1854; *Phil. Mag.* Dec. 1854; *Comptes Rendus*, XXXIX. Oct. 1854.]

THE mutual actions and motions of the heavenly bodies have long been regarded as the grandest phenomena of mechanical energy in nature. Their light has been seen, and their heat has been felt, without the slightest suspicion that we had thus a direct perception of mechanical energy at all. Even after it has been shown * that the almost inconceivably minute fraction [a one hundred and forty thousand millionth] of the Sun's heat and light reaching the earth is the source of energy from which all the

---

* Herschel's *Astronomy*, edition 1833.—See last ed., § (399).

mechanical actions of organic life, and nearly every motion of inorganic nature at its surface, are derived, the energy of this source has been scarcely thought of as a development of mechanical power.

Little more than ten years ago the true relation of heat to force, in every electric, magnetic, and chemical action, as well as in the ordinary operations of mechanics, was pointed out * ; and it is a simple corollary from this that the Sun, within the historical period of human observation, has emitted hundreds of times as much mechanical energy† as that of the motions of all the known planets taken together. The energy, that of light and radiant heat, thus emitted, is dissipated always more and more widely through endless space, and never has been, probably never can be, restored to the Sun, without acts as much beyond the scope of human intelligence as a creation or annihilation of energy, or of matter itself, would be. Hence the question arises, What is the source of mechanical energy, drawn upon by the Sun, in emitting heat, to be dissipated through space? In speculating on the answer, we may consider whether the source in question consists of dynamical energy [kinetic energy], that is, energy of motion ‡, or of "potential energy," (as Mr Rankine has called the energy of force acting between bodies, which will give way to it unless held); or whether it consists partly of dynamical [kinetic] and partly of potential energy.

And again, we may consider whether the source in question, or any part of it, is in the Sun, or exists in surrounding matter, until taken and sent out again by the Sun, or exists as energy

---

* Joule "On the Generation of Heat in the Galvanic Circuit," communicated to the Royal Society of London, Dec. 17, 1840, and published *Phil. Mag.*, Oct. 1841. "On the Heat evolved during the Electrolysis of Water," Literary and Phil. Soc. of Manchester, 1843, Vol. vii., Part 3, Second Series. "On the Calorific Effects of Magneto-Electricity, and the Mechanical Value of Heat," communicated to the British Association, August 1843, and published *Phil. Mag.*, Sept. 1843. "On the Changes of Temperature produced by the Rarefaction and Condensation of Air," communicated to the Royal Soc., June 1844, and published *Phil. Mag.*, May 1845. Joule and Scoresby, "On the Powers of Electromagnetism, Steam, and Horses," *Phil. Mag.*, June 1846. [All these articles are to be found in the collection of Joule's scientific papers, now in print, and published, or, very soon it is hoped, to be published, by the Physical Society of London. W. T. Nov. 9, 1882.]

† Once every 20 years or so.—See Table of Mechanical Energies of the Solar System, appended.

‡ "Actual Energy," as Mr Rankine has called it.

only convertible into heat by mutual actions between the Sun and surrounding matter.

If it be dynamical and entirely in the Sun, it can only be primitive heat; if potential and in the Sun, it can only be energy of chemical forces ready to act. If not in the Sun, it must be due to matter coming to the Sun; (for it certainly is not a mere communication of motion to solar particles from external energy, as such could only be effected by undulations like sound or radiant heat, and we know that no such anti-radiation can be experienced by a body in the Sun's circumstances); but whether intrinsically in such external matter, or developed by mutual action between this matter and the Sun, and whether dynamical [kinetic] or potential in either case, requires careful consideration, as will be shown in the course of this communication. We see, then, that all the theories which have been yet proposed, as well as every conceivable theory, must be one or other, or a combination of the following three :—

I. That the Sun is a heated body, losing heat.

II. That the heat emitted from the Sun is due to chemical action among materials originally belonging to his mass, or that the Sun is a great fire.

III. That meteors falling into the Sun give rise to the heat which he emits.

In alluding to theories of solar heat in former communications to the Royal Society, I pointed out that the first hypothesis is quite untenable*. In fact, it is demonstrable that, unless the Sun be of matter inconceivably more conductive for heat, and less volatile, than any terrestrial meteoric matter we know, he would become dark in two or three minutes, or days, or months, or years, at his present rate of emission, if he had no source of energy to draw from but primitive heat†. The second has been not only

---

* [Note of Nov. 9, 1882. I soon was forced to abandon this conclusion, and to definitely adopt prop. I. as the true theory of solar heat and light, that the Sun is merely a vast fluid mass, cooling by radiation into space. See extract from Presidential Address to the British Association, 1871, appended to the present Article.]

† This assertion was founded on the supposition that conduction is the only means by which heat could reach the Sun's surface from the interior, and perhaps requires limitation. For it might be supposed that, as the Sun is no doubt a melted mass, the brightness of his surface is constantly refreshed by incandescent fluid rushing from below to take the place of matter falling upon the surface after

held by the Fire-worshippers, but has probably been conceived of by all men in all times, and considered as more or less probable by every philosopher who has ever speculated on the subject. The third may have occurred at any time to ingenious minds, and may have occurred and been set aside as not worth considering; but was never brought forward in any definite form, so far as I am aware*, until Mr Waterston communicated to the British Association, during its last meeting at Hull, a remarkable speculation on cosmical dynamics, in which he proposed the Theory that solar heat is produced by the impact of meteors falling from extra-planetary space, and striking his surface with velocities which they have acquired by his attraction. This is a form of what may be called the Gravitation Theory of Solar Heat, which is itself included in the general meteoric theory.

The objects of the present communication are to consider the relative capabilities of the second and third hypothesis to account for the phenomena; to examine the relation of the gravitation theory to the meteoric theory in general; and to determine what form of the gravitation theory is required to explain solar heat consistently with other astronomical phenomena.

In the first place, it may be remarked, that in all probability there must always be meteors falling into the Sun, since the fact of meteors coming to the earth † proves the existence of such bodies moving about in space; and even if the motions of these

becoming somewhat cooled and consequently denser—a process which might go on for many years without any sensible loss of brightness. If we consider, however, the whole annual emission at the present actual rate, we find, even if the Sun's thermal capacity were as great as that of an equal mass of water, that his mean temperature would be lowered by about $3°$ cent. in two years. We may, I think, safely conclude that primitive heat within the Sun is not a sufficient source for the emission which has continued without sensible (if any) abatement for 6000 years.— (May 4, 1854.) [For a reversal of this conclusion founded on a thermo-dynamic proof that "the mean specific heat of the Sun's mass is probably more than ten times, and less than ten thousand times, that of water, see my paper on " the Age of the Sun's Heat" in Macmillan's *Magazine* for March, 1862, republished as Appendix (E) of Thomson and Tait's *Natural Philosophy*, 2nd Edition, Part II., 1883. W. T. Nov. 9, 1882.]

* [Note of Nov. 9, 1882. Mayer, as I have since learned, had previously suggested this hypothesis.]

† To make the argument perfectly conclusive, it would have to be assumed that meteors not only are, but have been, always falling to the earth for some immense period of time. The conclusion, however, appears sufficiently probable with the facts we know.

bodies are at any instant such as to correspond to elliptical or circular orbits round the Sun, the effects of the resisting medium would gradually bring them in to strike his surface. Also, it is easy to prove dynamically that meteors falling into the Sun, whatever may have been their previous state of motion, must enter his atmosphere, or strike his surface, with, on the whole, immensely greater relative velocities than those with which meteors falling to the earth enter the earth's atmosphere, or strike the earth's surface. Now, Joule has shown what enormous quantities of heat must be generated from this relative motion in the case of meteors coming to the earth; and by his explanation* of "falling stars," has made it all but certain that, in a vast majority of cases, this generation of heat is so intense as to raise the body in temperature gradually up to an intense white heat, and cause it ultimately to burst into sparks in the air (and burn if it be of metallic iron) before it reaches the surface. Such effects must be experienced to an enormously greater degree before reaching his surface, by meteors falling to the Sun, if, as is highly probable, he has a dense atmosphere; or they would take place yet more intensely on striking his solid or liquid surface, were they to reach it still possessing great velocities. Hence, it is certain that *some* heat and light radiating from the Sun is due to meteors. It is excessively probable that there is much more of this from any part of the Sun's surface than from an equal area of the earth's, because of the enormously greater action that an equal amount of meteoric matter would produce in entering the Sun, and because the Sun, by his greater attraction, must draw in meteoric matter much more copiously with reference to equal areas of surface. We should have no right then, as was done till Mr Waterston brought forward his theory, to neglect meteoric action in speculating on solar heat, unless we could prove, which we certainly cannot do, that its influence is insensible. It is in fact not only proved to exist as a cause of solar heat, but it is the only one of all conceivable causes which we know to exist from independent evidence.

* See *Philosophical Magazine*, May 1848, for reference to a lecture in Manchester, on the 28th April, 1847, in which Mr Joule said, that " the velocity of a meteoric stone is checked by the atmosphere and its *vis viva* converted into heat, which at last becomes so intense as to melt the body and dissipate it in fragments too small probably to be noticed in their fall to the ground, in most cases." [See also above, Vol. I. Art. XLIX. Part III.]

To test the possibility of this being the *principal or the sole cause* of the phenomenon, let us estimate at what rate meteoric matter would have to fall on the Sun, to generate as much heat as is emitted. According to Pouillet's data*, ·06 of a thermal unit [pound-water-degree] centigrade is the amount of heat incident per second on a square foot directly exposed to solar radiation at the earth's distance from the Sun, which being 95,000,000 miles, and the Sun's radius being 441,000 miles, we infer that the rate of emission of heat from the Sun is

$$·06 \times \left(\frac{95,000,000}{441,000}\right)^2 = 2781 \text{ thermal units per}$$

second per square foot of his surface.

The mechanical value of this (obtained by multiplying it by Joule's equivalent, 1390) is

$$83·4 \times \left(\frac{95,000,000}{441.000}\right)^2 = 386,900 \text{ ft. lbs}$$

Now if, as Mr Waterston supposes, a meteor either strikes the Sun, or enters an atmosphere where the luminous and thermal excitation takes place, *without having previously experienced any sensible resistance,* it may be shown dynamically (the velocity of rotation of the Sun's surface, which at his equator is only a mile and a quarter per second, being neglected) that the least relative velocity which it can have is the velocity it would acquire by solar gravitation in falling from an infinite distance, which is equal to the velocity it would acquire by the action of a constant force equal to its weight at the Sun's surface, operating through a space equal to his radius. The force of gravity at the Sun's surface being about 28 times that at the earth's surface, this velocity is

$$\sqrt{\frac{2 \times 28 \times 32·2 \times 441,000}{5280}} = 390 \text{ miles per second;}$$

and its mechanical value per pound of meteoric matter is

$$28 \times 441,000 \times 5280 = 65,000,000,000 \text{ ft. lbs.}$$

Hence the quantity of meteoric matter that would be required, according to Mr Waterston's form of the Gravitation Theory, to strike the Sun per square foot is 0·000060 pounds per second (or about a pound every five hours). At this rate the surface

* *Mémoire sur la Chaleur Solaire, &c.,* Paris, 1838; see *Comptes Rendus,* July 1838; or Pouillet, *Traité de Physique,* Vol. II.

would be covered to a depth of thirty feet in a year, if the density of the deposit is the same as that of water, which is a little less than the mean density of the Sun*. A greater rate of deposit than this could not be required, if the hypothesis of no resistance, except in the locality of resistance with luminous reaction, were true ; but a less rate would suffice if, as is probable enough, the meteors in remote space had velocities relative to the Sun not incomparably smaller than the velocity calculated above as due to solar gravitation.

But it appears to me that the hypothesis of no sensible resistance until the " Sun's atmosphere " is reached, or the Sun's surface struck, is not probable † ; because if meteors were falling into the Sun in straight lines, or in parabolic or hyperbolic paths, in anything like sufficient quantities for generating all the heat he emits, the earth in crossing their paths would be, if not intolerably pelted, at least struck much more copiously by meteors than we can believe it to be from what we observe ; and because the meteors we see appear to come generally in directions corresponding to motions which have been elliptic or circular, and rarely if ever in such directions as could correspond to previous parabolic, hyperbolic, or rectilineal paths towards the Sun. If this opinion and the first mentioned reason for it be correct, the meteors containing the stores of energy for future Sun light must be principally within the earth's orbit: and we actually see them there as the " Zodiacal Light," an illuminated shower or rather tornado of stones (Herschel, § 897). The inner parts of this tornado are always getting caught in the Sun's atmosphere, and drawn to his mass by gravitation. The bodies in all parts of it, in consequence of the same actions, must be approaching the Sun, although but very gradually ; yet, in consequence of their comparative minuteness, much more rapidly than the planets. The outer edge of the zodiacal light appears to reach to near the earth at present (Herschel, § 897) ; and in past times it may be that the earth has been in a dense enough part of it to be kept hot, just as the Sun is now, by drawing in meteors to its surface.

---

* This is rather more than double the estimate Mr Waterston has given. The velocity of impact which he has taken is 545 miles per second, in the calculation of which, unless I am mistaken, there must be some error.

† For a demonstration that it is not possible, see Addition, No. 1.

According to this form of the gravitation theory, a meteor would approach the Sun by a very gradual spiral, moving with a velocity very little more than that corresponding to a circular path at the same distance, until it begins to be much more resisted, and to be consequently rapidly deflected towards the Sun; then the phenomenon of ignition commences; after a few seconds of time all the dynamical energy the body had at the commencement of the sudden change is converted into heat and radiated off; and the mass itself settles incorporated in the Sun. It appears, therefore, that the velocity which a meteor loses in entering the Sun is that of a satellite at his surface, which (being $\frac{1}{\sqrt{2}}$ of that due to gravitation from an infinite distance) is 276 miles per second. The mechanical value (being half that of a body falling to the Sun from a state of comparatively slow motion in space) is about 32,500,000,000 ft. lb. per pound of meteoric matter; hence the fall of meteors must be just twice that which was determined above according to Mr Waterston's form of the theory, and must consequently amount to 3800 lbs. annually per square foot. If, as was before supposed, the density of the deposit is the same as that of water, the whole surface would be covered annually to a depth of 60 feet, from which the Sun would grow in diameter by a mile in 88 years. It would take 4000 years at this rate to grow a tenth of a second in apparent diameter, which could scarcely be perceived by the most refined of modern observations, or 40,000 years to grow 1″, which would be utterly insensible by any kind of observation (that of eclipses included) unassisted by powerful telescopes. We may be confident, then, that the gradual augmentation of the Sun's bulk required by the meteoric theory to account for this heat, may have been going on in time past during the whole existence of the human race, and yet could not possibly have been discovered by observation, and that at the same rate it may go on for thousands of years yet without being discoverable by the most refined observations of modern astronomy. It would take, always at the same rate, about 2,000,000 years for the Sun to grow in reality as much as he appears to grow from June to December by the variation of the earth's distance, which is quite imperceptible to ordinary observation. This leaves for the speculations of geologists on ancient natural history a wide enough range of time with a Sun not sensibly less than our present luminary : Still more, the meteoric theory affords the simplest possible explanation of past changes of climate on the earth.   For a time the earth may have been kept melted by the heat of meteors striking it.   A period may have followed when the earth was not too hot for vegetation, but was still kept, by the heat of meteors falling through its atmosphere, at a much higher temperature than at present, and illuminated in all regions, polar as well as equatorial, before the existence of night and day.   Lastly ; although a very little smaller, the Sun may have been at some remote period much hotter than at present by having a more copious meteoric supply.

A dark body of dimensions such as the Sun, in any part of space, might, by entering a cloud of meteors, become incandescent as intensely in a few seconds as it could in years of continuance of the same meteoric circumstances ; and on again getting to a position in space comparatively free from meteors, it might almost as suddenly become dark again.   It is far from improbable that this is the explanation of the appearance and disappearance of bright stars, and of the strange variations of brilliancy of others which have caused so much astonishment*.

The amount of matter, drawn by the Sun in any time from surrounding space, would be such as in $47\frac{1}{2}$ years to amount to a mass equal to that of the earth.   Now there is no reason whatever to suppose that 100 times the earth's mass drawn into the Sun, would be missed from the zodiacal light (or from meteors revolving inside the orbit of Mercury, whether visible as the " zodiacal light " or not) ; and we may conclude that there is no difficulty whatever in accounting for a constancy of solar heat during 5000 years of time past or to come.   Even physical astronomy can raise no objection by showing that the Sun's mass has not experienced such an augmentation ; for according to the form of the gravitation theory which I have proposed, the added matter is drawn from a space where it acts on the planets with very nearly the same forces as when incorporated in the Sun.   This form of the gravitation theory then, which may be proved to require a greater

---

* The star which Mr Hind discovered in April 1848, and which only remained visible for a few weeks, during which period it varied considerably in appearance and brightness, but was always of a " ruddy " colour, may not have experienced meteoric impact enough to make its surface more than red hot.

mass of meteoric matter to produce the solar heat than would be required on any other assumption that could be made regarding the previous positions and motions of the meteors, requires not more than it is perfectly possible does fall into the Sun. Hence I think we may regard the adequacy of the meteoric theory to be fully established.

Let us now consider how much chemical action would be required to produce the same effects, with a view both to test the adequacy of the theory that the Sun is merely a burning mass without a supply of either fuel or dynamical energy from without, and to ascertain the extent to which, in the third theory, the combustion of meteors may contribute, along with their dynamical energies, to the supply of solar heat. Taking the former estimate [p. 6 above], 2781 thermal units centigrade, or 3,869,000 foot-lbs. as the rate per second of emission of energy from a square foot of the Sun's surface, equivalent to 7000 horse power*, we find that more than ·42 of a lb. of coal per second, or 1500 lbs. per hour would be required to produce heat at the same rate. Now if all the fires of the whole Baltic fleet were heaped up and kept in full combustion, over one or two square yards of surface, and if the surface of a globe all round had every square yard so occupied, where could a sufficient supply of air come from to sustain the combustion? yet such is the condition we must suppose the Sun to be in, according to the hypothesis now under consideration, at least if one of the combining elements be oxygen or any other gas drawn from the surrounding atmosphere. If the products of combustion were gaseous, they would in rising check the necessary supply of fresh air; or if they be solid or liquid (as they might be wholly or partly if the fuel be metallic) they would interfere with the supply of the elements from below. In either or in both ways the fire would be choked, and I think it may be safely affirmed that no such fire could keep alight for more than a few minutes, by any conceivable adaptation of air and fuel. If then the Sun be a burning mass, it must be more analogous to burning gunpowder than to a fire burning in air; and it is quite conceivable that a solid mass, containing within itself all the elements required for combustion, *provided the products of combustion are*

[* Note of Nov. 11, 1882. This is sixty-seven times the rate per unit of radiant surface, at which energy is emitted from the incandescent filament of the Swan electric lamp when at the temperature which gives about 240 candles per horse power.]

permanently gaseous*, could burn off at its surface all round, and actually emit heat as copiously as the Sun. Thus an enormous globe of gun-cotton might, if at first cold, and once set on fire round its surface, get to a permanent rate of burning, in which any internal part would become heated by conduction, sufficiently to ignite, only when nearly approached by the diminishing surface. It is highly probable indeed that such a body might for a time be as large as the Sun, and give out luminous heat as copiously, to be freely radiated into space, without suffering more absorption from its atmosphere of transparent gaseous products† than the light of the Sun actually does experience from the dense atmosphere through which it passes. Let us therefore consider at what rate such a body, giving out heat so copiously, would diminish by burning away. The heat of combustion could probably not be so much as 4000 thermal units per pound of matter burned ‡, the greatest thermal equivalent of chemical action yet ascertained falling considerably short of this. But 2781 thermal units (as found above) are emitted per second from each square foot of the Sun ; hence there would be a loss of about ·7 of a pound of matter per square foot per second. Such a loss of matter from every square foot, if of the mean density of the Sun (a little more than that of water), would take off from the mass a layer of about ·5 of a foot thick in a minute, or of about 55 miles thick in a year. At the same rate continued, a mass as large as the Sun is at present would burn away in 8000 years. If the Sun has been burning at that rate in past time, he must have been of double diameter, of quadruple heating power, and of eight-fold mass, only 8000 years ago. We may quite safely conclude then that the Sun does not get its heat by chemical action among particles of matter primitively belonging to his own mass, and we must therefore look to the meteoric theory for fuel, even if we retain the idea of a fire. Now, according to Andrews, the heat of combustion of a pound of iron in oxygen gas is 1301 thermal units, and of a pound of potassium in chlorine 2655 ; a pound of potassium in oxygen 1700 according to Joule ; and carbon in oxygen, according to various observers, 8000. The

---

* On this account gunpowder would not do.

† These would rise and be regularly diffused into space.

‡ Both the elements that enter into combination are of course included in the weight of the burning matter.

greatest of these numbers, multiplied by 1390 to reduce to foot-pounds, expresses only the 6000th part, according to Mr Waterston's theory, and, according to the form of the Gravitation Theory now proposed, only the 3000th part, of the least amount of dynamical energy a meteor can have on entering the region of ignition in the Sun's atmosphere. Hence a mass of carbon entering the Sun's atmosphere, and there burning with oxygen, could only by combustion give out heat equal to the 3000th part of the heat it cannot but give out from its motion. Probably no kind of known matter (and no meteors reaching the earth have yet brought us decidedly new elements) entering the Sun's atmosphere from space, whatever may be its chemical nature, and whatever its dynamical antecedents, could emit by combustion as much as $\frac{1}{1000}$ of the heat inevitably generated from its motion. It is highly probable that many, if not all, meteors entering the Sun's atmosphere do burn, or enter into some chemical combination with substances which they meet. Probably meteoric iron comes to the Sun in enormous quantities, and burns in his atmosphere just as it does in coming to the earth. But (while probably nearly all the heat and light of the sparks which fly from a steel struck by a flint is due to combustion alone) only $\frac{1}{18000}$ part of the heat and light of a mass of iron entering the Sun's atmosphere or $\frac{1}{5}$th of the heat and light of such a meteor entering our own, can possibly be due to combustion. Hence the combustion of meteors may be quite disregarded as a source of solar heat.

At the commencement of this communication, it was shown that the heat radiated from the Sun is either taken from a stock of primitive solar heat, or generated by chemical action among materials originally belonging to his mass, or due to meteors falling in from surrounding space. We saw that there are sufficient reasons for utterly rejecting* the first hypothesis; we have now proved that the second is untenable; and we may consequently conclude that the third is true, or that meteors falling in from space give rise to the heat which is continually radiated off by the Sun. We have also seen that no appreciable portion of the heat thus produced is due to chemical action, either between the meteors and substances which they meet at the Sun, or among elements of the meteors themselves; and that whatever may have been their original positions or motions relatively to one another

* [See note on page 3.]

or to the Sun, the greater part of them fall in gradually from a state of approximately circular motion, and strike the Sun with the velocity due to half the potential energy of gravitation lost in coming in from an infinite distance to his surface. The other half of this energy goes to generate heat very slowly and diffusely in the resisting medium. Many a meteor, however, we cannot doubt, comes in to the Sun at once in the course of a rectilineal or hyperbolic path, without having spent any appreciable energy in the resisting medium; and, consequently, enters the region of ignition at his surface with a velocity due to the descent from its previous state of motion or rest, and there converts both the dynamical effect of the potential energy of gravitation, and the energy of its previous motion, if it had any, into heat which is instantly radiated off to space. But the reasons stated above make it improbable that more than a very small fraction of the whole solar heat is obtained by meteors coming in thus directly from extra-planetary space.

In conclusion, then, the source of energy from which solar heat is derived is undoubtedly meteoric. It is not any intrinsic energy in the meteors themselves, either potential, as of mutual gravitation or chemical affinities among their elements; or actual, as of relative motions among them. It is altogether dependent on mutual relations between those bodies and the Sun. A portion of it, although very probably not an appreciable portion, is that of motions relative to the Sun, and of independent origin. The principal source, perhaps the sole appreciably efficient source, is in bodies circulating round the Sun at present inside the earth's orbit, and probably seen in the sunlight by us and called "the Zodiacal Light." The store of energy for future sunlight is at present partly dynamical, that of the motions of these bodies round the Sun; and partly potential, that of their gravitation towards the Sun. This latter is gradually being spent, half against the resisting medium, and half in causing a continuous increase of the former. Each meteor thus goes on moving faster and faster, and getting nearer and nearer the centre, until some time, very suddenly, it gets so much entangled in the solar atmosphere, as to begin to lose velocity. In a few seconds more, it is at rest on the Sun's surface, and the energy given up is vibrated in a minute or two across the district where it was gathered during so many ages, ultimately to penetrate as light the remotest regions of space.

Explanation of Tables.

The following Tables exhibit the principal numerical data regarding the Mechanical Energies of the Solar System.

In Table I., the mass of the Earth is estimated on the assumption that its mean

TABLE I. *Forces and Motions in the Solar System.*

	Masses in pounds.	Distances from the Sun's centre, in miles.	Forces of attraction towards the Sun, in terrestrial pounds.	Velocities, in miles per second.
Sun	$4,230,000,000 \times 10^{21}$	(surface) 411,000	$28 \cdot 61$ per lb. of matter	(equator) $1 \cdot 27$
Imaginary solid planet close to the Sun	1×10^{21}	411,000	$286,100 \times 10^{7}$	277
Mercury	870×10^{21}	36,800,000	$35,710 \times 10^{7}$	$30 \cdot 36$
Venus	$10,530 \times 10^{21}$	68,700,000	$124,200 \times 10^{7}$	$22 \cdot 22$
Earth	$11,920 \times 10^{21}$	95,000,000	$73,490 \times 10^{7}$	$18 \cdot 89$
Mars	$1,579 \times 10^{21}$	144,800,000	$4,211 \times 10^{7}$	$15 \cdot 28$
Jupiter	$4,037,000 \times 10^{21}$	494,300,000	$919,400 \times 10^{7}$	$8 \cdot 28$
Saturn	$1,208,000 \times 10^{21}$	906,200,000	$81,855 \times 10^{7}$	$6 \cdot 11$
Uranus	$201,490 \times 10^{21}$	1,822,000,000	$3,377 \times 10^{7}$	$4 \cdot 31$
Neptune	$236,380 \times 10^{21}$	2,854,000,000	$1,615 \times 10^{7}$	$3 \cdot 44$

		Distances from Earth's centre.	Attraction towards Earth in terrestrial pounds.	Velocities relatively to Earth's centre, in miles.
Moon	136×10^{21}	237,000	378×10^{7}	$0 \cdot 615$
Earth's equator		3,956	1 per lb. of matter.	$0 \cdot 291$

density is five times that of water, and the other masses are shown in their true proportions to that of the Earth, according to data which Professor Piazzi Smyth has kindly communicated to the author.

In Table II., the mechanical values of the rotations of the Sun and Earth are computed on the hypothesis, that the moment of inertia of each sphere is equal the

TABLE II. *Mechanical Energies of the Solar System.*

	Potential Energy of gravitation to Sun's surface.		Actual Energy relatively to Sun's centre.	
	In foot-pounds.	Equivalent to supply of Solar Heat, at the present rate of radiation for a period of	In foot-pounds.	Equivalent to supply of Solar heat, at the present rate of radiation for a period of
Sun	0	0	$976{,}000 \times 10^{30}$	116 yrs. 6 days
Imaginary planet, of 10^{21} lb. of matter, close to the Sun	0	0	333×10^{29}	1·44 ...
Mercury	57×10^{33}	6 yrs. 214 days	347×10^{30}	15·2 ...
Venus	697×10^{33}	83 ... 227 ...	$2{,}252 \times 10^{30}$	98·5 ...
Earth	790×10^{33}	94 ... 303 ...	$1{,}843 \times 10^{30}$	80·7 ...
Mars	105×10^{33}	12 ... 252 ...	160×10^{30}	7·0 ...
Jupiter	$268{,}800 \times 10^{33}$	32,240	$119{,}980 \times 10^{30}$	14 yrs. 144 ...
Saturn	$80{,}440 \times 10^{33}$	9,650	$19{,}580 \times 10^{30}$	2 ... 127 ...
Uranus	$13{,}430 \times 10^{33}$	1,610	$1{,}625 \times 10^{30}$	71·2 ...
Neptune	$15{,}750 \times 10^{33}$	1,890	$1{,}217 \times 10^{30}$	53·3 ...
	To the Earth's surface.		Relatively to Earth's centre.	
Moon	$2{,}846 \times 10^{27}$	3·0 hours	$2{,}347 \times 10^{25}$	1·48 minutes
Earth (rotation)			$14{,}310 \times 10^{25}$ $= 6\cdot4 \times 10^{25}$ ft. tons.	9·03 ...
Total	$380{,}000 \times 10^{33}$	45,589 years	$1{,}114{,}004 \times 10^{30}$	134 years.

square of its radius multiplied by only one-third of its mass, instead of two-fifths of its mass as would be the case if its matter were of uniform density. These two estimates are only introduced for the sake of comparison with other mechanical values shown in the Table, not having been used in the reasoning.

The numbers in the last column of Table II., showing the times during which the Sun emits quantities of heat mechanically equivalent to the Earth's motion in its orbit, and to its motion of rotation, were first communicated to the Royal Society on the 9th January, 1852, in a paper "On the Sources Available to Man for the production of Mechanical Effect." [Vol. I. Art. LVIII.] These, and the other numbers in the same column, are the only part of the numerical data either shown in the Tables, or used directly or indirectly in the reasoning on which the present theory is founded, that can possibly require any considerable correction; depending as they do on M. Pouillet's estimate of Solar Heat in thermal units. The extreme difficulties in the way of arriving at this estimate, notwithstanding the remarkably able manner in which they have been met, necessarily leave much uncertainty as to the degree of accuracy of the result. But even if it were two or three times too great or too small (and there appears no possibility that it can be so far from the truth), the general reasoning by which the Theory of Solar Heat at present communicated is supported, would hold with scarcely altered force.

The mechanical equivalent of the thermic unit, by which the Solar radiation has been reduced to mechanical units is Mr Joule's result—1390 foot-pounds for the thermal unit centigrade—which he determined by direct experiment with so much accuracy, that any correction it may be found to require can scarcely amount to $\frac{1}{200}$ or $\frac{1}{300}$ of its own value.

11

Reprinted from Hermann von Helmholtz, *Popular Lectures on Scientific Subjects*, E. Atkinson, trans., D. Appleton and Co., New York, 1897, pp. 173–196

Contraction Theory of the Sun's Heat

Hermann von Helmholtz

[*Ed. note:* In the original, material precedes this excerpt.]

The general principle which I have sought to lay before you has conducted us to a point from which our view is a wide one ; and aided by this principle, we can now at pleasure regard this or the other side of the surrounding world according as our interest in the matter leads us. A glance into the narrow laboratory of the physicist, with its small appliances and complicated abstractions, will not be so attractive as a glance at the wide heaven above us, the clouds, the rivers, the woods, and the living beings around us. While regarding the laws which have been deduced from the physical processes of terrestrial bodies as applicable also to the heavenly bodies, let me remind you that the same force which, acting at the earth's surface, we call gravity (*Schwere*), acts as gravitation in the celestial spaces, and also manifests its power in the motion of the immeasurably distant double stars, which are governed by exactly the same laws as those subsisting between the earth and moon ; that therefore the light and heat of terrestrial bodies do not in any way differ essentially from those of the sun or of the most distant fixed star ; that the meteoric stones which sometimes fall from external space upon the earth are composed of exactly the same simple chemical substances as those with which we are acquainted. We need, therefore, feel no scruple in granting that general laws to which all terrestrial natural processes are subject are also valid for other bodies than the earth. We will, therefore, make use of our law to glance over the household of the universe with respect to the store of force, capable of action, which it possesses.

A number of singular peculiarities in the structure of our planetary system indicate that it was once a connected mass, with a uniform motion of rotation. Without such an assumption it is impossible to explain why all the planets move in the same direction round the sun, why they all rotate in the same direction round their axes, why the planes of their orbits and those of their satellites and rings all nearly coincide, why all their orbits differ but little from circles, and much besides. From these remaining indications of a former state astronomers have shaped an hypothesis regarding the formation of our planetary system, which, although from the nature of the case it must ever remain an hypothesis, still in its special traits is so well supported by analogy, that it certainly deserves our attention ; and the more so, as this notion in our own home, and within the walls of this town,[1] first found utterance. It was Kant who, feeling great interest in the physical description of the earth and the planetary system, undertook the labour of studying the works of Newton ; and, as an evidence of the depth to which he had penetrated into the fundamental ideas of Newton, seized the notion that the same attractive force of all ponderable matter which now supports the motion of the planets must also aforetime have been able to form from matter loosely scattered in space the planetary system. Afterwards, and independent of Kant, Laplace, the great author of the ' Mécanique céleste,' laid hold of the same thought, and introduced it among astronomers.

The commencement of our planetary system, including the sun, must, according to this, be regarded as an immense nebulous mass which filled the portion of space now occupied by our system far beyond the

[1] Königsberg.

limits of Neptune, our most distant planet. Even now we discern in distant regions of the firmament nebulous patches the light of which, as spectrum analysis teaches, is the light of ignited gases ; and in their spectra we see more especially those bright lines which are produced by ignited hydrogen and by ignited nitrogen. Within our system, also, comets, the crowds of shooting stars, and the zodiacal light exhibit distinct traces of matter dispersed like powder, which moves, however, according to the law of gravitation, and is, at all events, partially retarded by the larger bodies and incorporated in them. The latter undoubtedly happens with the shooting stars and meteoric stones which come within the range of our atmosphere.

If we calculate the density of the mass of our planetary system, according to the above assumption, for the time when it was a nebulous sphere, which reached to the path of the outermost planet, we should find that it would require several millions of cubic miles of such matter to weigh a single grain.

The general attractive force of all matter must, however, impel these masses to approach each other, and to condense, so that the nebulous sphere became incessantly smaller, by which, according to mechanical laws, a motion of rotation originally slow, and the existence of which must be assumed, would gradually become quicker and quicker. By the centrifugal force, which must act most energetically in the neighbourhood of the equator of the nebulous sphere, masses could from time to time be torn away, which afterwards would continue their courses separate from the main mass, forming themselves into single planets, or, similar to the great original sphere, into planets with satellites and rings, until finally the principal mass condensed itself into the sun. With regard to the origin of heat and light this theory originally gave no information.

When the nebulous chaos first separated itself from other fixed star masses it must not only have contained all kinds of matter which was to constitute the future planetary system, but also, in accordance with our new law, the whole store of force which at a future time ought to unfold therein its wealth of actions. Indeed, in this respect an immense dower was bestowed in the shape of the general attraction of all the particles for each other. This force, which on the earth exerts itself as gravity, acts in the heavenly spaces as gravitation. As terrestrial gravity when it draws a weight downwards performs work and generates *vis viva*, so also the heavenly bodies do the same when they draw two portions of matter from distant regions of space towards each other.

The chemical forces must have been also present, ready to act ; but as these forces can only come into operation by the most intimate contact of the different masses, condensation must have taken place before the play of chemical forces began.

Whether a still further supply of force in the shape of heat was present at the commencement we do not know. At all events, by aid of the law of the equivalence of heat and work, we find in the mechanical forces existing at the time to which we refer such a rich source of heat and light, that there is no necessity whatever to take refuge in the idea of a store of these forces originally existing. When, through condensation of the masses, their particles came into collision and clung to each other, the *vis viva* of their motion would be thereby annihilated, and must reappear as heat. Already in old theories it has been calculated that cosmical masses must generate heat by their collision, but it was far from anybody's thought to make even a guess at the amount of heat to be generated in this way. At present we can give definite numerical values with certainty.

Let us make this addition to our assumption—that, at the commencement, the density of the nebulous matter was a vanishing quantity as compared with the present density of the sun and planets : we can then calculate how much work has been performed by the condensation ; we can further calculate how much of this work still exists in the form of mechanical force, as attraction of the planets towards the sun, and as *vis viva* of their motion, and find by this how much of the force has been converted into heat.

The result of this calculation[1] is, that only about the 454th part of the original mechanical force remains as such, and that the remainder, converted into heat, would be sufficient to raise a mass of water equal to the sun and planets taken together, not less than twenty-eight millions of degrees of the Centigrade scale. For the sake of comparison, I will mention that the highest temperature which we can produce by the oxyhydrogen blowpipe, which is sufficient to fuse and vaporise even platinum, and which but few bodies can endure without melting, is estimated at about 2,000 degrees. Of the action of a temperature of twenty-eight millions of such degrees we can form no notion. If the mass of our entire system were pure coal, by the combustion of the whole of it only the 3,500th part of the above quantity would be generated. This is also clear, that such a great development of heat must have presented the greatest obstacle to the speedy union of the masses ; that the greater part of the heat must have been diffused by radiation into space, before the masses could form bodies possessing the present density of the sun and planets, and that these bodies must once have been in a state of fiery fluidity. This notion is corroborated by the geological phænomena of our planet ; and with regard to the other planetary bodies, the flat-

[1] See note on page 193.

tened form of the sphere, which is the form of equilibrium of a fluid mass, is indicative of a former state of
fluidity. If I thus permit an immense quantity of heat
to disappear without compensation from our system, the
principle of the conservation of force is not thereby in-
vaded. Certainly for our planet it is lost, but not for the
universe. It has proceeded outwards, and daily proceeds
outwards into infinite space; and we know not whether
the medium which transmits the undulations of light
and heat possesses an end where the rays must return, or
whether they eternally pursue their way through infinitude.

The store of force at present possessed by our system is
also equivalent to immense quantities of heat. If our
earth were by a sudden shock brought to rest in her orbit
—which is not to be feared in the existing arrangement
of our system—by such a shock a quantity of heat would
be generated equal to that produced by the combustion of
fourteen such earths of solid coal. Making the most unfavourable assumption as to its capacity for heat—that
is, placing it equal to that of water—the mass of the earth
would thereby be heated 11,200 degrees; it would, therefore, be quite fused, and for the most part converted into
vapour. If, then, the earth, after having been thus
brought to rest, should fall into the sun—which, of
course, would be the case—the quantity of heat developed by the shock would be 400 times greater.

Even now from time to time such a process is repeated
on a small scale. There can hardly be a doubt that
meteors, fireballs, and meteoric stones are masses which
belong to the universe, and before coming into the
domain of our earth, moved like the planets round the
sun. Only when they enter our atmosphere do they
become visible and fall sometimes to the earth. In order
to explain the emission of light by these bodies, and the
fact that for some time after their descent they are very

hot, the friction was long ago thought of which they experience in passing through the air. We can now calculate that a velocity of 3,000 feet a second, supposing the whole of the friction to be expended in heating the solid mass, would raise a piece of meteoric iron 1,000° C. in temperature, or, in other words, to a vivid red heat. Now the average velocity of the meteors seems to be thirty to fifty times the above amount. To compensate this, however, the greater portion of the heat is doubtless carried away by the condensed mass of air which the meteor drives before it. It is known that bright meteors generally leave a luminous trail behind them, which probably consists of severed portions of the red-hot surfaces. Meteoric masses which fall to the earth often burst with a violent explosion, which may be regarded as a result of the quick heating. The newly-fallen pieces have been for the most part found hot, but not red-hot, which is easily explainable by the circumstance, that during the short time occupied by the meteor in passing through the atmosphere, only a thin superficial layer is heated to redness, while but a small quantity of heat has been able to penetrate to the interior of the mass. For this reason the red heat can speedily disappear.

Thus has the falling of the meteoric stone, the minute remnant of processes which seem to have played an important part in the formation of the heavenly bodies, conducted us to the present time, where we pass from the darkness of hypothetical views to the brightness of knowledge. In what we have said, however, all that is hypothetical is the assumption of Kant and Laplace, that the masses of our system were once distributed as nebulæ in space.

On account of the rarity of the case, we will still further remark in what close coincidence the results of science here stand with the earlier legends of the human family, and the forebodings of poetic fancy. The cosmogony of ancient nations generally commences with chaos and darkness. Thus for example Mephistopheles says :—

> Part of the Part am I, once All, in primal night,
> Part of the Darkness which brought forth the Light,
> The haughty Light, which now disputes the space,
> And claims of Mother Night her ancient place.

Neither is the Mosaic tradition very divergent, particularly when we remember that that which Moses names heaven, is different from the blue dome above us, and is synonymous with space, and that the unformed earth and the waters of the great deep, which were afterwards divided into waters above the firmament and waters below the firmament, resembled the chaotic components of the world :—

'In the beginning God created the heaven and the earth.

'And the earth was without form, and void; and darkness was upon the face of the deep. And the spirit of God moved upon the face of the waters.'

And just as in nebulous sphere, just become luminous, and in the new red-hot liquid earth of our modern cosmogony light was not yet divided into sun and stars, nor time into day and night, as it was after the earth had cooled.

'And God divided the light from the darkness.

'And God called the light day, and the darkness He called night. And the evening and the morning were the first day.'

And now, first, after the waters had been gathered together into the sea, and the earth had been laid dry, could plants and animals be formed.

Our earth bears still the unmistakeable traces of its old fiery fluid condition. The granite formations of her mountains exhibit a structure, which can only be produced by the crystallisation of fused masses. Investigation still shows that the temperature in mines and borings increases as we descend; and if this increase is uniform, at the depth of fifty miles a heat exists sufficient to fuse all our minerals. Even now our volcanoes project from time to time mighty masses of fused rocks from their interior, as a testimony of the heat which exists there. But the cooled crust of the earth has already become so thick, that, as may be shown by calculations of its conductive power, the heat coming to the surface from within, in comparison with that reaching the earth from the sun, is exceedingly small, and increases the temperature of the surface only about $\frac{1}{30}$th of a degree Centigrade; so that the remnant of the old store of force which is enclosed as heat within the bowels of the earth has a sensible influence upon the processes at the earth's surface only through the instrumentality of volcanic phænomena. Those processes owe their power almost wholly to the action of other heavenly bodies, particularly to the light and heat of the sun, and partly also, in the case of the tides, to the attraction of the sun and moon.

Most varied and numerous are the changes which we owe to the light and heat of the sun. The sun heats our atmosphere irregularly, the warm rarefied air ascends, while fresh cool air flows from the sides to supply its place : in this way winds are generated. This action is most powerful at the equator, the warm air of which incessantly flows in the upper regions of the atmosphere towards the poles; while just as persistently at the earth's surface, the trade-wind carries new and cool air to the equator. Without the heat of the sun, all winds must of necessity cease. Similar currents are produced by the same cause in the waters of the sea. Their power may be inferred from the influence which in some cases they exert upon climate. By them the warm water of the Antilles is carried to the British Isles, and confers upon them a mild uniform warmth, and rich moisture; while, through similar causes, the floating ice of the North Pole is carried to the coast of Newfoundland and produces raw cold. Further, by the heat of the sun a portion of the water is converted into vapour, which rises in the atmosphere, is condensed to clouds, or falls in rain and snow upon the earth, collects in the form of springs, brooks, and rivers, and finally reaches the sea again, after having gnawed the rocks, carried away light earth, and thus performed its part in the geologic changes of the earth; perhaps besides all this it has driven our water-mill upon its way. If the heat of the sun were withdrawn, there would remain only a single motion of water, namely, the tides, which are produced by the attraction of the sun and moon.

How is it, now, with the motions and the work of organic beings? To the builders of the automata of the last century, men and animals appeared as clockwork which was never wound up, and created the force which they exerted out of nothing. They did not know how to establish a connexion between the nutriment consumed and the work generated. Since, however, we have learned to discern in the steam-engine this origin of mechanical force, we must inquire whether something similar does not hold good with regard to men. Indeed, the continuation of life is dependent on the consumption of nutritive materials: these are combustible substances, which, after digestion and being passed into the blood, actually undergo a slow combustion, and finally enter into almost the same combinations with the oxygen of the atmosphere that are produced in an open fire. As the quantity of heat generated by combustion is independent of the duration of the combustion and the steps in which it occurs, we can calculate from the mass of the consumed material how much heat, or its equivalent work, is thereby generated in an animal body. Unfortunately, the difficulty of the experiments is still very great; but within those limits of accuracy which have been as yet attainable, the experiments show that the heat generated in the animal body corresponds to the amount which would be generated by the chemical processes. The animal body therefore does not differ from the steam-engine as regards the manner in which it obtains heat and force, but does differ from it in the manner in which the force gained is to be made use of. The body is, besides, more limited than the machine in the choice of its fuel; the latter could be heated with sugar, with starch-flour, and butter, just as well as with coal or wood; the animal body must dissolve its materials artificially, and distribute them through its system; it must, further, perpetually renew the used-up materials of its organs, and as it cannot itself create the matter necessary for this, the matter must come from without. Liebig was the first to point out these various uses of the consumed nutriment. As material for the perpetual renewal of the body, it seems that certain definite albuminous substances which appear in plants, and form the chief mass of the animal body, can alone be used. They form only a portion of the mass of nutriment taken daily; the remainder, sugar, starch, fat, are really only materials for warming, and are perhaps not to be superseded by coal, simply because the latter does not permit itself to be dissolved.

If, then, the processes in the animal body are not in this respect to be distinguished from inorganic processes, the question arises, whence comes the nutriment which constitutes the source of the body's force? The answer is, from the vegetable kingdom; for only the material of plants, or the flesh of herbivorous animals, can be made use of for food. The animals which live on plants occupy a mean position between carnivorous animals, in which we reckon man, and vegetables, which the former could not make use of immediately as nutriment. In hay and grass the same nutritive substances are present as in meal and flour, but in less quantity. As, however, the digestive organs of man are not in a condition to extract the small quantity of the useful from the great excess of the insoluble, we submit, in the first place, these substances to the powerful digestion of the ox, permit the nourishment to store itself in the animal's body, in order in the end to gain it for ourselves in a more agreeable and useful form. In answer to our question, therefore, we are referred to the vegetable world. Now when what plants take in and what they give out are made the subjects of investigation, we find that the principal part of the former consists in the products of combustion which are generated by the animal. They take the consumed carbon given off in respiration, as carbonic acid, from the air, the consumed hydrogen as water, the nitrogen in its simplest and closest combination as ammonia; and from these materials, with the assistance of small ingredients which they take from the soil, they generate anew the compound combustible substances, albumen, sugar, oil, on which the animal subsists. Here, therefore, is a circuit which appears to be a perpetual store of force. Plants prepare fuel and nutriment, animals consume these, burn them slowly in their lungs, and from the products of combustion the plants again derive their nutriment. The latter is an eternal source of chemical, the former of mechanical forces. Would not the combination of both organic kingdoms produce the perpetual motion? We must not conclude hastily: further inquiry shows, that plants are capable of producing combustible substances only when they are

206

under the influence of the sun. A portion of the sun's rays exhibits a remarkable relation to chemical forces,—it can produce and destroy chemical combinations; and these rays, which for the most part are blue or violet, are called therefore chemical rays. We make use of their action in the production of photographs. Here compounds of silver are decomposed at the place where the sun's rays strike them. The same rays overpower in the green leaves of plants the strong chemical affinity of the carbon of the carbonic acid for oxygen, give back the latter free to the atmosphere, and accumulate the other, in combination with other bodies, as woody fibre, starch, oil, or resin. These chemically active rays of the sun disappear completely as soon as they encounter the green portions of the plants, and hence it is that in Daguerreotype images the green leaves of plants appear uniformly black. Inasmuch as the light coming from them does not contain the chemical rays, it is unable to act upon the silver compounds. But besides the blue and violet, the yellow rays play an important part in the growth of plants. They also are comparatively strongly absorbed by the leaves.

Hence a certain portion of force disappears from the sunlight, while combustible substances are generated and accumulated in plants; and we can assume it as very probable, that the former is the cause of the latter. I must indeed remark, that we are in possession of no experiments from which we might determine whether the *vis viva* of the sun's rays which have disappeared corresponds to the chemical forces accumulated during the same time; and as long as these experiments are wanting, we cannot regard the stated relation as a certainty. If this view should prove correct, we derive from it the flattering result, that all force, by means of which our bodies live and move, finds its source in the purest sunlight; and hence we are all, in point of nobility, not behind the race of the great monarch of China, who heretofore alone called himself Son of the Sun. But it must also be conceded, that our lower fellow-beings, the frog and leech, share the same æthereal origin, as also the whole vegetable world, and even the fuel which comes to us from the ages past, as well as the youngest offspring of the forest with which we heat our stoves and set our machines in motion.

You see, then, that the immense wealth of ever-changing meteorological, climatic, geological, and organic processes of our earth are almost wholly preserved in action by the light- and heat-giving rays of the sun; and you see in this a remarkable example, how Proteus-like the effects of a single cause, under altered external conditions, may exhibit itself in nature. Besides these, the earth experiences an action of another kind from its central luminary, as well as from its satellite the moon, which exhibits itself in the remarkable phænomenon of the ebb and flow of the tide.

Each of these bodies excites, by its attraction upon the waters of the sea, two gigantic waves, which flow in the same direction round the world, as the attracting bodies themselves apparently do. The two waves of the moon, on account of her greater nearness, are about $3\frac{1}{2}$ times as large as those excited by the sun. One of these waves has its crest on the quarter of the earth's surface which is turned towards the moon, the other is at the opposite side. Both these quarters possess the flow of the tide, while the regions which lie between have the ebb. Although in the open sea the height of the tide amounts to only about three feet, and only in certain narrow channels, where the moving water is squeezed together, rises to thirty feet, the might of the phænomenon is nevertheless manifest from the calculation of Bessel, according to which a quarter of the earth covered by the sea possesses, during the flow of the tide, about 22,000 cubic miles of water more than during the ebb, and that therefore such a mass of water must, in 6¼ hours, flow from one quarter of the earth to the other.

The phænomenon of the ebb and flow, as already recognised by Mayer, combined with the law of the conservation of force, stands in remarkable connexion with the question of the stability of our planetary system. The mechanical theory of the planetary motions discovered by Newton teaches, that if a solid body in absolute *vacuo*, attracted by the sun, move around him in the same manner as the planets, this motion will endure unchanged through all eternity.

Now we have actually not only one, but several such planets, which move around the sun, and by their mutual attraction create little changes and disturbances in each other's paths. Nevertheless Laplace, in his great work, the 'Mécanique céleste,' has proved that in our planetary system all these disturbances increase and diminish periodically, and can never exceed certain limits, so that by this cause the eternal existence of the planetary system is unendangered.

But I have already named two assumptions which must be made: first, that the celestial spaces must be absolutely empty; and secondly, that the sun and planets must be solid bodies. The first is at least the case as far as astronomical observations reach, for they have never been able to detect any retardation of the planets, such as would occur if they moved in a resisting medium. But on a body of less mass, the comet of Encke, changes are observed of such a nature: this comet describes ellipses round the sun which are becoming gradually smaller. If this kind of motion, which certainly corresponds to that through a resisting medium, be actually

due to the existence of such a medium, a time will come
when the comet will strike the sun; and a similar end
threatens all the planets, although after a time, the
length of which baffles our imagination to conceive of it.
But even should the existence of a resisting medium
appear doubtful to us, there is no doubt that the planets
are not wholly composed of solid materials which are
inseparably bound together. Signs of the existence of an
atmosphere are observed on the Sun, on Venus, Mars,
Jupiter, and Saturn. Signs of water and ice upon Mars;
and our earth has undoubtedly a fluid portion on its
surface, and perhaps a still greater portion of fluid within
it. The motions of the tides, however, produce friction,
all friction destroys *vis viva*, and the loss in this case can
only affect the *vis viva* of the planetary system. We
come thereby to the unavoidable conclusion, that every
tide, although with infinite slowness, still with certainty
diminishes the store of mechanical force of the system;
and as a consequence of this, the rotation of the planets
in question round their axes must become more slow.
The recent careful investigations of the moon's motion
made by Hansen, Adams, and Delaunay, have proved that
the earth does experience such a retardation. According
to the former, the length of each sidereal day has increased since the time of Hipparchus by the $\frac{1}{81}$ part of a
second, and the duration of a century by half a quarter
of an hour; according to Adams and Sir W. Thomson,
the increase has been almost twice as great. A clock
which went right at the beginning of a century, would
be twenty-two seconds in advance of the earth at the end
of the century. Laplace had denied the existence of
such a retardation in the case of the earth; to ascertain
the amount, the theory of lunar motion required a greater
development than was possible in his time. The final
consequence would be, but after millions of years, if in

210

the mean time the ocean did not become frozen, that one side of the earth would be constantly turned towards the sun, and enjoy a perpetual day, whereas the opposite side would be involved in eternal night. Such a position we observe in our moon with regard to the earth, and also in the case of the satellites as regards their planets; it is, perhaps, due to the action of the mighty ebb and flow to which these bodies, in the time of their fiery fluid condition, were subjected.

I would not have brought forward these conclusions, which again plunge us in the most distant future, if they were not unavoidable. Physico-mechanical laws are, as it were, the telescopes of our spiritual eye, which can penetrate into the deepest night of time, past and to come.

Another essential question as regards the future of our planetary system has reference to its future temperature and illumination. As the internal heat of the earth has but little influence on the temperature of the surface, the heat of the sun is the only thing which essentially affects the question. The quantity of heat falling from the sun during a given time upon a given portion of the earth's surface may be measured, and from this it can be calculated how much heat in a given time is sent out from the entire sun. Such measurements have been made by the French physicist Pouillet, and it has been found that the sun gives out a quantity of heat per hour equal to that which a layer of the densest coal 10 feet thick would give out by its combustion; and hence in a year a quantity equal to the combustion of a layer of 17 miles. If this heat were drawn uniformly from the entire mass of the sun, its temperature would only be diminished thereby $1\frac{1}{3}$ of a degree Centigrade per year, assuming its capacity for heat to be equal to that of water. These results can give us an idea of the magnitude of the emission, in relation to the surface and mass of the sun; but they cannot inform us whether the sun radiates heat as a glowing body, which since its formation has its heat accumulated within it, or whether a new generation of heat by chemical processes is continually taking place at the sun's surface. At all events, the law of the conservation of force teaches us that no process analogous to those known at the surface of the earth can supply for eternity an inexhaustible amount of light and heat to the sun. But the same law also teaches that the store of force at present existing, as heat, or as what may become heat, is sufficient for an immeasurable time. With regard to the store of chemical force in the sun, we can form no conjecture, and the store of heat there existing can only be determined by very uncertain estimations. If, however, we adopt the very probable view, that the remarkably small density of so large a body is caused by its high temperature, and may become greater in time, it may be calculated that if the diameter of the sun were diminished only the ten-thousandth part of its present length, by this act a sufficient quantity of heat would be generated to cover the total emission for 2,100 years. So small a change it would be difficult to detect even by the finest astronomical observations.

Indeed, from the commencement of the period during which we possess historic accounts, that is, for a period of about 4,000 years, the temperature of the earth has not sensibly diminished. From these old ages we have certainly no thermometric observations, but we have information regarding the distribution of certain cultivated plants, the vine, the olive tree, which are very sensitive to changes of the mean annual temperature, and we find that these plants at the present moment have the same limits of distribution that they had in the times of Abraham and Homer; from which we may infer backwards the constancy of the climate.

In opposition to this it has been urged, that here in Prussia the German knights in former times cultivated the vine, cellared their own wine and drank it, which is no longer possible. From this the conclusion has been drawn, that the heat of our climate has diminished since the time referred to. Against this, however, Dove has cited the reports of ancient chroniclers, according to which, in some peculiarly hot years, the Prussian grape possessed somewhat less than its usual quantity of acid. The fact also speaks not so much for the climate of the country as for the throats of the German drinkers.

But even though the force store of our planetary system is so immensely great, that by the incessant emission which has occurred during the period of human history it has not been sensibly diminished, even though the length of the time which must flow by before a sensible change in the state of our planetary system occurs is totally incapable of measurement, still the inexorable laws of mechanics indicate that this store of force, which can only suffer loss and not gain, must be finally exhausted. Shall we terrify ourselves by this thought? Men are in the habit of measuring the greatness and the wisdom of the universe by the duration and the profit which it promises to their own race; but the past history of the earth already shows what an insignificant moment the duration of the existence of our race upon it constitutes. A Nineveh vessel, a Roman sword, awake in us the conception of grey antiquity. What the museums of Europe show us of the remains of Egypt and Assyria we gaze upon with silent astonishment, and despair of being able to carry our thoughts back to a period so remote. Still must the human race have existed for ages, and multiplied itself before the Pyramids or Nineveh could have been erected. We estimate the duration of human history at 6,000 years; but immeasurable as this time may appear to us, what is it in comparison with the time during which the earth carried successive series of rank plants and mighty animals, and no men; during which in our neighbourhood the amber-tree bloomed, and dropped its costly gum on the earth and in the sea; when in Siberia, Europe, and North America groves of tropical palms flourished; where gigantic lizards, and after them elephants, whose mighty remains we still find buried in the earth, found a home? Different geologists, proceeding from different premises, have sought to estimate the duration of the above-named creative period, and vary from a million to nine million years. The time during which the earth generated organic beings is again small when compared with the ages during which the world was a ball of fused rocks. For the duration of its cooling from 2,000° to 200° Centigrade the experiments of Bishop upon basalt show that about 350 millions of years would be necessary. And with regard to the time during which the first nebulous mass condensed into our planetary system, our most daring conjectures must cease. The history of man, therefore, is but a short ripple in the ocean of time. For a much longer series of years than that during which he has already occupied this world, the existence of the present state of inorganic nature favourable to the duration of man seems to be secured, so that for ourselves and for long generations after us we have nothing to fear. But the same forces of air and water, and of the volcanic interior, which produced former geological revolutions, and buried one series of living forms after another, act still upon the earth's crust. They more probably will bring about the last day of the human race than those distant cosmical alterations of which we have spoken, forcing us perhaps to make way for new and more complete living forms, as the lizards and the mammoth have given place to us and our fellow-creatures which now exist.

Thus the thread which was spun in darkness by those who sought a perpetual motion has conducted us to a universal law of nature, which radiates light into the distant nights of the beginning and of the end of the history of the universe. To our own race it permits a long but not an endless existence; it threatens it with a day of judgment, the dawn of which is still happily obscured. As each of us singly must endure the thought of his death, the race must endure the same. But above the forms of life gone by, the human race has higher moral problems before it, the bearer of which it is, and in the completion of which it fulfils its destiny.

NOTE TO PAGE 177.

I must here explain the calculation of the heat which must be produced by the assumed condensation of the bodies of our system from scattered nebulous matter. The other calculations, the results of which I have mentioned, are to be found partly in J. R. Mayer's papers, partly in Joule's communications, and partly by aid of the known facts and method of science: they are easily performed.

The measure of the work performed by the condensation of the mass from a state of infinitely small density is the potential of the condensed mass upon itself. For a sphere of uniform density of the mass M, and the radius R, the potential upon itself V—if we call the mass of the earth m, its radius r, and the intensity of gravity at its surface g—has the value

$$V = \frac{3}{5} \cdot \frac{r^2 M^2}{Rm} \cdot g.$$

Let us regard the bodies of our system as such spheres, then the total work of condensation is equal to the sum of all their potentials on themselves. As, however, these potentials for different spheres are to each other as the quantity $\frac{M^2}{R}$, they all vanish in comparison with the sun; even that of the greatest planet, Jupiter, is only about the one hundred-thousandth part of that of the sun; in the calculation, therefore, it is only necessary to introduce the latter.

To elevate the temperature of a mass M of the specific heat σ, t degrees, we need a quantity of heat equal to

$\mathrm{M}\sigma t$; this corresponds, when $\mathrm{A}g$ represents the mechanical equivalent of the unit of heat, to the work $\mathrm{A}g\mathrm{M}\sigma t$. To find the elevation of temperature produced by the condensation of the mass of the sun, let us set

$$\mathrm{A}g\mathrm{M}\sigma t = \mathrm{V};$$

we have then

$$t = \frac{3}{5} \cdot \frac{r^2\mathrm{M}}{\mathrm{A} \cdot \mathrm{R} \cdot m \cdot \sigma}.$$

For a mass of water equal to the sun we have $\sigma = 1$; then the calculation with the known values of $\mathrm{A}, \mathrm{M}, \mathrm{R}, m,$ and r, gives

$$t = 28611000° \text{ Cent.}$$

The mass of the sun is 738 times greater than that of all the planets taken together; if, therefore, we desire to make the water mass equal to that of the entire system, we must multiply the value of t by the fraction $\frac{738}{739}$, which makes hardly a sensible alteration in the result.

When a spherical mass of the radius R condenses more and more to the radius R_1, the elevation of temperature thereby produced is

$$\vartheta = \frac{3}{5} \cdot \frac{r^2\mathrm{M}}{\mathrm{A} \cdot m\sigma} \left\{ \frac{1}{\mathrm{R}_1} - \frac{1}{\mathrm{R}_0} \right\},$$

or

$$= \frac{3}{5} \cdot \frac{r^2\mathrm{M}}{\mathrm{A}\mathrm{R}_1 m\sigma} \left\{ 1 - \frac{\mathrm{R}_1}{\mathrm{R}_0} \right\}.$$

Supposing, then, the mass of the planetary system to be at the commencement, not a sphere of infinite radius, but limited, say of the radius of the path of Neptune, which is six thousand times greater than the radius of the sun, the magnitude $\frac{\mathrm{R}_1}{\mathrm{R}_0}$ will then be equal to $\frac{1}{6000}$, and the above value of t would have to be diminished by this inconsiderable amount.

From the same formula we can deduce that a diminution of $\frac{1}{10000}$ of the radius of the sun would generate work in a water mass equal to the sun, equivalent to 2,861 degrees Centigrade. And as, according to Pouillet, a quantity of heat corresponding to $1\frac{1}{4}$ degree is lost annually in such a mass, the condensation referred to would cover the loss for 2,289 years.

If the sun, as seems probable, be not everywhere of the same density, but is denser at the centre than near the surface, the potential of its mass and the corresponding quantity of heat will be still greater.

Of the now remaining mechanical forces, the *vis viva* of the rotation of the heavenly bodies round their own axes is, in comparison with the other quantities, very small, and may be neglected. The *vis viva* of the motion of revolution round the sun, if μ be the mass of a planet, and ρ its distance from the sun, is

$$L = \frac{gr^2 M\mu}{m} \left\{ \frac{1}{R} - \frac{1}{2\rho} \right\}.$$

Omitting the quantity $\frac{1}{2\rho}$ as very small compared with $\frac{1}{R}$, and dividing by the above value of V, we obtain

$$\frac{L}{V} = \frac{5}{3}\frac{\mu}{M}.$$

The mass of all the planets together is $\frac{1}{738}$ of the mass of the sun; hence the value of L for the entire system is

$$L = \frac{1}{453} \cdot V.$$

Part IV

ENERGY IN ELECTRICITY
AND MAGNETISM

Editor's Comments
on Papers 12 Through 17

By the middle of the nineteenth century much was known about electricity and magnetism. In the latter and historically older field, the admirable summarizations of William Gilbert, as well as his own significant discoveries set forth in the celebrated work *De Magnete* (1600), had been supplemented in the eighteenth century by Coulomb's inverse square law for the attraction and repulsion of magnetic poles. In the early development of electricity the investigations of such scientists as Cabeo, Franklin, DuFay, Gray, and Cavendish had put electrostatics on a firm experimental foundation.

An elaborate theory of electrostatic phenomena had been developed by S. D. Poisson in France and George Green in England in the early part of the nineteenth century. It is of interest in connection with the relation between energy and electricity to note that both Poisson and Green took advantage of the fact that the law of attraction and repulsion for electric and magnetic charges is the same inverse square law as that for gravitational attraction, to use the analysis developed in the mechanics of Lagrange and Laplace. They both introduced the function ∇ of Lagrange, which is the space integral of the force, and which if it exists we now call the potential energy function; Green indeed termed it the electrical potential, a terminology that has persisted to this day. This use of the potential function by Poisson and Green constituted an association between electricity and magnetism, on the one hand, and mechanics, on the other, with respect to the concept of energy. Of course, at the time in which they worked the concept of energy had not been generalized beyond its use in mechanics, and even in the latter field its full significance had not been realized. Moreover, Green and Poisson restricted their electrical and magnetic studies to statics or cases of equilibrium in which the energy concept does not appear to play such an important role.

It would appear that electric current phenomena would have provided a more fertile field for an investigation of the role of the energy concept. Current electricity got its start with the epoch-making work of Galvani and Volta in Italy at the end of the eighteenth century. Although it was early realized that such currents produce heat, chemical effects and, by H. C. Oersted's researches in 1819, magnetic effects, there was at first not enough real understanding of what was going on to encourage an effort to bring in the concept of mechanical work. One would have supposed that this would happen in Ampere's development in the early 1820s of the laws of the interaction of current-carrying conductors, a field he denominated electrodynamics. But he confined his attention to interaction forces.

G. S. Ohm in 1826 first made clear the necessity of introducing something corresponding to a driving force to account for the flow of electricity through a conductor. Hence arose the concept of electromotive force and the law of Ohm connecting it with the magnitude of the current.

Michael Faraday's discovery in 1831 of electromagnetic induction advanced still further the knowledge and utility of the relation between electricity and magnetism. Faraday's further discoveries in the same decade of the laws governing the chemical action of electric currents put electrochemistry on a firm phenomenological foundation.

221

Hence, by the time the concept of energy and its conservation had been put on its feet and generalized by the labors of Mayer, Joule, Colding, Helmholtz, Kelvin, and others in the 1840s, there was a natural impulse to apply the concept to the phenomena of electricity and magnetism. Joule had very early indeed been convinced of the importance of bringing electric current phenomena within the domain of the energy concept. His work with electric currents led to the enunciation in 1840 of his famous law for the rate of heat development in a conductor as a function of the current. In 1843, he first evaluated the mechanical equivalent of heat from electric current measurements. This work, like the more or less contemporaneous theoretical researches of Mayer, was ahead of its time and for several years was not taken seriously. (For Joule's 1843 paper and associated editorial commentary see Paper 30A in Lindsay, *Energy: Concept.*)

It is interesting to recall that Mayer realized the importance of the concept of energy in electricity and magnetism. (See Lindsay, *Energy: Concept,* Paper 29B.) Mayer's inadequate acquaintance with electrical phenomena did not encourage him to go into details. This task was left to Helmholtz, who in his 1847 memoir, of which Paper 1 reproduces the first four sections, devoted the last two sections to electricity and magnetism. This part of the memoir is reprinted here as Paper 12; it is the most important initial publication in a series of significant papers continued by William Thomson (Lord Kelvin) and Rudolf Clausius in the early 1850s. These two were the most active mid-century workers in this field. Helmholtz himself made more elaborate contributions in this area later in the century.

In his 1847 memoir, Helmholtz is astonishingly detailed in his application of the principle of the conservation of energy to magnetic and electrical phenomena. Beginning with electrostatics, he covers both experimental results and relevant theory. He then moves on to current electricity, referred to in his article as galvanism; the principal source of currents at that time was the voltaic cell or batteries thereof. Here Helmholtz's treatment is almost more elaborate than the contemporary state of knowledge justified. The somewhat involved and confusing relation between the chemical action of a voltaic cell and the concept of contact difference in potential of metals remained a subject of controversy for many years after the publication of Helmholtz's memoir. Helmholtz's treatment of magnetism and electromagnetism is much more sketchy than his discussion of galvanism. Nevertheless, the basic importance of the energy concept in these fields is clearly brought out.

In line with the purpose of the Benchmark papers, we find it advisable to retain chronological order in the presentation of papers in any given category. We therefore turn next to Lord Kelvin's (at that time still William Thomson) significant note (Paper 13) of 1848 based on a presentation to the British Association for the Advancement of Science meeting of that year. This paper indicates briefly how the principle of conservation of energy (not stated in this way but rather in terms of the conservation of "mechanical effect," which however is extended to include heat) may be used effectively to derive Joule's law for the rate of heat production in a current-carrying conductor. He also provided in this same note a simple derivation of Franz Ernst Neumann's formula for electromagnetic induction, which was deduced theoretically by the latter in 1845 from Ampère's theory of the interaction of current-carrying conductors. Paper 13 is a very interesting early application of the energy idea when the concept was still not precisely formulated and the terminology had not been settled on.

A natural successor to Paper 13 is Lord Kelvin's 1851 article (Paper 14), which is a more detailed exposition of the idea set forth in Paper 13. Again we note that in modern terms "the principle of mechanical effect" means the principle of conservation of energy. Paper 14 is notable for establishing the law that the product of electromotive force and current is the rate at which work is being done in an electric circuit. The later part on units reflects Kelvin's keen interest in electrical measurements for which he devised many instruments.

Kelvin's preoccupation with the application of the energy concept to electrical problems and the fast pace at which he worked are well illustrated by Paper 15, also written in 1851. This was a natural facet of the subject to tackle in view of the relatively large amount of earlier literature on electric currents from voltaic cells, as well as the availability of Faraday's famous laws governing electrolysis (1834). Kelvin makes no mention of Helmholtz's 1847 memoir and was obviously unacquainted with it. He leans rather heavily on the earlier experimental work of Joule on the heat involved in electrolytic and voltaic cells. Kelvin uses the principle of the conservation of energy to write the equation conncecting heat and mechanical work in a cell. He then combines this with Joule's experimental law for the rate of heat production in a current-carrying conductor as a function of the current, and obtains thereby an expression for the current flowing through the cell. In Paper 15, Kelvin goes into much more analytical and numerical detail than Helmholtz in his 1847 memoir; among other things, he shows how one can calculate the electromotive force of a cell from energy considerations. As a small matter of scientific terminology, it is interesting to note that Kelvin uses the letter *J* to denote the mechanical equivalent of heat, a notation that has persisted in English-speaking countries and has even been adopted internationally. We reproduce the first 10 pages of this article. The remainder deals with details that are not particularly relevant to our purpose.

Rudolf Clausius was working simultaneously with Kelvin on the application of the energy concept to electrical phenomena and was right on his heels with his publications in this field. In 1852 he published in Poggendorff's *Annalen* a paper entitled "Uber die bei einem stationärem Strom in dem Leiter gethane Arbeit und erzengte Wärme." This is in some respects more fundamental than the preceding paper of Kelvin. In particular it provides a theoretical derivation of Joule's law for the rate of heat production in a current-carrying conductor. This article is in some sense a continuation of a previous article [Poggendorff's *Annalen*, **86**, 337–374 (1852)] on the mechanical equivalent of an electric discharge, in which Clausius investigates static electricity from the standpoint of energy. We reproduce the later paper in full in English translation (Paper 16).

In 1821 the German physicist J. T. Seebeck discovered thermoelectricity, i.e., the direct production of an electromotive force and electric current by means of heat. If in a circuit made up of two dissimilar metals, one junction is heated to a higher temperature than the other, an electric current flows. In 1834 the French physicist Jean Peltier discovered the inverse effect, i.e., if a current from a cell or other source is passed through a circuit consisting of two different metals, one junction gets hot and the other cool. This production of heat is in addition to and independent of the standard Joule heat. It was inevitable that these effects would be investigated from the standpoint of the energy concept. Both Kelvin and Clausius worked on this problem. Since Kelvin's results were published first we present here his paper of 1852 (Paper 17). Kelvin begins by writing the equation for the conservation of energy in the thermoelectric circuit. He adds to this an equation that applies a Carnot cycle to find the relation between the external electrical work done and the temperature differences involved in the circuit. This implies the role of the second law of thermodynamics in the thermoelectric circuit. It is indeed considered as a kind of engine. It is of interest that this paper shows for the first time the presence of temperature differences throughout a thermoelectric circuit and not merely at the junctions. This came to be known as the Thomson heat effect.

By 1853 the main outlines of the role of the concept of energy in electrical and magnetic phenomena were rather well established. In this connection attention may be called to an excellent summary article by Kelvin, "On the Mechanical Values of Distributions of Electricity, Magnetism and Galvanism" [*Proceedings of the Glasgow Philosophical Society*, **3** (Jan. 1853)]. It was reprinted in Kelvin's *Mathematical and Physical Papers of William Thomson* (Vol. 1, Cambridge University Press, Cambridge, 1882, pp. 521–533), with numerous additions made at a later date. We do not reproduce the paper here, but call special attention to the free use of the words energy, kinetic energy, and potential energy. Terminology was gradually becoming standardized, and this helped to make possible the valid comparison of the work of different investigators.

We also call attention to the further important work in the 1850s and early 1860s of Rudolf Clausius in Germany on energy in electricity and magnetism. These investigations were summarized in a large two-part volume, *Abhandlungen über die Mechanische Wärmetheorie*, (Verlag Friedrich Vieweg und Sohn, Braunschweig, 1864). The first part is devoted to the general concepts of the theory with applications to gases and vapors. The second part has many sections on energy in electricity and magnetism, as well as applications to the kinetic theory of gases. This work wa extensively revised and enlarged and brought out in a second edition in 1876. For many years it served as the principal German text on thermodynamics.

225

12

Energy Effects in Electricity and Magnetism

Hermann von Helmholtz

*This excerpt was translated expressly for this Benchmark volume
by R. Bruce Lindsay, Brown University, from "Uber die Erhaltung der Kraft," in H. von Helmholtz,* Wissenschafliche Abhandlungen, *Vol. 1, Johann Ambrosius Barth, Leipzing, 1892, pp.
42–68*

V. The Energy Equivalent of Electrical Effects

Static Electricity

The electricity from a static machine can be a cause of energy production in two ways. First, if the electricity moves with the object carrying it, it can provide mechanical energy through its attractive and repulsive forces. Second, if the electricity moves *through* a conductor, it produces heat. The first-mentioned mechanical effects have been derived from the attractive and repulsive forces varying as the inverse square of the distance from the electrified bodies or fluids. Insofar as experience can be compared with the theory, it is found to be in agreement. In accordance with our original deduction, conservation of energy must hold for such forces. Therefore, we shall examine the more special laws for the mechanical action of electricity only insofar as it is necessary for our deduction of the laws for the development of heat by electricity.

Let e_1 and e_2 be two electric charges of opposite sign. [*Ed. note:* The author considers effectively point charges, although necessarily attached to material particles.] If we assume that these are measured in electrostatic units and that their distance of separation is r, the magnitude of the force of attraction between them is

$$\phi = -\frac{e_1 e_2}{r^2}.$$

If the charged particles move from distance R to distance r, the gain in *vis viva* is

$$-\int_R^r \phi \, dr = \frac{e_1 e_2}{R} - \frac{e_1 e_2}{r}.$$

If the particles move from an infinite separation to separation r, the above becomes

$$-\frac{e_1 e_2}{r}.$$

If we designate this quantity, which is the sum of the tension forces [*Ed. note:* in modern terminology we should say the works done] expended in the motion of the particles or the *vis viva* gained in the motion, by the term potential (which Gauss introduced into magnetism) and call it the potential of the two charges at separation r, then the increase in the *vis viva* due to any motion of the charges is equal to the excess of the potential in the final position over its value in the initial position. [*Ed. note:* Helmholtz seems not to have been aware of or at any rate chose not to mention George Green's celebrated memoir *An Essay on the Application of Mathematical Analysis to the Theories of Electricity and Magnetism* (Nottingham, 1828), to say nothing of the earlier work of Laplace and Poisson.]

Let us designate the sum of the potentials of an electrically charged particle with respect to all the elementary parts of a finite charged body as the potential of the particle with respect to the body. We also designate the sum of the potentials of all the elements of one electrically charged body with respect to all the elements of another electrically charged body as the [total] potential of the two bodies. Then the gain in the *vis viva* by the two bodies will still be the difference in potential. It is here assumed that the distribution of electricity in the bodies is not changed, i.e., they remain charged uniformly. If the distribution changes, the magnitude of the electrical tension forces will also change in the bodies, and the gain in *vis viva* will then also have to change.

In all methods of electrification, equal quantities of positive and negative electricities are produced. In the exchange of electricity between two charged bodies [*Ed. note:* the author seems to be tacitly assuming that they are conductors], of which the one, A, has as much positive electricity as the other, B, has negative electricity, half of the positive electricity goes from A to B and half of the negative electricity goes from B to A. If we call the self-potentials of the bodies W_a and W_b, respectively, and the mutual potential of the two, V, we find[1] the whole *vis viva* that is gained when we subtract the potential of the moving electric charges with respect to themselves and with respect to the other charges from the same potential after the transfer. In this connection it should be noted that the sign of the potential changes when one of the charges changes sign.

We then have the following:

1. Potential of the moved charged

$E/2$ from A, with respect to itself	$\frac{1}{4}(W_b - W_a)$
With respect to moved charged $-E/2$	$\frac{1}{4}(V - V)$
With respect to resting charge $+E/2$	$\frac{1}{4}(-V - W_a)$
With respect to resting charge $-E/2$	$\frac{1}{4}(-W_b - V)$

2. Potential of the moved charge

$-E/2$ from B, with respect to itself	$\frac{1}{4}(W_a - W_b)$
With respect to moved charge $+E/2$	$\frac{1}{4}(V - V)$
With respect to resting charge $-E/2$	$\frac{1}{4}(-V - W_a)$
With respect to resting charge $+E/2$	$\frac{1}{4}(-W_a - V)$

$$\text{Sum} \qquad -\left(V + \frac{W_a + W_b}{2}\right)$$

This quantity therefore gives us the maximum *vis viva* and equivalent tension force (potential energy) that can be obtained in this process.

---

[1] See Appendix 6 (p. 31).

To introduce into the analysis more familiar ideas than that of the potential, we employ the following considerations. We imagine the construction of surfaces for which the potential of a charged element lying on it with respect to one or more electrified bodies has the same value (for all points on the surface). We call these equilibrium surfaces. [*Ed. note:* In modern terminology they are equipotential surfaces.] The motion of a charged particle from any point on such a surface to any point on any other such surface always corresponds to the same change in *vis viva*. On the other hand, the motion of a charge *along* such a surface leads to no change in its velocity. Consequently, the resultant of all the attractive forces on any charge in space must lie along the normal to the equilibrium surface on which the charge is located, and every surface to which such resultant forces are perpendicular must be an equilibrium surface.

Electrical equilibrium will not exist in a conductor until all attractive forces due to its own charge and the charges of other neighboring bodies are normal to its surfaces, since otherwise the electric charges in the conductor would have to move along the conductor. Consequently, the surface of a charged conductor must itself be an equilibrium surface. The *vis viva* that a vanishingly small electric charge gains in moving from the surface of one conductor to the surface of another is constant. Let us call C_a the *vis viva* that a unit positive charge gains in its transfer from the surface of conductor A to infinity. For positive electric charges, C_a is positive. A_a is the potential of the same quantity of charge (1 electrostatic unit) with respect to conductor A when it is on the surface of A. For conductor B, A_b has the same significance. W_a is the potential of A with respect to itself. W_b has the same significance for B. V is the potential of A relative to B. Q_a is the quantity of electricity on conductor A, and Q_b that on conductor B. The *vis viva* that the elementary charge e gains in its passage from infinity to the conductor A is therefore

$$-eC_a = e(A_a + A_b).$$

If, in place of e, we set one after another all the elementary charges making up the total charge on A, and for A_a and A_b substitute the appropriate corresponding potentials and sum over all, we get

$$-Q_a C_a = V + W_a.$$

Similarly, for conductor B we have

$$-Q_b C_b = V + W_b.$$

The constant C must be the same not only for all points on one and the same conductor, but also for separated conductors which are joined together in such a way that the charge distribution is not altered and no exchange of charge takes place between them; i.e., the C's must be the same for all conductors at the same free potential. As a measure of the free potential of an electrified body, we can use that quantity of electricity which when placed on a conducting sphere of unit radius well outside the induction range is in electrical equilibrium with the electrified body. If the electric charge is uniformly distributed over the surface of the unit sphere, it acts, as is well known, as if the whole charge were concentrated at the center. If the quantity of electric charge on the conductor is denoted by E, we have

$$C = \frac{E}{R} = E,$$

since R has been assumed to be unity. This confirms the earlier statement.

The potential of two conductors that contain equal quantities Q of positive and negative electricity becomes

$$-\left(V + \frac{W_a + W_b}{2}\right) = Q\left(\frac{C_a - C_b}{2}\right).$$

Since C_b is negative, the difference $C_a - C_b$ is actually equal to their absolute sum. Suppose that we have approximately $C_b = 0$. Then the magnitude of the potential is $\frac{1}{2}QC_a = \frac{1}{2}(-V + W_a)$. If the separation of the conductors is very great, this reduces to $W_a/2$.

We have found the *vis viva* produced in the motion of two electrically charged particles to be equal to the decrease in the sum $\frac{1}{2}(Q_aC_a + Q_bC_b)$. This *vis viva* appears as mechanical energy if the velocity with which the electricity moves inside the bodies is vanishingly small compared with the propagation velocity of the particle motion. If the latter is not the case, the *vis viva* appears as heat. Consequently, the quantity of heat Θ produced by the discharge of equal quantities of electricity Q of opposite sign is

$$\Theta = \frac{1}{2a}(C_a - C_b)Q,$$

where a is the mechanical equivalent of heat. If $C_b = 0$, as in batteries of Leyden jars in which the outer coating is grounded, and if we denote the capacitance of the battery by S, we have $CS = Q$; hence

$$\Theta = \frac{QC}{2a} = \frac{Q^2}{2aS}.$$

P. T. Riess[1] has shown through his experiments that for different charges and for a different number of Leyden jars of the same kind the heat produced in the connecting wires in every part is proportional to the quantity Q^2/S. It is true that he uses S to denote the area of the coating of the jars. But for jars of the same construction this must be proportional to the capacitance. From their researches, Vorselmann de Heer[2] and Knochenhauer[3] have concluded that the heat production from

[1] Poggendorff's *Annalen*, **43**, 47.
[2] Poggendorff's *Annalen*, **48**, 292.
[3] Poggendorff's *Annalen*, **63**, 364; **64**, 64.

the same charge on the same battery of Leyden jars is the same, no matter how the connecting wire is changed. The latter has found the same law to hold even for branched wires. No observations have as yet been reported on the magnitude of the quantity *a*. [*Ed. note:* This of course ignores the results of Mayer and Joule, and is difficult to understand.]

It is easy to explain this law as soon as we give up looking at the discharge of a battery of jars as a simple motion of electricity in one direction, but rather think of it as a to and fro oscillation between the two coatings, an oscillation that grows steadily smaller, until the *vis viva* is entirely destroyed by the resistance of the connecting wire. That the discharge current is actually an alternating current is shown by the oscillatory magnetic effects associated with the current, as well as by the experiment of Wollaston, who endeavored to decompose water by the discharge from a static machine and found that both kinds of gases were produced at both electrodes. At the same time, this assumption explains why in this experiment the electrodes must have the smallest possible surfaces.

Galvanism

In dealing with galvanic phenomena we have to distinguish between two kinds of conductors. The first are those that conduct like metals and follow the law of the galvanic potential series. The second class is made up of those that do not follow this law. The latter are compound liquids; in conduction they always suffer a decomposition whose magnitude is proportional to the quantity of charge that passes.

We can divide the experimental phenomena into two groups: (1) those that take place only between conductors of the first kind, differently charged metals in contact, and (2) those that take place between conductors of both classes, the differences in electric potential in open circuits and the electric currents in closed circuits. Electric currents can never be produced by an arbitrary combination of conductors of the first class; these produce only electrical potential differences. These potential differences are not, however, equivalent to a certain quantity of force, such as we have previously considered and which denoted a disturbance in electrical equilibrium. The galvanic potential differences arise rather through the establishment of electrical equilibrium; through this, no motion of electricity can be produced save by configuration changes in the conductor itself brought about by a change in the distribution of the bound electricity. If we think of all the metals of the earth brought into contact, with a corresponding distribution of electricity taking place, there are no other connections of these by which any change in the free potentials can take place, before a contact has been made with a conductor of the second class. The concept of contact force [*Ed. note:* now referred to as contact potential], or the force that comes into play when two different metals are brought into contact with each other, has not been closely investigated hitherto, because people sought to combine the phenomena of the contact of conductors of both first and second kinds at a time when they did not recognize the importance of the essential difference between the phenomena in the two classes of conductors, i.e., the chemical process. In this indefinite state of conceptualization, the contact potential appears as something that could lead to the production of infinite quantities of free electricity, with corresponding quantities of mechanical energy, heat, and light, if only there were a single conductor of the second kind that would not be electrolyzed by conduction. It is probably this circumstance that has aroused so much decisive resistance to the contact theory, in spite of its simple and practical explanation of phenomena.[1]

The concept of contact force held up to now directly contradicts the principle we are trying to maintain (i.e., that of conservation of energy), at any rate if the necessity of incorporating the chemical processes is not taken into account. If this is actually done, however, let us assume that the conductor of the second kind does not follow the galvanic potential series because it conducts only through electrolysis. In this case the concept of contact potential becomes essentially simplified and can be attributed to attractive and repulsive forces. Clearly, in this case all phenomena in conductors of the first kind can be deduced from the assumption that the various chemical elements have different attractive forces for the two kinds of electricity, and that these attractive forces act only at vanishingly small distances, whereas electrically charged bodies act on each other at much greater distances. From this point of view, contact potential would be due to the difference in the attractive forces that the metallic particles in the contact layer exert on the electric charges there. Electrical equilibrium then prevails when an electrified particle that goes across the boundary from one metal to the other neither loses nor gains *vis viva*. Let c_1 and c_2 be the free potentials of the two metals, and let $a_1 e$ and $a_2 e$ be the quantities of *vis viva* that an electric charge e gains in going from the one metal or the other, respectively. Then the energy gained in its transmission from the one metal to the other becomes

$$e(a_1 - a_2) - e(c_1 - c_2).$$

For equilibrium, this must be zero; hence

$$a_1 - a_2 = c_1 - c_2.$$

This means that the potential difference for different pieces of the same metal must be constant (zero) and for different metals must follow the law of the galvanic potential series.

We have now to consider the following principal effects concerning galvanic currents insofar as they relate to the conservation of energy, i.e., heat production, chemical processes, and polarization. We shall take up electrodynamic effects when we discuss magnetism. The production of heat is common to all currents. For our purposes we can divide the other two effects into three parts: (1) those that merely produce chemical decomposition, (2) those that merely produce polarization, and (3) those that produce both.

We first investigate the conditions for the conservation of energy in those series circuits in which polarization is annulled, since these are the only ones for which at the present time definite laws prevail, verified by experiment. The magnitude J of the current flowing through a series circuit of n elements [*Ed. note:* cells or galvanic sources of electromotive force] is given by Ohm's law as follows:

[1] See M. Faraday, Experimental Investigations in Electricity, 17th Series, *Philosophical Transactions of the Royal Society*, no. 2071, p. 1 (1840). See also Poggendorff's *Annalen*, 53, 568.

$$J = \frac{nA}{W}.$$

Here the constant A is the electromotive force of each individual element [*Ed. note:* the author here assumes tacitly that they are all the same] and W is the resistance of the circuit. In such circuits, A and W are independent of the current magnitudes. Since in a given interval during which activity takes place in the circuit the only changes in it are the chemical processes and the production of heat, the law of the conservation of energy demands that the heat which corresponds to these chemical processes shall be that whose development is actually observed. According to Lenz[1] in a single segment of a metallic conductor of resistance w, the heat developed in time t is

$$\Theta = J^2 wt$$

if for the unit of w one takes the length of wire in which unit current in unit time produces unit heat. [*Ed. note:* The author credits E. Lenz with the discovery of this law. But J. P. Joule had already discovered it in 1840. Presumably, Lenz obtained the law independently. It seems curious that Helmholtz should not have been aware of Joule's work on electric currents, since he refers earlier in this memoir to the latter's experimental measurements of the mechanical equivalent of heat]. For branched or parallel circuits in which the resistance of the various branches is denoted by w_a, the total resistance is given by the formula

$$\frac{1}{w} = \sum \frac{1}{w_a}.$$

The magnitude of the current in branch a is

$$J_a = \frac{Jw}{w_a},$$

and the heat Θ_a developed in the same branch in time t is

$$\Theta_a = J^2 \frac{w^2}{w_a} \cdot t.$$

The heat developed in time t in the whole branched conductor becomes

$$\Theta = \sum \Theta_a = J^2 w^2 \sum \frac{1}{w_a} \cdot t = J^2 wt.$$

Consequently, the heat developed in any circuit consisting of arbitrary parallel conductors (assuming that Lenz's law holds also for liquid conductors) is given by

---

[1] Poggendorff's *Annalen*, **59**, 203. Also *Bulletin of the Academy of Sciences in St. Petersburg*, p. 407 (1843).

$$\Theta = J^2 Wt = nAJt.$$

We have two kinds of galvanic sources of constant electromotive force, the Daniell and Grove cells. The chemical effect in the first is produced by a positive metal electrode, which dissolves in an acid, while the negative electrode is precipitated in a salt solution of that acid. [*Ed. note:* Actually, there are several types of Daniell cell. One common variety has a negative electrode (positive pole) of copper immersed in a saturated solution of copper sulfate. The positive electrode (negative pole) is amalgamated zinc immersed in a solution of one part sulfuric acid to four parts of water.] If we take as a unit of current that which will decompose 1 gram equivalent of water in unit time, then nJt gram equivalents of the positive metal will be dissolved in time t and an equal number of gram equivalents of the negative electrode will be precipitated. If now we call a_z the quantity of heat developed by a gram equivalent of the positive metal through its solution, and denote by a_c the corresponding heat absorbed at the negative electrode, the total heat developed by the chemical processes in the battery of n cells is

$$nJt(a_z - a_c).$$

The chemically produced heat will therefore be equal to the heat produced through electrical resistance if

$$A = a_z - a_c,$$

i.e., if the electromotive force produced by the two metals is proportional to the difference in the heat developed and absorbed in the cell or battery of cells.

In the elements of a cell of the Grove variety, the polarization is annulled by the fact that the hydrogen which is produced reduces the components rich in oxygen which surround the negative metal electrode. To this general variety belong not only the Grove elements, but also those of the Bunsen cell, i.e., amalgamated zinc, dilute sulfuric acid, fuming nitric acid, and platinum or carbon. To these we may add the constant electromotive force cells formed with chromic acid. These have been subjected to more precise measurements. These elements are amalgamated zinc, dilute sulfuric acid, solution of potassium bichromate with sulfuric acid, and copper or platinum. The chemical processes are in both cases equivalent to those in cells formed with nitric acid. It would also follow from the above deduction that the electromotive forces would be the same. According to the measurements of Poggendorff[1] this is indeed the case. The chromic acid cell formed with carbon has a very variable electromotive force, although it produces substantially higher values than the others, at any rate initially. We do not count this in the present group but rather with those exhibiting polarization. In these constant cells the electromotive force is independent of the negative metal electrode. We could make it revert to the Daniell cell type by regarding as the negative element the particles of nitric acid and chromium oxide lying next to the platinum. In this way we may explain the Grove and Bunsen cells as cells with elements effectively between zinc and nitric

---

[1] Poggendorff's *Annalen*, 54, 429; 57, 104.

acid, whereas those with chromic acid may be considered as zinc–chromic oxide cells.

Among the cells exhibiting polarization, we can distinguish between those that show polarization alone with no chemical decomposition and those that involve both. To the first class of those which produce a small initial variable current that soon reduces to practically zero belong the simple cells of Faraday.[1] These are formed with solutions of potassium hydroxide, potassium sulfate, and nitric acid. Another would be the case of strongly negative metals in the usual acids. Positive metals are those that are unable to decompose the acids; as examples we have copper, silver, gold, platinum, and carbon in sulfuric acid. Other illustrations are provided by cells in which the polarization is in excess of the normal electromotive force of the cell elements. It has not yet been possible to make precise measurements on the output of such cells because of the large variability of the currents produced. In general, the magnitude of their currents appears to depend on the nature of the metal electrodes used. Their duration of activity increases with the size of the surfaces and with the decrease in current magnitude. Even when such cells are almost completely exhausted, they can be renewed by moving the plates in the liquid and in air to remove the layer of hydrogen producing the polarization. The whole effect is accordingly a production of electrical equilibrium between the liquid particles and the metals. Here the particles of the liquid appear to undergo some rearrangement, and at the same time chemical changes, at least in many cases,[2] take place on the surface layers of the metals. In compound cells, in which the polarization of plates originally alike is produced by the action of the current from other elements, we can think of the energy of the original current lost in this way as retrieved by a secondary current by removing the relevant elements and forming a closed circuit with the polarized cells. The application of the principle of the conservation of energy to this case has not so far proved possible because of the lack of special data.

The most complicated case is provided by those cells in which both polarization and chemical decomposition enter. To this class belong the cells with the development of gas. The current from such is the same as that in the case of pure polarization; i.e., it is strongest initially and then decreases more or less rapidly to a rather steady value. In individual cells of this kind or in batteries made up only of such cells, the polarization current ceases only very slowly. On the other hand, it is easier to secure steady currents by the combination of constant cells with individual variable cells if the plates of the latter are comparatively small. Up to now, however, few measurements have been made on such combinations. From the few that I have noted by Lenz[3] and Poggendorff[4] it turns out that the current values from such combinations with different connector resistances do not obey the simple formula of Ohm, in the sense that when the constants in the formula are calculated for small current magnitudes, the values for larger current magnitudes turn out to be

[1] Experimental Investigations on Electricity, 16th series, *Philosophical Transactions*, p. 1 (1840). See also Poggendorff's *Annalen*, **52**, 163, 547.
[2] See G. S. Ohm, Poggendorff's *Annalen*, **63**, 389.
[3] Poggendorff's *Annalen*, **59**, 224.
[4] Poggendorff's *Annalen*, **67**, 531.

too great. Hence one must treat the numerator or denominator in the formula (or both) as functions of current magnitude. The data so far available do not allow us to decide which alternative to follow.

If we try to apply the principle of the conservation of energy to these currents, we must divide them into two classes; the first is the variable or polarization current governed by what we have just said above, and the second is the constant or decomposition-associated current. To the latter we can apply the same considerations as apply to constant currents without the development of gas. The heat developed by the current must be equal to that developed by the chemical processes. For example, if in a combination of zinc and a negative metal in dilute sulfuric acid the heat developed by an atom of zinc going into solution with the emission of an atom of hydrogen is $a_z - a_h$, then the heat developed in time dt is

$$J(a_z - a_h)\, dt.$$

If now the heat development in all parts of such a circuit were to be proportional to the square of the current, i.e., of the form $J^2 W\, dt$, we would have, as before,

$$J = \frac{a_z - a_h}{W},$$

i.e., the simple formula of Ohm. Since, however, this formula does not apply here, it follows that there are cross sections in the circuit in which the heat development must follow another law, in which the resistance, therefore, cannot be considered constant. Thus, for example, if the development of heat in any cross section of the circuit is directly proportional to the current magnitude, as must be the case with the heat associated with change in state of aggregation, in which accordingly $\Theta = \mu J\, dt$, we then have

$$J(a_z - a_h) = J^2 w + J\mu$$

or

$$J = \frac{a_z - a_h - \mu}{w}.$$

In this case the quantity μ must appear in the numerator in Ohm's law. The resistance of such a section would be $\Theta/J^2 = \mu/J$. If, however, the heat development in such a section is not precisely proportional to the current magnitude, which means that the quantity μ is not precisely constant but increases with the current, we get the case to which the observations of Lenz and Poggendorf correspond. In analogy with constant cells in which the polarization current has ceased, we should have to assume the electromotive force of such a circuit to be denoted as that between zinc and hydrogen. In the terminology of contact theory, it would correspond to that between zinc and the negative metal decreased by the polarization of the latter in hydrogen. We must therefore only look upon the maximum of the polarization as independent of the current magnitude and differing in different metals exactly in proportion to the electromotive forces of those metals. The numerator in the formula of Ohm, calculated from current measurements for different resistances, can contain an additional term besides the electromotive force. This additional term has its origin in the resistance appearing at the points of transition and is probably different for different metals. That a transition resistance exists follows from the principle of the conservation of energy, in accordance with the fact that the current magnitudes in such a circuit cannot be calculated by means of Ohm's law, since the chemical processes remain the same. I have been able to find no satisfactory observations to indicate that, in circuits in which the polarization current has ceased, the numerator in Ohm's law depends on the negative metals. To get rid of the polarization current quickly, it is necessary to increase the current density at the polarized plates as much as possible, partly through the introduction of cells with constant electromotive force and partly through decrease in the surface area of these plates.

In the investigations of Lenz and Saweljew[1] pertaining to this matter, according to their statements constancy of current was not attained, and hence the electromotive force calculated by them was that due to the polarization currents. They find 0.51 for zinc–copper in sulfuric acid, for zinc–iron, 0.176, and for zinc–mercury, 0.93 [*Ed. note:* the units are not specified, though they could be in volts].

Finally, I remark that the attempt to demonstrate experimentally the equivalence of the heat developed by the chemical processes and the electricity has been made by Joule.[2] Nevertheless objections of many kinds can be raised against his methods of measurement. For example, in the use of the tangent galvanometer he assumes that the tangent law is valid up to the highest values, and does not operate with constant currents but calculates their magnitude by taking the average of the initial and final values; he assumes the electromotive force of the cells is constant. Hess has already called attention to the deviation of Joules's quantitative heat determinations from those obtained in other ways. E. Becquerel has already deduced the same law as Joule empirically according to a report in *Comptes Rendus* (no. 16, 1843).

In our discussion above we have found it necessary to attribute the concept of contact potential to simple attractive and repulsive forces in order to bring the concept into agreement with the fundamental principle [of conservation of energy]. Let us now try to refer the electrical motions between metals and liquids to the same principle. Let us think of the component parts of the compound atoms of a liquid endowed with different attractive forces with respect to electricity, and hence themselves endowed with different electric charges. If these atomic constituents are separated out at the metallic electrodes, then according to the laws of electrolysis each atom gives up at the electrode a quantity of electricity = $\pm E$, independently of its electromotive force. We can therefore imagine that even in the chemical compounds the atoms have attached to them equivalent charges $\pm E$, which are equal for all, like the stoichiometric equivalents of the weighable materials in different compounds. If we now immerse two differently electrified metals in a liquid without having a chemical process take place, the positive components of the liquid will be attracted to the negative metal and the negative components to the positive

[1] *Bulletin de la Classe Phys. Math. de l'Academie de Science de St. Petersburg*, **5**, 1. See also Poggendorff's *Annalen*, **57**, 497.
[2] *Philosophical Magazine*, **19**, 275 (1841); **20**, 204 (1843).

metal. The consequence will be a changed direction and distribution of the differently electrified component particles of the liquid. The appearance of this we recognize as the polarization current. The force causing the motion of this current will be the electrical potential difference of the metals. Its initial magnitude must therefore be proportional to this potential difference. For equal current magnitude, its deviation must be proportional to the number of atoms that appear on the surface of the metal plates, and hence proportional to their area. In the case of currents from chemical decomposition, on the other hand, we are not concerned with a lasting equilibrium between the liquid particles and the metals because the positively charged surface of the metal continually recedes, becoming in itself a component part of the liquid. Accordingly, a continual renewal of the charge must take place behind it. For every atom of the positive metal that enters the solution united with an equivalent positive charge, whereby an atom of the negative portion is neutralized, an acceleration of the motion once commenced is called into play, as soon as the attractive force of the first atom for $\pm E$, designated by a_z, is greater than that of the latter, a_c. The velocity of the motion would thereby increase indefinitely, if at the same time the loss in *vis viva* through heat development did not grow. It will continue to increase until the loss $J^2W\,dt$ is equal to the expenditure of potential energy $J(a_z - a_c)\,dt$, or until

$$J = \frac{a_z - a_c}{W}.$$

I believe that this separation of the galvanic currents into the two groups, one based on polarization and the other on chemical decomposition, conditioned by the principle of conservation of energy, is the only way to get around the difficulties posed by the chemical and contact theories.

Thermoelectric Currents

We must look for the source of energy in the case of these currents in the effects discovered by Peltier in the contact places [*Ed. note:* of the *different* metals in the circuit] where a current directed opposite to the original one is produced.

Let us think of a constant hydroelectric current in whose wire conductor a piece of another metal is inserted with the points of contact at temperatures t_1 and t_2, respectively. The electric current in time dt will then develop in the conductor as a whole the quantity of heat $J^2W\,dt$. In addition to this a quantity of heat $q_1\,dt$ will be developed at the first junction and a quantity of heat $q_2\,dt$ will be absorbed at the second junction. If A is the electromotive force of the circuit, and hence $AJ\,dt$ is the chemically produced heat, the principle of the conservation of energy requires that

$$AJ = J^2W + q_1 - q_2. \tag{1}$$

If B_t is the electromotive force of the thermoelectric circuit when one of the junctions is kept at temperature t and the other at any definite constant [different] temperature, say 0, then for the whole circuit

$$J = \frac{A - B_{t_1} + B_{t_2}}{W}. \qquad (2)$$

If $t_1 = t_2$, we have $B_{t_1} = B_{t_2}$ and

$$J = \frac{A}{W}.$$

If this is inserted in equation (1), we get

$$q_1 = q_2.$$

This means that for the same temperature at the two junctions (with the same metals involved at each junction) and the same current magnitude, the heats developed and absorbed at the junctions must be the same, independent of cross section. If we may assume that this effect is the same at every point of the cross section, it follows that the quantities of heat developed by the same current in equal surface space of different cross sections are in proportion to the current density. From this it follows again that the amounts of heat developed by different currents in the whole cross section are proportional to the current magnitudes.

If the junctions are at different temperatures, it follows from equations (1) and (2) that

$$(B_{t_1} - B_{t_2})J = q_1 - q_2.$$

This means that with the same current magnitude the force associated with the development and absorption of heat increases with the temperature in the same manner as the electromotive force.

Up to now I have learned of no investigation to test these results.

VI. Energy Equivalent of Magnetism and Electromagnetism

A magnet by virtue of its attractive and repulsive forces on other magnets and on unmagnetized iron is able to produce a certain amount of *vis viva*. Since the attraction phenomena of magnets are completely derivable from the assumption of two fluids, which attract and repel each other inversely as the square of the distance of separation, it follows directly from the deduction given at the beginning of this memoir that conservation of energy must prevail in the motion of magnetized bodies with respect to each other. Because of the theory of induction discussed in what follows we must examine more closely the laws of this motion.

1. If m_1 and m_2 are two magnetic elements (whose unit is the element that repels an equal and identical element at unit distance from it with unit force) which possess magnetism of opposite sign, and if r is the distance separating the elements, the magnitude of the central force between them is

$$\phi = -\frac{m_1 m_2}{r^2}.$$

The gain in *vis viva* when the elements move in from infinity to distance r is $-m_1m_2/r$.

2. Let us designate this quantity as the potential of the two elements and employ the concept of potential in magnetic problems, as was done previously in electrical problems. Then in the motions of two bodies whose magnetism does not change (i.e., which are composed of permanent magnets like steel), we obtain the gain in *vis viva* if we subtract the value of the potential at the beginning of the motion from that at the end. On the other hand, as in the case of electricity, in the motion of magnetic bodies in which the distribution of magnetism changes, we calculate the gain in *vis viva* by the change in the sum

$$V + \tfrac{1}{2}(W_a + W_b),$$

where V is the potential of the bodies with respect to each other, and W_a and W_b are the self-potentials of each. If the body B is a permanent steel magnet, the approach of a body with nonuniform magnetism yields a gain in *vis viva* equal to the sum $V + W_a/2$.

3. It is well known that the external action of a magnet can always be replaced by that of a certain distribution of magnetic fluid on its surface. We can accordingly replace the potential of a magnet by that of such a surface. If then we follow the analogy of a surface distribution of electricity, we find that, for a piece of soft iron A which is magnetized by a magnet B, the gain in *vis viva* when a unit of positive magnetic material moves from the surface of A to infinity is given by

$$-QC - V' + W_a.$$

[*Ed. note:* The author does not say what Q means, but it evidently is the number of units of magnetism on A. From the analogy with the corresponding case in electrostatics, C is the *vis viva* associated with unit magnetism on A.] Since every magnet must contain as much north magnetism as south magnetism, the net Q on every magnet is zero. It follows that, for such a piece of iron or an equivalent piece of steel of the same shape, position, and distribution of magnetism produced by magnet B, we have

$$V = -W_a.$$

4. V is, however, the *vis viva* that the steel magnet produces through its approach to B until B has acquired its magnetism. From this it follows that the *vis viva* must be the same no matter what magnet the piece of steel approaches, as long as it comes to complete magnetization, because W_a always remains the same. On the other hand, the *vis viva* acquired by a piece of iron that approaches an equal distribution of magnetism is, as shown above,

$$V + \frac{W}{2} = -\frac{W}{2},$$

i.e., only half as great as that of the piece already magnetized. In this connection it is to be noted that W is negative, so that $-W/2$ is positive.

If an unmagnetized piece of steel approaches an inducing magnet and retains the magnetism it has acquired, as it is drawn away from the inducing magnet mechanical work equal to $-W/2$ must be done, and for that the inducing magnet is in a position to contribute $-W/2$ more work than the piece of steel could do previously.

Electromagnetism

Ampere has explained electrodynamic phenomena by the attractive and repulsive forces between current elements, the magnitude of the forces depending on the velocity and direction of the currents. His derivation, however, does not include induction phenomena. On the other hand, W. Weber has explained the latter along with the purely electrodynamic phenomena by attractive and repulsive forces of the electric fluids themselves, whose magnitude depends on the velocities of approach or recession and the increase in the latter. At the moment no hypothesis has been found by which we can explain these phenomena by means of constant central forces. The laws of induced currents have been formulated by Neumann[1] [*Ed. note:* why is there no mention of Faraday?] by applying the laws for whole circuits found experimentally by Lenz to the smallest elements of the circuits. The results for closed circuits agree with the experimental results of Weber. The laws of Ampere and Weber also agree with their deduction on the basis of rotation forces by Grassmann.[2] Experience gives us no further clues, since the only experiments carried out so far have been with closed or almost closed circuits. Hence we shall apply our principle [conservation of energy] to closed circuits only and show that the same laws follow from it.

It has already been shown by Ampere that the electrodynamic effects of a closed current-carrying circuit are equivalent to those resulting from a certain distribution of magnetic fluid on an arbitrary surface bounded by the circuit. Neumann has therefore extended the concept of potential to the closed current-carrying circuit by replacing it by the potential of such a surface.

5. If a magnet moves under the influence of a current, the *vis viva* that it thereby gains must come out of the potential energy associated with the current. To use the terminology introduced earlier, in time dt this is $AJ\,dt$ in heat units and $aJA\,dt$ in mechanical units, if a is the mechanical equivalent of heat. The *vis viva* produced in the current path is $aJ^2W\,dt$ and that gained from the magnet is $J(dV/dt)$, where V is the potential of the latter with respect to the conductor through which unit current flows. Accordingly, we have

$$aAJ\,dt = aJ^2W\,dt + \frac{J\,dV}{dt}\,dt,$$

from which it follows that

$$J = \frac{A - \dfrac{1}{a}\dfrac{dV}{dt}}{W}.$$

[1] Poggendorff's *Annalen*, **67**, 31.
[2] Poggendorff's *Annalen*, **64**, 1.

We can designate the quantity $(1/a)$ (dV/dt) as a new electromotive force, that of the induced current. It always acts against that which would move the magnet in its path or increase the velocity of the latter. Since this electromotive force is independent of the magnitude of the current, it must also remain the same if there had been no current at all before the motion of the magnet. If the current's magnitude is variable, the total induced current in a given time becomes

$$\int J \, dt = -\frac{1}{aW} \int \frac{dV}{dt} \, dt = \frac{1}{a} \frac{V_1 - V_2}{W}$$

[*Ed. note:* the author evidently means the total charge that passes, not the "total current."], where V_1 means the potential at the beginning of the motion and V_2 that at the end. If the magnet moves in from a very great distance, we have

$$\int J \, dt = -\frac{1}{a} \frac{V_2}{W}$$

independent of the path and the velocity of the magnet.

We can express the law in the following words: The total electromotive force of the induction current that the change in position of a magnet with respect to a current circuit brings about is equal to the change in the potential of the magnet with respect to the circuit, if the latter is considered to have the current $-1/a$ flowing through it. [*Ed. note:* There is a problem of units and dimensions involved here. It is hard to see how $-1/a$ can be a current, if a is the mechanical equivalent of heat. The rest of the dimensions are hidden away in $-1/a$ to make this possible.] The unit of electromotive force is that by which the arbitrary unit of current is produced in unit resistance. The latter, however, is the resistance in which unit current produces unit heat in unit time. The same law will be found in Neumann (l.c. para. 9), only in place of $1/a$ he uses the undetermined constant c.

6. If now a magnet moves under the influence of a conductor with respect to which its potential for the magnetism is ϕ, as well as under the influence of a piece of iron magnetized by this conductor with respect to which its potential for the magnetism excited by unit current is χ, we have as previously

$$aAJ = aJ^2W + J\frac{d\phi}{dt} + J\frac{d\chi}{dt},$$

and therefore

$$J = \frac{A - \frac{1}{a}\left(\frac{d\phi}{dt} + \frac{d\chi}{dt}\right)}{W}.$$

The electromotive force of the induction current that results from the presence of the piece of iron is therefore

$$-\frac{1}{a}\frac{d\chi}{dt}.$$

241

If in an electromagnet the current n produces the same distribution of magnetism as is brought about by the approach of a magnet, then, according to what was said in paragraph 4 above, the potential of the current with respect to the magnet, $n\chi$, is equal to its potential with respect to the current-carrying conductor, nV, if V is taken for unit current. Accordingly, we have $\chi = V$. If then an induction current is produced by having the piece of iron magnetized by induction by the magnet, the electromotive force becomes

$$-\frac{1}{a} \cdot \frac{d\chi}{dt} = -\frac{1}{a} \frac{dV}{dt},$$

and, as in paragraph 5, we have for the total current [*Ed. note:* he means total charge]

$$\int J\, dt = \frac{\frac{1}{a}(V_1 - V_2)}{W},$$

where V_1 and V_2 are the potentials of the magnetized iron with respect to the current-carrying circuit before and after the magnetization, respectively. Neumann arrives at this law by analogy with the previous case.

7. If an electromagnet is magnetized under the influence of a current, heat is lost through the induction current. If the piece of iron (core) is soft, by opening the circuit the induction current will go in the opposite direction and the heat that was lost will be won again. If the core is a piece of steel, which retains its magnetism, the heat remains lost and in its place we get magnetic energy, equal to half the potential the magnet would have on complete magnetization, as was shown in paragraph 4. From analogy with the previous case, it would not be improbable that the electromotive force should correspond to the full potential, as Neumann concluded, and that part of the motion of the magnetic fluid gets lost as heat on account of its quickness.

8. If two closed current-carrying circuits move with respect to each other, the magnitude of the currents in both can be changed. If V is the mutual potential for unit currents, then by reasoning from previous cases we must have

$$A_1 J_1 + A_2 J_2 = J_1^2 W_1 + J_2^2 W_2 + \frac{1}{a} \cdot J_1 J_2 \frac{dV}{dt}.$$

If now the magnitude of the current in one circuit, let us say that with resistance W_2, is much smaller than that in the other whose resistance is W_1, so that the electromotive force of induction A_2, which is excited in W_2 by W_1, is vanishingly small compared with the electromotive force A_1, and we can therefore set $J = A_1/W_1$, we obtain from the previous equation

$$J_2 = \frac{A_2 - \frac{1}{a}J_1 \frac{dV}{dt}}{W_2}.$$

242

The electromotive force of induction is accordingly the same as that which a magnet would excite if it were to have the same electrodynamic force as the inducing current. W. Weber[1] has confirmed this law experimentally.

If, on the other hand, the current magnitude in W_1 is vanishingly small compared with that in W_2, we find by the same reasoning

$$J_1 = \frac{A_1 - \frac{1}{a} J_2 \frac{dV}{dt}}{W_1}.$$

The electromotive forces induced by each circuit in the other are therefore equal if the current magnitudes are equal, no matter what form the circuits may take.

The total electromotive force of induction that produces a current during a certain relative motion of the circuits, a current which is not itself changed by the induction, is accordingly again equal to the change in the potential of the same with respect to the other circuit with $-1/a$ flowing through it. It was in this form that Neumann deduced the law from the analogy between magnetic and electrodynamic forces (l.c. Sec. 10), and extended it also to the case in which induction takes place in immovable circuits by increase or decrease in the currents. W. Weber has shown the agreement of his assumption of electrodynamic forces with these theorems (l.c., pp. 147–153). We can get no determination for this case from the law of the conservation of energy. Through the reaction of the induced current on the inducing current there must take place a decrease in the latter, which corresponds to a heat loss just as great as that won in the induced current. The same relation must exist in the inductive action of a current on itself between the initial weakening and the "extra" current (on breaking the circuit). However, from this we can draw no further conclusions, since the form of the increase incurred is not known, and, moreover, Ohm's law is not immediately applicable since these currents may not take on simultaneously the full extent of the available conduction.

[1] *Electrodynamische Maassbestimmungen*, pp. 71–75.

13

Reprinted from *Mathematical and Physical Papers of William Thomson*, Vol. 1,
Cambridge University Press, London, 1882, pp. 91–92

ART. XXXV. ON THE THEORY OF ELECTRO-MAGNETIC INDUCTION.

William Thomson (Lord Kelvin)

[From the *British Association Report*, 1848 (Part II.).]

THE theory of electro-magnetic induction, founded on the elementary experiments of Faraday and Lenz, has been subjected to mathematical analysis by Neumann, who has recently laid some very valuable researches on this subject before the Berlin Academy of Sciences. The case of a closed linear conductor (a bent metallic wire with its ends joined) under the influence of a magnet in a state of relative motion is considered in Neumann's first memoir*, and a very beautiful theorem is demonstrated, completely expressing the circumstances which determine the intensity of the induced current. It has appeared to me that a very simple *à priori* demonstration of this theorem may be founded on the axiom that the amount of work expended in producing the relative motion on which the electro-magnetic induction depends must be equivalent to the mechanical effect lost by the current induced in the wire.

In the first place, it may be proved that the amount of the mechanical effect continually *lost* or spent in some physical agency (according to Joule the generation of heat) during the existence of a galvanic current in a given closed wire is, for a given time, proportional to the square of the intensity of the current. For, whatever be the actual source of the galvanism, an equivalent current might be produced by the motion of a magnetic body in the neighbourhood of the closed wire. If now, other circumstances remaining the same, the intensity of the magnetism in the influencing body be altered in any ratio, the intensity of the induced current must be proportionately changed; hence the amount of work spent in the motion, as it depends on the mutual influence of the magnet and the induced current, is altered in the

---

* A translation of this memoir into French is published in the last April number of Liouville's *Journal des Mathématiques*.

duplicate ratio of that in which the current is altered; and therefore the amount of mechanical effect lost in the wire, being equivalent to the work spent in the motion, must be proportional to
the square of the intensity of the current. Hence if i denote the
intensity of a current existing in a closed conductor, the amount
of work lost by its existence for an interval of time dt, so small
that the intensity of the current remains sensibly constant during
it, will be $k \cdot i^2 \cdot dt$; where k is a certain constant depending on
the resistance of the complete wire.

Let us now suppose this current to be actually produced by
induction in the wire, under the influence of a magnetic body in a
state of relative motion. The entire mutual force between the
magnetic and the galvanic wire may, according to Ampère's theory,
be expressed by means of the differential coefficients of a certain
"force function." This function, which may be denoted by U, will
be a quantity depending solely on the form and position of the
wire at any instant, and on the magnetism of the influencing body.
During the very small time dt, let U change from U to $U + dU$,
by the relative motion which takes place during that interval.
Then idU will be the amount of work spent in sustaining the
motion; but the mechanical effect lost in the wire during the
same interval is equal to $k i^2 dt$ [if we neglect "self-induction"];
and therefore we must have

$$i d\mathrm{U} = k i^2 dt.$$

Hence, dividing both members by $ki\,dt$, we deduce

$$i = \frac{1}{k} \cdot \frac{d\mathrm{U}}{dt},$$

which expresses the theorem of Neumann, the subject of the present communication. We may enunciate the result in general
language thus:—

When a current is induced in a closed wire by a magnet in
relative motion [and when "self-induction" is negligible], the intensity of the current produced is proportional to the actual rate of
variation of the "force function" by the differential coefficients of
which the mutual action between the magnet and the wire would be
represented if the intensity of the current in the wire were unity.

[For more on this subject, and particularly for the correction to take "self-
induction" into the account, see Articles on "Electromagnetic Induction"
below.]

245

Reprinted from *Mathematical and Physical Papers of William Thomson*, Vol. 1, Cambridge University Press, London, 1882, pp. 490–502

ART. LIV. APPLICATIONS OF THE PRINCIPLE OF MECHANICAL EFFECT TO THE MEASUREMENT OF ELECTRO-MOTIVE FORCES, AND OF GALVANIC RESISTANCES, IN ABSOLUTE UNITS.

William Thomson (Lord Kelvin)

[*Phil. Mag.* Dec. 1851.]

1. IN a short paper "On the Theory of Electro-magnetic Induction," [Art. XXXV. above], communicated to the British Association in 1848*, I demonstrated that "the amount of mechanical effect continually *lost* or spent in some physical agency (according to Joule, the generation of heat) during the existence of a galvanic current in a given closed wire, is, for a given time, proportional to the square of the strength of the current;" and I showed that Neumann's beautiful analytical expression for the electro-motive force experienced by a linear conductor moving relatively to a magnet of any kind, is, in virtue of this proposition, an immediate consequence of the general principle of mechanical effect. At that time I did not see clearly how the reasoning could be extended to inductive effects produced by a magnet (either of magnetized matter or an electro-magnet) of varying power upon a fixed conductor in its neighbourhood, or to "the induction of a varying current on itself;" but I have recently succeeded in making this extension, and found that the same general principle of mechanical effect is sufficient to enable us to found on a few elementary facts, a complete theory of electro-magnetic or electro-dynamic induction. The present communication, which is necessarily very brief, contains some propositions belonging to that part of the theory which was communicated to the British Association; but it is principally devoted to practical applications with reference to the measurement of electro-motive forces arising from chemical action, and to the system of measurement of "galvanic resistance in absolute units," recently introduced by Weber†.

2. PROP. I.—*If a current of uniform strength be sustained in a linear conductor, and if an electro-motive force act in this*

---

* *Report*, 1848; *Transactions of Sections*, p. 9.

† " Messungen galvanischer Leitungswiderstände nach einem absoluten Maasse;" von Wilhelm Weber.—Poggendorff's *Annalen*, March 1851, No. 3.

conductor in the same direction as the current, it will produce
work at a rate equal to the number measuring the force multiplied
by the number measuring the strength of the current.

3.   Let the electro-motive force considered be produced by the
motion of a straight conductor of unit-length, held at right angles
to the lines of force of a magnetic field of unit-intensity, and
carried in a direction perpendicular to its own length and to those
lines of force.   The velocity of the motion will be numerically
equal to the electro-motive force, which will be denoted by F, thus
inductively produced, since the unit of electro-motive force
adopted by those who have introduced or used absolute units in
electro-dynamics is that which would be produced in the same
circumstances if the velocity of the motion were unity.   If the
ends of the moveable conductor be pressed on two fixed conductors,
connected with one another either simply by a wire, or through
any circuit excited by electro-motive forces, so that a current of
strength γ is sustained through it, it will experience an electro-
magnetic force in a direction perpendicular to its own length and
to the lines of magnetic force in the field across which it is moving,
of which the amount will be the product of γ into the intensity
of the magnetic force, or, since this is unity, simply to γ *.   The
motion of the conductor being in that line, the force will be
directly opposed to it when the current is in the direction in which
it would be if it were produced solely by the electro-motive force
we are considering ; and therefore, if we regard γ as positive when
this is the case, the work done in moving the conductor during
any time will be equal to the product of γ into the space through
which it is moved, and will therefore in the unit of time be $F\gamma$,
since F is numerically equal to the velocity of the motion.   But
this work produces no other effect than making the electro-motive
force act, and therefore the electro-motive force must produce
some kind of effect mechanically equivalent to it.   Now if an
equal electro-motive force were produced in any other way (whether
chemically, thermally, or by a common frictional electrical machine)
between the same two conductors, connected in the same way, it
would produce the same effects.   Hence, universally, the mechanical value of the work done in a unit of time by an electro-motive

* This statement virtually expresses the definition of the " strength " of a
current, according to the electro-magnetic unit now generally adopted.

force F, on a circuit through which a current of strength γ is passing, is $F\gamma$.

4. If the algebraic signs of F and γ be different, that is if the electro-motive force act against the direction of the current, the amount of work done by it is negative, or effect is gained by allowing it to act. This is the case with the inductive re-action, by which an electro-magnetic engine at work resists the current by which it is excited, or with the electrolytic resistance experienced in the decomposition of water.

5. The application of the proposition which has just been proved, to chemical and thermal electro-motive forces is of much importance. I hope to make a communication to the Royal Society of Edinburgh before the end of this year, in which, by the application to thermal electro-motive forces, the principles explained in a previous communication * "On the Dynamical Theory of Heat," will be extended so as to include a mechanical theory of thermo-electric currents. The application to chemical electro-motive forces leads immediately to the expression for the electro-motive force of a galvanic battery, which was obtained by virtually the same reasoning, in another paper published in this Volume of the Magazine† (p. 429) [Art. LIII. above]: for if ϵ be the electro-chemical equivalent of one of the substances concerned in the chemical action; if θ be the quantity of heat evolved by as much of the chemical action concerned in producing the current as takes place during the consumption of a unit of mass of this substance; and if J be the mechanical equivalent of the thermal unit, the mechanical value of the chemical action which goes on in a unit of time will be $J\theta\epsilon\gamma$, and this must therefore be equal to $F\gamma$, the work done by the electro-motive force which results. Hence we have

$$F = J\theta\epsilon,$$

which is the expression given in the paper referred to above, for the electro-motive force of a galvanic battery in absolute measure.

6. In applying this formula to the case of Daniell's battery, I used a value for θ derived from experiments made by Mr Joule,

* March, 1851. Published in the *Transactions*, Vol. **xx**. Part II. [Art. **xlviii**. Parts I. II. III. above.]

† "On the Mechanical Theory of Electrolysis." [Art. LIII. above.]

the details of which have not yet been published, but which I believe to have consisted of observations of phenomena depending on the actual working electro-motive forces of the battery. I am now enabled to compare that value of the thermal equivalent, with the results of observations made directly on the heat of combination, by Dr Andrews *, who has kindly communicated to me the following *data* :—

(1) The heat evolved by the combination of one grain of zinc with gaseous oxygen amounts to

1301 units.

(2) The heat evolved by the combination of the 1·246 grains of oxide thus formed with dilute sulphuric acid amounts to

369 units.

(3) The heat evolved by the combination of the equivalent quantity, ·9727 of a grain of copper, with oxygen, amounts to

588·6 units.

(4) The heat evolved by the combination of the 1·221 grains of oxide thus formed, with dilute sulphuric acid, amounts to

293 units.

Hence the thermal equivalent of the whole chemical action which goes on in a Daniell's battery during the consumption of a grain of zinc is

$$1301 + 369 - (588 \cdot 6 + 293), \text{ or } 788 \cdot 4 \ldots \ldots \ldots \ldots (\text{I}):$$

the thermal equivalent of the part of it which consists of oxidation and deoxidation alone is

$$1301 - 588 \cdot 6, \text{ or } \qquad 712 \cdot 4 \ldots \ldots \ldots \ldots (\text{II}).$$

The thermal equivalent which I used formerly is

$$769 \ldots \ldots \ldots \ldots \ldots \ldots \ldots \ldots (\text{III}).$$

If the opinion expressed by Faraday, in April, 1834 (*Exper. Researches*, 919), with reference to the galvanic batteries then known, that the oxidation alone is concerned in producing the current, and the dissolution of the oxide in acid is electrically inoperative, be true for Daniell's battery, the number (II) is the thermal equivalent of the electrically effective chemical action. Joule's number (III) is considerably greater than this, and falls but little short of (I), the thermal equivalent of the *whole* chemi-

---

* Published in his papers "On the Heat disengaged during the Combination of Bodies with Oxygen and Chlorine" (*Phil. Mag.* May and June, 1848), "On the Heat disengaged during Metallic Substitutions" (*Phil. Transactions*, Part I. for 1848), "On the Heat developed during the Combination of Acids and Bases" (*Trans. Royal Irish Academy*, Vol. XIX. Part II.), &c.

cal action that goes on during the consumption of a grain of zinc. If we take successively (I), (II), (III) as the value of θ, and take for ϵ and J the values ·07284 and 44758, which were used in my former paper, we find the following values for the product $J\theta\epsilon$:—

(I)   2570300, which would be the electro-motive force (in
[= 1·101 Volts]   British absolute units) of a single cell of Daniell's battery if the whole chemical action were electrically efficient.

(II)   2322550, which would be the electro-motive force of a
[= ·995 Volts]   single cell of Daniell's battery if only the oxidation and deoxidation of the metals were electrically efficient.

(III)   2507100, which is the electro-motive force of a single cell
[= 1·074 Volts]   of Daniell's battery, according to Joule's experiments.

7.   The thermal equivalent of the whole chemical action in a cell of Smee's battery (zinc and platinized silver in dilute sulphuric acid), or of any battery consisting of zinc and a less oxidizable metal immersed in dilute sulphuric acid, is found by subtracting the quantity of heat that might be obtained by burning in gaseous oxygen the hydrogen that escapes, from the quantity of heat that would be obtained in the formation of the sulphate if the zinc were oxidized in gaseous oxygen instead of by combination with oxygen derived from the decomposition of water. Now the quantity of hydrogen that escapes during the consumption of a grain of zinc is $\frac{1}{32\cdot53}$ of a grain (if 32·53, which corresponds to the equivalents used by Dr Andrews, be taken as the equivalent of zinc, instead of 32·3 which I used in my former paper). According to Dr Andrews' experiments, the combination of this with gaseous oxygen would evolve

$$\frac{1}{32\cdot53} \times 33808, \text{ or } 1039\cdot3 \text{ units of heat.}$$

Hence the thermal equivalent of the whole chemical action corresponding to the consumption of a grain of zinc in Smee's battery is

$$1301 + 369 - 1039\cdot3, \text{ or } 630\cdot7\ldots\ldots\ldots\ldots\ldots(I).$$

250

The equivalent of that part which consists of the oxidation of zinc and the deoxidation of hydrogen is

$$1301 - 1039 \cdot 3, \text{ or } \qquad 261 \cdot 7 \ldots\ldots\ldots\ldots\ldots\text{(II)}.$$

Hence (I) if the whole chemical action be efficient in producing the current, the electro-motive force is 2056200.

(II)   If only the oxidation and deoxidation be efficient, the electro-motive force is 853190.

The *external* electro-motive force (or the electro-motive force with which the battery operates on a very long thin wire connecting its plates), according to either hypothesis, would be found by subtracting the "chemical resistance*" due to the evolution of hydrogen at the platinized silver, from the whole electro-motive force: but, on account of the feeble affinity of the platinized surface for oxygen, it is probable that this opposing electro-motive force, if it exist at all, is but very slight.

(III)   The external electro-motive force of a single cell of Smee's battery is, according to Joule's experiments †, ·65 of that of a single cell of Daniell's; and therefore if we take the preceding number (III), derived from his own experiments, as the true external electro-motive force of a single cell of Daniell's, that of a single cell of Smee's is

$$1,629,600.$$

This number is nearly double that which was found for the electro-motive force on the supposition that the oxidation and deoxidation alone are electrically efficient; but it falls considerably short of what was found on the suppositions that the whole chemical action is efficient, and that there is no "chemical resistance."

8.   It is to be remarked that the external electro-motive force determined for a single cell of Smee's, according to the preceding principles, by subtracting the "chemical resistance" from the value of $J\theta\epsilon$, is the *permanent working* external electro-motive force. The electro-statical tension, which will determine the initial working external electro-motive force, depends on the

---

* See foot note on § 6 of my paper "On the Mechanical Theory of Electrolysis." [Art. LIII. above. See also Art. LV. below.]

† *Phil. Mag.*, Jan.—June, 1844, XXIV. p. 115, and Dove's *Rep.*, Vol. VIII. p. 841.

primitive state of the platinized silver plate. It could never be greater than to make the initial working force be

$$J \times 1670 \times \epsilon, \text{ or } 5444500,$$

corresponding to the combination of zinc with gaseous oxygen and of the oxide with sulphuric acid. It might possibly reach this limit if the platinized surface had been carefully cleaned, and kept in oxygen gas until the instant of immersion, or if it had been used as the positive electrode of an apparatus for decomposing water, immediately before being connected with the zinc plate; and then it could only reach it if the whole chemical action were electrically efficient, and if there were no "chemical resistance" due to the affinity of the platinized surface for oxygen.

9. It is also to be remarked, that the permanent working electro-motive force of a galvanic element, consisting of zinc and a less oxidizable metal immersed in sulphuric acid, can never exceed the number 2056200, derived above from the *full* thermal equivalent for the single cell of Smee's, since the chemical action is identical in all such cases, and the mechanical value of the external effect can never exceed that of the chemical action. In a pair consisting of zinc and tin, the electro-motive force has been found by Poggendorf* to be only about half that of a pair consisting of zinc and copper, and consequently less than half that of a single cell of Smee's. There is therefore an immense loss of mechanical effect in the external working of a galvanic battery composed of such elements; which *must* be compensated by heat produced within the cells. I believe with Joule, that this compensating heat is produced at the surface of the tin in consequence of hydrogen being forced to bubble up from it, instead of the metal itself being allowed to combine with the oxygen of the water in contact with it. A most curious result of this theory of "chemical resistance" is, that in experiments (such as those of Faraday, *Exp. Researches*, 1027, 1028) in which an electrical current passing through a trough containing dilute sulphuric acid, is made to traverse a diaphragm of an oxidizable metal (zinc or tin), dissolving it on one side and evolving bubbles of hydrogen

---

* "Berl. Acb. 46, 242," Pogg. *Ann.*, LXX. 60. Dove's *Repertorium*, Vol. VII. p. 341.

on the other; part (if not all) of the heat of combination will be evolved, not on the side on which the metal is eaten away, but on the side at which the bubbles of hydrogen appear. It will be very interesting to verify this conclusion, by comparing the quantities of heat evolved in two equal and similar electrolytic cells, in the same circuit, each with zinc for the positive electrode, and one with zinc, the other with platinum or platinized silver for the positive electrode. The electro-motive force of the latter cell would be sufficient to excite a current through the circuit, but it might be found convenient to add electro-motive force from some other source*.

10. PROP. II. *The resistance of a metallic conductor, in terms of Weber's absolute unit, is equal to the product of the quantity of heat developed in it in a unit of time by a current of unit strength, into the mechanical equivalent of a thermal unit.*

11. If H denote the quantity of heat developed in the conductor in a unit of time, by a current of strength γ, the mechanical value of the whole effect produced in it will, according to the principles established by Joule, be JH. But this effect is produced by the electro-motive force, F, and therefore, by Prop. I., we have

$$JH = F\gamma.$$

Now, according to Ohm's original definition of galvanic resistance, if k denote the resistance of the given conductor, we have

$$\gamma = \frac{F}{k}.$$

If the electro-motive force and the strength of the current be measured in absolute units of the kind explained above, the

---

* An examination of the thermal effects of a current through four equal and similar vessels containing dilute sulphuric acid, and connected by means of electrodes [immersed plates] of zinc and platinum, varied according to the four permutations of double zinc, double platinum, zinc-platinum, platinum-zinc, in one circuit, excited by an independent galvanic battery or other electromotor, would throw great light on the theory of chemical electro-motive forces and resistances. Vessels containing electrodes of other metals, such as tin, variously combined, and direct and reverse cells of Daniell's battery, might all be introduced into the same circuit. If the exteriors of all the cells were equal and similar, the excesses of their permanent temperatures above that of an equal and similar cell in the neighbourhood, containing no source of heat within it, would be very nearly proportional to the rates at which heat is developed in them. [Compare Article LV. below.]

number k, expressing the resistance in this formula, will express it in terms of the absolute unit introduced by Weber. Using the value $k\gamma$ derived from this, for F, in the preceding equation, we have

$$JH = k\gamma^2.$$

This equation expresses the law of the excitation of heat in the galvanic circuit discovered by Joule; and if we take $\gamma = 1$, it expresses the proposition to be proved.

12.   In Mr Joule's original paper on the heat evolved by metallic conductors of electricity[*], experiments are described, in which the strengths of the currents used are determined in absolute measure, the unit employed being the strength which a current must have to decompose 9 grains of water in an hour of time. But the electro-chemical equivalent of water, according to the system of absolute measurement introduced by Weber, is, in British units, very nearly ·02, and therefore a current of unit strength would decompose 72 grains of water in an hour. Hence Joule's original unit is very exactly ⅛th of the British electro-magnetic unit for measuring current electricity. By using the formula $k = JH/\gamma^2$, and taking for γ one-eighth the number of Mr Joule's "degrees of current;" for H the quantity of heat (measured by grains of water raised 1° Cent.) evolved by the current through the conductor experimented on; and for J the value 44758; I have found

$$k = 13,240,000$$

as the absolute resistance of a certain wire used by Mr Joule for an absolute standard of resistance in the experiments on the heat evolved in electrolysis, described in the second part of the same paper[†].

13.   The "specific resistance" of a metal referred to unity of volume, may be defined as the absolute resistance of a unit length

[*] *Proceedings of the Royal Society*, Dec. 17, 1840; *Philosophical Magazine*, Vol. XIX. (Oct. 1841), p. 260.

[†] The three experiments from which the number in the text was deduced as a mean result (described in §§ 25, 26, 27 of the paper, *Phil. Mag.* Vol. XIX. Oct. 1841, p. 266), lead separately to the following values for the resistance :—

13260000
13360000
13090000;

none of which differs by as much as $\frac{1}{50}$th from the mean given in the text.

of a conductor of unit section; and the specific resistance of a metal referred to unity of mass, or simply "the specific resistance of a metal" (since the term, which was introduced by Weber, is, when unqualified, so used by him), is defined as the absolute resistance of a conductor of uniform section, and of unit length and unit weight. Hence, since the resistance of conductors of similar substance are inversely proportional to their sections, and directly proportional to their lengths, we have

$$\sigma_v = k\omega/l^*, \quad \sigma = km/l^2;$$

if l be the length, ω the area of the section, and m the mass (or weight) of a conductor, k its absolute resistance, and σ_v and σ the specific resistances of its substance referred respectively to unity of volume and to unity of mass.

14. The absolute resistance of a certain silver wire, and of a column of mercury contained in a spiral glass tube, may be determined from experimental *data* extracted from a paper of **Mr** Joule's laid before the French Institute (*Comptes Rendus*, Feb. 9, 1846), and communicated to me by the author. In four experiments on the silver wire, and in four similar experiments on the mercury tube, a current measured by a tangent galvanometer was passed through the conductor, and, in each experiment, the quantity of heat evolved during ten minutes was determined by the elevation of temperature produced in a measured mass of water, the temperature of the conductors during all the experi-

---

* By means of this I have found 4·1 for the specific resistance of copper, according to the statement made in § 24 of Mr Joule's paper, that his standard conductor was "10 feet long and ·024 of an inch thick;" but there must be some mistake here, as it will be seen below that this is about double what we might expect it to be. [Note of July 27, 1882. It is more probable that the wire was of less than half the proper conductivity for copper wire than that Joule had made any mistake in stating its dimensions. Such deficiencies of conductivity in ordinary copper wire as, nine years later, I found even in wires supplied for submarine telegraph cables, some of which I found to have less than 40 per cent. of the conductivity of others, were not imagined possible at the date (1851) of this paper.] I have found 2·17 for the specific resistance of copper referred to unity of volume, according to the experiment described in § 9, on a wire stated to be 2 yards long and $\frac{1}{24}$th of an inch thick; and 1·78 and 1·98, according to the experiments described in §§ 9 and 11, on a wire stated to be 2 yards long and $\frac{1}{16}$th of an inch thick; also 7·7 for that of iron, in a wire stated (§ 11) to be 2 yards long and $\frac{1}{27}$th of an inch thick. It is to be remarked, however, that no attempt was made by Mr Joule to determine the sections of his wires with accuracy, and that the "thicknesses" are merely mentioned in round numbers, as descriptive of the kinds of wire used in his different experiments.

ments having been nearly 50° Fahr.   The mean result of the four experiments on each conductor is expressed in terms of the square root of the sum of the squares of the tangents of the galvanometer-deflections, and the mean quantity of heat evolved in ten minutes. The weight of the silver wire in air and in water, the weight of the mercury contained in the glass tube, and the exact length of each conductor, were determined a short time ago, at my request, by Mr Joule, and the areas of the sections of the conductors have been deduced.   The same galvanometer having been used as was employed in the experiments on electrolysis, referred to in the "Note on Electro-chemical Equivalents," contained in this Volume of the Magazine, [Art. LIII. above], and the experiments at present referred to having also been made at Manchester in 1845, the strength of the current in absolute measure is found by multiplying the tangent of deflection by ·28186.   The various experimental data thus obtained are as follows:

Conductor.	Length in feet.	Mass in grains.	Sectional area in square feet.	Mean corrected tangent of deflection.	Mean strength of current in absolute units.	Mean quantity of heat produced in 10 minutes.
Silver wire..	27⅔	434·51	·0000034462	1·4526	·40943	19375 grs. of water raised 1°·7718 C. in temperature.
Mercury in glass tube }	} 5⅛	1511·5	·000048119			
				The resistance of the mercury conductor was found to be ·74964 of that of the silver wire.		

Taking as the thermal unit the quantity of heat required to raise the temperature of a grain of water by 1° Cent., we find 57·213 as the heat generated in the silver wire in one second, of which the mechanical equivalent is $44758 \times 57\cdot213$.   Dividing this by the square of the strength of the current, we find 15276000 for the absolute resistance of the silver wire; and by multiplying by ·74964, we deduce 11451000 for the absolute resistance of the mercury conductor.   Multiplying each absolute resistance by the sectional area of the conductor to which it corresponds, and dividing by the length; and again, multiplying each resistance by the mass, and dividing by the square of the length, we obtain the following results with reference to the specific resistances of silver and mercury at about 10° Cent. of temperature.

Metal.	Specific resistance referred to unity of volume.		"Specific resistance."
	British system.	[C. G. S.]	
Silver	1·9028	[1768]	8671500
Mercury	106·65	[99081]	648410000

15. The "conducting powers" of metals, as ordinarily defined, are inversely proportional to their specific resistances referred to unity of volume. Hence, according to the preceding results, the conducting powers of silver and mercury at about 10° Cent. of temperature are in the proportion of 1 to ·01784. According to the experiments of M. E. Becquerel (Dove's *Repertorium*, Vol. VIII. p. 193), the conducting powers of silver and mercury at 0° Cent. are in the proportion of 1 to ·017387; and at 100° Cent., of 1 to ·022083: at 10° Cent. they must therefore be nearly in the proportion of 1 to ·01786, which agrees very closely with the preceding comparative result. Again, according to M. Becquerel's experiments, the conducting powers of silver and copper are,—

at 0° in the proportion of 1 to ·91517,
    at 100° ...   1 to ·91030,
and therefore at 10° ...   1 to ·915.

Hence the specific resistance of copper at about 10° Cent. referred to unity of volume, may be found by dividing that of silver by ·915; and from the preceding result, it is thus found to be 2·080. Multiplying this by 3810500, the weight in grains of a cubic foot of copper (found by taking 8·72 as the specific gravity of copper), we obtain for the "specific resistance" of copper the value 7925800.

16. Weber, in first introducing the measurement of resistances in absolute units, gave two experimental methods, both founded virtually on a comparison of the electromotive forces with the strengths of the currents produced by them, in the conductors examined; and he actually applied them to various conductors, and obtained results which, reduced to British units, are shown in the following table. The first four numbers in the second column are deduced from M. Weber's results, on the hypothesis that the specific gravity of each specimen of copper is 8·72. The only numbers given on the authority of M. Weber are the first four of the column headed "Specific resistance." Some of the specific resistances derived above from Mr Joule's experiments are shown in the same table for the sake of comparison.

Quality of metal, &c.		Specific resistance referred to unity of volume.		"Specific resistance."
		British system.	[C. G. S.]	
No. 1.	Jacobi's copper wire.....................	2·851	[2649]	10870000
No. 2.	Kirchhoff's copper wire.................	2·365	[2197]	9225000
No. 3.	Weber's copper wire.....................	2·303	[2139]	8778000
No. 4.	Wire of electrolytically precipitated copper........................	2·079	[1931]	7924000
No. 5.	Copper at about 10⁰ Cent., according to Joule and Becquerel........	2·080	[1932]	7926000
	[One of Joule's copper wires]	[4·1]	[3809]	
	[Another of Joule's copper wires] ...	[1·78]	[1653]	
	[Pure copper at 0⁰ Cent.]		[1640]	
No. 6.	Joule's silver wire at about 10⁰ C.....	1·903	[1768]	8671000
No. 7.	Mercury at about 10⁰ Cent.	106·65	[99081]	648400000

The great discrepancies among the first four numbers of the third column, each of which is probably correct in three of its significant figures, show how very much the specific resistances of the substance of different specimens of copper wire may differ from one another. The specific resistance of copper (No. 5), deduced indirectly from Joule's absolute by means of Becquerel's relative determinations, agrees very closely with that of the electrolytically precipitated copper (No. 4) experimented on by Weber.

17.   It is very much to be desired that Weber's direct process, and the indirect method founded on estimating, according to Joule's principles, the mechanical value of the thermal effects of a galvanic current, should be both put in practice to determine the absolute resistance of the same conductor, or that the resistance of two conductors to which the two methods have been separately applied, should be accurately compared.   Such an investigation could scarcely be expected to give a more approximate value of the mechanical equivalent of a thermal unit than has been already found by means of experiments on the friction of fluids; but it would afford a most interesting illustration of those principles by which Mr Joule has shown how to trace an equivalence between work spent and mechanical effect produced, in all physical agencies in which heat is concerned.

GLASGOW COLLEGE, Nov. 19, 1851.

[Note of June 1, 1882. In the preceding paper as originally published, values stated in absolute measure were given on the British system, with the foot, grain and second as the fundamental units. Where it seemed advisable there has now been added, in square brackets, beside the original figures, the corresponding values on the C. G. S. system of units.]

15

Reprinted from *Mathematical and Physical Papers of William Thomson*, Vol. 1, Cambridge University Press, London, 1882, pp. 472–481

ART. LIII. ON THE MECHANICAL THEORY OF ELECTROLYSIS.

William Thomson (Lord Kelvin)

[*Phil. Mag.* Dec. 1851.]

1. CERTAIN principles discovered by Mr Joule, and published for the first time in his various papers in this Magazine, must ultimately become an important part of the foundation of a mechanical theory of chemistry. The object of the present communication is to investigate, according to those principles, the relation, in any case of electrolysis, between the electro-motive intensity, the electro-chemical equivalents of the substances operated on, and the mechanical equivalent of the chemical effect produced in the consumption of a given amount of the materials; and by means of it to determine in absolute measure the electro-motive intensity of a single cell of Daniell's battery, and the electro-motive intensity required for the electrolysis of water, from experimental data which Mr Joule has kindly communicated to me.

2. If a galvanic current, produced by means of a magneto-electric machine, be employed in electrolysis, it will generate, in any time, less heat throughout its entire circuit than the equivalent of the work spent, by an amount which may be called the thermal equivalent of the chemical action which has been effected, being the quantity of heat which would be obtained by recombining the elements of the decomposed substance, and reducing the compound to its primitive condition in every respect; or generally, by undoing all the action which has been done in the electro-chemical apparatus. Now the quantity of heat which is equivalent to the work done is obtained by dividing the number which measures the work by the number which measures by the same unit the mechanical equivalent of the unit of heat. Hence if the mechanical equivalent of the thermal unit be denoted by J, the work done in any time by W, the total quantity of heat evolved in the same time throughout the circuit by H, and the thermal equivalent of the chemical effect produced by Θ, we have

$$H = \frac{W}{J} - \Theta \dots\dots\dots\dots\dots\dots\dots(1);$$

an equation which may also be written in the form

$$W = JH + M \dots\dots\dots\dots\dots\dots(2),$$

if M be used to denote the value of $J\Theta$, or, as it may be called, the mechanical equivalent of the chemical effect produced in the stated period of time.

3.   To avoid the necessity of considering variable or discontinuous currents, let us suppose the "machine" to consist of a metallic disc, touched at its centre and at its circumference by fixed wires, and made to revolve in its own plane about an axis through its centre, held in any position not at right angles to the direction of the earth's magnetic force*. [Note of April 16, 1882. Better have said *an axis coincident with the direction of the earth's magnetic force.*] If these wires be connected by contact between their ends, there will, as is known, be a current produced in them of a strength proportional directly to the angular velocity of the disc, and inversely to the resistance through the whole circuit. Hence there will be between the ends of the wires, if separated by an insulating medium, an electromotive force the intensity of which will be constant and proportional to the angular velocity of the disc.

4.   Let us now suppose the wires to be connected with the electrodes of an electro-chemical apparatus, for instance a galvanic battery of any kind, or an apparatus for the decomposition of water; and let us conceive the electro-motive intensity between them to be sufficient to produce a current in its own direction. The preceding equations, when applied to this case, will have each of their terms proportional to the time, since the action is continuous and uniform, and therefore it will be convenient to consider the unit of time as the period during which the amounts of work and heat denoted by W and H, and the amount of chemical action of which the thermal and the mechanical equivalents are denoted respectively by Θ and M, are produced. If r denote the radius of the disc, ω the angular velocity with which it is moved, F the component of the earth's magnetic force perpendicular to its plane, and γ the strength of the current which is induced; the work done in a unit of time in moving the disc against the resistance which it experiences in virtue of the earth's

---

* This is in fact the "new electrical machine" suggested by Faraday in the Bakerian Lecture of 1832. (*Experimental Researches*, § 154.)

magnetic action on the current through it, will be expressed by the integral $\int_0^r \omega z \,.\, F \,.\, \gamma dz$; as is easily proved, whether the current be supposed to pass directly between the centre of the disc and the point of its circumference touched by the fixed wire, or to be, as it in reality must be, more or less diffused from the direct line, on account of the lateral extension of the revolving conductor. Hence we have

$$W = \frac{1}{2} r^2 F \gamma \omega \quad \dots\dots\dots\dots\dots\dots\dots(3).$$

5. Let E denote the quantity (in units of matter, as grains for instance) of one of the elements concerned in the chemical action, which is electrolysed or combined in the unit of time, and let θ denote the quantity of heat absorbed in the chemical action during the electrolysis or combination of a unit quantity of that element.   Then we have

$$\Theta = \theta \,.\, E \dots\dots\dots\dots\dots\dots\dots\dots(4),$$
$$M = J \,.\, \theta E \dots\dots\dots\dots\dots\dots\dots\dots(5).$$

Now it has been shown by Faraday, that in electro-chemical action of any known kind, produced by means of a continuous current, the amount of the action in a given time is approximately if not rigorously proportional to the strength of the current; and all subsequent researches on the subject have tended to confirm this conclusion. The only exception to it which, so far as I am aware, has yet been discovered, is the fact established by Faraday, that various electrolytes can conduct a continuous current, when the electro-motive intensity is below certain limits, without experiencing any continued decomposition*; but from it we may infer as probable, that in general the quantity decomposed with high or low electro-motive intensities is not quite rigorously proportional to the strength of the current.

* It is probable that when an electromotor of an intensity below a certain limit is put in connexion with two platinum electrodes immersed in water, there is at the first instant no electrolytic resistance; and a decomposing current passes which gradually falls off in strength, until the electrodes are, by the separated oxygen and hydrogen, put into a certain state, such that with the water between them, they exert a resisting electric force very nearly equal to that of the electromotor; after which a uniform current of excessively reduced strength passes without producing further decomposition. I hope before long to be able to communicate to the Magazine an account of some experiments I have made to illustrate these circumstances.

This non-electrolytic conducting power is, however, at least in the case of water, found to be excessively feeble; and it is not probable that when electrolysis is actually going on in any ordinary case, the quantity of electricity conducted by means of it is ever considerable compared with that which is electrically conducted; and the normal law of true electrolytic conduction will therefore be assumed as applicable to the conduction through the electro-chemical apparatus, subject to modification in any case in which the deviations from it can be determined. If, then, we denote by ϵ the electro-chemical equivalent of the particular element referred to for measuring the chemical action, that is, the quantity of it which is electrolysed or combined in a unit of time by the operation of a current of unit strength, since the actual strength of the current is γ, we have

$$E = \epsilon\gamma \dots\dots\dots\dots\dots\dots\dots\dots\dots(6).$$

The deviations from the normal law which may exist in any particular case may be represented by giving ϵ a variable value. For instance, if it were true that when the electro-motive intensity in an apparatus for the decomposition of water exceeds a certain limit, there is decomposition at a rate precisely proportional to the strength of the current; and when the intensity is below that limit, a slight current passes without any decomposition; ϵ would be a discontinuous function of the intensity, having a constant value when the intensity is above, and being zero when the intensity is below, the limit for decomposition.

6.   According to Joule's law of the generation of heat in the galvanic circuit, the quantity of heat developed in a unit of time would be rigorously proportional to the square of the strength of the current, if the total resistance were constant in all the circumstances considered; and therefore we may conveniently assume

$$H = R\gamma^2 \dots\dots\dots\dots\dots\dots\dots\dots(7);$$

but as we are not sure that the whole resistance is independent of the strength of the current when an electrolysed fluid forms part of the circuit, we must not assume that R is constant. In what follows, all that is assumed regarding the value of R is, that it is neither infinitely great nor infinitely small in any of the circumstances considered*.

7. If we substitute the expressions (3), (4) and (6), (7) for the three terms of the original equation (1), we have

$$R\gamma^2 = \frac{\frac{1}{2}r^2 F\gamma\omega}{J} - \theta\epsilon\gamma \dots\dots\dots\dots\dots(8),$$

from which we deduce

$$\gamma = \frac{\frac{1}{2}r^2 F\omega - J\theta\epsilon}{JR} \dots\dots\dots\dots\dots(9).$$

8. It appears from this result that the value of γ will be positive or negative according as the angular velocity of the disc exceeds or falls short of a certain value Ω, given by the equation

$$\Omega = \frac{J\theta\epsilon}{\frac{1}{2}r^2 F} \dots\dots\dots\dots\dots(10);$$

and therefore we conclude that, when the angular velocity has exactly this value, the electro-motive intensity of the disc is just equal to the intensity of the reverse electro-motive force exerted on the fixed wires, by the electro-chemical apparatus with which they are connected.

9. If we adopt as the unit of electro-motive intensity that which is produced by a conductor of unit length, carried, in a

---

* Since the present article was put into the Editor's hands, I have become acquainted with a paper by Mr Joule "On the Heat evolved during the Electrolysis of Water," published by the Literary and Philosophical Society of Manchester in 1843 (Vol. VII. part 3, second series), in which it is shown, that in some cases of electro chemical action (for instance, when hydrogen is evolved at an electrode or battery-plate of a metal possessing a considerable affinity for oxygen) there is a "resistance to electrolysis without chemical change," producing "a reaction on the intensity of the battery," and causing the evolution of heat to an amount exactly equivalent to the loss of heating power, or of external electro-motive force, which the battery thus suffers. [Note of April 17, 1882. For further development of this subject see Art. LV. below.] In any electro-chemical apparatus in which this kind of resistance occurs, the quantity of heat developed by a current of strength γ will be expressible in the form $A\gamma + B\gamma^2$, where A and B are finite when γ is infinitely small. Consequently what is denoted in the text by R will be equal to $\frac{A}{\gamma} + B$, and will therefore be infinitely great when γ is infinitely small. The modification required for such cases will be simply to use B in place of R, and to diminish the value of I found in the text (12) by JA; but the assumption that R does not become infinite in any of the circumstances considered is, I believe, quite justifiable in the two special cases which form the subject of the present communication.—W. T., Nov. 12, 1851.

magnetic field of unit force, with unit velocity, in a direction which is both perpendicular to its own length and to the lines of force in the magnetic field, it is easily shown that the electro-motive force of the disc, in the circumstances specified above, is given by the equation

$$i = \frac{1}{2} r^2 F \omega \dots\dots\dots\dots\dots\dots(11).$$

Hence if I denote the electro-motive force of the disc when it just balances that of the chemical apparatus, we have by (10)

$$I = J\theta\epsilon\dots\dots\dots\dots\dots\dots(12).$$

This equation comprehends a general expression of the conclusion long since arrived at by Mr Joule, that the quantities of heat developed by different chemical combinations are, for quantities of the chemical action electrically equivalent, proportional to the intensities of galvanic arrangements adapted to allow the combinations to take place without any evolution of heat in their own localities; and it may be stated in general terms thus :—

The intensity of an electro-chemical apparatus is, in absolute measure, equal to the mechanical equivalent of as much of the chemical action as goes on with a current of unit strength during a unit of time.

10.   When ω is less than Ω, γ is (§ 8) negative; and hence equations (3), (5) and (6), show W and M to be negative also. In this case the direction of the current is contrary to the electro-motive force of the disc; the chemical action is the source of the current instead of being an effect of it; and the disc by its rotation produces mechanical effect as an electro-magnetic engine, instead of requiring work to be spent upon it to keep it moving as a magneto-electric machine.   If we assume

$$\gamma = -\gamma', \quad M = -M', \quad W = -W',$$

so that when γ, M, and W are negative their absolute values may be represented by γ', M' and W', we find by (9), (10), (5), (6), (2), (3) the following expressions for these quantities :

$$\gamma' = \frac{\frac{1}{2} r^2 F}{JR} (\Omega - \omega)\dots\dots\dots\dots\dots(13),$$

$$M' = J\theta\epsilon\gamma' = \frac{\frac{1}{2} r^2 F . \theta\epsilon}{R} (\Omega - \omega)\dots\dots\dots(14),$$

$$W' = M' - JH = \frac{1}{2} r^2 F \omega . \gamma' = \frac{\omega}{\Omega} M'\dots\dots(15).$$

The first of the three expressions (15) for W' merely shows that the mechanical effect produced by the disc in any period of time is less than M', the full mechanical equivalent of the consumption of materials in the electro-chemical apparatus, by the mechanical equivalent of the heat generated in the whole circuit during that period. From the third we infer, that the fraction of the entire duty of the consumption which is actually performed by the engine is equal to $\frac{\omega}{\Omega}$. If ω were precisely equal to Ω, the electro-motive force of the battery would be precisely balanced, and there could be no current, and hence the performance of the engine cannot be perfect; but if ω be less than Ω by an infinitely small amount, the battery will be allowed to act very slowly; a very slight current, with a very small consumption of materials, will be generated; and the mechanical effect produced from it will be infinitely nearly equal to the whole duty, and infinitely greater than the portion of the effect wasted in the creation of heat throughout the circuit.

11.   A condition precisely analogous to that of *reversibility*, established by Carnot and Clausius as the criterion of perfection for a thermo-dynamic engine*, is applicable to this electro-magnetic engine; and is satisfied by it when the disc revolves with an angular velocity infinitely nearly equal to Ω, since then γ', M', and W' are each of them proportional to $\Omega - \omega$, whether this quantity be positive or negative; and consequently if the motion of the disc relatively to a state of rotation with the angular velocity Ω be reversed, all the physical and mechanical agencies are reversed.

12.   From experiments made at Manchester in the year 1845 by Mr Joule, on the quantity of zinc electrolysed from a solution of sulphate of zinc by means of a galvanic current measured by his tangent galvanometer, I have found the electro-chemical equivalent of zinc to be ·07284† [= ·003311 c. g. s.]; and I am

* "If an engine be such that, when it is worked backwards, the physical and mechanical agencies in every part of its motions are all reversed, it produces as much mechanical effect as can be produced by any thermo-dynamic engine, with the same temperatures of source and refrigerator, from a given quantity of heat." (From § 9 of "Dynamical Theory of Heat." [Art. XLVIII. above.] *Transactions of the Royal Society of Edinburgh*, March 17, 1851, Vol. XX. part 2.)

† See note on "Electro-chemical Equivalents" published at the end of this paper.

informed by him, that from other experiments which he has made, he finds that the entire heat developed by the consumption of a grain of zinc in a Daniell's battery is as much as would raise the temperature of 769 grains of water from $0°$ to $1°$ Cent.* Hence, if we wish to apply the preceding investigations to the case in which the electro-chemical apparatus (§ 4) is a single cell of Daniell's battery, we may consider the consumption of a grain of zinc as the unit of the chemical action which takes place, and therefore we have

$$\epsilon = \cdot 07284, \quad \theta = 769.$$

Again, according to Mr Joule's last researches on the mechanical equivalent of heat, the work done by a grain of matter in descending through 1390 feet is capable of raising the temperature of a grain of water from $0°$ to $1°$. Hence, since the unit of force adopted in the measurement of galvanic strength on which the preceding value of ϵ is founded, is that force which, operating during one second of time upon one grain of matter, would generate a velocity of one foot per second, and is consequently $\dfrac{1}{32\cdot2}$ of the weight of a grain at Manchester, we have

$$J = 1390 \times 32\cdot2 = 44758.$$

Substituting these values for ϵ, θ, and J in (12), we have

$$I = 2507100 \ [\ = 1\cdot074 \ \text{Volts}]$$

for the "intensity" or "electro-motive force" of a cell of Daniell's battery in absolute measure. To compare this with the electromotive intensity of a revolving disc such as we have considered (§ 3), let the axis of rotation of the disc be vertical or nearly vertical, and, the vertical component of the terrestrial magnetic force at Manchester being about $9\cdot94$, let us suppose that we have

---

* By experiments on the friction of fluids, Mr Joule has found that the quantity of work necessary to raise the temperature of a pound, or 7000 grains, of water from $0°$ to $1°$ Cent. is 1390 foot-pounds. Hence the mechanical equivalent of the consumption of a grain of zinc in Daniell's battery is $152\cdot7$, or nearly 153 foot-pounds. Messrs Scoresby and Joule, in their paper "On the Powers of Electro-magnetism, Steam and Horses" (*Phil. Mag.*, Vol. xxvi. 1846, p. 451), use 158 as the number expressing this equivalent according to earlier experiments made by Mr Joule. The experiments from which he deduced the thermal equivalents of chemical action, communicated to me for this paper, are described in a paper communicated to the French Institute, and acknowledged in the *Comptes Rendus* for Feb. 9, 1846, but not yet published.

$F = 10$ exactly, which would be the case with a disc exactly horizontal in localities a little north of Manchester, and might be made the case in any part of Great Britain by a suitable adjustment of the axis of the disc. Then we have by (11),

$$i = 5\omega r^2 ;$$

or if n be the number of turns per second,

$$i = 5 \times 2\pi n r^2 = 31{\cdot}416 \times n r^2.$$

Hence

$$\frac{i}{I} = \frac{31{\cdot}416 \times n r^2}{2507100} = \frac{n r^2}{79803}.$$

It appears, therefore, that if the radius of the disc be one foot, it would, when revolving at the rate of one turn per second, produce an intensity $\frac{1}{79803}$ of that of a single cell of Daniell's and it would consequently have to make more than 79803 turns per second to reverse the action of such a cell in the arrangement described in § 4.* We conclude also, that a disc of one foot radius, touched at its centre and circumference by the electrodes of a single cell of Daniell's, and allowed to turn about a vertical axis by the action of the earth upon the current passing through it, would revolve with a continually accelerated motion approaching to the limiting rate of 79803 turns per second, if it were subject to no frictional or other resistance; and that if, by resisting forces, it were kept steadily revolving at the rate of n turns per second, it would, in overcoming those forces, be performing $\frac{n}{79803}$ of the whole work due to the consumption of zinc and deposition of copper in the battery.

13. If the electro-chemical apparatus mentioned in § 4 be a vessel of pure water with two plates of platinum immersed in it, we may consider a grain of hydrogen electrolysed as the unit for measuring the chemical action which takes place. Now Mr Joule finds that, in the electrolysis of one grain of hydrogen from

---

* Hence in the multiple form of "the new electrical machine" suggested by Faraday, about 800 discs, each one foot in radius, would be required, so that with a rotation at the rate of 100 turns per second about a vertical axis in any part of Great Britain, it might give an intensity equal to that of a single cell of Daniell's.

water acidulated with sulphuric acid, as much heat is absorbed as would raise the temperature of 33553 grains of water from 0° to 1°. Hence θ must be less than 33553 by the quantity of heat evolved when as much pure water as contains one grain of hydrogen is mixed with acidulated water, such as that used by Mr Joule; but, without appreciable error on this account, we may take

$$\theta = 33553.$$

I have found also, from results of experiments on the electrolysis of water made by Mr Joule at Manchester in 1845, that the electro-chemical equivalent of hydrogen is ·002201. Using this value for ϵ, and the values indicated above for θ and J, we have by (12),

$$I = 3305400 \ [\ = 1\text{·}416 \text{ Volts}]$$

for the electro-motive force, in absolute measure, required for the decomposition of water. This exceeds the electro-motive force of a single cell of Daniell's battery, found above, in the ratio of 1·318 to 1. Hence at least two cells of Daniell's battery are required for the electrolysis of water; but fourteen cells of Daniell's battery connected in one circuit with ten electrolytic vessels of water with platinum electrodes would be sufficient to effect gaseous decomposition in each vessel.

[*Ed. note:* material omitted]

16

Reprinted from *Scientific Memoirs—Selected from the Transactions of Foreign Academies of Science and Foreign Journals*, Vol. 6, John Tyndall and William Francis, eds., Taylor & Francis Ltd., London, 1853, pp. 200–209

On the Work performed and the Heat generated in a Conductor by a Stationary Electric Current. By R. CLAUSIUS.

[From Poggendorff's *Annalen*, vol. lxxxvii. p. 415.]

THE following is a continuation of the paper contained in the last part of these Memoirs (p. 1). The inquiry there instituted into the effects of a sudden discharge I have here endeavoured to extend to the case of a continuous electric current. At present, however, I will confine myself to an especial case. I assume that the current, which I suppose to be constant, is confined to a definite conductor, and regarding the latter I make the following assumptions :—1st, that the conductor suffers neither mechanical nor chemical change by the passage of the current; 2ndly, that nowhere, within the conductor, a source of electromotive power exists, which will be the case when the conductor is composed of one material, in the same condition throughout; and 3rdly, that no inducing actions be exerted between it and other conductors or magnets.

In this case the only effect produced by the electric current is the heating of the conductor. The laws which regulate the generation of heat, in the ordinary case where the conductor possesses the form of a wire, have been empirically established by Joule[*], Lenz[†] and Becquerel[‡], who have found that the heat developed in a wire in the unit of time is proportional to its resistance, and to the square of the intensity of the current. Among the theoretic investigations connected with this subject, I must particularly mention a paper by W. Thomson in the Philosophical Magazine[§]. The results of this paper coincide, as far as they refer to the same points, with those contained in the present memoir, for in both of them the theoretic necessity

[*] Phil. Mag., S. 3. vol. xix. p. 264, and S. 4. vol. iii. p. 486.
[†] Poggendorff's *Annalen*, vol. lxi. p. 44.
[‡] *Ann. de Chim. et de Phys.*, S. 3. vol. ix. p. 21.
[§] S. 4. vol. ii. p. 551.

of the above empirical law is established. The way, however, by which Thomson arrived at this proposition, as well as the form which he has given to it, are very different from mine. He proceeds from the laws of electro-magnetic induction, and makes use of the law of Ohm, while I make use of the latter only in the form which Kirchhoff has given to it. His attention is further exclusively confined to a lineal conductor, while my results are independent of the form of the conductor, and hence comprehend the lineal ones as a special case. This reason alone would have been a sufficient inducement to me to publish my inquiry, although his has preceded it; but I have a further inducement in the fact, that the principle established in the following pages derives additional interest from its great similarity with that already proved in the case of machine electricity*.

The law of Ohm, so far as it refers to the process within a homogeneous conductor, may be expressed quite generally in the following manner. Let dw be any element of surface within the conductor, N the normal upon it, and idw the quantity of electricity which passes through it during the unit of time, where i is to be regarded as positive or negative, according as the electricity, in reference to the normal N, passes from the negative to the positive side of the element, or in a direction contrary to this; we have then the equation

$$i = k \frac{dV}{dN}, \quad \cdot \quad \cdot \quad \cdot \quad \cdot \quad \cdot \quad \cdot \quad (1)$$

where k represents the conductibility of the body, and V is a function which, as soon as the stationary condition has commenced, is dependent solely on the coordinates of space.

For in every point of the traversed conductor a force must act sufficient to retain the electricity in motion, notwithstanding the resistance continually opposed to it, and the differential coefficient $\frac{dV}{dN}$ evidently represents the component of this force in the direction of the normal. Nevertheless, the physical signification of this function V was formerly far from certain. Ohm called the quantity represented by it, the *electroscopic force*, and defined it as the *density of the electricity* at any

* Pogg. *Ann.* vol. lxxxvi. p. 345.

particular point of the conductor*. Against this view, however, Kirchhoff† justly urged that it is in direct contradiction to
a known electro-statical theorem ; for according to Ohm's view,
the electricity in a conductor would remain at rest if it were distributed equally throughout the whole volume of the conductor,
whereas it is sufficiently well known that the free electricity
of a body—which of course can alone here enter into consideration, as it alone exercises any force—is, in a condition of rest,
distributed *only over the surface* of the body.

This objection might, perhaps, create some mistrust as to the
general admissibility of Ohm's law ; nevertheless, Kirchhoff
himself has proved that the law can be made to harmonize very
well with the fundamental laws of electro-statics, and has likewise shown what meaning must be attached to the function V
in order that this may be the case.

As already stated, $\frac{dV}{dN}$ represents the component of the accelerating force at any particular point, in the direction of the
normal N ; and similarly, the components of the same force
in the directions of the three coordinate axes will be represented
by $\frac{dV}{dx}, \frac{dV}{dy}, \frac{dV}{dz}$. This denotes that the force is caused by
attractions and repulsions proceeding from fixed points, both of
which are dependent, as far as their intensity is concerned,
solely on the distance, and not on the position of the acting
point, the law of this dependence remaining for the present
arbitrary. This, however, can be inferred from other grounds,
namely, in our case it is evident that such attractions and repulsions can only be exercised by the electricity itself, and its
attractions and repulsions are subject to the law of *the inverse
square of the distance*. Hence it follows that the function V is
to be considered simply as the potential function of the whole
free electricity ‡.

---

* Die galvanische Kette, mathematisch bearbeitet von Dr. G. S. Ohm,
p. 95, and Scientific Memoirs, 1st Series, vol. ii. p. 401.

† Pogg. *Ann.* vol. lxxviii. p. 506 ; and Phil. Mag. S. 3. vol. xxxvii. p. 463.

‡ I have chosen the letter V to represent this function instead of the letter
U, which Ohm and Kirchhoff have employed, because in my former memoir
this letter was used for this function ; and to make the agreement with my
former memoir more complete, I have also changed its sign.

The above-mentioned contradiction therefore disappears ; for according to this signification of the function V, the equation V=const., which in (1) denotes that no current exists, is the same as that which in electro-statics is known as the conditional equation for a state of equilibrium.

Further, this signification of V being adopted, it is easy to determine, as Kirchhoff has shown, where the free electricity is distributed in the conductor during a stationary current. For, in order that a current may be stationary, the quantity of electricity contained in each element of space must be constant, hence the quantities of electricity entering and issuing from any element must be equal. Let $dx\, dy\, dz$ be such an element, situated at the point (x, y, z), then, according to equation (1), the quantity of electricity entering the element through the first of the two surfaces $dy\, dz$, in the unit of time

$$= k \cdot dy\, dz\, \frac{dV}{dx},$$

and the quantity issuing from the element through the opposite surface

$$= k \cdot dy\, dz \left(\frac{dV}{dx} + \frac{d^2V}{dx^2}\, dx \right);$$

hence the excess of the latter over the former

$$= k\, dx\, dy\, dz\, \frac{d^2V}{dx^2}.$$

Similarly, for the pair of surfaces $dx\, dz$ we obtain the excess

$$k\, dx\, dy\, dz\, \frac{d^2V}{dy^2},$$

and for the pair of surfaces $dx\, dy$,

$$k\, dx\, dy\, dz\, \frac{d^2V}{dz^2}.$$

The sum of these three last expressions gives the excess of the total quantity of electricity issuing from the element over the quantity entering it in the unit of time, and as this excess must be null, we have

$$\frac{d^2V}{dx^2} + \frac{d^2V}{dy^2} + \frac{d^2V}{dz^2} = 0. \quad \cdot \quad \cdot \quad \cdot \quad \cdot \quad (2)$$

From a well-known theorem of the potential function, however, it follows from this equation, that the point (x, y, z) must be situated *without* the mass, of which V is the potential function; and as the same conclusion applies to every point of the conductor, it follows further, that there can be no free electricity within it, and hence, that during a stationary current, just as in a state of equilibrium, the free electricity is distributed solely over the surface of the conductor.

According as the hypothesis of *two*, or only of one electricity is admitted, the circumstance, that the electricity passing along the interior of a conductor exercises no attraction or repulsion, must receive a different interpretation. By the first hypothesis, we must assume that each element of space within the conductor contains an equal amount of both electricities, which flow with equal strength of current in opposite directions. The second hypothesis involves the supposition, that an element of space, when it contains a certain normal quantity of electricity, exercises no action on another particle of electricity, inasmuch as the electrical repulsion is compensated by some other force; and further, that an actual attraction or repulsion *then* only occurs when the element of space contains too much or too little electricity; by this hypothesis, therefore, we must assume, that during a stationary current each element of space within the conductor contains the normal quantity of electricity.

This is not the place to discuss the probability of either the one or the other hypothesis, for as far as the validity of the following conclusions are concerned, it is a matter of perfect indifference to which of the two we attach ourselves; our choice, therefore, may be governed entirely by convenience. In my former memoir on machine electricity, I adopted, for convenience of illustration, the first hypothesis; for a similar reason I will here employ the second. In order to translate all conclusions hereafter to be given so as to be in accordance with the first hypothesis, we have merely, wherever one current conveying the quantity of electricity Q in one direction occurs, to substitute two currents conveying the quantities of electricity $\frac{1}{2}Q$ and $-\frac{1}{2}Q$ in opposite directions, and then to apply to both currents the same conclusions which here have reference to one current only.

We proceed now to determine the quantity of work produced by the force acting within the conductor during the motion of the electricity.

For this purpose, let us consider any element of electricity

dq during its motion along the path s. The component of the *accelerating* force in the direction of its motion, will for every point of its path be represented by $\dfrac{dV}{ds}$, and hence the component of the *moving* force acting on dq by $dq\,\dfrac{dV}{ds}$. The work produced by the force during the motion along the element ds will therefore be

$$= dq \cdot \frac{dV}{ds} \cdot ds, \quad \cdot \quad \cdot \quad \cdot \quad \cdot \quad \cdot \quad (3)$$

and consequently, the work produced along the way from s_0 to s_1 will be

$$= dq \int_{s_0}^{s_1} \frac{dV}{ds}\, ds = (V_1 - V_0)dq\,; \cdot \quad \cdot \quad \cdot \quad \cdot \quad (4)$$

wherein V_0 and V_1 denote the values of V corresponding to s_0 and s_1.

From this it is at once evident, that this quantity of work is completely defined by the values of the potential function at the extreme points of the path described, without its being necessary to know the path followed between these points. Further, the product $V.\,dq$ is the *potential* * of the free electricity upon the element dq, so that the foregoing expression represents the increase of the potential between s_0 and s_1; and as a like expression applies to every other element of electricity, and can therefore be extended to a finite quantity of electricity, we can deduce the following theorem :—

The quantity of work produced by a force in the conductor during any definite motion of a quantity of electricity, is equal to the corresponding increase of the potential of this quantity of electricity, and of the free electricity upon each other.

In this development we have conceived the motion of the electricity to be such, that one and the same quantity of electricity traverses the whole path under consideration; the actual motion of the electricity, however, may be of a quite different character. For instance, let us assume each particle of mass to

---

* I here make the distinction between the terms *potential* and *potential function*, introduced in my former memoir (Pogg. *Ann.* vol. lxxxvi., pp. 163 and 342. Scien. Mem. 2nd Ser. vol. i. part 1).

be provided with a certain quantity of electricity, and conceive a number of such particles, 1, 2, 3, 4, &c., situated in a row; the motion of electricity may take place in such a manner, that a small quantity will pass over from 1 to 2, an equal but different quantity from 2 to 3 ; again, an equal but still a different quantity from 3 to 4, and so forth.   For the validity of the foregoing theorem, however, it is of no importance which of these two kinds of motion we assume, for the theorem merely requires that all parts of the entire path be traversed by an *equal*, but not by the *same* quantity of electricity.

By this theorem, it is now easy to determine the work produced within any portion of a conductor traversed by a stationary current during the unit of time.

Let a closed surface be given, bounding a part of the space filled by the conductor, then we have merely to determine the increase of the potential for every particle of electricity traversing this enclosed space during the unit of time, or, in other words, to multiply the element of electricity by the values of the potential function corresponding to the points of entrance and exit, and then to take the difference of these two products. The sum of all these differences, which gives the required quantity of work, can be conveniently represented in the following manner. Let dw be an element of the surface of the space enclosed, and idw the quantity of electricity passing through the same in the unit of time, which must be taken as positive or negative, according as it is leaving or entering the space in question; then, if W represent the work produced within the space,

$$W = \int V i dw, \quad \ldots \quad \ldots \quad (I)$$

where the integration is to be extended over the entire surface. If herein we set, according to equation (1),

$$i = k \frac{d V}{d N},$$

whereby the external direction of the normal is to be considered as positive, then equation (I) can be also written thus:

$$W = k \int V \frac{d V}{d N} dw. \quad \ldots \quad \ldots \quad (Ia)$$

Immediately connected with these equations are those which express the quantity of *heat generated* within the enclosed surface.

The work produced within the same must be accompanied by just as great an increase of *vis viva*. In our case, inasmuch as we have agreed to disregard all extraneous actions, such as, for instance, electrolytic action, the work produced is fully expressed by the equation (I) or (I*a*). Strictly speaking, in considering the *vis viva*, we should regard not only the material mass of the conductor, but the electricity also. In other words, the particles of electricity may be accelerated or retarded on their way through the space in question; for although the condition of being stationary implies that the velocity at any particular place must be constant, yet it does not follow that in different places it must be equal. For instance, if the current pass through a conductor with different transverse sections, the electricity may move more quickly through the narrow than through the wider places; just as the water of a river moves with greater velocity through places where the river-bed is contracted than through others. Nevertheless, as it is not yet certain whether electricity possesses inertia or not, and hence whether or not we may ascribe *vis viva* to the moved electricity, and as, even if this were assumed, we have here but to consider the changes in *vis viva*, and not its total value, we may, for the present at any rate, disregard this possibility *. We have therefore to consider the *vis viva* of the material mass alone; and as by hypothesis no perceptible exterior motion is produced, the increase or decrease of the quantity of heat alone remains. This may be briefly expressed thus :—The whole work is employed in overcoming the resistance opposed by the conductor, and this, just as when friction is overcome, necessarily engenders a quantity of heat equivalent to the work consumed.

Let A be the equivalent of heat for the unit of work, and H the heat generated in the enclosed space during the unit of

* I may here remark, that, in assuming the correctness of Ohm's law, the same is tacitly admitted. For if the equation (1), $i = k \dfrac{d\,V}{d\,N}$, be true, the magnitude and direction of the velocity of the electricity at any given point depends only on the acting force at that point; and hence the inertia of the electricity must either be null, or at any rate so small, that the force necessary to produce such changes of velocity as occur in the conductor may be neglected, in presence of the force necessary to overcome the resistance opposed by the conductor.

time, we shall then have

$$H = A.W, \quad \cdots \quad \cdots \quad (5)$$

and hence, according to (I) and (Ia),

$$H = A . \int V . i dw \quad \cdots \quad \cdots \quad (II)$$

$$H = A . k . \int V . \frac{dV}{dN} dw. \quad \cdots \quad (IIa)$$

The integrals contained in equations (I), (Ia), (II), and (IIa) are, in most cases which occur in practice, capable of great simplification.

If a part of the surface enclosing the space under consideration form at the same time the surface of the conductor, and if, in comparison to the whole quantity of electricity passing through the conductor, we neglect the small quantity lost in the surrounding air during the current, then in the integration we may entirely neglect this portion of the surface. When, for example, as is usually the case, the conductor is an elongated body traversed longitudinally by the electric current, and when we consider a portion of it situated between two transverse sections, it will only be necessary to effect the integration for these two transverse sections.

If, further, the form of the conductor at one of the transverse sections be approximately that of a prism or cylinder, so that we may assume that here all particles of electricity move parallel to each other and to the axis, then the force urging them must also have this direction. Let us now place our rectangular system of coordinate axes, so that the x axis may be parallel to the axis of the conductor, then $\frac{dV}{dx}$ represents the whole urging force, and $\frac{dV}{dy}$ and $\frac{dV}{dz}$ vanish. From this position it also follows, that when the transverse section is taken perpendicular to the axis, V must be constant throughout the same, and we may write,

$$\int V \, i dw = V \int i dw.$$

The integral $\int i dw$,—which must be taken negative or positive, according as the transverse section is the first or second in reference to the direction of the current,—represents the whole quantity of electricity passing through the transverse section in the unit of time. It is usually termed the *intensity* of the current, and may here therefore be represented by J, whereby the foregoing expression becomes

$$\mp V.J.$$

Let us now assume that at the other transverse section the same conditions are fulfilled, and let the values of V corresponding to the first and second transverse sections be denoted by V_0 and V_1, then the work accomplished within the entire portion will be

$$W = (V_1 - V_0) . J, \quad \ldots \quad \ldots \quad (6)$$

and the heat produced

$$H = A (V_1 - V_0) . J, \quad \ldots \quad \ldots \quad (7)$$

But, according to Ohm's law,

$$J = \frac{V_1 - V_0}{l}, \quad \ldots \quad \ldots \quad (8)$$

in which l denotes the resistance to conduction of the portion occurring between the two transverse sections, and consequently the two preceding equations pass into

$$W = l. J^2 \quad \ldots \quad \ldots \quad (9)$$

$$H = A.l. J^2 \quad \ldots \quad \ldots \quad (10)$$

The last of these equations contains the two laws discovered by Joule, and subsequently confirmed by Lenz and Becquerel.

17

Reprinted from *Mathematical and Physical Papers of William Thomson*, Vol. 1,
Cambridge University Press, London, 1882, pp. 316–323

On a Mechanical Theory of Thermoelectric Currents

William Thomson (Lord Kelvin)

[From *Proceedings of the Royal Society of Edinburgh*, Dec. 1851.]

It was discovered by Peltier that heat is absorbed at a surface of contact of bismuth and antimony in a compound metallic conductor, when electricity traverses it from the bismuth to the antimony, and that heat is generated when electricity traverses it in the contrary direction. This fact, taken in connection with Joule's law of the electrical generation of heat in a homogeneous

279

metallic conductor, suggests the following assumption, which is the foundation of the theory at present laid before the Royal Society.

When electricity passes in a current of uniform strength γ through a heterogeneous linear conductor, no part of which is permitted to vary in temperature, the heat generated in a given time is expressible by the formula

$$A\gamma + B\gamma^2,$$

where A, which may be either positive or negative, and B, which is essentially positive, denote qualities independent of γ.

The fundamental equations of the theory are the following :—

$$F\gamma = J\left(\gamma \Sigma a_t + B\gamma^2\right) \dots\dots\dots\dots\dots\dots\dots\dots\dots (a),$$

$$\Sigma a_t = \Sigma a_t \left(1 - \epsilon^{-\frac{1}{J}\int_T^t \mu dt}\right) \dots\dots\dots\dots\dots\dots (b),$$

where F denotes the electromotive force (considered as of the same sign with γ, when it acts in the direction of the current) which must act to produce or to permit the current γ to circulate uniformly through the conductor; J the mechanical equivalent of the thermal unit; $a_t\gamma$ the quantity of heat evolved in the unit of time in all parts of the conductor which are at the temperature t when γ is infinitely small; μ "Carnot's function*" of the temperature t; T the temperature of the coldest part of the circuit; and Σ a summation including all parts of the circuit.

The first of these equations is a mere expression of the equivalence, according to the principles established by Joule, of the work, $F\gamma$†, done in a unit of time by the electromotive force, to the heat developed, which, in the circumstances, is the sole effect produced. The second is a consequence of the first and of the following equation :—

$$\phi \,.\, \gamma = \mu \Sigma a_t \gamma \,.\, (t - T) \dots\dots\dots\dots\dots\dots\dots\dots (c),$$

where ϕ denotes the electromotive force when γ is infinitely small, and when the temperatures in all parts of the circuit are infinitely

---

* The values of this function, calculated from Regnault's observations, and the hypothesis that the density of saturated steam follows the "gaseous laws," for every degree of temperature from 0^0 to 230^0 cent., are shown in Table I. of the author's "Account of Carnot's Theory" [Art. xli., above], *Transactions*, vol. xvi., p. 541.

† See *Philosophical Magazine*, Dec. 1851, "On Applications of the Principle of Mechanical Effect," &c. [Art. liv., below].

nearly equal. This latter equation is an expression, for the present circumstances, of the proposition* (first enunciated by Carnot and first established in the dynamical theory by Clausius) that the obtaining of mechanical effect from heat, by means of a perfectly reversible arrangement, depends in a definite manner on the transmission of a certain quantity of heat from one body to another at a lower temperature. There is a degree of uncertainty in the present application of this principle, on account of the conduction of heat that must necessarily go on from the hotter to the colder parts of the circuit; an agency which is not reversed when the direction of the current is changed. As it cannot be shown that the thermal effect of this agency is infinitely small, compared with that of the electric current, unless γ be so large that the term $B\gamma^2$, expressing the thermal effect of another irreversible agency, cannot be neglected, the conditions required for the application of Carnot and Clausius's principle, according to the demonstrations of it which have been already given, are not completely fulfilled : the author therefore considers that at present this part of the theory requires experimental verification.

1.   A first application of the theory is to the case of antimony and bismuth; and it is shown that the fact discovered by Seebeck is, according to equation (c), a consequence of the more recent discovery of Peltier referred to above,—a partial verification of the only doubtful part of the theory being thus afforded.

2.   If $\Theta\gamma$ denote the quantity of heat evolved, [or $-\Theta\gamma$ the quantity absorbed,] at the surface of separation of two metals in a compound circuit, by the passage of a current of electricity of strength γ across it, when the temperature t is kept constant; and if ϕ denote the electromotive force produced in the same circuit by keeping the two junctions at temperatures t and t', which differ from one another by an infinitely small amount, the magnitude of this force is given by the equation

$$\phi = \Theta\mu\,(t' - t) \dots\dots\dots\dots\dots\dots\dots\dots\dots\dots\dots\dots \;(d),$$

and its direction is such, that a current produced by it would cause the absorption of heat at the hotter junction, and the evolution of heat at the colder. A complete experimental verification of this conclusion would fully establish the theory.

* "Dynamical Theory of Heat" [§ 9, above] (*Transactions*, vol. xx., part ii.), Prop. II., &c.

3. If a current of electricity, passing from hot to cold, or from cold to hot, in the same metal produced the same thermal effects ; that is, if no term of Σa_t depended upon variation of temperature from point to point of the same metal; we should have, by equation (a),

$$\phi = J \frac{d\Theta}{dt} (t' - t); \text{ and therefore, by } (d), \frac{d\Theta}{dt} = \frac{1}{J} \Theta \mu.$$

From this we deduce

$$\Theta = \Theta_0 \, \epsilon^{\frac{1}{J} \int_0^t \mu dt}; \text{ and } \phi = (t' - t) \, \mu \Theta_0 \, \epsilon^{\frac{1}{J} \int_0^t \mu dt}.$$

A table of the values of $\dfrac{\phi}{\Theta_0 (t' - t)}$ for every tenth degree from 0 to 230 is given, according to the values of μ*, used in the author's previous papers; showing, that if the hypothesis just mentioned were true, the thermal electromotive force corresponding to a given very small difference of temperatures would, for the same two metals, increase very slowly, as the mean absolute temperature is raised.   Or, if Mayer's hypothesis, which leads to the expression $\dfrac{JE}{1 + Et}$ for μ, were true, the electromotive force of the same pair of metals would be the same, for the same difference of temperatures, whatever be the absolute temperatures.   Whether the values of μ previously found were correct or not, it would follow, from the preceding expression for ϕ, that the electromotive force of a thermo-electric pair is subject to the same law of variation, with the temperatures of the two junctions, whatever be the metals of which it is composed.   This result being at variance with known facts, the hypothesis on which it is founded must be false ; and the author arrives at the remarkable conclusion, that *an electric current produces different thermal effects, according as it passes from hot to cold, or from cold to hot, in the same metal.*

4. If $\Im (t' - t)$ be taken to denote the value of the part of Σa_t which depends on this circumstance, and which corresponds to all parts of the circuit of which the temperatures lie within an

---

* The unit of force adopted in magnetic and electro-magnetic researches, being that force which, acting on a unit of matter, generates a unit of velocity in the unit of time, the values of μ and J used in this paper are obtained by multiplying the values used in the author's former papers, by 32·2.

infinitely small range t to t'; the equations to be substituted for the preceding are

$$\phi = J \frac{d\Theta}{dt} (t' - t) + J\Im (t' - t) \dots\dots\dots\dots\dots(e),$$

and therefore, by (d),

$$\frac{d\Theta}{dt} + \Im = \frac{1}{J} \Theta\mu \dots\dots\dots\dots\dots\dots\dots\dots\dots(f).$$

5. The following expressions for F, the electromotive force in a thermo-electric pair, with the two junctions at temperatures S and T differing by any finite amount, are then established in terms of the preceding notations, with the addition of suffixes to denote the particular values of Θ for the temperatures of the junctions.

$$\left.\begin{array}{l} F = \displaystyle\int_T^S \mu\Theta dt = J \left\{ \Theta_S - \Theta_T + \int_T^S \Im dt \right\} \\[3mm] = J \left\{ \Theta_S (1 - \epsilon^{-\frac{1}{J}\int_T^S \mu dt}) + \int_T^S \Im (1 - \epsilon^{-\frac{1}{J}\int_T^t \mu dt}) \, dt \right\} \end{array}\right\} \dots\dots\dots(g).$$

6. It has been shown by Magnus, that no sensible electromotive force is produced by keeping the different parts of a circuit of one homogeneous metal at different temperatures, however different their sections may be. It is concluded that for this case $\Im = 0$; and therefore that, for a thermo-electric element of two metals, we must have

$$\Im = \Psi_1 (t) - \Psi_2 (t),$$

where Ψ_1 and Ψ_2 denote functions depending solely on the qualities of the two metals, and expressing the thermal effects of a current passing through a conductor of either metal, kept at different uniform temperatures in different parts. Thus, with reference to the metal to which Ψ_1 corresponds, if a current of strength γ pass through a conductor consisting of it, the quantity of heat *absorbed* in any infinitely small part PP' is $\Psi_1 (t) (t' - t) \gamma$, if t and t' be the temperatures at P and P' respectively, and if the current be in the direction from P to P'. An application to the case of copper and iron is made, in which it is shown that, if Ψ_1, and Ψ_2 refer to these metals respectively, if S be a certain temperature defined below (which, according to Regnault's observations, cannot differ much from 240 cent.), and if T be any lower temperature;

we have

$$\int_{T}^{S} \{\Psi_1(t) - \Psi_2(t)\}dt = \Theta_r + \frac{1}{J}\dot{F},$$

since the experiments made by Becquerel lead to the conclusion, that at a certain high temperature iron and copper change their places in the thermo-electric series (a conclusion which the author has experimentally verified), and if this temperature be denoted by S, we must consequently have $\Theta^s = 0$.

The quantities denoted by Θ_r and F in the preceding equation being both positive, it is concluded that, *when a thermo-electric current passes through a piece of iron from one end kept at about 240° cent., to the other end kept cold, in a circuit of which the remainder is copper, including a long resistance wire of uniform temperature throughout or an electro-magnetic engine raising weights, there is heat evolved at the cold junction of the copper and iron, and (no heat being either absorbed or evolved at the hot junction) there must be a quantity of heat absorbed on the whole in the rest of the circuit. When there is no engine raising weights, in the circuit, the sum of the quantities evolved, at the cold junction, and generated in the " resistance wire," is equal to the quantity absorbed on the whole in the other parts of the circuit. When there is an engine in the circuit, the sum of the heat evolved at the cold junction and the thermal equivalent of the weights raised, is equal to the quantity of heat absorbed on the whole in all the circuit except the cold junction.*

7.   An application of the theory to the case of a circuit consisting of several different metals, shows that if

$$\phi(A, B), \quad \phi(B, C), \quad \phi(C, D),\ldots\ldots\ldots\ldots\ldots\ldots\phi(Z, A)$$

denote the electromotive forces in single elements, consisting respectively of different metals taken in order, with the same absolute temperatures of the junctions in each element, we have

$$\phi(A, B) + \phi(B, C) + \phi(C, D)\ldots\ldots\ldots\ldots\ldots\ldots+ \phi(Z, A) = 0,$$

which expresses a proposition, the truth of which was first pointed out and experimentally verified by Becquerel. A curious experimental verification of this proposition (so far as regards the signs of the terms of the preceding equation) was made by the author, with reference to certain specimens of platinum wire, and iron and copper wires. He had observed that the platinum wire, with iron wires bent round its ends, constituted a less powerful thermo-electric element than an iron wire with copper wires bent round its ends, for temperatures within atmospheric limits. He tried, in consequence, the platinum wire with copper wires bent round its ends, and connected with the ends of a galvanometer coil; and he found that, with temperatures within atmospheric limits, a current passed from the copper to the platinum through the hot junction, and concluded that, in the thermo-electric series

$$+ \qquad\qquad\qquad\qquad\qquad\qquad -$$
$$\text{Antimony, Iron, } \left\{ \begin{array}{l} \text{Copper,} \\ \text{Platinum,} \end{array} \right\} \text{ Bismuth,}$$

this platinum wire must, at ordinary temperatures, be between iron and copper. He found that the platinum wire retained the same properties after having been heated to redness in a spirit-lamp and cooled again; but with temperatures above some limit itself considerably below that of boiling water, he found that the iron and platinum constituted a more powerful thermo-electric element than the iron and copper; and he verified that for such temperatures, in the platinum and copper element the current was from the platinum to the copper through the hot junction, and therefore that the copper now lay between the iron and the platinum of the series, or in the position in which other observers have generally found copper to lie with reference to platinum. A second somewhat thinner platinum wire was found to lie invariably on the negative side of copper, for all temperatures above the freezing point; but a third, still thinner, possessed the same property as the first, although in a less marked degree, as the superior limit of the range of temperatures for which it was positive towards copper was lower than in the case of the first wire. By making an element of the first and third platinum wire, it was found that the former was positive towards the latter, as was to be expected.

In conclusion, various objects of experimental research regarding thermo-electric forces and currents are pointed out, and methods of experimenting are suggested. It is pointed out that, failing direct data, the absolute value of the electromotive force in an element of copper and bismuth, with its two junctions kept at the temperatures 0° and 100° cent., may be estimated indirectly from Pouillet's comparison of the strength of the current it sends through a copper wire 20 metres long and 1 millimetre in diameter, with the strength of a current decomposing water at an observed rate ; by means of determinations by Weber, and of others, of the specific resistance of copper and the electro-chemical equivalent of water, in absolute units. The specific resistances of different specimens of copper having been found to differ considerably from one another, it is impossible, without experiments on the individual wire used by M. Pouillet, to determine with much accuracy the absolute resistance of his circuit, but the author has estimated it on the hypothesis that the specific resistance of its substance is $2\frac{1}{4}$ British units. Taking ·02 as the electro-chemical equivalent of water in British absolute units, the author has thus found 16300 as the electromotive force of an element of copper and bismuth, with the two junctions at $0°$ and $100°$ respectively. About 154 of such elements would be required to produce the same electromotive force as a single cell of Daniell's ; if, in Daniell's battery, the whole chemical action were electrically efficient. A battery of 1000 copper and bismuth elements, with the two sets of junctions at $0°$ and $100°$ cent., employed to work a galvanic engine, if the resistance in the whole circuit be equivalent to that of a copper wire of about 100 feet long and about one-eighth of an inch in diameter, and if the engine be allowed to move at such a rate as by inductive reaction to diminish the strength of the current to the half of what it is when the engine is at rest, would produce mechanical effect at the rate of about one fifth of a horse-power. The electromotive force of a copper and bismuth element, with its two junctions at $0°$ and $1°$, being found by Pouillet to be about $\frac{1}{100}$ of the electromotive force when the junctions are at $0°$ and $100°$, must be about 163. The value of Θ_0 for copper and bismuth, according to these results (and to the value 160·16 of μ at $0°$), or the quantity of heat absorbed in a second of time by a current of unit strength in passing from bismuth to copper, when the temperature is kept at $0°$, is $\frac{163}{160·16}$, or very nearly equal to the quantity required to raise the temperature of a grain of water from $0°$ to $1°$ cent.

Part V

ENERGY IN THE FIELD

Editor's Comments
on Papers 18 Through 20

In the evolution of the concept of energy in classical mechanics the energy is always assumed to be associated with a particle or aggregation of particles (see Lindsay, *Energy: Concept*). The very form of the *vis viva* (Mv^2) or kinetic energy ($\frac{1}{2}mv^2$) emphasizes this, as does indeed the potential energy also, as is illustrated in the case of a particle of mass m subject to the earth's gravitational field, where the potential energy with respect to the earth's surface is mgx at height x above the surface (g is the acceleration of gravity).

The association of energy with heat, as required by the mechanical theory of heat, might seem to provide a problem as to the "location" of the energy in the heat. In the early stages of the development of the theory, however, the problem was avoided by treating heat purely calorimetrically. This was, of course, the point of view adopted by Joule in his measurement of the mechanical equivalent of heat and also that of Mayer in his theoretical derivation of the quantity. It is true that earlier scientists like Boyle and Rumford had insisted that heat is really some form of motion in the heated body. This concept was later refined and made scientifically useful in the molecular theory of matter.

In the application of the mechanical theory of heat to other physical phenomena like electricity and magnetism, the tendency, as is clear from Papers 12 through 17, was still to associate energy with matter, e.g., with solid and liquid conductors and nonconductors in the case of electricity and with magnets and magnetizable material in the case of magnetism. This situation eventually changed, however, in the light of the new idea introduced into electricity and magnetism by Michael Faraday in the 1830s, that of the *field*.

Rather than look upon the interaction of magnets and electric charges and currents as simple action at a distance, as the Continental physicists chose to do, Faraday considered the region surrounding an electric charge or magnetic pole as a domain at every point of which influence will be exerted on other charges or poles that happen to be there. This domain was called a field of force. The field concept was adopted and elaborated by Clerk Maxwell in his detailed investigations in electricity and magnetism. His first public announcement of his theory came in a paper in the *Philosophical Transactions of the Royal Society* [**155**, 459 (1865)] with the title "A Dynamical Theory of the Electromagnetic Field." In the development of the theory, Maxwell realized that it was essential to introduce the concept of energy, and he decided to locate the energy in the field itself. The introduction to this paper is well worth reading, since in it Maxwell set forth in physical terms his reasons for adopting the field idea. The details were presented later in fully organized form in Maxwell's famous book *A Treatise on Electricity and Magnetism* (Clarendon Press, Oxford, 1873), in which Chapter Eleven was specifically devoted to the discussion of energy and stress in the electromagnetic field. Here Maxwell showed how the concept of electric displacement, perhaps his greatest contribution to the science of electricity and magnetism, could be used in the definition of electromagnetic field energy. We reprint here as Paper 18 the first seven pages of this chapter as an indication of Maxwell's method. Our extract is taken from the third edition of his treatise (1896).

It became essential to understand how the field energy is transmitted from one place to another. This problem was solved by J. H. Poynting in the derivation of a famous theorem, which has since borne his name and which first appeared in a paper in the *Philosophical Transactions of the Royal Society* [**195**, Pt. 1, 343–361 (1885)], portions of which we reprint as Paper 19. In this paper Poynting first gives a general physical discussion of the way in which electromagnetic energy is transmitted through a field. His theorem is then stated and demonstrated in the fashion made familiar in all modern books on the subject. He introduces the well-known Poynting vector for the rate of energy flow across a surface. However, he does not employ modern conventional vector notation. Poynting's paper is of particular interest because he applies his theorem to special examples. The one we reprint relates to the propagation of light in the electromagnetic theory of light invented by Maxwell.

The concept of field energy takes a somewhat less esoteric form in the case of acoustic wave propagation, i.e., the transmission of a mechanical disturbance through an elastic medium. It is uncertain who was the first to apply the energy idea to elastic wave propagation, although it was probably William Thomson (Lord Kelvin) [*Philosophical Magazine,* **9**(4), 36 (1855)]. The first formal mathematical development in modern terms, however, was probably due to Lord Rayleigh, who in his famous *Theory of Sound* (Macmillan, London, 1877–1878) provided expressions for the kinetic and potential energies for any region traversed by an elastic wave. We here reprint as Paper 20 paragraph 245 of his treatise, which is indeed restricted to plane harmonic waves, but is adequately illustrative of the fundamental idea involved. The reader should note that the function ϕ in Rayleigh's analysis is the velocity potential, whose negative gradient is the medium disturbance velocity. The quantity s is the condensation, defined as the fractional change in medium density associated with the disturbance. Finally, the quantity a is the wave velocity.

The great importance of the introduction of the energy concept in wave propagation came in its use in the definition of the intensity of a wave as the average flow of energy per unit time across unit area of the wave front. The intensity is one of the most significant quantities connected with wave propagation, since its attenuation with time or distance can be precisely measured and provides useful information about the interaction of the wave and the medium through which it passes.

18

Reprinted from James Clerk Maxwell, *A Treatise on Electricity and Magnetism*, Vol. 2, unabridged 3rd ed., Dover Publications, Inc., New York, 1954, pp. 270–276

On Energy and Stress in the Electromagnetic Field

James Clerk Maxwell

Electrostatic Energy.

630.] THE energy of the system may be divided into the Potential Energy and the Kinetic Energy.

The potential energy due to electrification has been already considered in Art. 85. It may be written

$$W = \tfrac{1}{2} \Sigma (e\Psi), \tag{1}$$

where e is the charge of electricity at a place where the electric potential is Ψ, and the summation is to be extended to every place where there is electrification.

If f, g, h are the components of the electric displacement, the quantity of electricity in the element of volume $dx\,dy\,dz$ is

$$e = \left(\frac{df}{dx} + \frac{dg}{dy} + \frac{dh}{dz}\right) dx\,dy\,dz, \tag{2}$$

and

$$W = \tfrac{1}{2} \iiint \left(\frac{df}{dx} + \frac{dg}{dy} + \frac{dh}{dz}\right) \Psi\,dx\,dy\,dz, \tag{3}$$

where the integration is to be extended throughout all space.

631.] Integrating this expression by parts, and remembering that when the distance, r, from a given point of a finite electrified system becomes infinite, the potential Ψ becomes an infinitely small quantity of the order r^{-1}, and that f, g, h become infinitely small quantities of the order r^{-2}, the expression is reduced to

$$W = -\tfrac{1}{2} \iiint \left(f\frac{d\Psi}{dx} + g\frac{d\Psi}{dy} + h\frac{d\Psi}{dz}\right) dx\,dy\,dz, \tag{4}$$

where the integration is to be extended throughout all space.

If we now write P, Q, R for the components of the electro-motive intensity, instead of $-\dfrac{d\Psi}{dx}$, $-\dfrac{d\Psi}{dy}$ and $-\dfrac{d\Psi}{dz}$, we find

$$W = \tfrac{1}{2} \iiint (Pf + Qg + Rh)\, dx\, dy\, dz.* \qquad (5)$$

Hence, the electrostatic energy of the whole field will be the same if we suppose that it resides in every part of the field where electrical force and electrical displacement occur, instead of being confined to the places where free electricity is found.

The energy in unit of volume is half the product of the electro-motive force and the electric displacement, multiplied by the cosine of the angle which these vectors include.

In Quaternion language it is $-\tfrac{1}{2} S.\mathfrak{E}\mathfrak{D}$.

Magnetic Energy.

†632.] We may treat the energy due to magnetization in a way similar to that pursued in the case of electrification, Art. 85. If A, B, C are the components of magnetization and a, β, γ the components of magnetic force, the potential energy of the system of magnets is then, by Art. 389,

$$-\tfrac{1}{2} \iiint (A a + B \beta + C \gamma)\, dx\, dy\, dz, \qquad (6)$$

the integration being extended over the space occupied by mag-netized matter. This part of the energy, however, will be included in the kinetic energy in the form in which we shall presently obtain it.

633.] We may transform this expression when there are no electric currents by the following method.

We know that
$$\frac{da}{dx} + \frac{db}{dy} + \frac{dc}{dz} = 0. \qquad (7)$$

---

* { This expression for the electrostatic energy was deduced in the first volume on the assumption that the electrostatic force could be derived from a potential function. This proof will not hold when part of the electromotive intensity is due to electromagnetic induction. If however we take the view that this part of the energy arises from the polarized state of the dielectric and is per unit volume $\dfrac{1}{8\pi K}(f^2 + g^2 + h^2)$, the potential energy will then only depend on the polarization of the dielectric no matter how it is produced. Thus the energy will, since

$$\frac{f}{4\pi K} = P, \quad \frac{g}{4\pi K} = Q, \quad \frac{h}{4\pi K} = R,$$

be equal to $\tfrac{1}{2}(Pf + Qg + Rh)$ per unit volume.}
† See Appendix I at the end of this Chapter.

Hence, by Art. 97, if

$$a = -\frac{d\Omega}{dx}, \quad \beta = -\frac{d\Omega}{dy}, \quad \gamma = -\frac{d\Omega}{dz}, \tag{8}$$

as is always the case in magnetic phenomena where there are no currents,

$$\iiint (a\,a + b\,\beta + c\gamma)\,dx\,dy\,dz = 0, \tag{9}$$

the integral being extended throughout all space, or

$$\iiint \{(a + 4\pi A)\,a + (\beta + 4\pi B)\,\beta + (\gamma + 4\pi C)\gamma\}\,dx\,dy\,dz = 0. \tag{10}$$

Hence, the energy due to a magnetic system

$$-\tfrac{1}{2}\iiint (A\,a + B\beta + C\gamma)\,dx\,dy\,dz = \frac{1}{8\pi}\iiint (a^2 + \beta^2 + \gamma^2)\,dx\,dy\,dz,$$

$$= \frac{1}{8\pi}\iiint \mathfrak{H}^2\,dx\,dy\,dz. \tag{11}$$

Electrokinetic Energy.

634.] We have already, in Art. 578, expressed the kinetic energy of a system of currents in the form

$$T = \tfrac{1}{2}\Sigma\,(pi), \tag{12}$$

where p is the electromagnetic momentum of a circuit, and i is the strength of the current flowing round it, and the summation extends to all the circuits.

But we have proved, in Art. 590, that p may be expressed as a line-integral of the form

$$p = \int \left(F\frac{dx}{ds} + G\frac{dy}{ds} + H\frac{dz}{ds}\right)ds, \tag{13}$$

where F, G, H are the components of the electromagnetic momentum, $\mathfrak{A}$, at the point (x, y, z), and the integration is to be extended round the closed circuit s. We therefore find

$$T = \tfrac{1}{2}\Sigma i \int \left(F\frac{dx}{ds} + G\frac{dy}{ds} + H\frac{dz}{ds}\right)ds. \tag{14}$$

If u, v, w are the components of the density of the current at any point of the conducting circuit, and if S is the transverse section of the circuit, then we may write

$$i\frac{dx}{ds} = uS, \quad i\frac{dy}{ds} = vS, \quad i\frac{dz}{ds} = wS, \tag{15}$$

and we may also write the volume

$$S\,ds = dx\,dy\,dz,$$

and we now find

$$T = \tfrac{1}{2} \iiint (Fu + Gv + Hw)\,dx\,dy\,dz, \qquad (16)$$

where the integration is to be extended to every part of space where there are electric currents.

635.] Let us now substitute for u, v, w their values as given by the equations of electric currents (E), Art. 607, in terms of the components a, β, γ of the magnetic force. We then have

$$T = \frac{1}{8\pi} \iiint \left\{ F\left(\frac{d\gamma}{dy} - \frac{d\beta}{dz}\right) + G\left(\frac{da}{dz} - \frac{d\gamma}{dx}\right) + H\left(\frac{d\beta}{dx} - \frac{da}{dy}\right) \right\} dx\,dy\,dz, \quad (17)$$

where the integration is extended over a portion of space including all the currents.

If we integrate this by parts, and remember that, at a great distance r from the system, a, β, and γ are of the order of magnitude r^{-3}, {and that at a surface separating two media, F, G, H, and the tangential magnetic force are continuous,} we find that when the integration is extended throughout all space, the expression is reduced to

$$T = \frac{1}{8\pi} \iiint \left\{ a\left(\frac{dH}{dy} - \frac{dG}{dz}\right) + \beta\left(\frac{dF}{dz} - \frac{dH}{dx}\right) + \gamma\left(\frac{dG}{dx} - \frac{dF}{dy}\right) \right\} dx\,dy\,dz. \quad (18)$$

By the equations (A), Art. 591, of magnetic induction, we may substitute for the quantities in small brackets the components of magnetic induction a, b, c, so that the kinetic energy may be written

$$T = \frac{1}{8\pi} \iiint (a\,a + b\,\beta + c\,\gamma)\,dx\,dy\,dz, \qquad (19)$$

where the integration is to be extended throughout every part of space in which the magnetic force and magnetic induction have values differing from zero.

The quantity within brackets in this expression is the product of the magnetic induction into the resolved part of the magnetic force in its own direction.

In the language of quaternions this may be written more simply,

$$-S.\mathfrak{B}\mathfrak{H},$$

where $\mathfrak{B}$ is the magnetic induction, whose components are a, b, c, and $\mathfrak{H}$ is the magnetic force, whose components are a, β, γ.

636.] The electrokinetic energy of the system may therefore be expressed either as an integral to be taken where there are electric currents, or as an integral to be taken over every part of the field in which magnetic force exists. The first integral, however, is the natural expression of the theory which supposes the currents to act upon each other directly at a distance, while the second is appropriate to the theory which endeavours to explain the action between the currents by means of some intermediate action in the space between them. As in this treatise we have adopted the latter method of investigation, we naturally adopt the second expression as giving the most significant form to the kinetic energy.

According to our hypothesis, we assume the kinetic energy to exist wherever there is magnetic force, that is, in general, in every part of the field. The amount of this energy per unit of volume is $-\dfrac{1}{8\pi} S . \mathfrak{B} \mathfrak{H}$, and this energy exists in the form of some kind of motion of the matter in every portion of space.

When we come to consider Faraday's discovery of the effect of magnetism on polarized light, we shall point out reasons for believing that wherever there are lines of magnetic force, there is a rotatory motion of matter round those lines. See Art. 821.

Magnetic and Electrokinetic Energy compared.

637.] We found in Art. 423 that the mutual potential energy of two magnetic shells, of strengths ϕ and ϕ', and bounded by the closed curves s and s' respectively, is

$$-\phi\phi' \iint \frac{\cos \epsilon}{r} ds\, ds',$$

where ϵ is the angle between the directions of ds and ds', and r is the distance between them.

We also found in Art. 521 that the mutual energy of two circuits s and s', in which currents i and i' flow, is

$$i\, i' \iint \frac{\cos \epsilon}{r} ds\, ds'.$$

If i, i' are equal to ϕ, ϕ' respectively, the mechanical action between the magnetic shells is equal to that between the corresponding electric circuits, and in the same direction. In the case of the magnetic shells the force tends to diminish their mutual potential energy, in the case of the circuits it tends to increase their mutual energy, because this energy is kinetic.

It is impossible, by any arrangement of magnetized matter, to produce a system corresponding in all respects to an electric circuit, for the potential of the magnetic system is single valued at every point of space, whereas that of the electric system is many-valued.

But it is always possible, by a proper arrangement of infinitely small electric circuits, to produce a system corresponding in all respects to any magnetic system, provided the line of integration which we follow in calculating the potential is prevented from passing through any of these small circuits. This will be more fully explained in Art. 833.

The action of magnets at a distance is perfectly identical with that of electric currents. We therefore endeavour to trace both to the same cause, and since we cannot explain electric currents by means of magnets, we must adopt the other alternative, and explain magnets by means of molecular electric currents.

638.] In our investigation of magnetic phenomena, in Part III of this treatise, we made no attempt to account for magnetic action at a distance, but treated this action as a fundamental fact of experience. We therefore assumed that the energy of a magnetic system is potential energy, and that this energy is *diminished* when the parts of the system yield to the magnetic forces which act on them.

If, however, we regard magnets as deriving their properties from electric currents circulating within their molecules, their energy is kinetic, and the force between them is such that it tends to move them in a direction such that if the strengths of the currents were maintained constant the kinetic energy would *increase*.

This mode of explaining magnetism requires us also to abandon the method followed in Part III, in which we regarded the magnet as a continuous and homogeneous body, the minutest part of which has magnetic properties of the same kind as the whole.

We must now regard a magnet as containing a finite, though very great, number of electric circuits, so that it has essentially a molecular, as distinguished from a continuous structure.

If we suppose our mathematical machinery to be so coarse that our line of integration cannot thread a molecular circuit, and that an immense number of magnetic molecules are contained in our element of volume, we shall still arrive at results similar to those of Part III, but if we suppose our machinery of a finer order, and capable of investigating all that goes on in the interior of the molecules, we must give up the old theory of magnetism, and adopt that of Ampère, which admits of no magnets except those which consist of electric currents.

We must also regard both magnetic and electromagnetic energy as kinetic energy, and we must attribute to it the proper sign, as given in Art. 635.

In what follows, though we may occasionally, as in Art. 639, &c., attempt to carry out the old theory of magnetism, we shall find that we obtain a perfectly consistent system only when we abandon that theory and adopt Ampère's theory of molecular currents, as in Art. 644.

The energy of the field therefore consists of two parts only, the electrostatic or potential energy

$$W = \tfrac{1}{2} \iiint (Pf + Qg + Rh)\, dx\, dy\, dz,$$

and the electromagnetic or kinetic energy

$$T = \frac{1}{8\pi} \iiint (a\,a + b\,\beta + c\,\gamma)\, dx\, dy\, dz.$$

[*Ed. note:* material omitted]

19

Reprinted from *Phil. Trans. Roy. Soc. London*, **175**, pt. 2, 343–349, 358–360 (1885)

On the Transfer of Energy in the Electromagnetic Field

By J. H. POYNTING, *M.A., late Fellow of Trinity College, Cambridge, Professor of Physics, Mason College, Birmingham.*

Communicated by Lord RAYLEIGH, *M.A., D.C.L., F.R.S.*

Received December 17, 1883,—Read January 10, 1884.

A SPACE containing electric currents may be regarded as a field where energy is transformed at certain points into the electric and magnetic kinds by means of batteries, dynamos, thermoelectric actions, and so on, while in other parts of the field this energy is again transformed into heat, work done by electromagnetic forces, or any form of energy yielded by currents. Formerly a current was regarded as something travelling along a conductor, attention being chiefly directed to the conductor, and the energy which appeared at any part of the circuit, if considered at all, was supposed to be conveyed thither through the conductor by the current. But the existence of induced currents and of electromagnetic actions at a distance from a primary circuit from which they draw their energy, has led us, under the guidance of FARADAY and MAXWELL, to look upon the medium surrounding the conductor as playing a very important part in the development of the phenomena. If we believe in the continuity of the motion of energy, that is, if we believe that when it disappears at one point and reappears at another it must have passed through the intervening space, we are forced to conclude that the surrounding medium contains at least a part of the energy, and that it is capable of transferring it from point to point.

Upon this basis MAXWELL has investigated what energy is contained in the medium, and he has given expressions which assign to each part of the field a quantity of energy depending on the electromotive and magnetic intensities and on the nature of the matter at that part in regard to its specific inductive capacity and magnetic permeability. These expressions account, as far as we know, for the whole energy. According to MAXWELL's theory, currents consist essentially in a certain distribution of energy in and around a conductor, accompanied by transformation and consequent movement of energy through the field.

Starting with MAXWELL's theory, we are naturally led to consider the problem, How does the energy about an electric current pass from point to point—that is, by what paths and according to what law does it travel from the part of the circuit where

298

it is first recognisable as electric and magnetic to the parts where it is changed into heat or other forms?

The aim of this paper is to prove that there is a general law for the transfer of energy, according to which it moves at any point perpendicularly to the plane containing the lines of electric force and magnetic force, and that the amount crossing unit of area per second of this plane is equal to the product of the intensities of the two forces multiplied by the sine of the angle between them divided by 4π, while the direction of flow of energy is that in which a right-handed screw would move if turned round from the positive direction of the electromotive to the positive direction of the magnetic intensity. After the investigation of the general law several applications will be given to show how the energy moves in the neighbourhood of various current-bearing circuits.

The following is a general account of the method by which the law is obtained.

If we denote the electromotive intensity at a point (that is the force per unit of positive electrification which would act upon a small charged body placed at the point) by $\mathfrak{E}$, and the specific inductive capacity of the medium at that point by K, the magnetic intensity (that is, the force per unit pole which would act on a small north-seeking pole placed at the point) by $\mathfrak{H}$ and the magnetic permeability by μ, MAXWELL's expression for the electric and magnetic energies per unit volume of the field is

$$K\mathfrak{E}^2/8\pi + \mu.\mathfrak{H}^2/8\pi \quad . \quad . \quad . \quad . \quad . \quad . \quad . \quad (1)$$

If any change is going on in the supply or distribution of energy the change in this quantity per second will be

$$K\mathfrak{E}\frac{d\mathfrak{E}}{dt}/4\pi + \mu.\mathfrak{H}\frac{d\mathfrak{H}}{dt}/4\pi \quad . \quad . \quad . \quad . \quad . \quad . \quad (2)$$

According to MAXWELL the true electric current is in general made up of two parts, one the conduction current $\mathfrak{K}$, and the other due to change of electric displacement in the dielectric, this latter being called the displacement current. Now, the displacement is proportional to the electromotive intensity, and is represented by $K\mathfrak{E}/4\pi$, so that when change of displacement takes place, due to change in the electromotive intensity, the rate of change, that is, the displacement current, is $K\frac{d\mathfrak{E}}{dt}/4\pi$, and this is equal to the difference between the true current $\mathfrak{C}$ and the conduction current $\mathfrak{K}$. Multiplying this difference by the electromotive intensity $\mathfrak{E}$ the first term in (2) becomes

$$\frac{K\mathfrak{E}}{4\pi}\frac{d\mathfrak{E}}{dt} = \mathfrak{C}\mathfrak{E} - \mathfrak{K}\mathfrak{E} \quad . \quad . \quad . \quad . \quad . \quad . \quad (3)$$

The first term of the right side of (3) may be transformed by substituting for the components of the total current their values in terms of the components of the magnetic intensity, while the second term, the product of the conduction current and the electromotive intensity, by OHM's law, which states that $\mathfrak{K}=C\mathfrak{E}$, becomes $\mathfrak{K}^2/C$, where C is the specific conductivity. But this is the energy appearing as heat in the circuit per unit volume according to JOULE's law. If we sum up the quantity in (3) thus transformed, *for the whole space within a closed surface* the integral of the first term can be integrated by parts, and we find that it consists of two terms— one an expression depending on the surface alone to which each part of the surface contributes a share depending on the values of the electromotive and magnetic inten- sities at that part, the other term being the change per second in the magnetic energy (that is, the second term of (2)) with a negative sign. The integral of the second term of (3) is the total amount of heat developed in the conductors within the surface per second. We have then the following result.

The change per second in the electric energy within a surface is equal to a quantity depending on the surface—the change per second in the magnetic energy—the heat developed in the circuit.

Or rearranging.

The change per second in the sum of the electric and magnetic energies within a surface together with the heat developed by currents is equal to a quantity to which each element of the surface contributes a share depending on the values of the electric and magnetic intensities at the element. That is, the total change in the energy is accounted for by supposing that the energy passes in through the surface according to the law given by this expression.

On interpreting the expression it is found that it implies that the energy flows as stated before, that is, perpendicularly to the plane containing the lines of electric and magnetic force, that the amount crossing unit area per second of this plane is equal to the product

$$\frac{\text{electromotive intensity} \times \text{magnetic intensity} \times \text{sine included angle}}{4\pi}$$

while the direction of flow is given by the three quantities, electromotive intensity, magnetic intensity, flow of energy, being in right handed order.

It follows at once that the energy flows perpendicularly to the lines of electric force, and so along the equipotential surfaces where these exist. It also flows perpendicu- larly to the lines of magnetic force, and so along the magnetic potential surfaces where these exist. If both sets of surfaces exist their lines of intersection are the lines of flow of energy.

The following is the full mathematical proof of the law :—

The energy of the field may be expressed in the form (MAXWELL's 'Electricity,' vol. ii., 2nd ed., p. 253)

$$\tfrac{1}{2}\iiint(Pf+Qg+Rh)dxdydz+\frac{1}{8\pi}\iiint(a\alpha+b\beta+c\gamma)dxdydz$$

the first term the electrostatic, the second the electromagnetic energy.

But since $f = \dfrac{K}{4\pi} P$, with corresponding values for g and h, and $a = \mu\alpha$, $b = \mu\beta$, $c = \mu\gamma$, substituting, the energy becomes

$$\frac{K}{8\pi}\iiint(P^2+Q^2+R^2)dxdydz + \frac{\mu}{8\pi}\iiint(\alpha^2+\beta^2+\gamma^2)dxdydz \quad . \quad . \quad . \quad (1)$$

Let us consider the space within any fixed closed surface. The energy within this surface will be found by taking the triple integrals throughout the space.

If any changes are taking place the rate of increase of energy of the electric and magnetic kinds per second is

$$\frac{K}{4\pi}\iiint\left(P\frac{dP}{dt}+Q\frac{dQ}{dt}+R\frac{dR}{dt}\right)dxdydz + \frac{\mu}{4\pi}\iiint\left(\alpha\frac{d\alpha}{dt}+\beta\frac{d\beta}{dt}+\gamma\frac{d\gamma}{dt}\right)dxdydz. \quad . \quad (2)$$

Now MAXWELL'S equations for the components of the true current are

$$u = p + \frac{df}{dt} \qquad v = q + \frac{dg}{dt} \qquad w = r + \frac{dh}{dt}$$

where p, q, r are components of the conduction current.

But we may substitute for $\dfrac{df}{dt}$ its value $\dfrac{K}{4\pi}\dfrac{dP}{dt}$, and so for the other two, and we obtain

$$\left.\begin{array}{l} \dfrac{K}{4\pi}\dfrac{dP}{dt} = u - p \\[2mm] \dfrac{K}{4\pi}\dfrac{dQ}{dt} = v - q \\[2mm] \dfrac{K}{4\pi}\dfrac{dR}{dt} = w - r \end{array}\right\} \quad . \quad . \quad . \quad . \quad . \quad . \quad . \quad . \quad (3)$$

Taking the first term in (2) and substituting from (3) we obtain

$$\frac{K}{4\pi}\iiint\left(P\frac{dP}{dt}+Q\frac{dQ}{dt}+R\frac{dR}{dt}\right)dxdydz = \iiint\{P(u-p)+Q(v-q)+R(w-r)\}dxdydz$$

$$= \iiint(Pu+Qv+Rw)dxdydz - \iiint(Pp+Qq+Rr)dxdydz \quad . \quad . \quad . \quad (4)$$

Now the equations for the components of electromotive force are (MAXWELL, vol. ii., p. 222)

$$
\left.
\begin{aligned}
\mathrm{P} &= c\dot{y} - b\dot{z} - \frac{d\mathrm{F}}{dt} - \frac{d\psi}{dx} = c\dot{y} - b\dot{z} + \mathrm{P}' \\
\mathrm{Q} &= a\dot{z} - c\dot{x} - \frac{d\mathrm{G}}{dt} - \frac{d\psi}{dy} = a\dot{z} - c\dot{x} + \mathrm{Q}' \\
\mathrm{R} &= b\dot{x} - a\dot{y} - \frac{d\mathrm{H}}{dt} - \frac{d\psi}{dz} = b\dot{x} - a\dot{y} + \mathrm{R}'
\end{aligned}
\right\} \quad \ldots \ldots \quad (5)
$$

where P', Q', R' are put for the parts of P, Q, R which do not contain the velocities.
Then

$$
\begin{aligned}
\mathrm{P}u + \mathrm{Q}v + \mathrm{R}w &= (c\dot{y} - b\dot{z})u + (a\dot{z} - c\dot{x})v + (b\dot{x} - a\dot{y})w + \mathrm{P}'u + \mathrm{Q}'v + \mathrm{R}'w \\
&= -\{(vc - wb)\dot{x} + (wa - uc)\dot{y} + (ub - va)\dot{z}\} + \mathrm{P}'u + \mathrm{Q}'v + \mathrm{R}'w \\
&= -(\mathrm{X}\dot{x} + \mathrm{Y}\dot{y} + \mathrm{Z}\dot{z}) + \mathrm{P}'u + \mathrm{Q}'v + \mathrm{R}'w
\end{aligned}
$$

where X, Y, Z are the components of the electromagnetic force per unit of volume (MAXWELL, vol. ii., p. 227).

Now substituting in (4) and putting for u, v, w their values in terms of the magnetic force (MAXWELL, vol. ii., p. 233) and transposing we obtain

$$
\frac{\mathrm{K}}{4\pi} \iiint \left(\mathrm{P} \frac{d\mathrm{P}}{dt} + \mathrm{Q} \frac{d\mathrm{Q}}{dt} + \mathrm{R} \frac{d\mathrm{R}}{dt} \right) dx\,dy\,dz + \iiint \{(\mathrm{X}\dot{x} + \mathrm{Y}\dot{y} + \mathrm{Z}\dot{z}) + (\mathrm{P}p + \mathrm{Q}q + \mathrm{R}r)\} dx\,dy\,dz
$$

$$
= \iiint (\mathrm{P}'u + \mathrm{Q}'v + \mathrm{R}'w) dx\,dy\,dz
$$

$$
= \frac{1}{4\pi} \iiint \left\{ \mathrm{P}'\left(\frac{d\gamma}{dy} - \frac{d\beta}{dz} \right) + \mathrm{Q}'\left(\frac{d\alpha}{dz} - \frac{d\gamma}{dx} \right) + \mathrm{R}'\left(\frac{d\beta}{dx} - \frac{d\alpha}{dy} \right) \right\} dx\,dy\,dz
$$

$$
= \frac{1}{4\pi} \iiint \left(\mathrm{R}' \frac{d\beta}{dx} - \mathrm{Q}' \frac{d\gamma}{dx} \right) dx\,dy\,dz
$$

$$
+ \frac{1}{4\pi} \iiint \left(\mathrm{P}' \frac{d\gamma}{dy} - \mathrm{R}' \frac{d\alpha}{dy} \right) dx\,dy\,dz
$$

$$
+ \frac{1}{4\pi} \iiint \left(\mathrm{Q}' \frac{d\alpha}{dz} - \mathrm{P}' \frac{d\beta}{dz} \right) dx\,dy\,dz
$$

Integrating each term by parts]

$$
= \frac{1}{4\pi} \iint (\mathrm{R}'\beta - \mathrm{Q}'\gamma) dy\,dz + \frac{1}{4\pi} \iint (\mathrm{P}'\gamma - \mathrm{R}'\alpha) dz\,dx + \frac{1}{4\pi} \iint (\mathrm{Q}'\alpha - \mathrm{P}'\beta) dx\,dy
$$

$$
- \frac{1}{4\pi} \iiint \left\{ \beta \frac{d\mathrm{R}'}{dx} - \gamma \frac{d\mathrm{Q}'}{dx} + \gamma \frac{d\mathrm{P}'}{dy} - \alpha \frac{d\mathrm{R}'}{dy} + \alpha \frac{d\mathrm{Q}'}{dz} - \beta \frac{d\mathrm{P}'}{dz} \right\} dx\,dy\,dz
$$

[The double integral being taken over the surface]

$$
= \frac{1}{4\pi} \iint \{l(\mathrm{R}'\beta - \mathrm{Q}'\gamma) + m(\mathrm{P}'\gamma - \mathrm{R}'\alpha) + n(\mathrm{Q}'\alpha - \mathrm{P}'\beta)\} d\mathrm{S}
$$

$$
- \frac{1}{4\pi} \iiint \left\{ \alpha \left(\frac{d\mathrm{Q}'}{dz} - \frac{d\mathrm{R}'}{dy} \right) + \beta \left(\frac{d\mathrm{R}'}{dx} - \frac{d\mathrm{P}'}{dz} \right) + \gamma \left(\frac{d\mathrm{P}'}{dy} - \frac{d\mathrm{Q}'}{dx} \right) \right\} dx\,dy\,dz \quad \ldots \quad (6)
$$

where l, m, n are the direction cosines of the normal to the surface outwards.

But from the values of P', Q', R' in (5) we see that

$$\frac{dQ'}{dz} - \frac{dR'}{dy} = -\frac{d^2G}{dtdz} - \frac{d^2\psi}{dxdz} + \frac{d^2H}{dtdy} + \frac{d^2\psi}{dzdx}$$

$$= \frac{d}{dt}\left(\frac{dH}{dy} - \frac{dG}{dz}\right)$$

$$= \frac{da}{dt} = \mu \frac{d\alpha}{dt} \quad \text{(Maxwell, vol. ii., p. 216)}$$

similarly

$$\frac{dR'}{dx} - \frac{dP'}{dz} = \frac{db}{dt} = \mu \frac{d\beta}{dt}$$

$$\frac{dP'}{dz} - \frac{dQ'}{dx} = \frac{dc}{dt} = \mu \frac{d\gamma}{dt}$$

Whence the triple integral in (6) becomes

$$-\frac{\mu}{4\pi}\iiint\left(\alpha\frac{d\alpha}{dt} + \beta\frac{d\beta}{dt} + \gamma\frac{d\gamma}{dt}\right)dxdydz$$

Transposing it to the other side we obtain

$$\frac{K}{4\pi}\iiint\left(P\frac{dP}{dt} + Q\frac{dQ}{dt} + R\frac{dR}{dt}\right)dxdydz + \frac{\mu}{4\pi}\iiint\left(\alpha\frac{d\alpha}{dt} + \beta\frac{d\beta}{dt} + \gamma\frac{d\gamma}{dt}\right)dxdydz$$

$$+ \iiint(X\dot{x} + Y\dot{y} + Z\dot{z})dxdydz + \iiint(Pp + Qq + Rr)dxdydz$$

$$= \frac{1}{4\pi}\iint\{l(R'\beta - Q'\gamma) + m(P'\gamma - R'\alpha) + n(Q'\alpha - P'\beta)\}dS \quad . \quad . \quad . \quad . \quad (7)$$

The first two terms of this express the gain per second in electric and magnetic energies as in (2). The third term expresses the work done per second by the electromagnetic forces, that is, the energy transformed by the motion of the matter in which currents exist. The fourth term expresses the energy transformed by the conductor into heat, chemical energy, and so on; for P, Q, R are by definition the components of the force acting at a point per unit of positive electricity, so that P$p$dxdydz or Pdx$p$dydz is the work done per second by the current flowing parallel to the axis of x through the element of volume $dxdydz$. So for the other two components. This is in general transformed into other forms of energy, heat due to resistance, thermal effects at thermoelectric surfaces, and so on.

The left side of (7) thus expresses the total gain in energy per second within the closed surface, and the equation asserts that this energy comes through the bounding surface, each element contributing the amount expressed by the right side.

This may be put in another form for if $\mathfrak{E}'$ be the resultant of P', Q', R', and θ the angle between its direction and that of $\mathfrak{H}$, the magnetic intensity, the direction cosines L, M, N of the line perpendicular to the plane containing $\mathfrak{E}'$ and $\mathfrak{H}$ are given by

$$L = \frac{R'\beta - Q'\gamma}{\mathfrak{E}'\mathfrak{H}\sin\theta}; \quad M = \frac{P'\gamma - R'\alpha}{\mathfrak{E}'\mathfrak{H}\sin\theta}; \quad N = \frac{Q'\alpha - P'\beta}{\mathfrak{E}'\mathfrak{H}\sin\theta}$$

so that the surface integral becomes

$$\frac{1}{4\pi}\iint \mathfrak{E}'\mathfrak{H}\sin\theta(Ll + Mm + Nn)dS.$$

If at a given point dS be drawn to coincide with the plane containing $\mathfrak{E}'$ and $\mathfrak{H}$, it then contributes the greatest amount of energy to the space; or in other words the energy flows perpendicularly to the plane containing $\mathfrak{E}'$ and $\mathfrak{H}$, the amount crossing unit area per second being $\mathfrak{E}'\mathfrak{H}\sin\theta/4\pi$. To determine in which way it crosses the plane take $\mathfrak{E}'$ along Oz, $\mathfrak{H}$ along Oy. Then

$$P' = 0 \qquad Q' = 0 \qquad \frac{R'}{\mathfrak{E}'} = 1$$

$$\alpha = 0 \qquad \frac{\beta}{\mathfrak{H}} = 1 \qquad \gamma = 0$$

and if $\sin\theta = 1$

$$L = 1 \qquad M = 0 \qquad N = 0$$

If now the axis Ox be the normal to the surface outwards, $l = 1$, $m = 0$, $n = 0$, so that this element of the integral contributes a positive term to the energy within the surface on the negative side of the yz plane; that is, the energy moves along xO, or in the direction in which a screw would move if its head were turned round from the positive direction of the electromotive to the positive direction of the magnetic intensity. If the surface be taken where the matter has no velocity, $\mathfrak{E}'$ becomes equal to $\mathfrak{E}$, and the amount of energy crossing unit area perpendicular to the flow per second is

$$\frac{\text{electromotive intensity} \times \text{magnetic intensity} \times \text{sine included angle}}{4\pi}$$

Since the surface may be drawn anywhere we please, then wherever there is both magnetic and electromotive intensity there is flow of energy.

Since the energy flows perpendicularly to the plane containing the two intensities, it must flow along the electric and magnetic level surfaces, when these exist, so that the lines of flow are the intersections of the two surfaces.

We shall now consider the applications of this law in several cases.

[*Ed. note:* material omitted]

(7.) *The electromagnetic theory of light.*

The velocity of plane waves of polarised light on the electromagnetic theory may be deduced from the consideration of the flow of energy.   If the waves pass on unchanged in form with uniform velocity the energy in any part of the system due to the disturbance also passes on unchanged in amount with the same velocity.   If this velocity be v, then the energy contained in unit volume of cubical form with one face in a wave front will all pass out through that face in $1/v^{\text{th}}$ of a second.   Let us suppose that the direction of propagation is straightforward, while the displacements are up and down; then the magnetic intensity will be right and left.   If $\mathfrak{E}$ be the E.M.I. and $\mathfrak{H}$ the M.I. within the volume, supposed so small that the intensities may be taken as uniform through the cube, then the energy within it is $\mathrm{K}\mathfrak{E}^2/8\pi + \mu\mathfrak{H}^2/8\pi$.   The rate at which energy crosses the face in the wave front is $\mathfrak{E}\mathfrak{H}/4\pi$ per second, while it takes $1/v^{\text{th}}$ of a second for the energy in the cube to pass out.

Then

$$\frac{\mathfrak{E}\mathfrak{H}}{4\pi v} = \frac{\mathrm{K}\mathfrak{E}^2}{8\pi} + \frac{\mu\mathfrak{H}^2}{8\pi} \quad . \quad . \quad . \quad . \quad . \quad . \quad . \quad (1)$$

Now, if we take a face of the cube perpendicular to the direction of displacement, and therefore containing the M.I., the line integral of the M.I. round this face is equal to $4\pi \times$ current through the face.   If we denote distance in the direction of propagation from some fixed plane by z, the line integral of the M.I. is $-\frac{d\mathfrak{H}}{dz}$, while the current, being an alteration of displacement, is $\frac{K}{4\pi}\frac{d\mathfrak{E}}{dt}$

Therefore

$$-\frac{d\mathfrak{H}}{dz}=K\frac{d\mathfrak{E}}{dt} \qquad \dots \dots \dots \quad (2)$$

But since the displacement is propagated on unchanged with velocity v, the displacement now at a given point will alter in time dt to the displacement, now a distance dz behind, where $dz=vdt$.

Therefore

$$\frac{d\mathfrak{E}}{dt}=-v\frac{d\mathfrak{E}}{dz} \qquad \dots \dots \dots \quad (3)$$

Substituting in (2)

$$\frac{d\mathfrak{H}}{dz}=Kv\frac{d\mathfrak{E}}{dz}$$

whence

$$\mathfrak{H}=Kv\mathfrak{E} \qquad \dots \dots \dots \quad (4)$$

the function of the time being zero, since $\mathfrak{H}$ and $\mathfrak{E}$ are zero together in the parts which the wave has not yet reached.

If we take the line integral of the E.M.I. round a face perpendicular to the M.I. and equate this to the decrease of magnetic induction through the face, we obtain similarly

$$\mathfrak{E}=\mu v\mathfrak{H} \qquad \dots \dots \dots \quad (5)$$

It may be noticed that the product of (4) and (5) at once gives the value of v, for dividing out $\mathfrak{E} \mathfrak{H}$ we obtain

$$1=\mu Kv^2$$

or

$$v=\frac{1}{\sqrt{\mu K}}$$

But using one of these equations alone, say (4), and substituting in (1) K for $\mathfrak{H}$ and dividing by $\mathfrak{E}^2$, we have

$$\frac{K}{4\pi}=\frac{K}{8\pi}+\frac{\mu K^2 v^2}{8\pi}$$

or

$$1=\mu Kv^2$$

whence

$$v=\frac{1}{\sqrt{\mu K}}$$

This at once gives us the magnetic equal to the electric energy, for

$$\frac{\mu \mathfrak{H}^2}{8\pi} = \frac{\mu K^2 v^2 \mathfrak{E}^2}{8\pi} = \frac{K \mathfrak{E}^2}{8\pi}$$

It may be noted that the velocity $\dfrac{1}{\sqrt{\mu K}}$ is the greatest velocity with which the two energies can be propagated together, and that they must be equal when travelling with this velocity. For if v be the velocity of propagation and θ the angle between the two intensities, we have

$$\frac{\mathfrak{E}\mathfrak{H} \sin \theta}{4\pi v} = \frac{K \mathfrak{E}^2}{8\pi} + \frac{\mu \mathfrak{H}^2}{8\pi}$$

or

$$v = \frac{2 \sin \theta}{\dfrac{K \mathfrak{E}}{\mathfrak{H}} + \dfrac{\mu \mathfrak{H}}{\mathfrak{E}}}$$

The greatest value of the numerator is 2 when θ is a right angle, and the least value of the denominator is $2\sqrt{\mu K}$, when the two terms are equal to each other and to $\sqrt{\mu K}$.

The maximum value of v therefore is $\dfrac{1}{\sqrt{\mu K}}$, and occurs when $\theta = \dfrac{\pi}{2}$ and $K \mathfrak{E}^2 = \mu \mathfrak{H}^2$.

[Ed. note: material omitted]

20

Reprinted from John William Strutt, Baron Rayleigh, *The Theory of Sound*, Vol. 2, 2nd ed., rev. and enlarged, Dover Publications, Inc., New York, 1945, pp. 15–18

Energy Transfer in Elastic Radiation

John William Strutt (Lord Rayleigh)

[*Ed. note:* In the original, material precedes this excerpt.]

245.   The simplest kind of wave-motion is that in which the excursions of every particle are parallel to a fixed line, and are the same in all planes perpendicular to that line.   Let us therefore (assuming that $R = 0$) suppose that ϕ is a function of x (and t) only.   Our equation (9) § 244 becomes

$$\frac{d^2\phi}{dt^2} = a^2 \frac{d^2\phi}{dx^2} \quad \dots \dots \dots \dots \dots \dots \dots \dots (1),$$

the same as that already considered in the chapter on Strings. We there found that the general solution is

$$\phi = f(x - at) + F(x + at) \ \dots \dots \dots \dots \dots (2),$$

representing the propagation of independent waves in the positive and negative directions with the common velocity a.

Within such limits as allow the application of the approximate equation (1), the velocity of sound is entirely independent of the form of the wave, being, for example, the same for simple waves

$$\phi = A \cos \frac{2\pi}{\lambda} (x - at),$$

whatever the wave-length may be.   The condition satisfied by the positive wave, and therefore by the initial disturbance if a positive wave alone be generated, is

$$a \frac{d\phi}{dx} + \frac{d\phi}{dt} = 0,$$

or by (8) § 244

$$u - as = 0 \ \dots \dots \dots \dots \dots \dots (3).$$

Similarly, for a negative wave

$$u + as = 0 \ \dots \dots \dots \dots \dots \dots \ \dots \dots (4).$$

Whatever the initial disturbance may be (and u and s are both arbitrary), it can always be divided into two parts, satisfying respectively (3) and (4), which are propagated undisturbed.   In each component wave the direction of propagation is the same as that of the motion of the *condensed* parts of the fluid.

The rate at which energy is transmitted across unit of area of a plane parallel to the front of a progressive wave may be regarded as the mechanical measure of the intensity of the radiation. In the case of a simple wave, for which

$$\phi = A \cos \frac{2\pi}{\lambda} (x - at) \dotfill (5),$$

the velocity $\dot{\xi}$ of the particle at x (equal to $d\phi/dx$) is given by

$$\dot{\xi} = - \frac{2\pi}{\lambda} A \sin \frac{2\pi}{\lambda} (x - at) \dotfill (6),$$

and the displacement ξ is given by

$$\xi = - \frac{A}{a} \cos \frac{2\pi}{\lambda} (x - at) \dotfill (7).$$

The pressure $p = p_0 + \delta p$, where by (6) § 244

$$\delta p = - \frac{2\pi}{\lambda} \rho_0 a A \sin \frac{2\pi}{\lambda} (x - at) \dotfill (8).$$

Hence, if W denote the work transmitted across unit area of the plane x in time t,

$$\frac{dW}{dt} = (p_0 + \delta p) \dot{\xi} = \tfrac{1}{2} \rho_0 u \left(\frac{2\pi}{\lambda}\right)^2 A^2 + \text{periodic terms.}$$

If the integration with respect to time extend over any number of complete periods, or practically whenever its range is sufficiently long, the periodic terms may be omitted, and we may take

$$W : t = \tfrac{1}{2} \rho_0 a \left(\frac{2\pi}{\lambda}\right)^2 A^2 \dotfill (9);$$

or by (3) and (6), if $\dot{\xi}$ now denote the maximum value of the velocity and s the maximum value of the condensation,

$$W = \tfrac{1}{2} \rho_0 \dot{\xi}^2 at = \tfrac{1}{2} \rho_0 a^3 s^2 t \dotfill (10).$$

Thus the work consumed in generating waves of harmonic type is the same as would be required to give the maximum velocity $\dot{\xi}$ to the whole mass of air through which the waves extend[1].

---

[1] The earliest statement of the principle embodied in equation (10) that I have met with is in a paper by Sir W. Thomson, "On the possible density of the luminiferous medium, and on the mechanical value of a cubic mile of sun-light." *Phil. Mag.* IX. p. 36. 1855.

In terms of the maximum excursion ξ by (7) and (9)

$$W = 2\pi^2 \rho_0 \frac{a^3}{\lambda^2} \xi^2 t = 2\pi^2 \rho_0 a t \frac{\xi^2}{\tau^2} \dots\dots\dots\dots(11)[1],$$

where $\tau (= \lambda/a)$ is the periodic time. In a *given medium* the mechanical measure of the intensity is proportional to the square of the amplitude directly, and to the square of the periodic time inversely. The reader, however, must be on his guard against supposing that the mechanical measure of intensity of undulations of different wave lengths is a proper measure of the loudness of the corresponding sounds, as perceived by the ear.

In any plane progressive wave, whether the type be harmonic or not, the whole energy is equally divided between the potential and kinetic forms. Perhaps the simplest road to this result is to consider the formation of positive and negative waves from an initial disturbance, whose energy is wholly potential[2]. The total energies of the two derived progressive waves are evidently equal, and make up together the energy of the original disturbance. Moreover, in each progressive wave the condensation (or rarefaction) is one-half of that which existed at the corresponding point initially, so that the *potential* energy of each progressive wave is *one-quarter* of that of the original disturbance. Since, as we have just seen, the *whole* energy is *one-half* of the same quantity, it follows that in a progressive wave of any type one-half of the energy is potential and one-half is kinetic.

The same conclusion may also be drawn from the general expressions for the potential and kinetic energies and the relations between velocity and condensation expressed in (3) and (4). The potential energy of the element of volume dV is the work that would be gained during the expansion of the corresponding quantity of gas from its actual to its normal volume, the expansion being opposed throughout by the normal pressure p_0. At any stage of the expansion, when the condensation is s', the effective pressure δp is by § 244 $a^2 \rho_0 s'$, which pressure has to be multiplied by the corresponding increment of volume $dV . ds'$. The whole work gained during the expansion from dV to $dV(1+s)$ is therefore $a^2 \rho_0 dV . \int_0 s' ds'$ or $\frac{1}{2} a^2 \rho_0 dV . s^2$. The general expressions for the potential and kinetic energies are accordingly

[1] Bosanquet, *Phil. Mag.* xlv. p. 173. 1873.
[2] *Phil. Mag.* (5) i. p. 260. 1876.

$$\text{potential energy} = \tfrac{1}{2} a^2 \rho_0 \iiint s^2 \, dV \quad \ldots\ldots\ldots\ldots(12),$$

$$\text{kinetic energy} \quad = \quad \tfrac{1}{2}\rho_0 \iiint u^2 \, dV \ldots\ldots\ldots\ldots(13),$$

and these are equal in the case of plane progressive waves for which

$$u = \pm \, as.$$

If the plane progressive waves be of harmonic type, u and s at any moment of time are circular functions of one of the space co-ordinates (x), and therefore the mean value of their squares is one-half of the maximum value. Hence the total energy of the waves is equal to the kinetic energy of the whole mass of air concerned, moving with the maximum velocity to be found in the waves, or to the potential energy of the same mass of air when condensed to the maximum density of the waves.

[It may be worthy of notice that when terms of the second order are retained, a purely periodic value of u does not correspond to a purely periodic motion. The quantity of fluid which passes unit of area at point x in time dt is $\rho u \, dt$, or $\rho_0 (1 + s) \, u \, dt$. If u be periodic, $\int u \, dt = 0$, but $\int s u \, dt$ may be finite. Thus in a positive progressive wave

$$\int s u \, dt = a \int s^2 \, dt,$$

and there is a transference of fluid in the direction of wave propagation.]

[*Ed. note:* material omitted]

Part VI

THE SCIENCE OF ENERGETICS

Editor's Comments
on Papers 21 Through 24

Through the epoch-making researches of Helmholtz, Clausius, Lord Kelvin, Joule, Rankine, and others, the utility of the concept of energy in the scientific study of natural phenomena was decisively established in the early 1850s. It is not surprising that some scientists developed great enthusiasm for the concept and its ultimate significance not only in physical science but in the study of living things as well. To scientists with strong philosophical leanings, energy would naturally appear to have special importance as a unifying idea.

William J. M. Rankine, the Scottish engineering professor whose early important contributions to thermodynamics have been reprinted as Papers 5 and 6, had a somewhat surprising penchant for philosophizing. This was already evident in Paper 5 on the general law of the transformation of energy. He developed here a general point of view and tried to set up equations that would apply to the transformation of energy of all forms, consistent with the conservation principle. Still obsessed with the desire for generalization, he followed up this preliminary work with a paper read in May 1855 before the Philosophical Society of Glasgow, in which he outlined what he proposed to call "the Science of Energetics," with energy as the principal concept. The resulting memoir was originally printed in the *Proceedings of the Philosophical Society of Glasgow* [3(6), 1855]. This memoir, which is reprinted here in full as Paper 21, is of interest not merely for its emphasis on energy but also for the exposition of Rankine's views on the nature of a physical theory.

Rankine distinguishes between a theory based on hypotheses that assume the existence of entities outside of sensation experience, e.g., atoms and molecules, and a theory, which he calls abstractive, in which the elements are entities evident to our senses but demand careful symbolic definition, e.g., the mass of a body. On the whole, Rankine seems to prefer the latter method and therefore shows himself to be a kind of phenomenologist or positivist in the philosophical sense. However, he did not prove as thoroughly wedded to this point of view as Ernst Mach, who would not accept atoms as a valid element in trying to understand natural phenomena. In an earlier paper "On the Mechanical Action of Heat, Especially in Gases and Vapors" [*Transactions of the Royal Society of Edinburgh*, **20**, (1850)], reprinted in *Miscellaneous Scientific Papers of W. J. M. Rankine* (Charles Griffin and Co., London, 1881, pp. 234–284), Rankine had had no qualms about introducing a version of the molecular theory of gases which foreshadowed some of the atomic constitution theories of the early part of the twentieth century. Consistency is not necessarily a virtue in scientists!

There is no indication that Rankine followed up in any detail the development of his "energetics" idea, although he did use some of the ideas and nomenclature in his later papers on thermodynamics, particularly in connection with the second law. Like others in the 1860s and 1870s he felt that this law should be derivable from the principles of mechanics, if one were willing to introduce the hypothesis of molecular constitution and specifically his own idea of molecular vortices, in which the "atmosphere" of an atom was supposed to whirl about a central nucleus in a vortical motion. The details of this theory will be found in the article just referred to. Rankine seems to have felt that the entropy function introduced by Clausius could be represented by the so-called metamorphic function introduced in his outline of energetics. Rankine's early death in 1872 cut short his excursions into the development of thermodynamics through his ideas on energetics. The latter notions had little apparent influence on the working out of the details of thermodynamics by Kelvin, Clausius, Helmholtz, Maxwell, Gibbs, and others. They might well have been forgotten when in 1887 they were, to a certain extent, resurrected by a somewhat obscure German secondary school teacher, Georg Helm, in a book entitled *Die Lehre von der Energie* (Leipzig, 1887). Helm introduced the term *Energetik* in his discussion. He adapted the phenomenological approach of Mach and evidently felt that his development was simpler and easier to apply than the standard thermodynamics already current in his time. Helm was one of the early adherents to the positivistic philosophy of which Mach was a leading representative. Helm's book, although a rather slight affair, evidently attracted some attention, for around 1890, when the well-known German physical chemist Wilhelm Ostwald (1853–1932) became interested in energetics, he was favorably impressed with the positivistic, phenomenological leanings of Mach, whose critical study of mechanics, *Die Mechanik in Ihrer Entwicklung*, had already been published in 1883. Another bond between them was a mutual dislike of the growth of atomic theory in physics.

In 1891, Ostwald began a series of articles in the *Berichte über die Verhandlungen der Sächsische Akademie der Wissenschaften* in Leipzig with the general title *Studien zur Energetik*. We reprint here as Paper 22 the second of these articles as a satisfactory sample of Ostwald's fundamental thesis. It is clear that he felt very strongly the disadvantage of the standard plan of representing all physical quantities in terms of space, time, and mass, which was at that time coming into general use. Ostwald took as the program of energetics the replacement of mass by energy, which he considered to be a much more fundamental scientific quantity than mass. Ostwald then proceeds to lay down two fundamental principles of energetics. The first is the conservation of energy in all transformation or transfer processes and is essentially equivalent to the first law of thermodynamics. The second forbids the uncompensated flow of energy, even when the total remains constant, and is analogous to the second law of thermodynamics, although it is stated in a form different from those already set forth by Clausius and Kelvin. Ostwald then proceeds to introduce the idea of the decomposition of energy into the product of capacity and intensity factors, and discusses what these terms mean and how they may be determined for various forms of energy. His claim is that by his method one can obtain more directly and simply the results of standard thermodynamics. Some classical results, e.g., the Gibbs–Helmholtz equation, are indeed derived, if in a somewhat questionable fashion. No essentially new results are presented, but considerable claims are made.

This work of Ostwald attracted much attention and was undoubtedly favorably received in some quarters. However, it also stirred up criticism, particularly at the hands of Ludwig Boltzmann (1844–1906) and Max Planck (1858–1947). At the time of Ostwald's activity in energetics, Boltzmann was engaged in the development of statistical mechanics, while Planck was much involved in sys-

316

tematizing what has come to be called classical thermodynamics. In fact, he was preparing a standard text on the subject. Planck felt that there were serious faults in Ostwald's energetics, and Paper 23 is his reply. The interested reader is urged also to consult two papers by Boltzmann [*Annalen der Physik*, **57**, 39, 646 (1896)]. These were both rather devastating attacks though clothed in polite language. Planck points out that Ostwald apparently failed to recognize the difference between state variables in thermodynamics (e.g., volume and temperature) and quantities like work, which are not state variables but depend on the path between states. Ostwald ignored the important fact that these quantities must be handled mathematically in quite different fashion, as was pointed out by Clausius many years before. Planck also emphasized the fact that energetics had produced no new results that could be compared with experiment, whereas thermodynamics had shown conspicuous success in this respect. He concluded that energetics was "barking up the wrong tree" and was in danger of misleading many uncautious scientists.

Boltzmann in his articles showed that many of the mathematical developments of both Helm and Ostwald were completely invalid, even in the domain of mechanics, where with care energetics might expect to be applicable.

In spite of these adverse criticisms, Ostwald sailed serenely on. In his book *Grosse Manner*, published in Leipzig in 1909, in which he discussed the achievements of numerous famous scientists and stated his views of how they gained their success, he introduced much philosophizing; in the course of this, he reviewed the basic ideas of energetics, which in spite of the existence of mistakes in detail (which he readily admitted), he insisted was fundamentally sound and of great value in science.

The story of energetics is one of the most interesting episodes in the history of science. Although it failed to achieve its goal, it certainly excited a great interest in its day. It is often worthwhile to devote some attention to the failures of scientific speculation, particularly if some, at any rate, of the persons concerned are men of admitted competence. Wilhelm Ostwald was one of the most distinguished German physical chemists of the late nineteenth and early twentieth centuries. He was one of the founders of modern physical chemistry. In 1909 he was awarded the Nobel prize in chemistry for his work on chemical equilibrium, catalysis, and reaction velocities. It may well be that his zeal for purely philosophical considerations tempted him a bit too far in his concern for the energy concept. It was just a little too alluring. As a distinguished scientist, Ostwald certainly had some peculiarities. For most of his life he refused to accept the atomic theory. Here he

317

followed Mach. He probably had to come round in this matter in his extreme old age.

The question arises: Could anything really successful ever be made out of energetics? After the severe critiques of Planck and Boltzmann, this appears to be unlikely. Whatever of value resides in its notions has been fully absorbed in modern statistical thermodynamics and its modifications resulting from quantum mechanics.

We shall conclude our excursion into energetics by including the comments of Henri Poincaré (1854–1912), the distinguished French mathematician, astronomer, and philosopher. In his semipopular collection of essays on the philosophy of science, *La Science et l'hypothèse*, published in 1906, he paid his respects to energy, energetics, and thermodynamics. We reprint as Paper 24 his essay, "Energy and Thermodynamics."

It will be noted that Poincaré takes a somewhat dim view of our ability to define energy in any general sense. His views are cogent but have not had an adverse effect on the use of the energy concept in modern science. Perhaps they have encouraged good scientists to be more careful in their employment of it.

21

Reprinted from *Miscellaneous Scientific Papers of W. J. M. Rankine*, Charles Griffin and Co., London, 1881, pp. 209–228

OUTLINES OF THE SCIENCE OF ENERGETICS.*

William John Mcquorn Rankine

SECTION I.—WHAT CONSTITUTES A PHYSICAL THEORY.

AN essential distinction exists between two stages in the process of advancing our knowledge of the laws of physical phenomena; the first stage consists in observing the relations of phenomena, whether of such as occur in the ordinary course of nature, or of such as are artificially produced in experimental investigations, and in expressing the relations so observed by propositions called formal laws. The second stage consists in reducing the formal laws of an entire class of phenomena to the form of a science; that is to say, in discovering the most simple system of principles, from which all the formal laws of the class of phenomena can be deduced as consequences.

Such a system of principles, with its consequences methodically deduced, constitutes the PHYSICAL THEORY of a class of phenomena.

A physical theory, like an abstract science, consists of definitions and axioms as first principles, and of propositions, their consequences, but with these differences:—First, That in an abstract science, a definition assigns a name to a class of notions derived originally from observation, but not necessarily corresponding to any existing objects of real phenomena; and an axiom states a mutual relation amongst such notions, or the names denoting them: while in a physical science, a definition states properties common to a class of existing objects, or real phenomena; and a physical axiom states a general law as to the relations of phenomena. And, secondly, That in an abstract science, the propositions first discovered are the most simple; whilst in a physical theory, the propositions first discovered are in general numerous and complex, being formal laws, the immediate results of observation and experiment, from which the definitions and axioms are subsequently arrived at by a process of reasoning differing from that whereby one proposition is deduced from another in an abstract science, partly in being more complex and difficult, and partly in being, to a certain extent, *tentative*—that is to say, involving the trial of conjectural principles, and their acceptance or rejection, according as their consequences are found to agree or disagree with the formal laws deduced immediately from observation and experiment.

* Read before the Philosophical Society of Glasgow on May 2, 1855, and published in the *Proceedings* of that Society, Vol. III., No. VI.

SECTION II.—THE ABSTRACTIVE METHOD OF FORMING A PHYSICAL
THEORY DISTINGUISHED FROM THE HYPOTHETICAL METHOD.

Two methods of framing a physical theory may be distinguished,
characterised chiefly by the manner in which classes of phenomena are
defined.   They may be termed, respectively, the ABSTRACTIVE and the
HYPOTHETICAL methods.

According to the ABSTRACTIVE method, a class of objects or phenomena
is defined by describing, or otherwise making to be understood, and
assigning a name or symbol to, that assemblage of properties which is
common to all the objects or phenomena composing the class, as perceived
by the senses, without introducing anything hypothetical.

According to the HYPOTHETICAL method, a class of objects or phenomena is defined, according to a conjectural conception of their nature, as
being constituted, in a manner not apparent to the senses, by a modification of some other class of objects or phenomena whose laws are already
known.   Should the consequences of such a hypothetical definition be
found to be in accordance with the results of observation and experiment,
it serves as the means of deducing the laws of one class of objects or
phenomena from those of another.

The conjectural conceptions involved in the hypothetical method may
be distinguished into two classes, according as they are adopted as a probable representation of a state of things which may really exist, though
imperceptible to the senses, or merely as a convenient means of expressing
the laws of phenomena; two kinds of hypotheses, of which the former
may be called *objective*, and the latter *subjective*.   As examples of objective hypotheses may be taken, that of vibrations or oscillations in the
theory of light, and that of atoms in chemistry; as an example of a
subjective hypothesis, that of magnetic fluids.

SECTION III.—THE SCIENCE OF MECHANICS CONSIDERED AS AN
ILLUSTRATION OF THE ABSTRACTIVE METHOD.

The principles of the science of mechanics, the only example yet existing of a complete physical theory, are altogether formed from the data of
experience by the abstractive method.   The class of *objects* to which the
science of mechanics relates—viz., material bodies—are defined by
means of those sensible properties which they all possess—viz., the property of occupying space, and that of resisting change of motion.   The
two classes of *phenomena* to which the science of mechanics relates are
distinguished by two words, *motion* and *force*—*motion* being a word

denoting that which is common to the fall of heavy bodies, the flow of streams, the tides, the winds, the vibrations of sonorous bodies, the revolutions of the stars, and, generally, to all phenomena involving change of the portions of space occupied by bodies; and *force*, a word denoting that which is common to the mutual attractions and repulsions of bodies, distant or near, and of the parts of bodies, the mutual pressure or stress of bodies in contact, and of the parts of bodies, the muscular exertions of animals, and, generally, to all phenomena tending to produce or to prevent motion.

The laws of the composition and resolution of motions, and of the composition and resolution of forces, are expressed by propositions which are the consequences of the definitions of motion and force respectively. The laws of the relations between motion and force are the consequences of certain axioms, being the most simple and general expressions for all that has been ascertained by experience respecting those relations.

SECTION IV.—MECHANICAL HYPOTHESES IN VARIOUS BRANCHES OF PHYSICS.

The fact that the theory of motions and motive forces is the only complete physical theory, has naturally led to the adoption of *mechanical hypotheses* in the theories of other branches of physics; that is to say, hypothetical definitions, in which classes of phenomena are defined conjecturally as being constituted by some kind of motion or motive force not obvious to the senses (called *molecular* motion or force), as when light and radiant heat are defined as consisting in molecular vibrations, thermometric heat in molecular vortices, and the rigidity of solids in molecular attractions and repulsions.

The hypothetical motions and forces are sometimes ascribed to *hypothetical bodies*, such as the luminiferous ether; sometimes to *hypothetical parts*, whereof tangible bodies are conjecturally defined to consist, such as atoms, atomic nuclei with elastic atmospheres, and the like.

A mechanical hypothesis is held to have fulfilled its object, when, by applying the known axioms of mechanics to the hypothetical motions and forces, results are obtained agreeing with the observed laws of the classes of phenomena under consideration; and when, by the aid of such a hypothesis, phenomena previously unobserved are predicted, and laws anticipated, it attains a high degree of probability.

A mechanical hypothesis is the better the more extensive the range of phenomena whose laws it serves to deduce from the axioms of mechanics; and the perfection of such a hypothesis would be, if it could, by means of one connected system of suppositions, be made to form a basis for all branches of molecular physics.

Section V.—Advantages and Disadvantages of Hypothetical Theories.

It is well known that certain hypothetical theories, such as the wave theory of light, have proved extremely useful, by reducing the laws of a various and complicated class of phenomena to a few simple principles, and by anticipating laws afterwards verified by observation.

Such are the results to be expected from well-framed hypotheses in every branch of physics, when used with judgment, and especially with that caution which arises from the consideration, that even those hypotheses whose consequences are most fully confirmed by experiment never can, by any amount of evidence, attain that degree of certainty which belongs to observed facts.

Of mechanical hypotheses in particular, it is to be observed, that their tendency is to combine all branches of physics into one system, by making the axioms of mechanics the first principles of the laws of all phenomena— an object for the attainment of which an earnest wish was expressed by Newton.*

In the mechanical theories of elasticity, light, heat, and electricity, considerable progress has been made towards that end.

The neglect of the caution already referred to, however, has caused some hypotheses to assume, in the minds of the public generally, as well as in those of many scientific men, that authority which belongs to facts alone; and a tendency has, consequently, often evinced itself to explain away, or set aside, facts inconsistent with these hypotheses, which facts, rightly appreciated, would have formed the basis of true theories. Thus, the fact of the production of heat by friction, the basis of the true theory of heat, was long neglected, because inconsistent with the hypothesis of caloric; and the fact of the production of cold by electric currents, at certain metallic junctions, the key (as Professor William Thomson recently showed) to the true theory of the phenomena of thermo-electricity, was, from inconsistency with prevalent assumptions respecting the so-called "electric fluid," by some regarded as a thing to be explained away, and by others as a delusion.

Such are the evils which arise from the misuse of hypotheses.

* Utinam cætera naturæ phænomena ex principiis mechanicis eodem argumentandi genere derivare liceret. —(*Phil. Nat. Prin. Math.; Præf.*)

SECTION VI.—ADVANTAGES OF AN EXTENSION OF THE ABSTRACTIVE METHOD OF FRAMING THEORIES.

Besides the perfecting of mechanical hypotheses, another and an entirely distinct method presents itself for combining the physical sciences into one system; and that is, by an *extension of the* ABSTRACTIVE PROCESS in framing theories.

The abstractive method has already been partially applied, and with success, to special branches of molecular physics, such as heat, electricity, and magnetism. We are now to consider in what manner it is to be applied to physics generally, considered as one science.

Instead of supposing the various classes of physical phenomena to be constituted, in an occult way, of modifications of motion and force, let us distinguish the properties which those classes possess in common with each other, and so define more extensive classes denoted by suitable terms. For axioms, to express the laws of those more extensive classes of phenomena, let us frame propositions comprehending as particular cases the laws of the particular classes of phenomena comprehended under the more extensive classes. So shall we arrive at a body of principles, applicable to physical phenomena in general, and which, being framed by induction from facts alone, will be free from the uncertainty which must always attach, even to those mechanical hypotheses whose consequences are most fully confirmed by experiment.

This extension of the abstractive process is not proposed in order to supersede the hypothetical method of theorising; for in almost every branch of molecular physics it may be held, that a hypothetical theory is necessary, as a preliminary step, to reduce the expression of the phenomena to simplicity and order, before it is possible to make any progress in framing an abstractive theory.

SECTION VII.—NATURE OF THE SCIENCE OF ENERGETICS.

Energy, or the capacity to effect changes, is the common characteristic of the various states of matter to which the several branches of physics relate; if, then, there be general laws respecting energy, such laws must be applicable, *mutatis mutandis*, to every branch of physics, and must express a body of principles as to physical phenomena in general.

In a paper read before the Philosophical Society of Glasgow, on the 5th of January, 1853 (*see p. 203*), a first attempt was made to investigate such principles by defining *actual energy* and *potential energy*, and by demonstrating a general law of the mutual transformations of those kinds of energy, of which one particular case is a previously known law of the mechanical action of heat in elastic bodies, and another, a subsequently demonstrated law which forms the basis of Professor William Thomson's theory of thermo-electricity.

The object of the present paper is to present, in a more systematic form, both these and some other principles, forming part of a science whose subjects are, material bodies and physical phenomena in general, and which it is proposed to call the SCIENCE OF ENERGETICS.

SECTION VIII.—DEFINITIONS OF CERTAIN TERMS.

The peculiar terms which will be used in treating of the Science of Energetics are purely abstract; that is to say, they are not the names of any particular object, nor of any particular phenomena, nor of any particular notions of the mind, but are names of very comprehensive *classes* of objects and phenomena. About such classes it is impossible to think or to reason, except by the aid of examples or of symbols. General terms are symbols employed for this purpose.

Substance.

The term "*substance*" will be applied to all bodies, parts of bodies, and systems of bodies. The parts of a substance may be spoken of as distinct substances, and a system of substances related to each other may be spoken of as one complex substance. Strictly speaking, the term should be "*material substance;*" but it is easily borne in mind, that in this essay none but material substances are referred to.

Property.

The term "*property*" will be restricted to *invariable* properties; whether such as always belong to all material substances, or such as constitute the invariable distinctions between one kind of substance and another.

Mass.

Mass means "*quantity of substance.*" Masses of one kind of substance may be compared together by ascertaining the numbers of equal parts which they contain; masses of substances of different kinds are compared by means to be afterwards referred to.

Accident.

The term "*accident*" will be applied to every variable state of substances, whether consisting in a condition of each part of a substance, how small soever, (which may be called an *absolute accident*), or in a physical relation between parts of substances, (which may be called a *relative accident*). Accidents to be the subject of scientific inquiry, must be capable of being measured and expressed by means of quantities. The quantity, even of an absolute accident, can only be expressed by means of a mentally-conceived relation.

The whole condition or state of a substance, so far as it is variable, is a *complex accident;* the independent quantities which are at once *necessary* and *sufficient* to express completely this complex accident, are *independent accidents.* To express the same complex accident, different systems of independent accidents may be employed; but the number of independent accidents in each system will be the same.

Examples.—The variable thermic condition of an elastic fluid is a *complex accident,* capable of being completely expressed by *two independent accidents,* which may be any two out of these three quantities—the *temperature,* the *density,* the *pressure*—or any two independent functions of these quantities.

The condition of strain at a point in an elastic solid, is a *complex accident,* capable of being completely expressed by *six independent accidents,* which may be the three elongations of the dimensions and the three distortions of the faces of a molecule originally cubical, or the lengths and directions of the axes of the ellipsoidal figure assumed by a molecule originally spherical; or any six independent functions of either of those systems of quantities.

The distinction of accidents into absolute and relative is, to a certain extent, arbitrary; thus, the figure and dimensions of a molecule may be regarded as absolute accidents when it is considered as a whole, or as relative accidents when it is considered as made up of parts. Most kinds of accidents are necessarily relative; but some kinds can only be considered as relative accidents when some hypothesis is adopted as to the occult condition of the substances which they affect, as when heat is ascribed hypothetically to molecular motions; and such suppositions are excluded from the present inquiry.

Accidents may be said to be *homogeneous* when the quantities expressing them are capable of being put together, so that the result of the combination of the different accidents shall be expressed by one quantity. The number of heterogeneous kinds of accidents is evidently indefinite.

Effort, or Active Accident.

The term "*effort*" will be applied to every cause which varies, or tends to vary, an accident. This term, therefore, comprehends not merely *forces* or *pressures,* to which it is usually applied, but all causes of variation in the condition of substances.

Efforts may be homogeneous or heterogeneous.

Homogeneous efforts are compared by balancing them against each other.

An effort being a condition of the parts of a substance, or a relation between substances, is itself an accident, and may be distinguished as an "*active accident.*"

With reference to a given limited substance, *internal efforts* are those which consist in actions amongst its parts; *external efforts* those which consist in actions between the given substance and other substances.

Passive Accident.

The condition which an effort tends to vary may be called a "*passive accident,*" and when the word "accident" is not otherwise qualified, "passive accident" may be understood.

Radical Accident.

If there be a quantity such that it expresses at once the magnitude of the passive accident caused by a given effort, and the magnitude of the active accident or effort itself, let the condition denoted by that quantity be called a "*radical accident.*"

[The velocity of a given mass is an example of a radical accident, for it is itself a passive accident, and also the measure of the kind of effort called accelerative force, which, acting for unity of time, is capable of producing that passive accident.]

[The strength of an electric current is also a radical accident.]

Effort as a Measure of Mass.

Masses, whether homogeneous or heterogeneous, may be compared by means of the efforts required to produce in them variations of some particular accident. The accident conventionally employed for this purpose is *velocity.*

Work.

"*Work*" is the variation of an accident by an effort, and is a term comprehending all phenomena in which physical change takes place. *Quantity of work* is measured by the product of the variation of the passive accident by the magnitude of the effort, when this is constant; or by the integral of the effort, with respect to the passive accident, when the effort is variable.

Let x denote a passive accident;

X an effort tending to vary it;

W the work performed in increasing x from x_0 to x_1 : then,

$$W = \int_{x_0}^{x_1} X\,dx, \text{ and}$$

$$W = X\,(x_1 - x_0), \text{ if } X \text{ is constant.} \qquad \left.\right\} \qquad . \qquad . \quad (1.)$$

Work is represented geometrically by the area of a curve, whereof the abscissa represents the passive accident, and the ordinate, the effort.

Energy, Actual and Potential.

The term "*energy*" comprehends every state of a substance which constitutes a capacity for performing work. *Quantities of energy* are measured by the quantities of work which they constitute the means of performing.

"*Actual energy*" comprehends those kinds of capacity for performing work which consist in particular states of each part of a substance, how small soever; that is, in an *absolute accident*, such as heat, light, electric current, *vis viva*. Actual energy is essentially positive.

"*Potential energy*" comprehends those kinds of capacity for performing work which consist in relations between substances, or parts of substances; that is, in *relative accidents*. To constitute potential energy there must be a *passive accident* capable of variation, and an *effort* tending to produce such variation; the integral of this effort, with respect to the *possible variation* of the passive accident, is *potential energy*, which differs in work from this—that in work the change *has been effected*, which, in potential energy, is *capable of being effected*.

Let x denote an accident; x_1, its actual value; X, an effort tending to vary it; x_0, the value to which the effort tends to bring the accident; then

$$\int_{x_1}^{x_0} X\,dx = U, \text{ denotes potential energy.}$$

Examples of potential energy are, the chemical affinity of uncombined elements; the energy of gravitation, of magnetism, of electrical attraction and repulsion, of electro-motive force, of that part of elasticity which arises from actions between the parts of a body, and, generally, of all mutual actions of bodies, and parts of bodies.

Potential energy may be passive or negative, according as the effort in question is of the same sign with the variation of the passive accident, or of the opposite sign; that is, according as X is of the same sign with dx, or of the opposite sign.

It is to be observed, that the states of substances comprehended under the term *actual energy*, may possess the characteristics of potential energy also; that is to say, may be accompanied by a tendency or effort to vary relative accidents; as heat, in an elastic fluid, is accompanied by a tendency to expand; that is, an effort to increase the volume of the receptacle containing the fluid.

The states to which the term *potential energy* is especially applied, are those which are solely due to mutual actions.

To put a substance into a state of energy, or to increase its energy, is obviously a *kind of work*.

Section IX.—First Axiom.

All kinds of Work and Energy are Homogeneous.

This axiom means, that *any kind of energy may be made the means of performing any kind of work*. It is a fact arrived at by induction from experiment and observation, and its establishment is more especially due to the experiments of Mr. Joule.

This axiom leads, in many respects, to the same consequences with the hypothesis that all those kinds of energy which are not sensibly the results of motion and motive force are the results of occult modifications of motion and motive force.

But the axiom differs from the hypothesis in this, that the axiom is simply the generalised allegation of the facts proved by experience, while the hypothesis involves conjectures as to objects and phenomena which never can be subjected to observation.

It is the truth of this axiom which renders a science of energetics possible.

The efforts and passive accidents to which the branches of physics relate are varied and heterogeneous; but they are all connected with *energy*, a uniform species of quantity which pervades every branch of physics.

This axiom is also equivalent to saying, that *energy is transformable and transferable* (an allegation which, in the previous paper referred to, was included in the definition of energy); for, to *transform energy*, means to employ energy depending on accidents of one kind in putting a substance into a state of energy depending on accidents of another kind; and to *transfer energy*, means to employ the energy of one substance in putting another substance into a state of energy, both of which are kinds of work, and may, according to the axiom, be performed by means of any kind of energy.

SECTION X.—SECOND AXIOM.

The Total Energy of a Substance cannot be altered by the Mutual Actions of its Parts.

Of the truth of this axiom there can be no doubt; but some difference of opinion may exist as to the evidence on which it rests. There is ample experimental evidence from which it might be proved; but independently of such evidence, there is the argument, that the law expressed by this axiom is essential to the stability of the universe, such as it exists.

The special application of this law to mechanics is expressed in two ways, which are virtually equivalent to each other, the principle of *vis viva*, and that of the equality of action and reaction. The latter principle is demonstrated by Newton, from considerations connected with the stability of the universe (*Principia*, Scholium to the Laws of Motion); for he shows, that but for the equality of action and reaction, the earth, with a continually accelerated velocity, would fly away through infinite space.

It follows, from the second axiom, that *all work consists in the transfer and transformation of energy alone;* for otherwise the total amount of energy would be altered. Also, that the energy of a substance can be varied by *external efforts alone.*

SECTION XI.—EXTERNAL POTENTIAL EQUILIBRIUM.

The entire condition of a substance, so far as it is variable, as explained in Sect. VIII., under the head of *accident*, is a complex accident, which may be expressed in various ways by means of different systems of quantities denoting independent accidents; but the number of independent accidents in each system must be the same.

The quantity of work required to produce any change in the condition of the substance, that is to say, the potential energy received by it from without during that change, may in like manner be expressed in different ways by the sums of different systems of integrals of external efforts, each integrated with respect to the independent accident which it tends to augment; but the number of integrals in each system, and the number of efforts, like the number of independent accidents, must be the same; and so also must the sums of the integrals, each sum representing the same quantity of work in a different way.

The different systems of efforts which correspond to different systems of independent accidents, each expressing the same complex accident, may be called *equivalent systems of efforts;* and the finding of a system of efforts equivalent to another may be called conversion of efforts. *

When the law of variation of potential energy, by a change of condition of a substance, is known, the system of external efforts corresponding to any system of independent accidents is found by means of this principle:

Each effort is equal to the rate of variation of the potential energy with respect to the independent accident which that effort tends to vary; or, symbolically,

$$X = \frac{d\,U}{d\,x}. \qquad . \qquad . \qquad . \qquad . \qquad (2.)$$

EXTERNAL POTENTIAL EQUILIBRIUM *of a substance takes place, when the external effort to vary each of the independent accidents is null;* that is to say, when the rate of variation of the potential energy of the substance with the variation of each independent accident is null.

For a given substance there are as many conditions of equilibrium, of the form

$$\frac{d\,U}{d\,x} = 0, \qquad . \qquad . \qquad . \qquad . \qquad (3.)$$

as there are independent accidents in the expression of its condition.

The special application of this law to motion and motive force constitutes the *principle* of *virtual velocities*, from which the whole science of statics is deducible.

SECTION XII.—INTERNAL POTENTIAL EQUILIBRIUM.

The internal potential equilibrium of a substance consists in the equilibrium of each of its parts, considered separately; that is to say, in the nullity of the rate of variation of the potential energy of each part with respect to each of the independent accidents on which the condition of such part depends.

Examples of particular cases of this principle are, the laws of the equilibrium of elastic solids, and of the distribution of statical electricity.

SECTION XIII.—THIRD AXIOM.

The Effort to Perform Work of a Given Kind, caused by a Given Quantity of Actual Energy, is the Sum of the Efforts caused by the Parts of that Quantity.

A law equivalent to this axiom, under the name of the " GENERAL

---

* The conversion of efforts in physics is connected with the theory of lineal transformations in algebra.

LAW OF THE TRANSFORMATION OF ENERGY," formed the principal subject of the previous paper already referred to. (*See p. 203.*)

This axiom appears to be a consequence of the definition of actual energy, as a capacity for performing work possessed by each part of a substance independently of its relations to other parts, rather than an independent proposition.

Its applicability to natural phenomena arises from the fact, that there are states of substances corresponding to the definition of actual energy.

The mode of applying this third axiom is as follows :—

Let a homogeneous substance possess a quantity Q, of a particular kind of actual energy, uniformly distributed, and let it be required to determine the amount of the effort arising from the actual energy, which tends to perform a particular kind of work W, by the variation of a particular passive accident x.

The total effort to perform this kind of work is represented by the rate of its increase relatively to the passive accident, viz.,—

$$X = \frac{d\,W}{d\,x}.$$

Divide the quantity of actual energy Q into an indefinite number of indefinitely small parts δQ; the portion of the effort X due to each of those parts will be

$$\delta Q \frac{d\,X}{d\,Q},$$

and adding these partial efforts together, the effort caused by the whole quantity of actual energy will be

$$Q \frac{d\,X}{d\,Q} = Q \frac{d^2\,W}{d\,Q\,d\,x}. \qquad . \qquad . \qquad . \quad (4.)$$

If this be equal to the *effective effort* X, then that effort is simply proportional to, and wholly caused by, the actual energy Q. This is the case of the pressure of a perfect gas, and the centrifugal force of a moving body.

If the effort caused by the actual energy differs from the effective effort, their difference represents, when the former is the less, an additional effort,

$$\left(1 - Q\frac{d}{d\,Q}\right)X,$$

and when the former is the greater, a counter effort

$$\left(Q\frac{d}{d\,Q} - 1\right)X,$$

$$\left. \begin{array}{c} \\ \\ \\ \end{array} \right\} \quad (5.)$$

due to some other cause or causes.

SECTION XIV.—RATE OF TRANSFORMATION; METAMORPHIC FUNCTION.

The effort to augment a given accident x, caused by actual energy of a given kind Q, may also be called the *"rate of transformation"* of the given kind of actual energy, with increase of the given accident; for the limit of the amount of actual energy which disappears in performing work by an indefinitely small augmentation dx, of the accident, is

$$d\,H = Q \frac{d\,X}{a\,Q} dx \quad . \qquad . \qquad . \qquad . \quad (6.)$$

$$= Q \frac{d^2\,W}{d\,Q\,d\,x} \quad d\,x = Q\,d \frac{d\,W}{dQ}.$$

The *last* form of the above expression is obviously applicable when the work W is the result of the variation of any number of independent accidents, each by the corresponding effort. For example, let x, y, z, &c., be any number of independent accidents, and X, Y, Z, &c., the efforts to augment them; so that

$$d\,W = X\,dx + Y\,dy + Z\,dz + \&c.$$

Then,

$$d\,H = Q \left\{ \frac{d\,X}{d\,Q} d\,x + \frac{d\,Y}{d\,Q} d\,y + \frac{d\,Z}{d\,Q} d\,z + \&c. \right\} \quad . \quad (7.)$$

$$= Q\,d \frac{d\,W}{dQ}, \text{ as before.}$$

The function of actual energy, efforts, and passive accidents, denoted by

$$\frac{d\,W}{dQ} = \int \frac{d\,H}{Q} = F, \quad . \qquad . \qquad . \qquad . \quad (8.)$$

whose variation, multiplied by the actual energy, gives the amount of actual energy transformed in performing the work d W, may be called the "METAMORPHIC FUNCTION" of the kind of actual energy Q, relatively to the kind of work W.

When this metamorphic function is known for a given homogeneous substance, the quantity H of actual energy of the kind Q transformed to the kind of work W, during a given operation, is found by taking the integral

$$H = \int Q\,d\,F. \quad . \qquad . \qquad . \quad (9.)$$

The transformation of actual energy into work by the variation of passive accidents is a *reversible operation;* that is to say, if the passive accidents be made to vary to an equal extent in an opposite direction, potential energy will be exerted upon the substance, and transformed into actual energy: a case represented by the expression (9) becoming negative.

The metamorphic function of heat relatively to expansive power, was first employed in a paper on the Economy of Heat in Expansive Machines, read before the Royal Society of Edinburgh in April, 1851. (*Trans. Roy. Soc. Edin.*, Vol. XXI.)

The metamorphic function of heat relatively to electricity was employed by Professor William Thomson, in a paper on Thermo-Electricity, read before the Royal Society of Edinburgh in May, 1854 (*Trans. Roy. Soc. Edin.*, Vol. XXI.), and was the means of anticipating some most remarkable laws, afterwards confirmed by experiment.

Section XV.—Equilibrium of Actual Energy; Metabatic Function.

It is known by experiment, that a state of actual energy is directly transferable; that is to say, the actual energy of a particular kind (such as heat), in one substance, may be diminished, the sole work performed being an equal augmentation of the same kind of actual energy in another substance.

Equilibrium of actual energy of a particular kind Q between substances A and B, takes place when the tendency of B to transfer this kind of energy to B is equal to the tendency of B to transfer the same kind of energy to A.

Laws respecting the equilibrium of particular kinds of actual energy have been ascertained by experiment, and in some cases anticipated by means of mechanical hypotheses, according to which all actual energy consists in the *vis viva* of motion.

The following law will now be proved, respecting the equilibrium of actual energy of all possible kinds :—

Theorem.—If equilibrium of actual energy of a given kind take place between a given pair of substances, possessing respectively quantities of actual energy of that kind in a given ratio, then that equilibrium will subsist for every pair of quantities of actual energy bearing to each other the same ratio.

Demonstration.—The tendency of one substance to transfer actual energy of the kind Q to another, must depend on some sort of effort, whose nature and laws may be known or unknown. Let Y_A be this effort for the substance A, Y_B the corresponding effort for the substance B.   Then a condition of equilibrium of actual energy is

$$Y_A = Y_B. \qquad . \qquad . \qquad . \qquad . \qquad (10.)$$

The effort Y may or may not be proportionate to the actual energy Q multiplied by a quantity independent of Q.

Case first.—If it is so proportional, let

$$Y = \frac{1}{K} Q,$$

K being independent of Q ; then the condition of equilibrium becomes

$$\frac{1}{K_A} Q_A = \frac{1}{K_B} Q_B,$$

or

$$\frac{Q_B}{Q_A} = \frac{K_B}{K_A},$$

a ratio independent of the absolute amounts of actual energy.

Case second.—If the effort Y is not simply proportional to the actual energy Q, the portion of it caused by that actual energy, according to the principle of Sect. XIII., deduced from the third axiom, is, for each substance,

$$Q \frac{d Y}{d Q},$$

and a second condition of equilibrium of actual energy is furnished by the equation

$$Q_A \frac{d Y}{d Q_A} = Q_B \frac{d Y_B}{d Q_B}. \qquad . \qquad . \qquad . \qquad (11.)$$

In order that this condition may be fulfilled simultaneously with the condition (10), it is necessary that

$$\frac{d Q_A}{Q_A} = \frac{d Q_B}{Q_B},$$

that is to say, that the ratio of the quantities of actual energy in the two substances should be independent of those quantities themselves ; a condition expressed, as before, by

$$\frac{Q_B}{Q_A} = \frac{K_B}{K_A}. \qquad . \qquad . \qquad . \qquad (11.)$$

Q.E.D.

This ratio is a quantity to be ascertained by experiment, and may be called the ratio of the SPECIFIC ACTUAL ENERGIES of the substances A and B, for the kind of energy under consideration.

The function

$$\frac{Q_A}{K_A} = \frac{Q_B}{K_B} = \theta, \qquad \cdot \qquad \cdot \qquad \cdot \qquad (12.)$$

whose identity for the two substances expresses the condition of equilibrium of the actual energy Q between them, may be called the "METABATIC FUNCTION" for that kind of energy.

In the science of thermo-dynamics, the metabatic function is *absolute temperature;* and the factor K is *real specific heat.* The theorem stated above, when applied to heat, amounts to this : *that the real specific heat of a substance is independent of its temperature.*

SECTION XVI.—USE OF THE METABATIC FUNCTION; TRANSFORMATION OF ENERGY IN AN AGGREGATE.

From the mutual proportionality of the actual energy Q, and the metabatic function θ, it follows that the operations

$$Q\frac{d}{d\,Q}, \;\; \theta\frac{d}{d\,\theta}$$

are equivalent; and that the latter may be substituted for the former in all the equations expressing the laws of the transformation of energy. We have therefore

$$Q\frac{d\,X}{d\,Q} = \theta\frac{d\,X}{d\,\theta} = \theta\frac{d^2\,W}{d\,\theta\,d\,x}, \qquad \cdot \qquad \cdot \qquad (13.)$$

for the effort to transform actual energy of the kind Q into work of the kind W, when expressed in terms of the metabatic function; and

$$d\,H = \theta\,d\frac{d\,W}{d\,\theta}, \qquad \cdot \qquad \cdot \qquad \cdot \qquad (14.)$$

for the limit of the indefinitely small transformation produced by an indefinitely small variation of the accidents on which the kind of work W depends.

There is also a form of *metamorphic function,*

$$\phi = \frac{d\,W}{d\,\theta} = \int\frac{d\,H}{\theta} = K\,F, \qquad \cdot \qquad \cdot \qquad (15.)$$

suited for employment along with the metabatic function, in order to find, by the integration

$$H = \int \theta \, d\phi, \qquad . \qquad . \qquad . \qquad . \quad (16.)$$

the quantity of actual energy of a given kind Q transformed to the kind of work W during any finite variation of accidents.

The advantage of the above expressions is, that they are applicable not merely to a homogeneous substance, but to any *heterogeneous substance or aggregate*, which is internally in a state of equilibrium of actual and potential energy; for throughout all the parts of an aggregate in that condition, the metabatic function θ is the same, and each of the efforts X, &c., is the same, and consequently the metamorphic function ϕ is the same.

" *Carnôt's function* " in thermo-dynamics is proportional to the reciprocal of the metabatic function of heat.

Section XVII.—Efficiency of Engines.

An engine is a contrivance for transforming energy, by means of the periodical repetition of a cycle of variations of the accidents of a substance.

The *efficiency* of an engine is the proportion which the energy permanently transformed to a useful form by it, bears to the whole energy communicated to the working substance.

In a *perfect engine* the cycle of variations is thus :—

I. The metabatic function is increased, say from θ_0 to θ_1.

II. The metamorphic function is increased by the amount $\Delta \phi$.

III. The metabatic function is diminished from θ_1 back to θ_0.

IV. The metamorphic function is diminished by the amount $\Delta \phi$.

During the second operation, the energy received by the working substance, and transformed from the actual to the potential form is $\theta_1 \Delta \phi$. During the fourth operation energy is transformed back, to the amount $\theta_0 \Delta \phi$. So that the energy permanently transformed during each cycle is $(\theta_1 - \theta_0) \Delta \phi$; and the efficiency of the engine $\dfrac{\theta_1 - \theta_0}{\theta_1}$.

Section XVIII.—Diffusion of Actual Energy; Irreversible or Frictional Operations.

There is a tendency in every substance, or system of substances, to the *equable diffusion* of actual energy; that is to say, to its transfer between the parts of the substance or system, until the value of the *metabatic function* becomes uniform.

This process is *not directly reversible;* that is to say, there is no such operation as a direct concentration of actual energy through a tendency of the metabatic function to become unequal in different parts of a substance or system.

Hence arises the impossibility of using the energy reconverted to the actual form at the lower limit of the metabatic function in an engine.

There is an analogy in respect of this property of *irreversibility*, between the diffusion of one kind of actual energy and certain irreversible transformations of one kind of actual energy to another, called by Professor William Thomson, "Frictional Phenomena"—viz., the production of heat by rubbing, and agitation, and by electric currents in a homogeneous substance at a uniform temperature.

In fact, a conjecture may be hazarded, that immediate diffusion of the actual energy produced in frictional phenomena, is the circumstance which renders them irreversible; for, suppose a small part of a substance to have its actual energy increased by the exertion of some kind of work upon it, then, if the increase of actual energy so produced be immediately diffused amongst other parts, so as to restore the uniformity of the metabatic function, the whole process will be irreversible. This speculation, however, is, for the present, partly hypothetical; and, therefore, does not, strictly speaking, form part of the science of energetics.

SECTION XIX.—MEASUREMENT OF TIME.

The general relations between energy and time must form an important branch of the science of energetics; but for the present, all that I am prepared to state on this subject is the following DEFINITION OF EQUAL TIMES :—

Equal times are the times in which equal quantities of the same kind of work are performed by equal and similar substances, under wholly similar circumstances.

SECTION XX.—CONCLUDING REMARKS.

It is to be observed, that the preceding articles are not the results of a new and hitherto untried speculation, but are the generalised expression of a method of reasoning which has already been applied with success to special branches of physics.

In this brief essay, it has not been attempted to do more than to give an outline of some of the more obvious principles of the science of energetics, or the abstract theory of physical phenomena in general; a science to which the maxim, true of all science, is specially applicable—that its subjects are boundless, and that they never can, by human labours, be exhausted, nor the science brought to perfection.

22

Studies in Energetics: II. Fundamentals of General Energetics

Wilhelm Ostwald

This article was translated expressly for this Benchmark volume by R. Bruce Lindsay, Brown University, from "Studien zur Energetik, II. Fundamenten der allgemeine Energetik," Sitzber. Sächs. Ges. Wiss., Math. Phys. Klasse, **44,** *211–237 (1892), with the permission of the publisher, Akademie-Verlag, GmbH, for the Sächisches Akademie der Wissenschaften*

1. First Fundamental Principle

The concepts that find application in all branches of science involving measurement are space, time, and energy. The significance of the first two has been accepted without question since the time of Kant. That energy deserves a place beside them follows from the fact that because of the laws of its transformation and its quantitative conservation it makes possible a measurable relation between all domains of natural phenomena. Its exclusive right to rank along with space and time is founded on the fact that, besides energy, no other general concept finds application in all domains of science.

Whereas we look upon time as unconditionally flowing and space as unconditionally at rest, we find energy appearing in both states. In the last analysis everything that happens is nothing but changes in energy.

Energy can decrease at one place and indeed disappear there, while it increases at another place. Experience shows that the decrease of energy at one place is always associated with an equal increase somewhere else. The expression of this experience forms the first fundamental principle of energetics, discovered about 50 years ago by J. R. Mayer. It says that the total amount of energy is constant. If energy disappears at one place, it must reappear at another place. It is not necessary, however, that it should reappear in the same form. We express the fact that another form of energy can appear in place of that which has disappeared by the word *transformation*. The first principle can then be phrased in the form: If a certain quantity of energy of form *A* is changed into another form *B*, and this in turn is transformed into form *C*, the same quantity of *C* will result as if *A* were transformed directly into *C*. If we call the energy quantities resulting from these transformations *equivalent*, the first principle takes the form: Two energy quantities that are equivalent to a third are equivalent to each other.

If, finally, a device by which work is done or energy is created without its decrease anywhere else is called a perpetual motion of the first kind, the content of the first principle can also be stated in the form: *A perpetual motion of the first kind is impossible*.

The analytic expression for these relations is very simple. If a is the quantity of energy of the form *A* (in appropriate units) while b is the quantity of energy of form *B* (again in appropriate units), which appears in its place, then we have

$$a = f(A, B)b,$$

which says that a and b are proportional to each other. The factor $f(A, B)$ depends on the relation of the two energy forms A and B to each other. It can be determined by any transformation investigation in which the quantities a and b are measured, so that

$$f(A, B) = \frac{a}{b}.$$

The transformation factor $f(B, C)$ is determined similarly; i.e.,

$$f(B, C) = \frac{b}{c}.$$

Hence there results

$$f(A, B) \cdot f(B, C) = \frac{a}{b} \cdot \frac{b}{c} = \frac{a}{c},$$

and hence

$$f(A, B) \cdot f(B, C) = f(A, C).$$

[*Ed. note:* The notation here is misleading. The implication is that the functional form of the proportionality factor is the same for all pairs of energy forms for which there is no a priori justification.]

It is obviously simplest to choose energy units so that all the factors $f(A, B)$, etc., are equal to unity, and in what follows, we shall assume that this is done. [*Ed. note:* It is not clear that this can be done for all forms of energy, at any rate without further elucidation.] Kinetic energy serves to provide a suitable reference unit. From the expression $E_k = \frac{1}{2} \cdot mv^2$, the unit of energy is therefore double the quantity of kinetic energy represented by 1 gram of mass with a velocity of 1 centimeter per second.

It is obvious that a quantity of energy can be transformed simultaneously into several different forms. If a is the original quantity of energy and b', b'', b''' are the quantities resulting from the transformation, we can resolve a into factors a_1, a_2, a_3, . . . , so that

$$a_1 = b', \qquad a_2 = b'', \qquad a_3 = b''', . . . ,$$

where

$$a = b' + b'' + b''' + \cdots .$$

In similar fashion, different energy forms A can be transformed into different energy forms B, so that

$$\sum a = \sum b$$

or

$$\sum a - \sum b = 0.$$

Here all energy is assumed to be positive. Thus energy that appears is positive, whereas that which disappears is negative.

2. Second Fundamental Principle

The first fundamental principle of energetics has as its purpose the expression of the fact that energy is an autonomous quantity in all its manifestations and that it is quantitatively invariant. It manifests itself through the transformations it undergoes from one form to another. The first principle leaves unanswered the question: What causes these transformations? The answer to this question is the content of the second fundamental principle of energetics.

Let us first concentrate our attention on the simplest case, i.e., when only one form of energy is present. The simplest possible transformation in this case is that involved when a certain amount of energy disappears at one place and an equal amount appears at another place. Experience teaches us that in certain cases such transfers take place, whereas in other circumstances they do not. To describe such situations, we shall ascribe to energy a definite property, which we shall call its intensity. The intensity stays the same when no transfer of energy takes place. A lower intensity will be ascribed to the energy at a place where the energy increases, and a higher intensity will be ascribed to the energy at a place where it decreases. If between two regions no energy transfer takes place, this will be said to be a case of energy equilibrium. We can then state the general principle: Two regions that are in energy equilibrium with respect to a third are in equilibrium with respect to each other. We can phrase this in terms of intensity as follows: Two intensities that are each equal to a third are equal to each other.

The very extensive experience on which this principle is grounded comes to mind most vividly if we assume that the principle is invalid. Let us, for example, take heat as the energy form in question. We bring a body A in contact with a body C and then bring C in contact with another body B, and wait until no more heat is transferred from A to C or from B to C. If then A and B were not in equilibrium with each other, if we brought A and B in contact, heat would pass from one to the other. Suppose then in this case that A loses heat and B gains it. But then the equilibrium between A and C, on the one hand, and B and C, on the other, would be disturbed. Heat would flow from C to A in order to replace the loss in the latter, and as well from B to C. Hence the equilibrium between A and B would again be disturbed and the whole flow process would repeat itself indefinitely.

If we call such a situation in which energy flows endlessly, even though the total amount is constant, a perpetual motion of the second kind, the content of the second fundamental principle becomes: *A perpetual motion of the second kind is impossible.*

These two fundamental principles govern all phenomena in the natural world.

341

The second principle has been stated in the first instance for only one kind of energy transfer, i.e., heat. It holds in appropriately changed form for the transformation of different forms of energy, but its general formulation demands further assumptions and the introduction of new concepts, which we now investigate.

3. Factors of Energy

The intensity of energy has been defined as a quantity that decreases at a place which is losing energy and increases at a place which is gaining energy. The transfer of energy can be interpreted in terms of a kind of intensity stepladder by which we can talk of higher, lower, or equal values. This intensity stepladder is unique for a given kind of energy. The scale on such a device is initially arbitrary, but will be so chosen that equal changes in energy correspond to equal steps on the ladder. This permits energy to be proportional to its intensity. Thus, if E denotes the energy and i the corresponding intensity, we have

$$E = ci,$$

where c is a proportionality coefficient. It is assumed that zero intensity corresponds to zero energy. We shall call c the capacity factor or, in short, the capacity of a system for energy. We can regard the factoring of the energy of a system into capacity and intensity factors as a general property of energy, which will be assumed for every kind of energy. The absolute values of energy are not in general available to our experience. The experimental values of the quantities in the equation $E = ci$ are therefore in general not measurable. Changes in energy, however, can be assumed measurable. Thus, from the above equation, we can write

$$dE = c\,di + i\,dc.$$

If we interpret this equation in the two cases

$$dE = c\,di \quad (c \text{ constant}),$$

$$dE = i\,dc \quad (i \text{ constant}),$$

we see the possibility of determining c and i through both kinds of simultaneous measurement of dc and di, respectively, and hence also the product or the total energy E. There are, however, cases in which the simultaneous measurement in question is not possible. We then have to give up the possibility of determining E or the two factors c and i.

4. Forms of Energy

It is not our purpose to present a complete listing of all forms of energy. The accompanying table is included primarily to provide examples for our later discussion. A more systematic table would have to await a more thorough treatment of the characteristic differences of different forms of energy and their factors.

Of all the kinds of energy, the mechanical variety deserves particular mention; for its determination only the unit of energy itself is needed, plus those of space and time. Mechanical energy falls into two categories: kinetic or energy of motion, on the one hand, and space energy, on the other. The last named is divided into distance, surface, and volume energy forms. Mechanical energy and its factors are therefore as shown in A and B of Table 1.

Table 1

Energy form	Capacity	Intensity
A. Energy of motion	Mass; momentum	Square of velocity, velocity
B. Space energy		
a. Distance energy	Distance	Force
b. Surface energy	Surface	Surface tension
c. Volume energy	Volume	Pressure
C. Heat energy	Heat capacity or entropy	Temperature
D. Electrical energy	Quantity of electricity	Potential
E. Magnetic energy	Quantity of magnetism	Magnetic potential
F. Chemical energy	Combining weight	Chemical potential or affinity
G. Radiant energy	Quantity of absorption or emission	Intensity of radiation

The following comments refer to the table:

C. The term "heat capacity" refers to the case in which transfer of heat energy leads to temperature change. If there is no change in temperature, the entropy serves as the capacity factor.

F. The capacity factor for chemical energy is proportional to mass and weight (as in the case of heat energy). From the term "combining weight," it should be clearly understood that the capacity in this case is not actually a weight. It is no more a weight than it is a mass. It is indeed proportional to these, and the proportionality factor is dependent on the nature of the material. It must be realized that for none of the capacity factors in the table is it possible to assign "dimensions" in terms of the usual units of space, time, and mass. Any assumption to the contrary leads to error.

The resolution of chemical energy into factors is due to Willard Gibbs. Chemical energy intensity is usually referred to as affinity, but goes much further than this term implies.

Kinetic (or motional) energy, $\frac{1}{2}Mv^2$, can be resolved into factors in two ways. The most important factoring is into mass and half the square of the velocity. A second type of resolution is into momentum (Mv) and one half the velocity ($v/2$), which is applicable under certain circumstances, but suffers the drawback that the two factors are not independent of each other.

Space energy must be divided into three separate parts as shown. [*Ed. note:* Actually, there seems to be no need for this, and it only adds to the complication of

Ostwald's scheme.] That distance energy has been taken to be the only form of energy in mechanics is one of the most serious oversights in the development of science. Hence there developed the need to express all other forms of energy in terms of this alone. [*Ed. note:* Ostwald here betrays an astonishing ignorance of mechanics. His "three" forms of "space" energy are all included in the space integral of the scalar product of force and displacement vectors.]

Additional forms of energy are presented in C–G of Table 1.

G. Radiation energy has a very special place among the kinds of energy, for this energy is not tied to matter. We shall later investigate the nature of matter and will see that it necessitates the existence of certain relations connecting the factors of the different forms of energy. However, it will turn out that radiant energy is that form which is not subject to such relations.

The capacity factor of radiant energy is here called an emission quantity. It is the product of the area of the radiating surface and what may be called the emission coefficient. The intensity factor of radiant energy is that quantity which is the same for two objects between which no radiant energy exchange takes place. If two bodies are individually in radiation equilibrium with respect to a third, they are in equilibrium with respect to each other. This is the basis of Kirchhoff's law of radiation. It follows at once from the second principle of energetics. [*Ed. note:* The definition is inadequate, as it provides no quantitative expression from which the intensity in question may be calculated. This inadequacy is partially rectified in the following paragraph.]

In general the intensity factor for radiant energy is a unique function of the temperature. Yet there are cases in which other energy forms than heat take part in radiation, when very different factors of radiant energy exist at the same temperature. [*Ed. note:* The author seems to be thinking of electromagnetic radiation.]

Radiant energy is often referred to as radiant heat. This is a mistaken designation. It rests on the fact that warm bodies do give rise to radiant energy. But radiant energy can exist in other forms, e.g., electrical and chemical energy, in which no heat is involved. It is true that radiant energy is easily transformed ultimately into heat, although not exclusively so. In any case, these two forms of energy follow quite different laws. It is part of the nature of radiant energy that it possesses a periodic character (for the most part of very short period).

5. Evaluation of Energy Factors

Of the factors of energy, the intensity is the easier to determine, since it is the factor on which depends all rest or motion of energy, i.e., effectively of everything that happens. From the standpoint of experience, we are therefore concerned with this quantity even before we consider the form of energy that is involved.

Suppose that we have a system which, within certain limits, can contain an arbitrary amount of energy of a certain kind, in which the quantity present is associated with a measurable phenomenon in such a way that we can readily recognize it. We then have at our disposal a measuring instrument for the intensity. For the amount of energy that is contained in this instrument, which is brought into energy exchange or equilibrium with some other system, is completely determined by the value of the intensity that prevails in this instrument.

Such an instrument permits us to recognize the existence of intensity quantities, as well as to distinguish larger and smaller values of intensity from each other. At first the instrument is unable to indicate equal intervals of intensity or the zero point of an intensity scale. It is merely able to associate an intensity value with each position read on it.

With the help of such an intensity measuring device we can also determine capacity values numerically. Suppose that we read on the scale of the instrument two intensity values, say i_1 and i_2, where $i_1 > i_2$. Bring the instrument in contact with the system whose capacity is desired so that energy flow can take place. If then ΔE is the quantity of energy that flows from intensity i_1 to i_2, we have

$$\Delta E = c(i_1 - i_2)$$

or

$$c = \frac{\Delta E}{i_1 - i_2}$$

By repetition of this process we can measure the capacities of different systems and get values

$$c', c'', c''' \ldots,$$

and hence set up a capacity scale. Suppose that we choose two capacities c' and c'' such that

$$\frac{\Delta E}{i_1 - i_2} = c',$$

$$\frac{\Delta E''}{i_1 - i_2} = c''.$$

Suppose now that we take a second system such that the initial intensity corresponding to the same energy flow ΔE has changed to i''. We then have

$$\frac{\Delta E}{i_1 - i_2} = c' \quad \frac{\Delta E}{i_1'' - i_2} = c'',$$

or

$$\frac{c'}{c''} = \frac{i_1'' - i_2}{i_1 - i_2} = \frac{\Delta i''}{\Delta i'}.$$

This shows that the intensity differences are in inverse ratio to the capacities. If, for example, we choose the latter so that

$$\frac{c'}{c''} = \frac{1}{2}$$

the series i_2, i''_1, i_1 will represent an equidistant intensity scale.

By application of the equations

$$i = \frac{dE}{dc} \quad (i \text{ constant}),$$

$$c = \frac{dE}{di} \quad (c \text{ constant}),$$

we can determine the absolute values of i and c and the initial points on each scale.

This general procedure holds only under the assumption that arbitrary variations of intensity and capacity are possible. However, the physical possibility of carrying out the indicated procedures is not available for all kinds of energy. There are certain forms of energy for which a change in capacity or a change in intensity is not possible. There is also the possibility that both will change simultaneously in a definite fashion. In this last case the energy is a function of one variable only.

In the case in which the change in energy can produce no change in capacity (or in which the capacity is a definitely constant quantity), we have

$$dE = c \, di,$$

and the scale of intensity is simply proportional to the quantity of energy. But the initial or zero point cannot be determined, since we obviously cannot now use the equation

$$i = \frac{dE}{dc}$$

since c does not change. An example of energy of this sort is *vis viva* or motional (kinetic) energy. Here the capacity is the mass, which cannot change. Hence the equation immediately above is not applicable. For this reason it is not possible to fix the intensity factor $v^2/2$ absolutely. We can only measure changes in it.

If i is not variable, we have the similar situation in which it is impossible to fix c absolutely. We can then only measure changes in c. A case of this sort is provided by gravitational energy; if we neglect the change of weight with height, we then have the equation

$$E = gh,$$

where g is the weight [*Ed. note:* the author is evidently talking about unit mass] and h is the height. Hence the only experimentally usable equation is

$$dE = g \, dh,$$

from which the value of g and the scale of h can follow, but not the absolute value of the height. Here, of course, the choice of a zero height is not important.

In the final case in which energy depends on only one variable, the above procedure for determining the factors becomes impossible; for then the intensity and capacity factors depend on each other, and we are unable to carry through a procedure in which one varies and the other stays constant. In this case one is forced to choose both quantities arbitrarily, trying to make the choice to meet one's purpose. It often happens that one or the other is the only really important variable in the problem.

In this case the analysis works out so that the energy depends on a single variable r, so

$$E = \phi(r, a),$$

where a is a constant. Then

$$dE = \frac{d\phi}{dr}\,dr.$$

If r can be considered in the light of a capacity factor, then the derivative can be thought of as the intensity factor, and conversely. A classical example of this case is gravitational energy. Newton showed that the motions of the heavenly bodies can be explained if we assume that a force exists between them which is proportional to the product of constants specific to the bodies concerned, and inversely proportional to the square of the distance between them. From our point of view this means that gravitational energy is a distance energy whose change with distance follows the law in question. If we call a_1 and a_2 the constants associated with the two bodies, respectively, and take r as the distance between them, then

$$\frac{d\phi(a_1, a_2, r)}{dr} = \frac{a_1 a_2}{r^2},$$

so that

$$E = \phi(a_1, a_2, r) = C - \frac{a_1 a_2}{r}$$

becomes the gravitational energy. C is a constant of integration, which cannot be determined from this equation alone.

6. Mutual Relations of the Energy Factors

The different forms of energy that are known to us are related to each other in a fashion exemplified by the fact that the factors of a given form of energy may not change without changes taking place in other energy forms. Thus the various energy factors are functionally related.

Of such relations, proportionality occurs most frequently. In particular, the capacity factor of the kinetic energy, i.e., the mass, is proportional to many others.

Through this circumstance it has come about that people have attributed a very general significance to mass, although it really belongs only to the domain of kinetic energy. In a quite mistaken way these people have chosen to treat mass as the third fundamental unit in the determination of the dimensions of physical quantities.

Since the energy factors proportional to each other, like mass, weight, volume, heat capacity, and capacity for chemical energy, all appear to be spatially related, it has become customary to assume that they are all associated with an energy carrier, to which the name *matter* has been assigned. Actually, we learn nothing about matter save through the energy quantities mentioned. After we have noticed that all these quantities always appear spatially separated, the content of a hypothetical carrier of energy, which is in itself somehow different from energy, becomes exhausted. It appears superfluous to set up a specialized hypothesis for a simple fact. We must also not fail to recognize that this hypothesis has had a restrictive influence on the development of a clear understanding of the nature of energy.

Matter is therefore nothing but a spatially distinguishable composite sum of energy quantities. We are accustomed to call fundamental properties of matter those factors of these energies which are proportional to each other and to the mass. In this we give preference to the mechanical properties: mass, weight, and impenetrability (volume), although, for example, the ability to undergo chemical change is associated with "matter" no less than the other properties. The other energy factors, which are not necessarily proportional, such as velocity, temperature and electrical potential, etc., we have become accustomed to call "states" of matter. When in what follows we wish to use with exactness the terms "matter," "material object," or just plain "object," it will be understood we are foregoing any hypothesis of a "carrier," and merely mean by these terms the existence of spatial and functional collections of energy collections.

In addition to these constant relations of energy factors, there exist arbitrary devices that can bring about (artificially) such connections. They are called machines. The "elementary powers" of the older machines, like the lever, pulley, inclined plane, etc., represent simple cases of such relations between energy factors. So also are the piston and cylinder of a steam engine, as well as the armature and magnet of a dynamo. The special feature of the relations in such cases is that within limits we can make the proportionality factors connecting the energy factor take on whatever values we like.

The great significance of these necessary mutual relations of energy factors lies in the fact that they are the necessary conditions for and indeed the causes of the mutual transformation of the various kinds of energy into each other. For if one changes the quantity of energy of any particular form, and hence the relevant corresponding energy factors, there is a corresponding simultaneous change in other factors; therefore, the necessity exists for the energy corresponding to the latter to also change. The first fundamental principle of energetics specifies that the total change of energy in such a process must be zero.

7. Condition of Energy Equilibrium

The condition for the equilibrium of a system with one kind of energy is that the intensity of the energy shall be the same everywhere. From this it follows that a finite system cannot possibly satisfy the condition. For at the boundaries of such a system where it joins others having energy of the same or different kind, it will in general encounter a different intensity of energy.

Since there actually exist finite systems with energy at rest, it must be possible to render differences in an energy form *A* ineffective or to compensate for them somehow. Such a compensation can follow from the joining of the energy factors, as discussed in the previous section. Suppose that at the phase at which energy *A* suffers a change, along with the corresponding intensity factor, another energy factor of energy *B* is joined to the first in such a way that it must suffer a corresponding change; then a change in energy *A* necessitates a change in energy *B*. If this is so arranged that energy *A* decreases and energy *B* increases by the same amount, the system is in equilibrium.

The demonstration of this important theorem follows from the understanding of what would happen if it were not true while the equality in question existed. We readily see that once such an energy exchange takes place the decrease in energy must be greater than that produced, since otherwise a creation of energy would have to take place, whereas here only the excess of the disappearing energy remains available for further transformation. Let us suppose that the condition equations for the system are such that the two energies are very close to equality, so that the quantity of energy which disappears from *A* is slightly greater than that which originates in *B*. Then *A* would have to be transformed into *B*. With a very slight difference in equality in the other direction, *B* would have to be transformed into *A*. This leads to the establishment of equilibrium.

The equation for the equilibrium of two energies *A* and *B* that are in contact may therefore be written (if it is assumed that increasing energy and decreasing energy have opposite signs) as

$$\Delta A + \Delta B = 0.$$

The two increments Δ are not arbitrary. Actually, we have

$$F_A = K \, \Delta F_B,$$

where F_A and F_B are factors of the energies *A* and *B*, respectively, and *K* is a coefficient governing the transformation of *A* and *B* in the particular system.

In the application of this law it is essential that the assumptions be kept in mind. These are the coexistence of two energy regions and the existence of a "machine" equation, which is independent of the first principle itself. For the first principle demands that under all circumstances the originating and disappearing energy quantities must be equal, whereas the equilibrium theory demands this equality for the kinds of energy related by the machine equation. If the latter condition is not fulfilled, a motion will ensue in which the first principle is satisfied but for which the quantity of disappearing energy is greater than that which is being developed; i.e., $\Delta A > \Delta B$. In this case the excess must be made up by the appearance of a third kind of energy, say of amount ΔC. In purely mechanical systems this would still take the form of mechanical energy, but in general systems it might have the form of heat.

It is easy to extend these considerations to the case of a whole group of energy varieties, which are related to each other through machine equations. Here the sum of all energy changes must vanish; i.e.,

$$\sum \Delta E = 0.$$

This equation holds not only when all the forms of energy are related by machine equations, but requires no more than that each form of energy shall stand in a definite relation with at least one other form. For to each individual energy exchange we have equations of the form

$$\sum_1 \Delta E = 0$$

$$\sum_2 \Delta E = 0, \quad \text{etc.}$$

with the total sum

$$\sum \Delta E = 0.$$

In applications one constantly uses the individual equations. $\sum_n \Delta E = 0$, leaving out those energy quantities which stay constant during the process in question.

In using the equation $\sum \Delta E = 0$, one must necessarily resolve the different energies into their factors, so that we can carry out the elimination of those energy factors which are related through the machine equation. Other equations then result, connecting the other energy factors, which are to be looked upon as the result of the calculation.

8. Generalized Intensity Law

The machine equations through which different forms of energy are made dependent on each other through their changes involve only capacity factors as experience teaches us.[1] Accordingly, the machine equation has the general form

$$c_1 = Kc_2,$$

and in the virtual motions of the machine the changes in energy will be expressed in the form $c\,di$. Therefore, from the equation for two energies in equilibrium, $\Delta E_1 + \Delta E_2 = 0$, we get

$$c_1\,di_1 + c_2\,di_2 = 0,$$

or

---

[1] This statement must be taken with some reservation. I have so far found no exceptions, but my investigations have not yet gone far enough to provide complete assurance on this point.

$$\frac{c_1}{c_2} di_1 + di_2 = 0.$$

From the machine equation above this becomes

$$\frac{c_1}{c_2} = K,$$

from which there results

$$K\,di_1 + di_2 = 0 \quad \text{or} \quad K\,di_1 = -di_2.$$

Hence equilibrium exists between two energies if the intensity of the one is equal and opposite in sign to the reduced intensity of the other. [*Ed. note:* This statement is strictly speaking incorrect. The relation in question is between *changes* in intensity.] By reduced intensity we mean here the intensity multiplied by the machine factor K.

We note the evident analogy between this theorem and that stated earlier for a single kind of energy, i.e., in a state of rest the intensity must be everywhere the same.

The equilibrium condition in this form is useful in many cases, for in every case in which a given form of energy shows a change in intensity it leads necessarily to the result that there must exist some other form of energy related to the first through a machine equation. If, as is very often the case, the machine equation is known, at once the sign and magnitude of the intensity change in the second energy form are given.

9. Heat

As a result of the freedom with which heat can be communicated to and extracted from systems, it is possible to apply experimentally both equations in Section 5 and hence to find numerical values for the capacity and intensity.

In the first place, it is well known that for the so-called permanent (ideal) gases, especially hydrogen, the heat capacity at constant volume (i.e., without external work) is independent of the temperature; i.e., the heat contained in the gas is proportional to the temperature as measured by the gas thermometer. [*Ed. note:* This statement is true only for room temperature and above. The dependence of heat capacity on temperature, now well known, had not been observed at the time when Ostwald was writing. Work in cryogenics by people like Dewar and Kamerlingh Onnes was just getting underway in the early 1890s.] If we call the latter t, we get for the ideal gas over wide ranges

$$\frac{dQ}{dT} = c \quad \text{(a constant)}.$$

Here the increment dt as measured on the gas thermometer is set equal to the increment dT on the absolute thermometric scale. That is, we set

$$dt = dT$$

or

$$T = t + k$$

where k is the constant of integration, whose value is at first unknown. [*Ed. note:* The author takes dQ as the quantity of heat communicated or extracted corresponding to the change in temperature dT.]

To find the initial fixed point on the absolute scale T, we utilize the property of an ideal gas that its total energy content is constant at constant temperature; i.e., it is not dependent on its volume. This emerges from the well-known researches of Gay-Lussac and Joule according to which a compressed gas that is allowed to stream out into a vacuum neither gains nor loses heat [*Ed. note:* These statements have to be greatly modified in the light of the existence of the Joule–Thomson effect and of modern quantum statistical mechanics.]

When the gas expands at constant temperature from volume v_0 to volume v, the volume energy decreases by the amount

$$\int_{v_0}^{v} p \, dv.$$

If we replace the pressure p from its gas equation in the form

$$p = \frac{R(273 + t)}{v},$$

we get for the decrease in the volume energy

$$R(273 + t) \ln \frac{v}{v_0}.$$

In order for the total energy to remain constant, the heat energy must increase by the same amount. If we call U the total energy and Q remains the heat energy, we have

$$Q = U + R(273 + t) \ln \frac{v}{v_0} + C,$$

where C is the integration constant determined by v_0. It can still be a function of the temperature. We can think of it as combined with U, which is a function of temperature alone, and write

$$Q = U_1 + R(273 + t) \ln \frac{v}{v_0}.$$

[*Ed. note:* The preceding statements constitute one of the weakest aspects of energetics in the eyes of Planck and Boltzmann, its severe critics; Ostwald fails to make a distinction between what in thermodynamics is called a *state* function, i.e., a quantity which depends only on the state of a system and not at all on how it got into that state, and a quantity like the work $\int p \, dv$, which depends on the path taken between states by the system. The concept of volume energy, whose change is measured by work done, is in direct contradiction to the principles of thermodynamics. However, we proceed with Ostwald's presentation.]

To work with the equation

$$\frac{dQ}{dc} = T \quad (T \text{ constant}),$$

we differentiate Q with respect to v at constant t and obtain

$$dQ = \frac{R(273 + t) \, dv}{v}.$$

On the other hand, since

$$\frac{dQ}{dt} = \frac{dQ}{dT} = c \quad (c \text{ constant}),$$

it follows that

$$\frac{dQ}{dT} = U_1 + R \ln \frac{v}{v_0} = c,$$

and from this

$$dc = R \frac{dv}{v} \quad (T \text{ constant}),$$

from which by division we obtain

$$\frac{dQ}{dc} = T = 273 + t.$$

This means that the Celsius temperature t decreased by 273 is the temperature on the absolute scale.

According to definition, the heat capacity c is given by

$$c = \frac{dQ}{dT},$$

and

$$dc = \frac{dQ}{T}.$$

Here dc has two designations: (1) the change in heat capacity, and (2) the change in entropy. The first holds for variable temperature, whereas the second holds for constant temperature. Other things being equal, both quantities are proportional to the mass or weight of the system. [*Ed. note:* Here again the author falls afoul of standard thermodynamics, in which dQ/T measures the change in entropy only for a reversible process, concerning which Ostwald has nothing to say here.]

To demonstrate the application of these considerations, we first determine the relation which must hold in order that energy equilibrium shall exist in the transformation of liquid into vapor. The two kinds of energy in question are heat energy and volume energy. Their capacity quantities are proportional to each other, since both are proportional to the quantity of substance in question. These quantities appear as entropy and volume energy. For equilibrium, we must therefore have

$$S \, dT = v \, dp$$

or, if we set for the entropy S its value ρ/T, where ρ is the latent heat of vaporization, we get

$$\rho \frac{dT}{T} = v \, dp$$

or

$$\frac{dp}{dT} = \frac{\rho}{vt}.$$

[*Ed. note:* There is carelessness here. Clearly t in the denominator on the right side should be T.] This is the well-known vapor pressure relation.

As a second illustration, let us take a galvanic element and find the condition for equilibrium between heat and electrical energy. We have

$$S \, dT = e \, dp,$$

where e is the quantity of electricity and p is the electrical potential. The entropy S is proportional to the quantity of electricity, for we have

$$S = \frac{w}{T},$$

where w is the heat taken up by the galvanic element (galvanic minus chemical heat), which in turn is proportional to the quantity of electricity that passes through. By substituting w/T for S, we find

$$\frac{w}{T} \, dT = e \, dp$$

or

$$\frac{dp}{dT} = \frac{w}{eT},$$

which is the Gibbs–Helmholtz formula. [*Ed. note:* This oversimplified procedure is scarcely a cogent derivation, since it is based on tacit assumptions, which may not always hold.]

As a third example, we seek for the equilibrium condition between heat and surface energy. If w is now the surface area and γ is the surface tension, we have

$$S\, dt = w\, d\gamma$$

or

$$\frac{I}{T}\, dt = w\, d\gamma,$$

whence

$$I = wT\frac{d\gamma}{dT},$$

where I is the latent heat of surface expansion per unit area, given in terms of the temperature coefficient of the surface tension.

10. Movable Energy

Let us imagine a system containing several different kinds of energy, $A, B, C, \ldots$, all in equilibrium. If energy in the form A is now introduced into the system, the equilibrium will be disturbed. The associated intensity quantity will become greater, and there will take place a transformation of some energy of form A into energy of form B with which it had formally been in equilibrium; i.e., the intensity increase in A will be compensated by an intensity change in B.

If the system can be so arranged that in the transformation certain parts do not suffer permanent change but return to their initial state, so that we have a cyclic process, then the device becomes a machine [*Ed. note:* he means an *engine*] for the transformation of energy from form A to form B. When we concentrate attention on the state to which the system completely returns, the energy contributed equals that transformed, so that no net energy is left in the machine [engine].

In order for such a process to be possible, the intensity of the energy of form A contributed to the system must be greater than the intensity of the energy of form A already in the system. Otherwise, the transfer of energy to the system would not be possible. The intensity difference can be arbitrarily small, however, and can be zero in the limit.

The energy of form B that is produced has a larger intensity than it had initially when it was in equilibrium with A. It will, therefore, be completely transformed back into A if the intensity of form A is kept continuously at its initial height. Similarly, If a part of energy of form B stands in equilibrium with a third energy form C, the newly produced energy B will be completely transformed into C and then in turn to a fourth form D, or back to the original A, but always without change in the total amount of energy in the system.

No matter what transformations one may bring about, that energy quantity which was originally brought into the system in equilibrium will remain available for subsequent transformation.

Now, however, in any system not in equilibrium we can separate out the maximum part of the various forms of energy that stand in equilibrium with each other and look upon the remainder as the "contributed" energy. If we call the latter the *movable* energy, the preceding considerations can be summarized in the form of the following theorem: *In an isolated system the quantity of movable energy is constant.*

A good example of this theorem is the motion of a planet around the sun. If the kinetic energy and the distance energy [potential energy in modern terminology] are exactly in equilibrium, the planet revolves around the sun in a circular pattern (really around the common center of gravity). Both energies remain constant and the movable energy is zero. If this condition is not fulfilled, the path becomes an ellipse, and at the same time a part of the energy becomes movable insofar as it periodically appears first as distance energy and then as kinetic energy. The distance energy can never be smaller than that which corresponds to perihelion and never greater than that which corresponds to aphelion. The distance energy oscillates back and forth between these two limits. The value of the kinetic energy oscillates between the same limits in such a way that the sum of the two energies is always constant. This difference between the maximum value of the distance energy and the minimum value of the kinetic energy is the movable energy.

11. Dissipation of Energy

The considerations of the previous sections have been developed under the assumption that the different forms of energy are initially in equilibrium. This assumption demands that the energy forms be related to each other by corresponding relations or "machine" equations, so that no form can change without the others changing in association with it.

Although energy in general shows itself to be in agreement with this condition, there is a form for which the assumption does not hold; this is *radiant energy*. In this form the energy is not subject to any "machine" equation. Radiant energy therefore follows the law of the compensation of its intensity differences.

The above statement means that radiant energy is not tied to matter. For by matter we understand nothing else than the presence of spatially connected and initially interdependent different forms of energy. As soon as energy leaves matter, it is free from its relation to other forms of energy and follows without restriction the general intensity law.

It follows from this that the theorem stated in the previous section on the conservation of movable energy is not a general one, but holds only as long as radiation energy is not involved, e.g., in the case of cosmic motions. In all cases in which transformation takes place from other energy forms to radiation energy, a part of the movable energy goes over into something in equilibrium with another form of energy and hence is no longer transformable. The quantity of this unusable energy is dependent on the intensity difference of the radiation energy and the time during which the difference exists.

Radiation energy originates most easily from heat, since every temperature difference causes a difference in the intensity factor of the radiation energy, and thereby produces an equilibrium of the same. Hence it has come about that we ascribe to the free equilibration of heat the chief characteristic of radiant energy. Nevertheless, one soon convinces oneself that there are many phenomena in which heat appears through finite temperature differences without (at least in the ideal limit) having the amount of movable energy decreased. As examples we have the elastic oscillations of solid, liquid, and gaseous bodies, if only they take place sufficiently rapidly.

The same effect that is brought about by the transformation of heat into radiant energy and conversely, i.e., the equilibration of energy differences, is also exhibited by the phenomenon of heat conduction. According to the view of Fourier, it is most convenient to think of this as taking place in a series of transformations of radiant energy and heat, which take place between the smallest particles of the conducting medium. This viewpoint is supported by the comparative slowness of heat conduction, since owing to the smallness of the particles concerned there must be an enormous number of such transformations before the energy can cover measurable stretches of the conduction medium.

The considerations pointed out here show that the content of the second fundamental principle of energetics along with the phenomena which are designated as degradation and dissipation of energy, increase in entropy, the predominance of uncompensated transformations, etc., and which because of their importance have attracted the attention of many investigators, actually are all closely connected with each other. The corresponding formula of Clausius, i.e., $\int (dQ/t) \geqslant 0$, has up to now had a scientific application only in the limiting case in which the equality sign holds, i.e., in which heat appears as energy compensatable by other forms of energy. It has been shown in Section 9 that in several cases the relations previously derived for handling reversible processes, or the application of the minimum condition for the thermodynamical potential or energy function, emerge in the same form from the simple equilibrium condition for the energies in question, and are everywhere referable to the impossibility of a perpetual motion of the second kind. The latter, however, demands the mutual interdependence of the energies in question, i.e., the existence of a "machine" condition, which does not exist for radiant energy.

The significance of the phenomenon of the dissipation of energy lies in the fact that because of it there is a definite decrease in movable energy in most natural processes. It is noteworthy that radiant energy, on whose properties dissipation phenomena rest, is at the same time that through which a replacement is provided continuously by the sun on the surface of the earth for the unavoidable loss of movable energy.

357

23

Attack on the New Energetics

Max Planck

*This article was translated expressly for this Benchmark volume by R. Bruce Lindsay, Brown University, from "Gegen die neuere Energetik," Ann. Phys., **57**, 72–78 (1896), with the permission of the publisher, Johann Ambrosius Barth, Leipzig*

Soon after the discovery of the mechanical equivalent of heat by R. Mayer and J. P. Joule, the English physicist [*Ed. note:* he should say Scottish engineer] W. J. M., Rankine published in the year 1853 a paper "On the General Law of the Transformation of Energy" in which, by the subdivision of energy in different forms and the separation of special forms of energy into two factors, he attempted to generalize Carnot's principle into a general law, which would embrace all natural phenomena. He followed this with other papers on the same theme. But neither he nor any other physicist succeeded in obtaining significant results with this method, so that it attracted no general attention and finally apparently was forgotten. For a long time this line of thought, called energetics by Rankine, remained dormant. In the meantime, Clausius discovered his second principle of the mechanical theory of heat and developed his concept of entropy, and then there began a long series of fruitful applications of this principle by Clausius himself, as well as by Lord Kelvin, Gibbs, Helmholtz and others. These applications, which have thrown new light in the most varied domains of physics and chemistry on the mutual interdependence of phenomena, have been without exception confirmed by experience.

Now, after through a series of outstanding investigations the firmest possible foundation has been laid for the extension of thermodynamics, energetics has been revived, independently of Rankine but essentially embodying the same ideas, with the aim of considering the principles of thermodynamics from a modified and more universal standpoint and deriving them so simply that one should be able to write down their content with scarcely any effort. Moreover, it is claimed that the new method cannot only handle the standard results of thermodynamics in the various fields of physics, but can solve other problems that standard thermodynamics is unable to handle. In fact, even more recently the adherents of the new method have attacked the mechanical view of nature, which has yielded to science some of its greatest successes.

In this place I do not intend to enter the lists in behalf of the mechanical theory of nature. For this, very profound and rather difficult investigations are called for. Here we shall consider much more elementary things, in particular the mathematical justification of the new energetics. For the examination of this preliminary question has convinced every competent worker in the field that the new energetics lacks a firm foundation and that its simple proofs, precisely in the cases in which proofs should be most important, are really sham proofs, so that it does not come anywhere near to the problems at issue, to say nothing of providing means of solving them.

In justification of this statement it will suffice to present a critique of one of the most characteristic concepts of energetics, *volume energy*. The adherents of energetics in their writings speak so often of volume energy that many physicists and chemists have become so accustomed to this name that they do not bother to investigate a test of the origin of the concept. But such a test shows at once, to put it bluntly, that volume energy represents a mathematical nonentity, that it is a quantity which in reality does not exist. For we must demand of a physical quantity, and especially one which is an energy quantity of fundamental significance in energetics, that it shall be definitely determined by the chemical and physical state of the system in question, in the sense that if the system through any arbitrary changes returns to the original state, the energy quantity must also return to its original value. If this is not the case, the energy principle loses its meaning completely.

Let us now ask, for example, about the volume energy of any arbitrary gas with given mass, temperature, and density.

The adherent of energetics answers that the volume energy is $\int p\,dv$, in which p is the pressure and v the volume. In the theory of energetics this integral represents the change in the volume energy that takes place when the gas undergoes a change of state. And its value is determined by the change in state. If we now carry the gas through a succession of state changes, e.g., through a Carnot cycle, and bring it back to its original state, the volume energy should return to its original value and the change in it should be zero. But it is well known that this in general is not the case with the integral in question, but in general in such a cyclic process the gas will do a certain amount of positive or negative work. This shows that it makes no sense to talk of volume energy as a genuine physical quantity with which one can make calculations.

There is no validity to the objection that in energetics it is not a question of the absolute value of the volume energy but only differences in it. For the difference in the volume energy for two different states must be a definitely determined one, and must not depend on the path taken between the two states, as the integral in question quite definitely does.

Clausius considered this circumstance so important that in his *Gesammelte Abhandlungen über mechanische Wärmetheorie* he

provided a mathematical introduction, "On the Treatment of Differential Equations Which Are Not Integrable in the Usual Sense." In
his preface he emphasized this matter with the following words:

> A further difficulty which I have often realized has affected adversely
> the use of my book has been the difficulty it presented of under-
> standing things right. The mechanical theory of heat has introduced
> new ideas into science which deviate from earlier views, and they
> have therefore demanded special mathematical considerations. In
> particular one must mention a certain kind of differential equa-
> tion, which I have applied in my investigations and which in certain
> essential points is different from the customary variety. If the
> difference is not realized certain misunderstandings will arise. The
> meaning and methods of operating with these equations were
> indeed long ago established by Monge, but they do not appear
> to be well enough known today, for an incorrect interpretation of
> these equations led to an attack on my theory.

The content of Clausius's introduction discusses precisely the method of handling differential forms that like *pdv* are not in general integrable and therefore cannot be considered the perfect differentials
of quantitites which may be considered *state* variables.

In the second edition of his book (1876), Clausius has also emphasized this point (paragraph 3 of the mathematical introduction), without unfortunately having secured the necessary attention, as is evident.

To the foregoing difficulties, which have led to the lack of validity
of one of the principal concepts of energetics, one can add a further
series with the same result. However, I can refrain here from a discussion of these points, since I shortly plan to discuss the concepts
and results of thermodynamics in a detailed presentation [*Ed. note:*
this refers to Planck's text on thermodynamics, first published in 1897
with numerous following editions].

On the other hand, it cannot be denied that energetics by reason
of its relation to the principle of the conservation of energy contains
a sound kernel of value within it. This explains the special attraction
that the whole idea of energetics has had for many scientists. However, it is not difficult for one accustomed to such investigations to
see that, when energetics is freed from its contemporary blossoming,
its applicability is limited to a domain of extremely modest extent as
compared with the elaborate claims that are currently made for it.
Indeed, it must be considered a cruel dispensation of fate that this
domain of application is precisely that which energetics would prefer
to disregard as a very special case, not deserving much consideration,
i.e., mechanics. At any rate, this is the case insofar as one can neglect
friction, the imperfections of elasticity, and related phenomena. It
can also handle electrodynamics including magnetism insofar as one
can neglect Joule heat and magnetic hysteresis. It can also apply to
optics insofar as one disregards absorption and dispersion of light. In
short, it applies to all those phenomena taking place in finite time
that possess the property of reversibility, and which therefore repre-

sent only ideal abstractions of the processes taking place in reality. Here a *correct* theory of energetics could provide a suitable picture of natural phenomena. Here the law of the decomposability of energy forms into capacity and intensity factors and its associated consequences possess validity, and on this basis all the examples are brought together through which energetics achieves closer understanding. Actually, it can hardly offer anything new in this domain, since it is precisely here that science has a method for handling all questions concerning the measurable course of phenomena and answering them much more completely than the theory of energetics can hope to do: this is Hamilton's principle of least action. [*Ed. note:* here Planck follows a common misunderstnding. Actually, two principles are involved. The first is the principle of least action of Maupertuis, put into logical, mathematical form by Lagrange, and the second is Hamilton's principle proper. They are closely related, but operate under different boundary conditions and cannot be considered precisely the same principle. See R. B. Lindsay and H. Margenau, *Foundations of Physics* (John Wiley & Sons Inc., New York, 1936, pp. 128ff).]

However, for thermodynamics, the theory of chemical change, and electrochemistry, as well as the other phenomena mentioned above, the pertinent concepts and laws of the theory of energetics lose all significance. In this domain energetics achieves the apparent and surprising simplicity of its proofs by the simple process of pushing the content of the laws to be demonstrated (which must always be known in advance) backward to their definitions. Of how these definitions turn out, we have given an example in the case of volume energy. Through such superficial operations the connections of things is not made clearer but rather more obscure. Above all, the theory of energetics has covered with confusion the principal contrasts between reversible and irreversible processes. It is my conviction that the progress of thermodynamics and its associated relations depends precisely on the extension and deepening of our understanding of these processes. To take an example, the fact that the equalization of the heights of a heavy liquid in two connecting tubes is somehow fundamentally different from the equalization of the temperature of two bodies in thermal contact never finds precise expression in energetics. Therefore, its adherents are never in a position to draw characteristic consequences from this difference.

And indeed the theory of energetics has up to the present day been able to show nothing in the way of positive results, although since Rankine there has been full time and occasion for this. [*Ed. note:* Planck is perhaps a bit hard on Rankine. His thermodynamics achievements were notable, even though his energetics was a bit faulty, largely because he failed to distinguish state functions from quantities that are not state functions.] One might indeed counter with the statement, "Energetics has never in any case led to a contradiction with experience." This is quite true for the simple reason that energetics, because of the uncertainity of its concepts, is unable to produce a new result which can be tested against experience. And this must be considered the most serious objection to it. For a theory that to preserve its existence is obliged to avoid the real problems can no longer have any roots in the domain of natural science, but must rest on metaphysical grounds where the weapons of empiricism are no longer available to it. Hence I consider it my duty to protest with all the vigor I can master against the further development of energetics in the direction taken by it recently, which with respect to the established results of scientific investigations represents a definite backward step. It can only have as a consequence that young people in science will be encouraged toward mere dilettante speculations instead of devoting themselves to the thorough study of the classics of science, therby allowing the fruitful field of theoretical physics to be uncultivated for years.

Berlin, December, 1895

24

Reprinted from *The Foundations of Science*, George Bruce Halsted, trans., The Science Press, Lancaster, Pa., 1946, pp. 115–123

Energy and Thermodynamics

Henri Poincaré

ENERGETICS.—The difficulties inherent in the classic mechanics have led certain minds to prefer a new system they call *energetics*.

Energetics took its rise as an outcome of the discovery of the principle of the conservation of energy. Helmholtz gave it its final form.

It begins by defining two quantities which play the fundamental rôle in this theory. They are *kinetic energy*, or *vis viva*, and *potential energy*.

All the changes which bodies in nature can undergo are regulated by two experimental laws:

1° The sum of kinetic energy and potential energy is constant. This is the principle of the conservation of energy.

2° If a system of bodies is at A at the time t_0 and at B at the time t_1, it always goes from the first situation to the second in such a way that the *mean* value of the difference between the two sorts of energy, in the interval of time which separates the two epochs t_0 and t_1, may be as small as possible.

This is Hamilton's principle, which is one of the forms of the principle of least action.

The energetic theory has the following advantages over the classic theory:

1° It is less incomplete; that is to say, Hamilton's principle and that of the conservation of energy teach us more than the fundamental principles of the classic theory, and exclude certain motions not realized in nature and which would be compatible with the classic theory:

2° It saves us the hypothesis of atoms, which it was almost impossible to avoid with the classic theory.

But it raises in its turn new difficulties:

The definitions of the two sorts of energy would raise difficulties almost as great as those of force and mass in the first system. Yet they may be gotten over more easily, at least in the simplest cases.

Suppose an isolated system formed of a certain number of material points; suppose these points subjected to forces depending only on their relative position and their mutual distances, and independent of their velocities. In virtue of the principle of the conservation of energy, a function of forces must exist.

In this simple case the enunciation of the principle of the conservation of energy is of extreme simplicity. A certain quantity, accessible to experiment, must remain constant. This quantity is the sum of two terms; the first depends only on the position of the material points and is independent of their velocities; the second is proportional to the square of these velocities. This resolution can take place only in a single way.

The first of these terms, which I shall call U, will be the potential energy; the second, which I shall call T, will be the kinetic energy.

It is true that if $T + U$ is a constant, so is any function of $T + U$,

$$\Phi(T + U).$$

But this function $\Phi(T + U)$ will not be the sum of two terms the one independent of the velocities, the other proportional to the square of these velocities. Among the functions which remain constant there is only one which enjoys this property, that is $T + U$ (or a linear function of $T + U$, which comes to the same thing, since this linear function may always be reduced to $T + U$ by change of unit and of origin). This then is what we shall call energy; the first term we shall call potential energy and the second kinetic energy. The definition of the two sorts of energy can therefore be carried through without any ambiguity.

It is the same with the definition of the masses. Kinetic energy, or *vis viva*, is expressed very simply by the aid of the masses and the relative velocities of all the material points with reference to one of them. These relative velocities are accessible to observation, and, when we know the expression of the kinetic energy as function of these relative velocities, the coefficients of this expression will give us the masses.

Thus, in this simple case, the fundamental ideas may be defined without difficulty. But the difficulties reappear in the more complicated cases and, for instance, if the forces, in lieu of depending only on the distances, depend also on the velocities. For example, Weber supposes the mutual action of two electric molecules to depend not only on their distance, but on their velocity and their acceleration. If material points should attract each other according to an analogous law, U would depend on the velocity, and might contain a term proportional to the square of the velocity.

Among the terms proportional to the squares of the velocities, how distinguish those which come from T or from U? Consequently, how distinguish the two parts of energy?

But still more; how define energy itself? We no longer have any reason to take as definition $T + U$ rather than any other function of $T + U$, when the property which characterized $T + U$ has disappeared, that, namely, of being the sum of two terms of a particular form.

But this is not all; it is necessary to take account, not only of mechanical energy properly so called, but of the other forms of energy, heat, chemical energy, electric energy, etc. The principle of the conservation of energy should be written:

$$T + U + Q = \text{const.}$$

where T would represent the sensible kinetic energy, U the potential energy of position, depending only on the position of the bodies, Q the internal molecular energy, under the thermal, chemic or electric form.

All would go well if these three terms were absolutely distinct, if T were proportional to the square of the velocities, U independent of these velocities and of the state of the bodies, Q independent of the velocities and of the positions of the bodies and dependent only on their internal state.

The expression for the energy could be resolved only in one single way into three terms of this form.

But this is not the case; consider electrified bodies; the electrostatic energy due to their mutual action will evidently depend upon their charge, that is to say, on their state; but it will equally depend upon their position. If these bodies are in motion, they will act one upon another electrodynamically and the electro-dynamic energy will depend not only upon their state and their position, but upon their velocities.

We therefore no longer have any means of making the separation of the terms which should make part of T, of U and of Q, and of separating the three parts of energy.

If $(T + U + Q)$ is constant so is any function $\Phi(T + U + Q)$.

If $T + U + Q$ were of the particular form I have above considered, no ambiguity would result; among the functions $\Phi(T + U + Q)$ which remain constant, there would only be one of this particular form, and that I should convene to call energy.

But as I have said, this is not rigorously the case; among the functions which remain constant, there is none which can be put rigorously under this particular form; hence, how choose among them the one which should be called energy? We no longer have anything to guide us in our choice.

There only remains for us one enunciation of the principle of the conservation of energy: *There is something which remains constant.* Under this form it is in its turn out of the reach of experiment and reduces to a sort of tautology. It is clear that if the world is governed by laws, there will be quantities which will remain constant. Like Newton's laws, and, for an analogous reason, the principle of the conservation of energy, founded on experiment, could no longer be invalidated by it.

This discussion shows that in passing from the classic to the energetic system progress has been made; but at the same time it shows this progress is insufficient.

Another objection seems to me still more grave: the principle of least action is applicable to reversible phenomena; but it is not at all satisfactory in so far as irreversible phenomena are concerned; the attempt by Helmholtz to extend it to this kind of phenomena did not succeed and could not succeed; in this regard everything remains to be done. The very statement of the principle of least action has something about it repugnant to the mind. To go from one point to another, a material molecule, acted upon by no force, but required to move on a surface, will take the geodesic line, that is to say, the shortest path.

This molecule seems to know the point whither it is to go, to foresee the time it would take to reach it by such and such a route, and then to choose the most suitable path. The statement presents the molecule to us, so to speak, as a living and free being. Clearly it would be better to replace it by an enunciation less objectionable, and where, as the philosophers would say, final causes would not seem to be substituted for efficient causes.

THERMODYNAMICS.[1]—The rôle of the two fundamental principles of thermodynamics in all branches of natural philosophy becomes daily more important. Abandoning the ambitious theories of forty years ago, which were encumbered by molecular hypotheses, we are trying to-day to erect upon thermodynamics alone the entire edifice of mathematical physics. Will the two principles of Mayer and of Clausius assure to it foundations solid enough for it to last some time? No one doubts it; but whence comes this confidence?

An eminent physicist said to me one day *à propos* of the law of errors: "All the world believes it firmly, because the mathematicians imagine that it is a fact of observation, and the observers that it is a theorem of mathematics." It was long so for the principle of the conservation of energy. It is no longer so to-day; no one is ignorant that this is an experimental fact.

But then what gives us the right to attribute to the principle itself more generality and more precision than to the experiments which have served to demonstrate it? This is to ask whether it is legitimate, as is done every day, to generalize empirical data, and I shall not have the presumption to discuss this question, after so many philosophers have vainly striven to solve it. One thing is certain; if this power were denied us, science could not exist or, at least, reduced to a sort of inventory, to the ascertaining of isolated facts, it would have no value for us, since it could give no satisfaction to our craving for order and harmony and since it would be at the same time incapable of foreseeing. As the circumstances which have preceded any fact will probably never be simultaneously reproduced, a first general-

---

[1] The following lines are a partial reproduction of the preface of my book *Thermodynamique*.

ization is already necessary to foresee whether this fact will be reproduced again after the least of these circumstances shall be changed.

But every proposition may be generalized in an infinity of ways. Among all the generalizations possible, we must choose, and we can only choose the simplest. We are therefore led to act as if a simple law were, other things being equal, more probable than a complicated law.

Half a century ago this was frankly confessed, and it was proclaimed that nature loves simplicity; she has since too often given us the lie. To-day we no longer confess this tendency, and we retain only so much of it as is indispensable if science is not to become impossible.

In formulating a general, simple and precise law on the basis of experiments relatively few and presenting certain divergences, we have therefore only obeyed a necessity from which the human mind can not free itself.

But there is something more, and this is why I dwell upon the point.

No one doubts that Mayer's principle is destined to survive all the particular laws from which it was obtained, just as Newton's law has survived Kepler's laws, from which it sprang, and which are only approximative if account be taken of perturbations.

Why does this principle occupy thus a sort of privileged place among all the physical laws? There are many little reasons for it.

First of all it is believed that we could not reject it or even doubt its absolute rigor without admitting the possibility of perpetual motion; of course we are on our guard at such a prospect, and we think ourselves less rash in affirming Mayer's principle than in denying it.

That is perhaps not wholly accurate; the impossibility of perpetual motion implies the conservation of energy only for reversible phenomena.

The imposing simplicity of Mayer's principle likewise contributes to strengthen our faith. In a law deduced immediately from experiment, like Mariotte's, this simplicity would rather seem to us a reason for distrust; but here this is no longer the case; we see elements, at first sight disparate, arrange themselves in an unexpected order and form a harmonious whole; and we refuse to believe that an unforeseen harmony may be a simple effect of chance. It seems that our conquest is the dearer to us the more effort it has cost us, or that we are the surer of having wrested her true secret from nature the more jealously she has hidden it from us.

But those are only little reasons; to establish Mayer's law as an absolute principle, a more profound discussion is necessary. But if this be attempted, it is seen that this absolute principle is not even easy to state.

In each particular case it is clearly seen what energy is and at least a provisional definition of it can be given; but it is impossible to find a general definition for it.

If we try to enunciate the principle in all its generality and apply it to the universe, we see it vanish, so to speak, and nothing is left but this: *There is something which remains constant.*

But has even this any meaning? In the determinist hypothesis, the state of the universe is determined by an extremely great number n of parameters which I shall call $x_1, x_2, \ldots x_n$. As soon as the values of these n parameters at any instant are known, their derivatives with respect to the time are likewise known and consequently the values of these same parameters at a preceding or subsequent instant can be calculated. In other words, these n parameters satisfy n differential equations of the first order.

These equations admit of $n-1$ integrals and consequently there are $n-1$ functions of $x_1, x_2, \ldots x_n$, which remain constant. *If then we say there is something which remains constant,* we only utter a tautology. We should even be puzzled to say which among all our integrals should retain the name of energy.

Besides, Mayer's principle is not understood in this sense when it is applied to a limited system. It is then assumed that p of our parameters vary independently, so that we only have $n - p$ relations, generally linear, between our n parameters and their derivatives.

To simplify the enunciation, suppose that the sum of the work of the external forces is null, as well as that of the quantities of heat given off to the outside. Then the signification of our principle will be:

There is a combination of these $n-p$ *relations whose first member is an exact differential;* and then this differential vanishing in virtue of our $n-p$ relations, its integral is a constant and this integral is called energy.

But how can it be possible that there are several parameters whose variations are independent? That can only happen under the influence of external forces (although we have supposed, for simplicity, that the algebraic sum of the effects of these forces is null). In fact, if the system were completely isolated from all external action, the values of our n parameters at a given instant would suffice to determine the state of the system at any subsequent instant, provided always we retain the determinist hypothesis; we come back therefore to the same difficulty as above.

If the future state of the system is not entirely determined by its present state, this is because it depends besides upon the state of bodies external to the system. But then is it probable that there exist between the parameters x, which define the state of the system, equations independent of this state of the external bodies? and if in certain cases we believe we can find such, is this not solely in consequence of our ignorance and because the influence of these bodies is too slight for our experimenting to detect it?

If the system is not regarded as completely isolated, it is probable that the rigorously exact expression of its internal energy will depend on the state of the external bodies. Again, I have above supposed the sum of the external work was null, and if we try to free ourselves from this rather artificial restriction, the enunciation becomes still more difficult.

To formulate Mayer's principle in an absolute sense, it is therefore necessary to extend it to the whole universe, and then we find ourselves face to face with the very difficulty we sought to avoid.

In conclusion, using ordinary language, the law of the conservation of energy can have only one signification, which is that there is a property common to all the possibilities; but on the determinist hypothesis there is only a single possibility, and then the law has no longer any meaning.

On the indeterminist hypothesis, on the contrary, it would have a meaning, even if it were taken in an absolute sense; it would appear as a limitation imposed upon freedom.

But this word reminds me that I am digressing and am on the point of leaving the domain of mathematics and physics. I check myself therefore and will stress of all this discussion only one impression, that Mayer's law is a form flexible enough for us to put into it almost whatever we wish. By that I do not mean it corresponds to no objective reality, nor that it reduces itself to a mere tautology, since, in each particular case, and provided one does not try to push to the absolute, it has a perfectly clear meaning.

This flexibility is a reason for believing in its permanence, and as, on the other hand, it will disappear only to lose itself in a higher harmony, we may work with confidence, supporting ourselves upon it, certain beforehand that our labor will not be lost.

Almost everything I have just said applies to the principle of Clausius. What distinguishes it is that it is expressed by an inequality. Perhaps it will be said it is the same with all physical laws, since their precision is always limited by errors of observation. But they at least claim to be first approximations, and it is hoped to replace them little by little by laws more and more precise. If, on the other hand, the principle of Clausius reduces to an inequality, this is not caused by the imperfection of our means of observation, but by the very nature of the question.

[*Ed. note:* material omitted]

Part VII

PROGRESS IN EQUILIBRIUM
THERMODYNAMICS

Editor's Comments
on Papers 25 Through 27

The preceding papers in this volume have portrayed the generalization of the concept of energy through the work of Helmholtz, Clausius, Kelvin, Rankine, and others. The successful application of the idea to many fields of natural science has also been stressed. Aided by the epoch-making but for long neglected theoretical insights of Sadi Carnot, these developments led to the founding of thermodynamics, perhaps the most remarkable of all scientific theories. Much, indeed, of what has already been presented in this volume constitutes a part of thermodynamics, although not always bearing that name. By the late 1860s and early 1870s, the fundamental principles of this new discipline were sufficiently understood so that the subject could be profitably presented in specific treatises and textbooks, among which may be mentioned those of Balfour Stewart (1866), P. G. Tait (1868), and J. C. Maxwell (1872).

It is true that the full extent of the possible applicability of thermodynamics was not generally recognized at that time. Among those who did see clearly the enormous future possibilities of the subject was the American theoretical physicist and mathematician J. Willard Gibbs (1839–1903). Except for two student years in Europe, Gibbs spent his entire professional career as professor of mathematical physics at Yale University. He early became interested in developing the theory of thermodynamics in a systematic fashion. Paper 25 is an excerpt from his earliest published scientific paper, and indicates clearly the profundity of his insight. In a sense it was a development of the earlier ideas of Rankine, as set forth in Paper 6, but Gibbs's approach was much more sophisticated than that of Rankine. He took advantage of the progress

374

made in the years following Rankine's work, particularly with respect to the introduction of the concept of entropy by Clausius. The role of this concept has not received much emphasis in the current volume. Subsequent volumes in the Benchmark Series on Energy will treat it in detail. Gibbs showed the great value of the entropy–temperature diagram in the understanding of thermodynamic processes as a supplement to the earlier and more common pressure–volume diagram.

In the years following the appearance of his first paper, Gibbs became increasingly concerned with the concept of thermodynamic equilibrium in the most general sense, i.e., as applied to systems of more complicated character than the simple ideal gas. His aim was to study systems consisting of many chemically different components and present in different phases (i.e., solid, liquid, or gaseous). The results of his investigation led to the production in 1878 of a remarkable memoir entitled *On the Equilibrium of Heterogeneous Substances*. In this book-length paper Gibbs immensely enlarged the scope of applicability of thermodynamics and indeed effectively made it the foundation of physical chemistry. The memoir contains Gibbs's statement of his famous phase rule, giving the number of independent variations of which a system of coexistent phases is capable, in terms of the number of phases and the number of independently variable components. Fortunately, Gibbs prepared an abstract of his lengthy memoir, which we reprint here as Paper 26.

Among those physicists who devoted considerable attention to thermodynamics during the last quarter of the nineteenth century must be mentioned Max Planck, whose critique of the theory of energetics is presented in Paper 23. Planck's first paper on thermodynamics was his inaugural dissertation at the University of Munich in 1879, where he examined in detail the second law and the concept of entropy. There followed a long list of important contributions, culminating in his well-known text on thermodynamics, the first edition of which appeared in 1897. This gave Planck the opportunity to organize in systematic fashion his own previous work, as well as that of other investigators. This book became a standard text on the subject and went into many editions. An English translation by Alexander Ogg cam out in 1903 and enjoyed wide popularity. In the preface to the first edition, Planck explains simply and clearly the various ways of looking at thermodynamics, concentrating on the way he proposed to treat the subject in his book. The translation of the greater part of this preface (presented here as Paper 27) provides a fitting conclusion to this volume on nineteenth century applications of the concept of energy.

25

Reprinted from *Trans. Conn. Acad.*, **2**, 309–325, 342 (Apr. 1873)

GRAPHICAL METHODS IN THE THERMODYNAMICS OF FLUIDS.
BY J. WILLARD GIBBS.

ALTHOUGH geometrical representations of propositions in the thermodynamics of fluids are in general use, and have done good service in disseminating clear notions in this science, yet they have by no means received the extension in respect to variety and generality of which they are capable. So far as regards a general graphical method, which can exhibit at once all the thermodynamic properties of a fluid concerned in reversible processes, and serve alike for the demonstration of general theorems and the numerical solution of particular problems, it is the general if not the universal practice to use diagrams in which the rectilinear co-ordinates represent volume and pressure. The object of this article is to call attention to certain diagrams of different construction, which afford graphical methods coextensive in their applications with that in ordinary use, and preferable to it in many cases in respect of distinctness or of convenience.

QUANTITIES AND RELATIONS WHICH ARE TO BE REPRESENTED BY THE DIAGRAM.

We have to consider the following quantities:—

v, the volume,
p, the pressure,
t, the (absolute) temperature,
ε, the energy,
η, the entropy,

of a given body in any state,

also W, the work done, and H, the heat received,* by the body in passing from one state to another.

These are subject to the relations expressed by the following differential equations:—

---

* Work spent upon the body is as usual to be considered as a negative quantity of work done by the body, and heat given out by the body as a negative quantity of heat received by it.

It is taken for granted that the body has a uniform temperature throughout, and that the pressure (or expansive force) has a uniform value both for all points in the body and for all directions. This, it will be observed, will exclude irreversible processes, but will not entirely exclude solids, although the condition of equal pressure in all directions renders the case very limited, in which they come within the scope of the discussion.

$$dW = \alpha p \, dv, \tag{a}$$
$$d\varepsilon = \beta dH - dW, \tag{b}$$
$$d\eta = \frac{dH^*}{t}, \tag{c}$$

where α and β are constants depending upon the units by which v, p, W and H are measured. We may suppose our units so chosen that $\alpha = 1$ and $\beta = 1$,† and write our equations in the simpler form,

$$d\varepsilon = dH - dW, \tag{1}$$
$$dW = p \, dv, \tag{2}$$
$$dH = t \, d\eta. \tag{3}$$

Eliminating dW and dH, we have

$$d\varepsilon = t \, d\eta - p \, dv. \tag{4}$$

The quantities v, p, t, ε and η are determined when the state of the body is given, and it may be permitted to call them *functions of the state of the body*. The state of a body, in the sense in which the term is used in the thermodynamics of fluids, is capable of two independent variations, so that between the five quantities v, p, t, ε and η there exist relations expressible by three finite equations, different in general for different substances, but always such as to be in harmony with the differential equation (4). This equation evidently signifies that if ε be expressed as function of v and η, the partial differential co-efficients of this function taken with respect to v and to η will be equal to $-p$ and to t respectively.‡

---

* Equation (a) may be derived from simple mechanical considerations. Equations (b) and (c) may be considered as defining the energy and entropy of any state of the body, or more strictly as defining the differentials $d\varepsilon$ and $d\eta$. That functions of the state of the body exist, the differentials of which satisfy these equations, may easily be deduced from the first and second laws of thermodynamics. The term *entropy*, it will be observed, is here used in accordance with the original suggestion of Clausius, and not in the sense in which it has been employed by Professor Tait and others after his suggestion. The same quantity has been called by Professor Rankine the *Thermodynamic function*. See Clausius, Mechanische Wärmetheorie, Abhnd. ix, § 14; or Pogg. Ann., Bd. cxxv (1865), p. 390; and Rankine, Phil. Trans., vol. 144, p. 126.

† For example, we may choose as the unit of volume, the cube of the unit of length, —as the unit of pressure the unit of force acting upon the square of the unit of length,—as the unit of work the unit of force acting through the unit of length,—and as the unit of heat the thermal equivalent of the unit of work. The units of length and of force would still be arbitrary as well as the unit of temperature.

‡ An equation giving ε in terms of η and v, or more generally any finite equation between ε, η and v for a definite quantity of any fluid, may be considered as the fundamental thermodynamic equation of that fluid, as from it by aid of equations (2), (3) and (4) may be derived all the thermodynamic properties of the fluid (so far as reversible

On the other hand W and H are not functions of the state of the body (or functions of any of the quantities v, p, t, ε and η), but are determined by the whole series of states through which the body is supposed to pass.

FUNDAMENTAL IDEA AND GENERAL PROPERTIES OF THE DIAGRAM.

Now if we associate a particular point in a plane with every separate state, of which the body is capable, in any continuous manner, so that states differing infinitely little are associated with points which are infinitely near to each other,* the points associated with states of equal volume will form lines, which may be called *lines of equal volume*, the different lines being distinguished by the numerical value of the volume, (as lines of volume 10, 20, 30, etc.) In the same way we may conceive of *lines of equal pressure, of equal temperature, of equal energy, and of equal entropy.* These lines we may also call *isometric, isopiestic, isothermal, isodynamic, isentropic,*† and if necessary use these words as substantives.

Suppose the body to change its state, the points associated with the states through which the body passes will form a line, which we may call the *path* of the body. The conception of a path must include the idea of direction, to express the order in which the body passes through the series of states. With every such change of state there is connected in general a certain amount of work done, W, and of heat received, H, which we may call the *work* and the *heat* of the *path*.‡

---

processes are concerned,) viz: the fundamental equation with equation (4) gives the three relations existing between v, p, t. ε and η, and these relations being known, equations (2) and (3) give the work W and heat H for any change of state of the fluid.

* The method usually employed in treatises on thermodynamics, in which the rectangular co-ordinates of the point are made proportional to the volume and pressure of the body, is a single example of such an association.

† These lines are usually known by the name given them by Rankine, *adiabatic*. If, however, we follow the suggestion of Clausius and call that quantity *entropy*, which Rankine called the *thermodynamic function*, it seems natural to go one step farther, and call the lines in which this quantity has a constant value *isentropic*.

‡ For the sake of brevity, it will be convenient to use language which attributes to the diagram properties which belong to the associated states of the body. Thus it can give rise to no ambiguity, if we speak of the volume or the temperature of a point in the diagram, or of the work or heat of a line, instead of the volume or temperature of the body in the state associated with the point, or the work done or the heat received by the body in passing through the states associated with the points of the line. In like manner also we may speak of the body moving along a line in the diagram, instead of passing through the series of states represented by the line.

The value of these quantities may be calculated from equations (2) and (3),

$$dW = pdv$$
$$dH = td\eta,$$

i. e.,

$$W = \int pdv \qquad (5)$$
$$H = \int td\eta, \qquad (6)$$

the integration being carried on from the beginning to the end of the path. If the direction of the path is reversed, W and H change their signs, remaining the same in absolute value.

If the changes of state of the body form a cycle, i. e., if the final state is the same as the initial, the path becomes a *circuit*, and the work done and heat received are equal, as may be seen from equation (1), which when integrated for this case becomes $0 = H - W$.

The circuit will enclose a certain area, which we may consider as positive or negative according to the direction of the circuit which circumscribes it. The direction in which areas must be circumscribed in order that their value may be positive, is of course arbitrary. In other words, if x and y are the rectangular co-ordinates, we may define an area either as $\int ydx$, or as $\int xdy$.

If an area be divided into any number of parts, the work done in the circuit bounding the whole area is equal to the sum of the work done in all the circuits bounding the partial areas. This is evident from the consideration, that the work done in each of the lines which separate the partial areas appears twice and with contrary signs in the sum of the work done in the circuits bounding the partial areas. Also the heat received in the circuit bounding the whole area is equal to the sum of the heat received in all the circuits bounding the partial areas.*

If all the dimensions of a circuit are infinitely small, the ratio of the included area to the work or heat of the circuit is independent of the shape of the circuit and the direction in which it is described, and varies only with its position in the diagram. That this ratio is independent of the direction in which the circuit is described, is evident from the consideration that a reversal of this direction simply changes the sign of both terms of the ratio. To prove that the ratio

---

* The conception of areas as positive or negative renders it unnecessary in propositions of this kind to state explicitly the direction in which the circuits are to be described. For the directions of the circuits are determined by the signs of the areas, and the signs of the partial areas must be the same as that of the area out of which they were formed.

is independent of the shape of the circuit, let us suppose the area ABCDE (fig. 1) divided up by an infinite number of isometrics v_1v_1, v_2v_2, etc., with equal differ-ences of volume dv, and an infinite number of isopiestics p_1p_1, p_2p_2, etc., with equal differences of pressure dp. Now from the principle of continuity, as the whole figure is infinitely small, the ratio of the area of one of the small quadrilaterals into which the figure is divided to the work done in passing around it is approximately the same for all the different quadrilaterals. Therefore the area

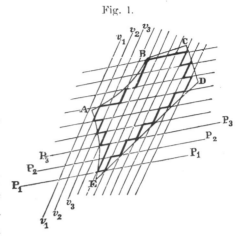

Fig. 1.

of the figure composed of all the complete quadrilaterals which fall within the given circuit has to the work done in circumscribing this figure the same ratio, which we will call γ. But the area of this figure is approximately the same as that of the given circuit, and the work done in describing this figure is approximately the same as that done in describing the given circuit, (eq. 5). Therefore the area of the given circuit has to the work done or heat received in that circuit this ratio γ, which is independent of the shape of the circuit.

Now if we imagine the systems of equidifferent isometrics and isopiestics, which have just been spoken of, extended over the whole diagram, the work done in circumscribing one of the small quadri-laterals, so that the increase of pressure directly precedes the increase of volume, will have in every part of the diagram a constant value, viz., the product of the differences of volume and pressure ($dv \times dp$), as may easily be proved by applying equation (2) successively to its four sides. But the area of one of these quadrilaterals, which we could consider as constant within the limits of the infinitely small cir-cuit, may vary for different parts of the diagram, and will indicate proportionally the value of γ, which is equal to the area divided by $dv \times dp$.

In like manner, if we imagine systems of isentropics and isother-mals drawn throughout the diagram for equal differences $d\eta$ and dt, the heat received in passing around one of the small quadrilaterals, so that the increase of t shall directly precede that of η, will be the constant product $d\eta \times dt$, as may be proved by equation (3), and the value of γ, which is equal to the area divided by the heat, will be indicated proportionally by the areas.*

This quantity γ, which is the ratio of the area of an infinitely small circuit to the work done or heat received in that circuit, and which we may call the scale on which work and heat are represented by areas, or more briefly, the *scale of work and heat*, may have a constant value throughout the diagram or it may have a varying value. The diagram in ordinary use affords an example of the first case, as the area of a circuit is everywhere proportional to the work or heat. There are other diagrams which have the same property, and we may call all such *diagrams of constant scale*.

In any case we may consider the scale of work and heat as known for every point of the diagram, so far as we are able to draw the isometrics and isopiestics or the isentropics and isothermals. If we

---

* The indication of the value of γ by systems of equidifferent isometrics and isopiestics, or isentropics and isothermals, is explained above, because it seems in accordance with the spirit of the graphical method, and because it avoids the extraneous consideration of the co-ordinates. If, however, it is desired to have analytical expressions for the value of γ based upon the relations between the co-ordinates of the point and the state of the body, it is easy to deduce such expressions as the following, in which x and y are the rectangular co-ordinates, and it is supposed that the sign of an area is determined in accordance with the equation $A = \int y\,dx$:—

$$\frac{1}{\gamma} = \frac{dv}{dx} \cdot \frac{dp}{dy} - \frac{dp}{dx} \cdot \frac{dv}{dy} = \frac{d\eta}{dx} \cdot \frac{dt}{dy} - \frac{dt}{dx} \cdot \frac{d\eta}{dy},$$

where x and y are regarded as the independent variables;—or

$$\gamma = \frac{dx}{dv} \cdot \frac{dy}{dp} - \frac{dy}{dv} \cdot \frac{dx}{dp},$$

where v and p are the independent variables;—or

$$\gamma = \frac{dx}{d\eta} \cdot \frac{dy}{dt} - \frac{dy}{d\eta} \cdot \frac{dx}{dt},$$

where η and t are the independent variables;—or

$$\frac{1}{\gamma} = \frac{-\dfrac{d^2\varepsilon}{dv\,d\eta}}{\dfrac{dx}{dv} \cdot \dfrac{dy}{d\eta} - \dfrac{dy}{dv} \cdot \dfrac{dx}{d\eta}},$$

where v and η are the independent variables.

These and similar expressions for $\frac{1}{\gamma}$ may be found by dividing the value of the work or heat for an infinitely small circuit by the area included. This operation can be most conveniently performed upon a circuit consisting of four lines, in each of which one of the independent variables is constant. E. g., the last formula can be most easily found from an infinitely small circuit formed of two isometrics and two isentropics.

write δW and δH for the work and heat of an infinitessimal circuit, and δA for the area included, the relations of these quantities are thus expressed :—*

$$\delta W = \delta H = \frac{1}{\gamma} \delta A. \tag{7}$$

We may find the value of W and H for a circuit of finite dimensions by supposing the included area A divided into areas δA infinitely small in all directions, for which therefore the above equation will hold, and taking the sum of the values of δH or δW for the various areas δA. Writing W^c and H^c for the work and heat of the circuit C, and Σ^c for a summation or integration performed within the limits of this circuit, we have

$$W^c = H^c = \Sigma^c \frac{1}{\gamma} \delta A. \tag{8}$$

We have thus an expression for the value of the work and heat of a circuit involving an integration extending over an area instead of one extending over a line, as in equations (5) and (6).

Similar expressions may be found for the work and the heat of a path which is not a circuit. For this case may be reduced to the preceding by the consideration that $W = 0$ for a path on an isometric or on the line of no pressure (eq. 2), and $H = 0$ for a path on an isentropic or on the line of absolute cold. Hence the work of any path S is equal to that of the circuit formed of S, the isometric of the final state, the line of no pressure and the isometric of the initial state, which circuit may be represented by the notation $[S, v'', p^0, v']$. And the heat of the same path is the same as that of the circuit $[S, \eta'', t^0, \eta']$. Therefore using W^s and H^s to denote the work and heat of any path S, we have

$$W^s = \Sigma^{[S, v'', p^0, v']} \frac{1}{\gamma} \delta A, \tag{9}$$

$$H^s = \Sigma^{[S, \eta'', t^0, \eta']} \frac{1}{\gamma} \delta A, \tag{10}$$

where as before the limits of the integration are denoted by the ex-

---

* To avoid confusion, as dW and dH are generally used and are used elsewhere in this article to denote the work and heat of an infinite short path, a slightly different notation, δW and δH, is here used to denote the work and heat of an infinitely small circuit. So δA is used to denote an element of area which is infinitely small in all directions, as the letter d would only imply that the element was infinitely small in one direction. So also below, the integration or summation which extends to all the elements written with δ is denoted by the character Σ, as the character $\int$ naturally refers to elements written with d.

pression occupying the place of an index to the sign Σ.* These equations evidently include equation (8) as a particular case.

It is easy to form a material conception of these relations. If we imagine, for example, mass inherent in the plane of the diagram with a varying (superficial) density represented by $\dfrac{1}{\gamma}$, then $\Sigma \dfrac{1}{\gamma} \delta A$ will evidently denote the mass of the part of the plane included within the limits of integration, this mass being taken positively or negatively according to the direction of the circuit.

Thus far we have made no supposition in regard to the nature of the law, by which we associate the points of a plane with the states of the body, except a certain condition of continuity. Whatever law we may adopt, we obtain a method of representation of the thermodynamic properties of the body, in which the relations existing between the functions of the state of the body are indicated by a net-work of lines, while the work done and the heat received by the body when it changes its state are represented by integrals extending over the elements of a line, and also by an integral extending over the elements of certain areas in the diagram, or, if we choose to introduce such a consideration, by the mass belonging to these areas.

The different diagrams which we obtain by different laws of association are all such as may be obtained from one another by a process of *deformation*, and this consideration is sufficient to demonstrate

---

* A word should be said in regard to the sense in which the above propositions should be understood. If beyond the limits, within which the relations of v, p, t, ϵ and η are known and which we may call the limits of the known field, we continue the isometrics, isopiestics, &c., in any way we please, only subject to the condition that the relations of v, p, t, ϵ and η shall be consistent with the equation $d\epsilon = td\eta - pdv$, then in calculating the values of quantities W and H determined by the equations $dW = pdv$ and $dH = td\eta$ for paths or circuits in any part of the diagram thus extended, we may use any of the propositions or processes given above, as these three equations have formed the only basis of the reasoning. We will thus obtain values of W and H, which will be identical with those which would be obtained by the immediate application of the equations $dW = pdv$ and $dH = td\eta$ to the path in question, and which in the case of any path which is entirely contained in the known field will be the true values of the work and heat for the change of state of the body which the path represents. We may thus use lines outside of the known field without attributing to them any physical signification whatever, without considering the points in the lines as representing any states of the body. If however, to fix our ideas, we choose to conceive of this part of the diagram as having the same physical interpretation as the known field, and to enunciate our propositions in language based upon such a conception, the unreality or even the impossibility of the states represented by the lines outside of the known field cannot lead to any incorrect results in regard to paths in the known field.

their properties from the well-known properties of the diagram in which the volume and pressure are represented by rectangular co-ordinates. For the relations indicated by the net-work of isometrics, isopiestics etc., are evidently not altered by deformation of the surface upon which they are drawn, and if we conceive of mass as belonging to the surface, the mass included within given lines will also not be effected by the process of deformation. If, then, the surface upon which the ordinary diagram is drawn has the uniform superficial density 1, so that the work and heat of a circuit, which are represented in this diagram by the included area, shall also be represented by the mass included, this latter relation will hold for any diagram formed from this by deformation of the surface on which it is drawn.

The choice of the method of representation is of course to be determined by considerations of simplicity and convenience, especially in regard to the drawing of the lines of equal volume, pressure, temperature, energy and entropy, and the estimation of work and heat. There is an obvious advantage in the use of diagrams of constant scale, in which the work and heat are represented simply by areas. Such diagrams may of course be produced by an infinity of different methods, as there is no limit to the ways of deforming a plane figure without altering the magnitude of its elements. Among these methods, two are especially important,—the ordinary method in which the volume and pressure are represented by rectilinear co-ordinates, and that in which the entropy and temperature are so represented. A diagram formed by the former method may be called, for the sake of distinction, a *volume-pressure* diagram,—one formed by the latter, an *entropy-temperature* diagram. That the latter as well as the former satisfies the condition that $\gamma = 1$ throughout the whole diagram, may be seen by reference to page 313.

THE ENTROPY-TEMPERATURE DIAGRAM COMPARED WITH THAT IN ORDINARY USE.

Considerations independent of the nature of the body in question.

As the general equations (1), (2), (3) are not altered by interchanging v, $-p$ and $-W$ with η, t and H respectively, it is evident that, so far as these equations are concerned, there is nothing to choose between a volume-pressure and an entropy-temperature diagram. In the former, the work is represented by an area bounded by the path which represents the change of state of the body, two ordinates and the axis of abscissas. The same is true of the heat received in the latter diagram. Again, in the former diagram the heat received is represented by an area bounded by the path and certain lines, the character of which depends upon the nature of the body under consideration. Except in the case of an ideal body, the properties of which are determined by assumption, these lines are more or less unknown in a part of their course, and in any case the area will generally extend to an infinite distance. Very much the same inconveniences attach themselves to the areas representing work in the entropy-temperature diagram.* There is, however, a consideration of a general character, which shows an important advantage on the side of the entropy-temperature diagram. In thermodynamic problems, heat received at one temperature is by no means the equivalent of the same amount of heat received at another temperature. For example, a supply of a million calories at 150ᶜ is a very different thing from a supply of a million calories at 50ᶜ. But no such distinction exists in regard to work. This is a result of the general law, that heat can only pass from a hotter to a colder body, while work can be transferred by mechanical means from one fluid to any other, whatever may be

---

* In neither diagram do these circumstances create any serious difficulty in the estimation of areas representing work or heat. It is always possible to divide these areas into two parts, of which one is of finite dimensions, and the other can be calculated in the simplest manner. Thus, in the entropy-temperature diagram, the work done in a path AB (fig. 2) is represented by the area included by the path AB, the isometric BC, the line of no pressure and the isometric DA. The line of no pressure and the adjacent parts of the isometrics in the case of an actual gas or vapor are more or less undetermined in the present state of our knowledge, and are likely to remain so; for an ideal gas the line of no pressure coincides with the axis of abscissas, and is an asymptote to the isometrics.

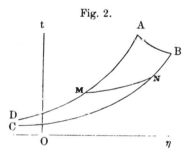

Fig. 2.

But, be this as it may, it is not necessary to examine the form of the remoter parts of the diagram. If we draw an isopiestic MN, cutting AD and BC, the area MNCD, which represents the work done in MN, will be equal to $p(v''-v')$, where p denotes the pressure in MN, and v'' and v' denote the volumes at B and A respectively (eq. 5). Hence the work done in AB will be represented by $ABNM + p(v''-v')$. In the volume-pressure diagram, the areas representing heat may be divided by an isothermal, and treated in a manner entirely analogous.

Or, we may make use of the principle, that, for a path which begins and ends on the same isodynamic, the work and heat are equal, as appears by integration of equation (1). Hence, in the entropy-temperature diagram, to find the work of any path, we may extend it by an isometric (which will not alter its work), so that it shall begin and end on the same isodynamic, and then take the heat (instead of the work) of the path thus extended. This method was suggested by that employed by Cazin (Théorie élémentaire des Machines à Air Chaud, p. 11) and Zeuner (Mechanische Wärmetheorie, p. 80) in the reverse case, viz: to find the heat of a path in the volume-pressure diagram.

the pressures. Hence, in thermodynamic problems, it is generally necessary to distinguish between the quantities of heat received or given out by the body at different temperatures, while as far as work is concerned, it is generally sufficient to ascertain the total amount performed. If, then, several heat-areas and one work-area enter into the problem, it is evidently more important that the former should be simple in form, than that the latter should be so. Moreover, in the very common case of a circuit, the work-area is bounded entirely by the path, and the form of the isometrics and the line of no pressure are of no especial consequence.

It is worthy of notice that the simplest form of a perfect thermodynamic engine, so often described in treatises on thermodynamics, is represented in the entropy-temperature diagram by a figure of extreme simplicity, viz: a rectangle of which the sides are parallel to the co-ordinate axes. Thús in figure 3, the circuit ABCD may represent the series of states through which the fluid is made to pass in such an engine, the included area representing the work done, while the area ABFE represents the heat received from the heater at the highest temperature AE, and the area CDEF represents the heat transmitted to the cooler at the lowest temperature DE.

Fig. 3.

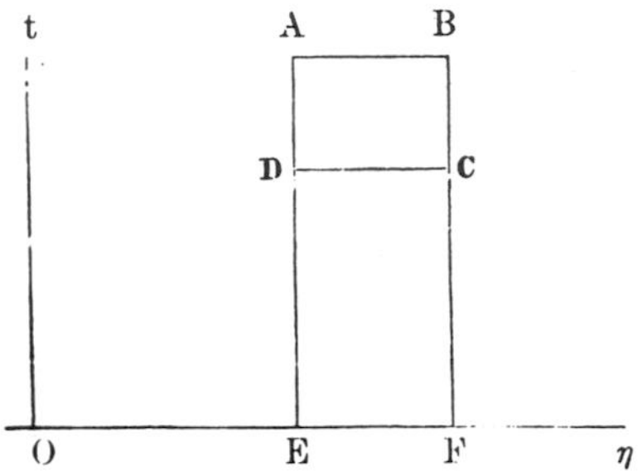

There is another form of the perfect thermodynamic engine, viz: one with a perfect regenerator as defined by Rankine (Phil. Trans. vol. 144, p. 140), the representation of which becomes peculiarly simple in the entropy-temperature diagram. The circuit consists of two equal straight lines AB and CD (fig. 4) parallel to the axis of abscissas, and two precisely similar curves of any form BC and AD. The included area ABCD represents the work done, and the areas ABba and CDdc represent respectively the heat received from the heater and that transmitted to the cooler. The heat imparted by the fluid to the regenerator in passing from B to C, and afterward restored to the fluid in its passage from D to A, is represented by the areas BCcb and DAad.

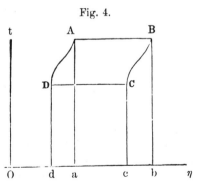

Fig. 4.

It is often a matter of the first importance in the study of any thermodynamic engine, to compare it with a perfect engine. Such a comparison will obviously be much facilitated by the use of a method in which the perfect engine is represented by such simple forms.

The method in which the co-ordinates represent volume and pressure has a certain advantage in the simple and elementary character of the notions upon which it is based, and its analogy with Watt's indicator has doubtless contributed to render it popular. On the other hand, a method involving the notion of *entropy*, the very existence of which depends upon the second law of thermodynamics, will doubtless seem to many far-fetched, and may repel beginners as obscure and difficult of comprehension. This inconvenience is perhaps more than counterbalanced by the advantages of a method which makes the second law of thermodynamics so prominent, and gives it so clear and elementary an expression. The fact, that the different states of a fluid can be represented by the positions of a point in a plane, so that the ordinates shall represent the temperatures, and the heat received or given out by the fluid shall be represented by the area bounded by the line representing the states through which the body passes, the ordinates drawn through the extreme points of this line, and the axis of abscissas,—this fact, clumsy as its expression in words may be, is one which presents a clear image to the eye, and which the mind can readily grasp and retain. It is, however, nothing more nor less than a geometrical expression of the second law of thermodynamics in its application to fluids, in a form exceedingly convenient for use, and from which the analytical expression of the same law can, if desired, be at once obtained. If, then, it is more important for purposes of instruction and the like to familiarize the learner with the second law, than to defer its statement as long as possible, the use of the entropy-temperature diagram may serve a useful purpose in the popularizing of this science.

The foregoing considerations are in the main of a general character, and independent of the nature of the substance to which the graphical method is applied. On this, however, depend the forms of the isometrics, isopiestics and isodynamics in the entropy-temperature diagram, and of the isentropics, isothermals and isodynamics in the volume-pressure diagram. As the convenience of a method depends largely upon the ease with which these lines can be drawn, and upon the peculiarities of the fluid which has its properties represented in the diagram, it is desirable to compare the methods under consideration in some of their most important applications. We will commence with the case of a perfect gas.

Case of a perfect gas.

A perfect or ideal gas may be defined as such a gas, that for any constant quantity of it the product of the volume and the pressure varies as the temperature, and the energy varies as the temperature, i. e.,

$$pv = at, \qquad \text{(A)}*$$
$$\varepsilon = ct. \qquad \text{(B)}$$

The significance of the constant a is sufficiently indicated by equation (A). The significance of c may be rendered more evident by differentiating equation (B) and comparing the result

$$d\varepsilon = c \, dt$$

with the general equations (1) and (2), viz:

$$d\varepsilon = dH - dW, \quad dW = p \, dv.$$

If $dv = 0$, $dW = 0$, and $dH = c \, dt$, i. e.,

$$\left(\frac{dH}{dt}\right)_v = c, \dagger \qquad \text{(C)}$$

i. e., c is the quantity of heat necessary to raise the temperature of the body one degree under the condition of constant volume. It will be observed, that when different quantities of the same gas are considered, a and c both vary as the quantity, and $c \div a$ is constant; also, that the value of $c \div a$ for different gases varies as their specific heat determined for equal volumes and for constant volume.

With the aid of equations (A) and (B) we may eliminate p and t from the general equation (4), viz:

$$d\varepsilon = t \, d\eta - p \, dv,$$

which is then reduced to

$$\frac{d\varepsilon}{\varepsilon} = \frac{1}{c} d\eta - \frac{a}{c}\frac{dv}{v},$$

and by integration to

$$\log \varepsilon = \frac{\eta}{c} - \frac{a}{c} \log v. \ddagger \qquad \text{(D)}$$

---

* In this article, all equations which are designated by arabic numerals subsist for any body whatever (subject to the condition of uniform pressure and temperature), and those which designated by small capitals subsist for any quantity of a perfect gas as defined above (subject of course to the same conditions).

† A subscript letter after a differential co-efficient is used in this article to indicate the quantity which is made constant in the differentiation.

‡ If we use the letter e to denote the base of the Naperian system of logarithms, equation (D) may also be written in the form

$$\varepsilon = e^{\frac{\eta}{c}} v^{-\frac{a}{c}}$$

This may be regarded as the fundamental thermodynamic equation of an ideal gas. See

The constant of integration becomes 0, if we call the entropy 0 for the state of which the volume and energy are both unity.

Any other equations which subsist between v, p, t, ε and η may be derived from the three independent equations (A), (B) and (D). If we eliminate ε from (B) and (D), we have

$$\eta = a \log v + c \log t + c \log c. \tag{E}$$

Eliminating v from (A) and (E), we have

$$\eta = (a+c) \log t - a \log p + c \log c + a \log a. \tag{F}$$

Eliminating t from (A) and (E), we have

$$\eta = (a+c) \log v + c \log p + c \log \frac{c}{a}. \tag{G}$$

If v is constant, equation (E) becomes

$$\eta = c \log t + \text{Const.},$$

i. e., the isometrics in the entropy-temperature diagram are logarithmic curves identical with one another in form,—a change in the value of v having only the effect of moving the curve parallel to the axis of η. If p is constant, equation (F) becomes

$$\eta = (a+c) \log t + \text{Const.},$$

so that the isopiestics in this diagram have similar properties. This identity in form diminishes greatly the labor of drawing any considerable number of these curves. For if a card or thin board be cut in the form of one of them, it may be used as a pattern or ruler to draw all of the same system.

The isodynamics are straight in this diagram (eq. B).

To find the form of the isothermals and isentropics in the volume-pressure diagram, we may make t and η constant in equations (A) and (G) respectively, which will then reduce to the well-known equations of these curves:—

$$pv = \text{Const.},$$

and

$$p^c v^{a+c} = \text{Const.}$$

The equation of the isodynamics is of course the same as that of the isothermals. None of these systems of lines have that property of identity of form, which makes the systems of isometrics and isopiestics so easy to draw in the entropy-temperature diagram.

the last note on page 310. It will be observed, that there would be no real loss of generality if we should choose, as the body to which the letters refer, such a quantity of the gas that one of the constants a and c should be equal to unity.

Case of condensable vapors.

The case of bodies which pass from the liquid to the gaseous condition is next to be considered. It is usual to assume of such a body, that when sufficiently superheated it approaches the condition of a perfect gas. If, then, in the entropy-temperature diagram of such a body we draw systems of isometrics, isopiestics and isodynamics, as if for a perfect gas, for proper values of the constants a and c, these will be asymptotes to the true isometrics, etc., of the vapor, and in many cases will not vary from them greatly in the part of the diagram which represents vapor unmixed with liquid, except in the vicinity of the line of saturation. In the volume-pressure diagram of the same body, the isothermals, isentropics and isodynamics, drawn for a perfect gas for the same values of a and c, will have the same relations to the true isothermals, etc.

In that part of any diagram which represents a mixture of vapor and liquid, the isopiestics and isothermals will be identical, as the pressure is determined by the temperature alone. In both the diagrams which we are now comparing, they will be straight and parallel to the axis of abscissas. The form of the isometrics and isodynamics in the entropy-temperature diagram, or that of the isentropics and isodynamics in the volume-pressure diagram, will depend upon the nature of the fluid, and probably cannot be expressed by any simple equations. The following property, however, renders it easy to construct equidifferent systems of these lines, viz: any such system will divide any isothermal (isopiestic) into equal segments.

It remains to consider that part of the diagram which represents the body when entirely in the condition of liquid. The fundamental characteristic of this condition of matter is that the volume is very nearly constant, so that variations of volume are generally entirely inappreciable when represented graphically on the same scale on which the volume of the body in the state of vapor is represented, and both the variations of volume and the connected variations of the connected quantities may be, and generally are, neglected by the side of the variations of the same quantities which occur when the body passes to the state of vapor.

Let us make, then, the usual assumption that v is constant, and see how the general equations (1), (2), (3) and (4) are thereby affected. We have first,

$$dv = 0,$$

then

$$dW = 0,$$

and

$$d\varepsilon = t\,d\eta.$$

If we add

$$dH = t\,d\eta,$$

these four equations will evidently be equivalent to the three independent equations (1), (2) and (3), combined with the assumption which we have just made. For a liquid, then, ε, instead of being a function of two quantities v and η, is a function of η alone,—t is also a function of η alone, being equal to the differential co-efficient of the function ε; that is, the value of one of the three quantities t, ε and η, is sufficient to determine the other two. The value of v, moreover, is fixed without reference to the values of t, ε and η (so long as these do not pass the limits of values possible for liquidity); while p does not enter into the equations, i. e., p may have any value (within certain limits) without affecting the values of t, ε, η or v. If the body change its state, continuing always liquid, the value of W for such a change is 0, and that of H is determined by the values of any one of the three quantities t, ε and η. It is, therefore, the relations between t, ε, η and H, for which a graphical expression is to be sought; a method, therefore, in which the co-ordinates of the diagram are made equal to the volume and pressure, is totally inapplicable to this particular case; v and p are indeed the only two of the five functions of the state of the body, v, p, t, ε and η, which have no relations either to each other, or to the other three, or to the quantities W and H, to be expressed.* The values of v and p do not really determine the state of an incompressible fluid,—the values of t, ε and η are still left undetermined, so that through every point in the volume-pressure diagram which represents the liquid there must pass (in general) an infinite number of isothermals, isodynamics and isentropics. The character of this part of the diagram is as follows:—the states of liquidity are represented by the points of a line parallel to the axis of pressures, and the isothermals, isodynamics and isentropics, which cross the field of partial vaporization and meet this line, turn upward and follow its course.†

In the entropy-temperature diagram the relations of t, ε and η are distinctly visible. The line of liquidity is a curve AB (fig. 5) determined by the relation between t and η. This curve is also an iso-

---

* That is, v and p have no such relations to the other quantities, as are expressible by equations; p, however, cannot be *less* than a certain function of t.

† All these difficulties are of course removed when the differences of volume of the liquid at different temperatures are rendered appreciable on the volume-pressure diagram. This can be done in various ways,—among others, by choosing as the body to which v, etc., refer, a sufficiently large quantity of the fluid. But, however we do it, we must evidently give up the possibility of representing the body in the state of vapor in the same diagram without making its dimensions enormous.

metric. Every point of it has a definite volume, temperature, entropy and energy. The latter is indicated by the isodynamics E_1E_1, E_2E_2, etc., which cross the region of par-

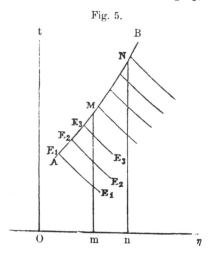

Fig. 5.

tial vaporization and terminate in the line of liquidity. (They do not in this diagram turn and follow the line.) If the body pass from one state to another, remaining liquid, as from M to N in the figure, the heat received is represented as usual by the area MN nm. That the work done is nothing, is indicated by the fact that the line AB is an isometric. Only the isopiestics in this diagram are superposed in the line of fluidity, turning downward where they meet this line and following its course, so that for any point in this line the pressure is undetermined. This is, however, no inconvenience in the diagram, as it simply expresses the fact of the case, that when all the quantities v, t, ε and η are fixed, the pressure is still undetermined.

[*Ed. note:* material omitted]

In the foregoing discussion, the equations which express the fundamental principles of thermodynamics in an analytical form have been
assumed, and the aim has only been to show how the same relations
may be expressed geometrically.   It would, however, be easy, starting
from the first and second laws of thermodynamics as usually enunciated,
to arrive at the same results without the aid of analytical formulæ,—to
arrive, for example, at the conception of energy, of entropy, of absolute temperature, in the construction of the diagram without the analytical definitions of these quantities, and to obtain the various properties of the diagram without the analytical expression of the thermodynamic properties which they involve.   Such a course would have
been better fitted to show the independence and sufficiency of a graphical method, but perhaps less suitable for an examination of the comparative advantages or disadvantages of different graphical methods.

The possibility of treating the thermodynamics of fluids by such
graphical methods as have been described evidently arises from the
fact that the state of the body considered, like the position of a point
in a plane, is capable of two and only two independent variations.
It is, perhaps, worthy of notice, that when the diagram is only used
to demonstrate or illustrate general theorems, it is not necessary,
although it may be convenient, to assume any particular method of
forming the diagram; it is enough to suppose the different states of
the body to be represented continuously by points upon a sheet.

26

Reprinted from *Am. J. Sci.*, Ser. 3, **16**(96), 441–458 (1878)

ART. LII.—*On the Equilibrium of Heterogeneous Substances;* by J. WILLARD GIBBS.* Abstract by the author.

IT is an inference naturally suggested by the general increase of entropy which accompanies the changes occurring in any isolated material system that when the entropy of the system has reached a maximum, the system will be in a state of equilibrium. Although this principle has by no means escaped the attention of physicists, its importance does not appear to have been duly appreciated. Little has been done to develop the principle as a foundation for the general theory of thermodynamic equilibrium.

The principle may be formulated as follows, constituting a criterion of equilibrium:

I. *For the equilibrium of any isolated system it is necessary and sufficient that in all possible variations of the state of the system which do not alter its energy, the variation of its entropy shall either vanish or be negative.*

The following form, which is easily shown to be equivalent to the preceding, is often more convenient in application:

II. *For the equilibrium of any isolated system it is necessary and sufficient that in all possible variations of the state of the system which do not alter its entropy, the variation of its energy shall either vanish or be positive.*

If we denote the energy and entropy of the system by ε and η respectively, the criterion of equilibrium may be expressed by either of the formulæ

$$(\delta \eta)_\varepsilon \lessgtr 0, \tag{1}$$
$$(\delta \varepsilon)_\eta \gtrless 0. \tag{2}$$

Again, if we assume that the temperature of the system is uniform, and denote its absolute temperature by t, and set

$$\psi = \varepsilon - t \eta, \tag{3}$$

the remaining conditions of equilibrium may be expressed by the formula

$$(\delta \psi)_t \gtrless 0, \tag{4}$$

the suffixed letter, as in the preceding cases, indicating that the quantity which it represents is constant. This condition, in connection with that of uniform temperature, may be shown to be equivalent to (1) or (2). The difference of the values of ψ for two different states of the system which have the same temperature represents the work which would be expended in bringing the system from one state to the other by a reversible process and without change of temperature.

* Transactions of the Connecticut Academy of Arts and Sciences, vol. iii, pp. 108–248 and 343–524.

If the system is incapable of thermal changes, like the systems considered in theoretical mechanics, we may regard the
entropy as having the constant value zero. Conditions (2) and
(4) may then be written

$$\delta\varepsilon \geqq 0, \qquad \delta\psi \geqq 0,$$

and are obviously identical in signification, since in this case
$\psi = \varepsilon$.

Conditions (2) and (4), as criteria of equilibrium, may therefore both be regarded as extensions of the criterion employed
in ordinary statics to the more general case of a thermodynamic system. In fact, each of the quantities $-\varepsilon$ and $-\psi$
(relating to a system without sensible motion) may be regarded
as a kind of force-function for the system,—the former as the
force-function *for constant entropy*, (i. e., when only such states
of the system are considered as have the same entropy,) and
the latter as the force-function *for constant temperature*, (i. e.,
when only such states of the system are considered as have the
same uniform temperature).

In the deduction of the particular conditions of equilibrium
for any system, the general formula (4) has an evident advantage over (1) or (2) with respect to the brevity of the processes
of reduction, since the limitation of constant temperature
applies to every part of the system taken separately, and
diminishes by one the number of independent variations in the
state of these parts which we have to consider. Moreover, the
transition from the systems considered in ordinary mechanics
to thermodynamic systems is most naturally made by this
formula, since it has always been customary to apply the
principles of theoretical mechanics to real systems on the supposition (more or less distinctly conceived and expressed) that
the temperature of the system remains constant, the mechanical
properties of a thermodynamic system maintained at a constant
temperature being such as might be imagined to belong to a
purely mechanical system, and admitting of representation by
a force-function, as follows directly from the fundamental laws
of thermodynamics.

Notwithstanding these considerations, the author has preferred in general to use condition (2) as the criterion of equilibrium, believing that it would be useful to exhibit the conditions of equilibrium of thermodynamic systems in connection
with those quantities which are most simple and most general
in their definitions, and which appear most important in the
general theory of such systems. The slightly different form in
which the subject would develop itself, if condition (4) had
been chosen as a point of departure instead of (2), is occasionally indicated.

Equilibrium of masses in contact.—The first problem to which the criterion is applied is the determination of the conditions of equilibrium for different masses in contact, when uninfluenced by gravity, electricity, distortion of the solid masses, or capillary tensions. The statement of the result is facilitated by the following definition.

If to any homogeneous mass in a state of hydrostatic stress we suppose an infinitesimal quantity of any substance to be added, the mass remaining homogeneous and its entropy and volume remaining unchanged, the increase of the energy of the mass divided by the quantity of the substance added is the *potential* for that substance in the mass considered.

In addition to equality of temperature and pressure in the masses in contact, it is necessary for equilibrium that the potential for every substance which is an independently variable component of any of the different masses shall have the same value in all of which it is such a component, so far as they are in contact with one another. But if a substance, without being an actual component of a certain mass in the given state of the system, is capable of being absorbed by it, it is sufficient if the value of the potential for that substance in that mass is not less than in any contiguous mass of which the substance is an actual component. We may regard these conditions as sufficient for equilibrium with respect to infinitesimal variations in the composition and thermodynamic state of the different masses in contact. There are certain other conditions which relate to the possible formation of masses entirely different in composition or state from any initially existing. These conditions are best regarded as determining the stability of the system, and will be mentioned under that head.

Anything which restricts the free movement of the component substances, or of the masses as such, may diminish the number of conditions which are necessary for equilibrium.

Equilibrium of osmotic forces.—If we suppose two fluid masses to be separated by a diaphragm which is permeable to some of the component substances and not to others, of the conditions of equilibrium which have just been mentioned, those will still subsist which relate to temperature and the potentials for the substances to which the diaphragm is permeable, but those relating to the potentials for the substances to which the diaphragm is impermeable will no longer be necessary. Whether the pressure must be the same in the two fluids will depend upon the rigidity of the diaphragm. Even when the diaphragm is permeable to all the components without restriction, equality of pressure in the two fluids is not always necessary for equilibrium.

Effect of gravity.—In a system subject to the action of gravity, the potential for each substance, instead of having a uniform value throughout the system, so far as the substance actually occurs as an independently variable component, will decrease uniformly with increasing height, the difference of its values at different levels being equal to the difference of level multiplied by the force of gravity.

Fundamental equations.—Let ε, η, v, t and p denote respectively the energy, entropy, volume, (absolute) temperature, and pressure of a homogeneous mass, which may be either fluid or solid, provided that it is subject only to hydrostatic pressures, and let m_1, m_2, . . . m_n denote the quantities of its independently variable components, and μ_1, μ_2, . . . μ_n the potentials for these components. It is easily shown that ε is a function of η, v, m_1, m_2, . . . m_n, and that the complete value of $d\varepsilon$ is given by the equation

$$d\varepsilon = t\,d\eta - p\,dv + \mu_1\,dm_1 + \mu_2\,dm_2 \ldots + \mu_n dm_n. \tag{5}$$

Now if ε is known in terms of η, v, m_1, . . . m_n, we can obtain by differentiation t, p, μ_1, . . . μ_n in terms of the same variables. This will make $n + 3$ independent known relations between the $2n + 5$ variables, ε, η, v, m_1, m_2, . . . m_n, t, p, μ_1, μ_2, . . . μ_n. These are all that exist, for of these variables, $n + 2$ are evidently independent. Now upon these relations depend a very large class of the properties of the compound considered,—we may say in general, all its thermal, mechanical, and chemical properties, so far as *active tendencies* are concerned, in cases in which the form of the mass does not require consideration. A single equation from which all these relations may be deduced may be called a fundamental equation. An equation between ε, η, v, m_1, m_2, . . . m_n is a fundamental equation. But there are other equations which possess the same property.

If we suppose the quantity ψ to be determined for such a mass as we are considering by equation (3), we may obtain by differentiation and comparison with (5)

$$d\psi = -\eta\,dt - p\,dv + \mu_1\,dm_1 + m_2\,dm_2 \ldots + \mu_n\,dm_n. \tag{6}$$

If, then, ψ is known as a function of t, v, m_1, m_2, . . . m_n, we can find η, p, μ_1, μ_2, . . . μ_n in terms of the same variables. If we then substitute for ψ in our original equation its value taken from equation (3) we shall have again $n + 3$ independent relations between the same $2n + 5$ variables as before.

Let

$$\zeta = \varepsilon - t\,\eta + p\,v, \tag{7}$$

then, by (5),

$$d\zeta = -\eta\,dt + v\,dp + \mu_1\,dm_1 + \mu_2\,dm_2 \ldots + \mu_n\,dm_n. \tag{8}$$

If, then, ζ is known as a function of $t, p, m_1, m_2, \ldots m_n$, we can find $\eta, v, \mu_1, \mu_2, \ldots \mu_n$ in terms of the same variables. By eliminating ζ, we may obtain again $n + 3$ independent relations between the same $2n + 5$ variables as at first.*

If we integrate (5), (6) and (8), supposing the quantity of the compound substance considered to vary from zero to any finite value, its nature and state remaining unchanged, we obtain

$$\varepsilon = t\eta - pv + \mu_1 m_1 + \mu_2 m_2 \ldots + \mu_n m_n \qquad (9)$$

$$\psi = -pv + \mu_1 m_1 + \mu_2 m_2 \ldots + \mu_n m_n, \qquad (10)$$

$$\zeta = \mu_1 m_1 + \mu_2 m_2 \ldots + \mu_n m_n. \qquad (11)$$

If we differentiate (9) in the most general manner, and compare the result with (5), we obtain

$$-v\,dp + \eta\,dt + m_1\,d\mu_1 + m_2\,d\mu_2 \ldots + m_n\,d\mu_n = 0, \qquad (12)$$

or

$$dp = \frac{\eta}{v}dt + \frac{m_1}{v}d\mu_1 + \frac{m_2}{v}d\mu_2 \ldots + \frac{m_n}{v}d\mu_n = 0. \qquad (13)$$

Hence, there is a relation between the $n + 2$ quantities $t, p, \mu_1, \mu_2, \ldots \mu_n$, which, if known, will enable us to find in terms of these quantities all the ratios of the $n + 2$ quantities $\eta, v, m_1, m_2, \ldots m_n$. With (9), this will make $n + 3$ independent relations between the same $2n + 5$ variables as at first.

Any equation, therefore, between the quantities

	$\varepsilon,$	$\eta,$	$v,$	$m_1,$	$m_2, \ldots m_n,$
or	$\psi,$	$t,$	$v,$	$m_1,$	$m_2, \ldots m_n,$
or	$\zeta,$	$t,$	$p,$	$m_1,$	$m_2, \ldots m_n,$
or		$t,$	$p,$	$\mu_1,$	$\mu_2, \ldots \mu_n,$

is a fundamental equation, and any such is entirely equivalent to any other.

Coëxistent phases.—In considering the different homogeneous bodies which can be formed out of any set of component substances, it is convenient to have a term which shall refer solely to the composition and thermodynamic state of any such body without regard to its size or form. The word *phase* has been chosen for this purpose. Such bodies as differ in composition or state are called different phases of the matter considered, all

---

* The properties of the quantities $-\psi$ and $-\zeta$ regarded as functions of the temperature and volume, and temperature and pressure, respectively, the composition of the body being regarded as invariable, have been discussed by M. Massieu in a memoir entitled "Sur les fonctions caractéristiques des divers fluides et sur la théorie des vapeurs" (*Mém. Savants Étrang.*, t. xxii.) A brief sketch of his method in a form slightly different from that ultimately adopted is given in *Comptes Rendus*, t. lxix. (1869) pp. 858 and 1057, and a report on his memoir by M. Bertrand in *Comptes Rendus*, t. lxxi. p. 257. M. Massieu appears to have been the first to solve the problem of representing all the properties of a body of invariable composition which are concerned in reversible processes by means of a single function.

bodies which differ only in size and form being regarded as different examples of the same phase. Phases which can exist together, the dividing surfaces being plain, in an equilibrium which does not depend upon passive resistances to change, are called *coëxistent.*

The number of independent variations of which a system of coëxistent phases is capable is $n+2-r$, where r denotes the number of phases, and n the number of independently variable components in the whole system. For the system of phases is completely specified by the temperature, the pressure, and the n potentials, and between these $n+2$ quantities there are r independent relations (one for each phase), which characterize the system of phases.

When the number of phases exceeds the number of components by unity, the system is capable of a single variation of phase. The pressure and all the potentials may be regarded as functions of the temperature. The determination of these functions depends upon the elimination of the proper quantities from the fundamental equations in p, t, μ_1, μ_2, etc., for the several members of the system. But without a knowledge of these fundamental equations, the values of the differential co-efficients such as $\dfrac{dp}{dt}$ may be expressed in terms of the entropies and volumes of the different bodies and the quantities of their several components. For this end we have only to eliminate the differentials of the potentials from the different equations of the form (12) relating to the different bodies. In the simplest case, when there is but one component, we obtain the well-known formula

$$\frac{dp}{dt} = \frac{\eta' - \eta''}{v' - v''} = \frac{Q}{t\,(v'' - v')},$$

in which v', v'', η', η'', denote the volumes and entropies of a given quantity of the substance in the two phases, and Q the heat which it absorbs in passing from one phase to the other.

It is easily shown that if the temperature of two coëxistent phases of two components is maintained constant, the pressure is in general a maximum or minimum when the composition of the phases is identical. In like manner, if the pressure of the phases is maintained constant, the temperature is in general a maximum or minimum when the composition of the phases is identical. The series of simultaneous values of t and p for which the composition of two coëxistent phases is identical separates those simultaneous values of t and p for which no coëxistent phases are possible from those for which there are two pairs of coëxistent phases.

If the temperature of three coëxistent phases of three components is maintained constant, the pressure is in general a maximum or minimum when the composition of one of the phases is such as can be produced by combining the other two. If the pressure is maintained constant, the temperature is in general a maximum or minimum when the same condition in regard to the composition of the phases is fulfilled.

Stability of fluids.—A criterion of the stability of a homogeneous fluid, or of a system of coëxistent fluid phases, is afforded by the expression

$$\varepsilon - t'\eta + p'v - \mu_1'm_1 - \mu_2'm_2 \quad . \quad . \quad . \quad - \mu_n'm_n \tag{14}$$

in which the values of the accented letters are to be determined by the phase or system of phases of which the stability is in question, and the values of the unaccented letters by any other phase of the same components, the possible formation of which is in question. We may call the former constants, and the latter variables. Now if the value of the expression, thus determined, is always positive for any possible values of the variables, the phase or system of phases will be stable with respect to the formation of any new phases of its components. But if the expression is capable of a negative value, the phase or system is at least *practically* unstable. By this is meant that, although, strictly speaking, an infinitely small disturbance or change may not be sufficient to destroy the equilibrium, yet a very small change in the initial state will be sufficient to do so. The presence of a small portion of matter in a phase for which the above expression has a negative value will in general be sufficient to produce this result. In the case of a system of phases, it is of course supposed that their contiguity is such that the formation of the new phase does not involve any transportation of matter through finite distances.

The preceding criterion affords a convenient point of departure in the discussion of the stability of homogeneous fluids. Of the other forms in which the criterion may be expressed, the following is perhaps the most useful.

If the pressure of a fluid is greater than that of any other phase of its independent variable components which has the same temperature and potentials, the fluid is stable with respect to the formation of any other phase of these components; but if its pressure is not as great as that of some such phase, it will be practically unstable.

Stability of fluids with respect to continuous changes of phase.— In considering the changes which may take place in any mass, we have often to distinguish between infinitesimal changes in existing phases, and the formation of entirely new phases. A phase of a fluid may be stable with respect to the former kind of change, and unstable with respect to the latter. In this case, it may be capable of continued existence in virtue of properties which prevent the commencement of discontinuous changes. But a phase which is unstable with respect to continuous changes is evidently incapable of permanent existence on a large scale except in consequence of passive resistances to change. To obtain the conditions of stability with respect to continuous changes, we have only to limit the application of the variables in (14) to phases adjacent to the given phase. We obtain results of the following nature.

The stability of any phase with respect to continuous changes depends upon the same conditions with respect to the second and higher differential coëfficients of the density of energy regarded as a function of the density of entropy and the densities of the several components, which would make the density of energy a minimum, if the necessary conditions with respect to the first differential coëfficients were fulfilled.

Again, it is necessary and sufficient for the stability with respect to continuous changes of all the phases within any given limits, that within those limits the same conditions should be fulfilled with respect to the second and higher differential coëfficients of the pressure regarded as a function of the temperature and the several potentials, which would make the pressure a minimum, if the necessary conditions with respect to the first differential coëfficients were fulfilled

The equation of the limits of stability with respect to continuous changes may be written

$$\left(\frac{d\mu_n}{d\gamma_n}\right)_{t,\,\mu_1,\,\ldots\,\mu_{n-1}} = 0, \text{ or } \left(\frac{d^2 p}{d\mu_n{}^2}\right)_{t,\,\mu_1,\,\ldots\,\mu_{n-1}} = \infty, \quad (15)$$

where γ_n denotes the density of the component specified or $m_n \div v$. It is in general immaterial to what component the suffix $_n$ is regarded as relating.

Critical phases.—The variations of two coëxistent phases are sometimes limited by the vanishing of the difference between them. Phases at which this occurs are called *critical phases.* A critical phase, like any other, is capable of $n+1$ independent variations, n denoting the number of independently variable components. But when subject to the condition of remaining a critical phase, it is capable of only $n-1$ independent variations. There are therefore two independent equations which characterize critical phases. These may be written

$$\left(\frac{d\mu_n}{d\gamma_n}\right)_{t,\,\mu_1,\,\ldots\,\mu_{n-1}} = 0, \left(\frac{d^2\mu_n}{d\gamma_n{}^2}\right)_{t,\,\mu_1,\,\ldots\,\mu_{n-1}} = 0. \quad (16)$$

It will be observed that the first of these equations is identical with the equation of the limit of stability with respect to continuous changes. In fact, stable critical phases are situated at that limit. They are also situated at the limit of stability with respect to discontinuous changes. These limits are in general distinct, but touch each other at critical phases.

Geometrical illustrations.—In an earlier paper,* the author has described a method of representing the thermodynamic properties of substances of invariable composition by means of surfaces. The volume, entropy, and energy of a constant quantity of the substance are represented by rectangular coördinates. This method corresponds to the first kind of fundamental equation described above. Any other kind of fundamental equation for a substance of invariable composition will suggest an analogous geometrical method. In the present paper, the method in which the coördinates represent temperature, pressure, and the potential, is briefly considered. But when the composition of the body is variable, the fundamental equation cannot be completely represented by any surface or finite number of surfaces. In the case of three components, if we regard the temperature and pressure as constant, as well as the total quantity of matter, the relations between ζ, m_1, m_2, m_3 may be represented by a surface in which the distances of a point from the three sides of a triangular prism represent the quantities m_1, m_2, m_3, and the distance of the point from the base of the prism represents the quantity ζ. In the case of two components, analogous relations may be represented by a plane curve. Such methods are especially useful for illustrating the combinations and separations of the components, and the changes in states of aggregation, which take place when the substances are exposed in varying proportions to the temperature and pressure considered.

Fundamental equations of ideal gases and gas-mixtures.—From the physical properties which we attribute to ideal gases, it is easy to deduce their fundamental equations. The fundamental equation in ε, η, v, and m for an ideal gas is

$$c \log \frac{\varepsilon - \mathrm{E}m}{cm} = \frac{\eta}{m} - \mathrm{H} + a \log \frac{m}{v}: \qquad (17)$$

that in ψ, t, v, and m is

$$\psi = \mathrm{E}m + m\,t\left(c - \mathrm{H} - c \log t + a \log \frac{m}{v}\right): \qquad (18)$$

that in p, t, and μ is

$$p = a\,e^{\frac{\mathrm{H}-c-a}{a}}\; t^{\frac{c+a}{a}}\; e^{\frac{\mu-\mathrm{E}}{at}}, \qquad (19)$$

where e denotes the base of the Naperian system of logarithms. As for the other constants, c denotes the specific heat of the

* Transactions of the Connecticut Academy, vol. ii, part 2.

gas at constant volume, a denotes the constant value of $pv \div mt$, E and H depend upon the zeros of energy and entropy. The two last equations may be abbreviated by the use of different constants. The properties of fundamental equations mentioned above may easily be verified in each case by differentiation.

The law of Dalton respecting a mixture of different gases affords a point of departure for the discussion of such mixtures and the establishment of their fundamental equations. It is found convenient to give the law the following form:

The pressure in a mixture of different gases is equal to the sum of the pressures of the different gases as existing each by itself at the same temperature and with the same value of its potential.

A mixture of ideal gases which satisfies this law is called an *ideal gas-mixture.* Its fundamental equation in p, t, μ_1, μ_2, etc. is evidently of the form

$$p = \Sigma_1 \left(a_1 e^{\frac{H_1 - c_1 - a_1}{a_1}} \; t^{\frac{c_1 + a_1}{a_1}} \; e^{\frac{\mu_1 - E_1}{a_1 t}} \right), \qquad (20)$$

where Σ_1 denotes summation with respect to the different components of the mixture. From this may be deduced other fundamental equations for ideal gas-mixtures. That in ψ, t, v, m_1, m_2, etc. is

$$\psi = \Sigma_1 \left(E_1 m_1 + m_1 t \left(c_1 - H_1 - c_1 \log t + a_1 \log \frac{m_1}{v} \right) \right). \quad (21)$$

Phases of dissipated energy of ideal gas-mixtures.—When the proximate components of a gas-mixture are so related that some of them can be formed out of others, although not necessarily in the gas-mixture itself at the temperatures considered, there are certain phases of the gas-mixture which deserve especial attention. These are the *phases of dissipated energy,* i. e., those phases in which the energy of the mass has the least value consistent with its entropy and volume. An atmosphere of such a phase could not furnish a source of mechanical power to any machine or chemical engine working within it, as other phases of the same matter might do. Nor can such phases be affected by any catalytic agent. A *perfect catalytic agent* would reduce any other phase of the gas-mixture to a phase of dissipated energy. The condition which will make the energy a minimum is that the potentials for the proximate components shall satisfy an equation similar to that which expresses the relation between the units of weight of these components. For example, if the components were hydrogen, oxygen and water, since one gram of hydrogen with eight grams of oxygen are chemically equivalent to nine grams of water, the potentials for these substances in a phase of dissipated energy must satisfy the relation

$$\mu_H + 8\mu_O = 9\mu_W.$$

Gas-mixtures with convertible components.—The theory of the phases of dissipated energy of an ideal gas-mixture derives an especial interest from its possible application to the case of those gas-mixtures in which the chemical composition and resolution of the components can take place in the gas-mixture itself, and actually does take place, so that the quantities of the proximate components are entirely determined by the quantities of a smaller number of ultimate components, with the temperature and pressure. These may be called *gas-mixtues with convertible components.* If the general laws of *ideal* gas-mixtures apply in any such case, it may easily be shown that the phases of dissipated energy are the only phases which can exist. We can form a fundamental equation which shall relate solely to these phases. For this end, we first form the equation in p, t, μ_1, μ_2, etc. for the gas-mixture, regarding its proximate components as *not* convertible. This equation will contain a potential for every proximate component of the gas-mixture. We then eliminate one (or more) of these potentials by means of the relations which exist between them in virtue of the convertibility of the components to which they relate, leaving the potentials which relate to those substances which naturally express the ultimate composition of the gas-mixture.

The validity of the results thus obtained depends upon the applicability of the laws of ideal gas-mixtures to cases in which chemical action takes place. Some of these laws are generally regarded as capable of such application, others are not so regarded. But it may be shown that in the very important case in which the components of a gas are convertible at certain temperatures, and not at others, the theory proposed may be established without other assumptions than such as are generally admitted.

It is, however, only by experiments upon gas-mixtures with convertible components, that the validity of any theory concerning them can be satisfactorily established.

The vapor of the peroxide of nitrogen appears to be a mixture of two different vapors, of one of which the molecular formula is double that of the other. If we suppose that the vapor conforms to the laws of an ideal gas-mixture in a state of dissipated energy, we may obtain an equation between the temperature, pressure, and density of the vapor, which exhibits a somewhat striking agreement with the results of experiment.

Equilibrium of stressed solids.—The second paper commences with a discussion of the conditions of internal and external equilibrium for solids in contact with fluids with regard to all possible states of strain of the solids. These conditions are deduced by analytical processes from the general condition of equilibrium (2). The condition of equilibrium which relates to the dissolving of the solid at a surface where it meets a fluid may be expressed by the equation

$$\mu_1 = \frac{\varepsilon - t\,\eta + p\,v}{m},\qquad(22)$$

where ε, η, v, and m_1 denote respectively the energy, entropy, volume, and mass of the solid, if it is homogeneous in nature and state of strain,—otherwise, of any small portion which may be treated as thus homogeneous,—μ_1 the potential in the fluid for the substance of which the solid consists, p the pressure in the fluid and therefore one of the principal pressures in the solid, and t the temperature. It will be observed that when the pressure in the solid is isotropic, the second member of this equation will represent the potential in the solid for the substance of which it consists [see (9)], and the condition reduces to the equality of the potential in the two masses, just as if it were a case of two fluids. But if the stresses in the solid are not isotropic, the value of the second member of the equation is not entirely determined by the nature and state of the solid, but has in general three different values (for the same solid at the same temperature, and in the same state of strain) corresponding to the three principal pressures in the solid. If a solid in the form of a right parallelopiped is sub-ject to different pressures on its three pairs of opposite sides by fluids in which it is soluble, it is in general necessary for equi-librium that the composition of the fluids shall be different.

¶The *fundamental equations* which have been described above are limited, in their application to solids, to the case in which the stresses in the solid are isotropic. An example of a more general form of fundamental equation for a solid, is afforded by an equation between the energy and entropy of a given quantity of the solid, and the quantities which express its state of strain, or by an equation between ψ [see (3)] as determined for a given quantity of the solid, the temperature, and the quantities which express the state of strain.

Capillarity.—The solution of the problems which precede may be regarded as a first approximation, in which the peculiar state of thermodynamic equilibrium about the surfaces of dis-continuity is neglected. To take account of the condition of things at these surfaces, the following method is used. Let us suppose that two homogeneous fluid masses are separated by a surface of discontinuity, i. e., by a very thin non-homogeneous film. Now we may imagine a state of things in which each of the homogeneous masses extends without variation of the densi-ties of its several components, or of the densities of energy and entropy, quite up to a geometrical surface (to be called the dividing surface) at which the masses meet. We may suppose this surface to be sensibly coincident with the physical surface of discontinuity. Now if we compare the actual state of things with the supposed state, there will be in the former in the vicinity of the surface a certain (positive or negative) excess of energy, of entropy, and of each of the component substances. These quantities are denoted by ε^s, η^s, m_1^s, m_2^s, etc. and are treated as belonging to the surface. The ^{s} is used simply as a distinguishing mark, and must not be taken for an algebraic exponent.

It is shown that the conditions of equilibrium already obtained relating to the temperature and the potentials of the homogeneous masses, are not affected by the surfaces of discontinuity, and that the complete value of $d\varepsilon^s$ is given by the equation

$$\delta\varepsilon^s = t\,\delta\eta^s + \sigma\,\delta s + \mu_1\,\delta m_1^s + \mu_2\,\delta m_2^s + \text{etc.} \tag{23}$$

in which s denotes the area of the surface considered, t the temperature, μ_1, μ_2, etc the potentials for the various components in the adjacent masses. It may be, however, that some of the components are found only at the surface of discontinuity, in which case the letter μ with the suffix relating to such a substance denotes, as the equation shows, the rate of increase of energy at the surface per unit of the substance added, when the entropy, the area of the surface, and the quantities of the other components are unchanged. The quantity σ we may regard as defined by the equation itself, or by the following, which is obtained by integration :

$$\varepsilon^s = t\,\eta^s + \sigma\,s + \mu_1\,m_1^s + \mu_2\,m_2^s + \text{etc.} \tag{24}$$

There are terms relating to variations of the curvatures of the surface which might be added, but it is shown that we can give the dividing surface such a position as to make these terms vanish, and it is found convenient to regard its position as thus determined. It is always sensibly coincident with the physical surface of discontinuity. (Yet in treating of plane surfaces, this supposition in regard to the position of the dividing surface is unnecessary, and it is sometimes convenient to suppose that its position is determined by other considerations.)

With the aid of (23), the remaining condition of equilibrium for contiguous homogeneous masses is found, viz :

$$\sigma\,(c_1 + c_2) = p' - p'', \tag{25}$$

where p', p'' denote the pressures in the two masses, and c_1, c_2 the principal curvatures of the surface. Since this equation has the same form as if a tension equal to σ resided at the surface, the quantity σ is called (as is usual) the *superficial tension*, and the dividing surface in the particular position above mentioned is called the *surface of tension*.

By differentiation of (24) and comparison with (23), we obtain

$$d\sigma = -\eta_s dt - \Gamma_1 d\mu_1 - \Gamma_2 d\mu_2 - \text{etc.}, \qquad (26)$$

where η_s, Γ_1, Γ_2, etc. are written for $\dfrac{\eta^s}{s}$, $\dfrac{m_1^s}{s}$, $\dfrac{m_2^s}{s}$, etc., and denote the superficial densities of entropy and of the various substances. We may regard σ as a function of t, μ_1, μ_2, etc., from which if known η_s, Γ_1, Γ_2, etc. may be determined in terms of the same variables. An equation between σ, t, μ_1, μ_2, etc. may therefore be called a *fundamental equation for the surface of discontinuity.* The same may be said of an equation between ϵ^s, η^s, s, m_1^s, m_2^s, etc.

It is necessary for the stability of a surface of discontinuity that its tension shall be as small as that of any other surface which can exist between the same homogeneous masses with the same temperature and potentials. Beside this condition, which relates to the nature of the surface of discontinuity, there are other conditions of stability, which relate to the possible motion of such surfaces. One of these is that the tension shall be positive. The others are of a less simple nature, depending upon the extent and form of the surface of discontinuity, and in general upon the whole system of which it is a part. The most simple case of a system with a surface of discontinuity is that of two coëxistent phases separated by a spherical surface, the outer mass being of indefinite extent. When the interior mass and the surface of discontinuity are formed entirely of substances which are components of the surrounding mass, the equilibrium is always unstable; in other cases, the equilibrium may be stable. Thus, the equilibrium of a drop of water in an atmosphere of vapor is unstable, but may be made stable by the addition of a little salt. The analytical conditions which determine the stability or instability of the system are easily found, when the temperature and potentials of the system are regarded as known, as well as the fundamental equations for the interior mass and the surface of discontinuity.

The study of surfaces of discontinuity throws considerable light upon the subject of the stability of such phases of fluids as have a less pressure than other phases of the same components with the same temperature and potentials. Let the pressure of the phase of which the stability is in question be denoted by p', and that of the other phase of the same temperature and potentials by p''. A spherical mass of the second phase and of a radius determined by the equation

$$2\sigma = (p'' - p')\, r, \qquad (27)$$

would be in equilibrium with a surrounding mass of the first phase. This equilibrium, as we have just seen, is instable, when the surrounding mass is indefinitely extended. A spherical mass a little larger would tend to increase indefinitely. The work required to form such a spherical mass, by a reversible process, in the interior of an infinite mass of the other phase, is given by the equation

$$W = \sigma s - (p'' - p') v''. \qquad (28)$$

The term σs represents the work spent in forming the surface, and the term $(p'' - p') v''$ the work gained in forming the interior mass. The second of these quantities is always equal to two-thirds of the first. The value of W is therefore positive, and the phase is in strictness stable, the quantity W affording a kind of measure of its stability. We may easily express the value of W in a form which does not involve any geometrical magnitudes, viz:

$$W = \frac{16 \, \pi \, \sigma^3}{3 (p'' - p')^2}, \qquad (29)$$

where p'', p' and σ may be regarded as functions of the temperature and potentials. It will be seen that the stability, thus measured, is infinite for an infinitesimal difference of pressures, but decreases very rapidly as the difference of pressures increases. These conclusions are all, however, practically limited to the case in which the value of r, as determined by equation (27) is of sensible magnitude.

With respect to the somewhat similar problem of the stability of the surface of contact of two phases with respect to the formation of a new phase, the following results are obtained. Let the phases (supposed to have the same temperature and potentials) be denoted by A, B, and C; their pressures by p_A, p_B and p_C; and the tensions of the three possible surfaces σ_{AB}, σ_{BC}, σ_{AC}. If p_C is less than

$$\frac{\sigma_{BC} p_A + \sigma_{AC} p_B}{\sigma_{BC} + \sigma_{AC}},$$

there will be no tendency toward the formation of the new phase at the surface between A and B. If the temperature or potentials are now varied until p_C is equal to the above expression, there are two cases to be distinguished. The tension σ_{AB} will be either equal to $\sigma_{AC} + \sigma_{BC}$ or less. (A greater value could only relate to an unstable and therefore unusual surface.) If $\sigma_{AB} = \sigma_{AC} + \sigma_{BC}$, a farther variation of the temperature or potentials, making p_C greater than the above expression, would cause the phase C to be formed at the surface between A and B. But if $\sigma_{AB} < \sigma_{AC} + \sigma_{BC}$, the surface between A and B would remain stable, but with rapidly diminishing stability, after p_C has passed the limit mentioned.

The conditions of stability for a line where several surfaces of discontinuity meet, with respect to the possible formation of a new surface, are capable of a very simple expression.   If the surfaces A-B, B-C, C-D, D-A, separating the masses A, B, C, D, meet along a line, it is necessary for equilibrium that their tensions and directions at any point of the line should be such that a quadrilateral α, β, γ, δ may be formed with sides representing in direction and length the normals and tensions of the successive surfaces.   For the stability of the system with reference to the possible formation of surfaces between A and C, or between B and D, it is farther necessary that the tensions σ_{AC} and σ_{BD} should be greater than the diagonals $\alpha\gamma$ and $\beta\delta$ respectively.   The conditions of stability are entirely analogous in the case of a greater number of surfaces.   For the conditions of stability relating to the formation of a new phase at a line in which three surfaces of discontinuity meet, or at a point where four different phases meet, the reader is referred to the original paper.

Liquid films.—When a fluid exists in the form of a very thin film between other fluids, the great inequality of its extension in different directions will give rise to certain peculiar properties, even when its thickness is sufficient for its interior to have the properties of matter in mass.   The most important case is where the film is liquid and the contiguous fluids are gaseous.   If we imagine the film to be divided into elements of the same order of magnitude as its thickness, each element extending through the film from side to side, it is evident that far less time will in general be required for the attainment of approximate equilibrium between the different parts of any such element and the contiguous gases than for the attainment of equilibrium between all the different elements of the film.

There will accordingly be a time, commencing shortly after the formation of the film, in which its separate elements may be regarded as satisfying the conditions of internal equilibrium, and of equilibrium with the contiguous gases, while they may not satisfy all the conditions of equilibrium with each other. It is when the changes due to this want of complete equilibrium take place so slowly that the film appears to be at rest, except so far as it accommodates itself to any change in the external conditions to which it is subjected, that the characteristic properties of the film are most striking and most sharply defined.   It is from this point of view that these bodies are discussed.   They are regarded as satisfying a certain well-defined class of conditions of equilibrium, but as not satisfying at all certain other conditions which would be necessary for complete equilibrium, in consequence of which they are subject to gradual changes, which ultimately determine their rupture.

The elasticity of a film (i. e., the increase of its tension when extended,) is easily accounted for.   It follows from the general relations given above that, when a film has more than one component, those components which diminish the tension will be found in greater proportion on the surfaces. When the film is extended, there will not be enough of these substances to keep up the same volume- and surface-densities as before, and the deficiency will cause a certain increase of tension. It does not follow that a thinner film has always a greater tension than a thicker formed of the same liquid. When the phases within the films as well as without are the same, and the surfaces of the films are also the same, there will be no difference of tension. Nor will the tension of the same film be altered, if a part of the interior drains away in the course of time, without affecting the surfaces. If the thickness of the film is reduced by evaporation, its tension may be either increased or diminished, according to the relative volatility of its different components.

Let us now suppose that the thickness of the film is reduced until the limit is reached at which the interior ceases to have the properties of matter in mass The elasticity of the film, which determines its stability with respect to extension and contraction, does not vanish at this limit. But a certain kind of instability will generally arise, in virtue of which inequalities in the thickness of the film will tend to increase through currents in the interior of the film. This probably leads to the destruction of the film, in the case of most liquids. In a film of soap-water, the kind of instability described seems to be manifested in the breaking out of the black spots. But the sudden diminution in thickness which takes place in parts of the film is arrested by some unknown cause, possibly by viscous or gelatinous properties, so that the rupture of the film does not necessarily follow.

Electromotive force.—The conditions of equilibrium may be modified by electromotive force. Of such cases a galvanic or electrolytic cell may be regarded as the type. With respect to the potentials for the ions and the electrical potential the following relation may be noticed :

When all the conditions of equilibrium are fulfilled in a galvanic or electrolytic cell, the electromotive force is equal to the difference in the values of the potential for any ion at the surfaces of the electrodes multiplied by the electro-chemical equivalent of that ion, the greater potential of an anion being at the same electrode as the greater electrical potential, and the reverse being true of a cation.

The relation which exists between the electromotive force of a *perfect electro-chemical apparatus* (i. e., a galvanic or electrolytic cell which satisfies the condition of reversibility,) and the changes in the cell which accompany the passage of electricity, may be expressed by the equation

$$d\varepsilon = (\mathrm{V}' - \mathrm{V}'')\,de + t\,d\eta + d\,\mathrm{W_G} + d\mathrm{W_P}, \qquad (30)$$

in which $d\varepsilon$ denotes the increment of the intrinsic energy in the apparatus, $d\eta$ the increment of entropy, de the quantity of electricity which passes through it, V' and V'' the electrical potentials in pieces of the same kind of metal connected with the anode and cathode respectively, $d\mathrm{W_G}$ the work done by gravity, and $d\mathrm{W_P}$ the work done by the pressures which act on the external surface of the apparatus. The term $d\mathrm{W_G}$ may generally be neglected. The same is true of $d\mathrm{W_P}$, when gases are not concerned. If no heat is supplied or withdrawn the term $t\,d\eta$ will vanish. But in the calculation of electromotive forces, which is the most important application of the equation, it is convenient and customary to suppose that the temperature is maintained constant. Now this term $t\,d\eta$, which represents the heat absorbed by the cell, is frequently neglected in the consideration of cells of which the temperature is supposed to remain constant. In other words, it is frequently assumed that neither heat or cold is produced by the passage of an electrical current through a perfect electro-chemical apparatus (except that heat which may be indefinitely diminished by increasing the time in which a given quantity of electricity passes), unless it be by processes of a secondary nature, which are not immediately or necessarily connected with the process of electrolysis.

That this assumption is incorrect is shown by the electromotive force of a gas battery charged with hydrogen and nitrogen, by the currents caused by differences in the concentration of the electrolyte, by electrodes of zinc and mercury in a solution of sulphate of zinc, by *a priori* considerations based on the phenomena exhibited in the direct combination of the elements of water or of hydrochloric acid, by the absorption of heat which M. Favre has in many cases observed in a galvanic or electrolytic cell, and by the fact that the solid or liquid state of an electrode (at its temperature of fusion) does not affect the electromotive force.

27

Methods of Developing Thermodynamics

Max Planck

This excerpt was translated expressly for this Benchmark volume by R. Bruce Lindsay, Brown University, from the preface to Vorlesungen über Thermodynamik, *1st ed., Viet and Co., Leipzig, 1897, with the permission of the publisher, Walter de Gruyter & Co., Berlin*

I received the first encouragement to prepare this book from the many requests that I should put together in one place my various periodical articles in the field of thermodynamics, and in this way present them in a more organized form. The mere assembly of the articles would have been much the simpler course, since I have seen no reason to change in any essential fashion the viewpoint expressed in my earlier works. However, I finally decided to work over the whole material. I was led to this decision partly by the thought that this course would provide the opportunity to present discussion and proofs in greater detail and more intelligibly than is usually possible in the normally concise style of scientific periodical papers. However, my principal ground for taking this step was the opportunity it provided of organizing the whole field of thermodynamics in a unified fashion. This course has indeed deprived the work of its character as an exercise in research, and has turned it into a textbook intended as an introduction to thermodynamics suitable for those who have had introductory courses in physics and chemistry and are familiar with the elements of differential and integral calculus.

In the development of thermodynamics up to this time we may distinguish three different approaches or methods of investigation. The first tries to delve most deeply into the nature of the phenomena being considered, so that if it could be carried through with exactness in every detail it would have to be considered the essentially complete method. According to this method, heat is due to definite motions of chemical molecules and atoms of discrete mass. For gaseous bodies these have relatively simple properties, whereas for solids and liquids their role up to now has been set forth only in rather broad outlines. Since its establishment by Joule, Waterston, Krönig, and Clausius, this kinetic theory has been substantially extended by Maxwell and Boltzmann. However, in its more recent development it appears to have encountered almost insuperable obstacles associated not merely with the highly complicated mathematics needed for the deductons from the basic hypotheses, but more particularly with dif-

ficulties in principle connected with the mechanical interpretation
of the principles of thermodynamics.

A second method of developing thermodynamics, due to Helmholtz,
avoids difficulties of the kind just mentioned. It restricts itself to the
most important assumption of the mechanical theory of heat, i.e., that
heat is due to motion, but in the first instance completely renounces
any attempt at a specialized representation of the nature of this motion. This standpoint rests on surer grounds than the former in that it
preserves the full philosophical satisfaction provided by the mechanical theory of natural phenomena. But the basis that it offers has up to
now not proved broad enough to permit the construction of a completely detailed theory. All that one can obtain so far from Helmholtz's
approach is the confirmation of some general laws already completely
established from experience.

There is a third way of handling thermodynamics, which up to the
present has actually proved to be the most fruitful. It is distinguished
from the first two mentioned by the fact that it does not place the
mechanical nature of heat in the foreground; rather, it abstains from
any specialized assumption as to the precise nature of heat. Actually,
it bases itself on some very general experimental facts, i.e., the two
great laws or principles of thermodynamics. From these can be derived in purely logical fashion a large number of new laws of physics
and chemistry, which have shown themselves capable of extensive
application without serious exception.

This last method may be looked upon as more inductive in nature
than the ones previously mentioned. It is the one that has been employed exclusively in this book. It conforms most satisfactorily to the
present state of science. However, it can hardly be considered as the
final word, but must probably ultimately give way to a mechanical
or even an electromagnetic way of looking at natural phenomena.
There may be for a time a certain advantage in treating the individual
natural phenomena, heat, motion, electricity, etc., as qualitatively different from each other and to suppress the question of their possible
common nature. Nevertheless, our striving toward a unified view of
nature, whether it will turn out to be on a mechanical or some other
basis, so strongly reinforced by the discovery of the conservation of
energy, cannot be indefinitely checked. Any present-day retreat from
the fundamental assumption of the essential unity of physical phenomena would be equivalent to the renunciation of any attempt to
understand a whole series of well-known regularities existing between
different domains of nature. The results so far obtained from the two
fundamental principles of thermodynamics would naturally not be
destroyed by the more general theory. What would happen is that
these principles would no longer have to be introduced as autonomous statements but would be derivable from other still more general
principles. However, it is not now possible to foresee the time when
the road to this goal may be successfully traveled.

413

AUTHOR CITATION INDEX

SUBJECT INDEX

Accident, in energetics, 324 ff.
Actinometer (Herschel), 156
Adiabatic process, 64
Atom, motion of component parts of, 23

Caloric, 21
Capacity, in energetics, 342
Carnot's function, 79, 280, 336
Carnot's theorem for heat engines, 70
Causality, principle of, 27
Central forces, 12 f.
Charge, electric, in current flow, 277 f.
Chemical affinity, 104
Chemical element, 8
Collisions
  elastic, 18
  inelastic, 20
Comets, 162
Condensation of vapor, 60
Conductivity of metals, 257
Contact potential, 230 f., 236
Coulomb's inverse-square law, 220, 226,
    238 f.
Current, electric, 220
  work done by, 274 ff.
Curve of absolute cold (Rankine), 110
Cycle, thermodynamic, in a gas (Clausius), 51

Daniell cell, 233 f., 266 f.
Determinism, in physics, 369

Earth
  age of, 214
  temperature of surface, 212

Efficiency of heat engine, 83, 103, 118, 336
Effort, in energetics, 325 f.
Elastic bodies, motion of, 18
Elastic strain, 325
Electrochemical equivalent, 254
Electrodynamics, 240
Electrolysis, 254 f.
  Faraday's laws of, 261
Electrolyte, conductivity of, 262
Electromotive force, 232, 242 f., 247
  produced by Faraday disk, 263 f.
  of voltaic cell, 252
Electrostatics, 220, 226
Encke's comet, 163
Energetics
  critique of (Planck), 358 ff.
  definition of (Rankine), 314 ff.
  principles of (Ostwald), 341
Energy
  actual (Rankine), 96
  association of, with matter, 288
  in chemical action in a cell, 264
  confusion with force, 1
  conservation of, 2 ff., 10, 12 ff., 17, 200, 339
    in charge of state of gas and vapor, 54 ff.
    critique (Poincaré), 364 ff.
    in electric currents, 231
    in electric phenomena, 222
    in energetics, 329
    in general dynamical systems, 14 f.
    in heat engines, 70
    in induced currents, 240
    in voltaic cell, 235
  definition of (Rankine), 96

417